Victorian

Aspects of English an

1837–1

Victorian England

Aspects of English and Imperial History
1837–1901

L. C. B. SEAMAN

Apart from the realm of letters and art – in
which, in my humble judgement, France is her
compeer, and even her superior – in everything that makes a people great, in
colonizing power, in trade and commerce,
in all the higher arts of civilization, England
not only excels all other nations of the
modern world, but all nations in ancient
history as well.

SIR WILFRID LAURIER, 1898
(quoted in C. H. D. Howard,
Splendid Isolation)

METHUEN & CO LTD
11 NEW FETTER LANE LONDON EC4P 4EE

First published 1973
by Methuen & Co Ltd
11 New Fetter Lane London EC4P 4EE
© *1973 L. C. B. Seaman*
Printed in Great Britain by
Cox & Wyman Ltd, Fakenham, Norfolk

SBN 416 07610 6 hardback
SBN 416 77550 0 paperback

Distributed in the U.S.A. by
BARNES & NOBLE IMPORT DIVISION
HARPER & ROW PUBLISHERS INC.

Contents

Acknowledgements

My thanks are due to my daughter-in-law, Christine, and my sister-in-law, Mary Smith, for turning much of my scribbled longhand into accurate typescript; to the Rev. P. N. Brooks for his observations on Chapter 1 and for being responsible in the first place for my decision to write this book; to my former colleague, Gilbert Talbot, for his help with one more set of proofs, and to Colin Parsons for material upon which to cling when I ventured into the troubled waters of Chapter 13; to Jack B. Watson for subjecting the book's first draft to that stern and thoughtful scrutiny which he has bestowed on so much of my efforts in other spheres of historical activity.

Finally my thanks are due to The Society of Authors as the literary representative of the Estate of A. E. Housman, Jonathan Cape Ltd., publishers of A. E. Housman's *Collected Poems*, and Holt, Rinehart & Winston, Inc., for permission to quote from A. E. Housman's the 'Lancer'.

L.C.B.S.

Introduction

> Above all things, let no unwary reader do me
> the injustice of believing in *me*.
>
> SAMUEL BUTLER

This book makes no claim either to be comprehensive or to be based on original research. It is a general introduction to various aspects of the Victorian age, written, as far as possible, on the basis of some of the more recently-published professional works on the period.

Whether they have studied the Victorian age at school or not, most people have some knowledge of it. School studies tend to concentrate either on the political activities of Peel, Palmerston, Disraeli and Gladstone and the failure of the Chartists, and rarely extend beyond 1885; or they concentrate heavily on the horrors of the factory system and the inadequacies of public health and hygiene. Among some adults, Victorianism is synonymous with the exploitation of the working class and the evils (or, increasingly of late, the absurdities) of Imperialism. Others see it mainly as a period of religious hypocrisy and cruelty to children. Over against these, others, believing what journalists tell them about the 'decline' of the British in the twentieth century and their failure to find a 'rôle' for themselves, see the Victorians, by contrast, as admirably full of bounce, bustle and achievement. Yet others see the period through a nostalgic haze as being cosily quaint, so that Victoriana of all sorts, dismissed as hideous by Edwardians and Georgians, become fashionable curiosities and receive the earnest attention of conservationists. Its machines, once seen as symbols of the enslavement of the masses, acquire aesthetic value; and industrial archaeology gives to early steam engines the status of Mycenaean pots.

The aim of this book is not so much to 'correct' or 'revise' these views as to seek to put them into perspective and to relate them to the economic and political background of the period as a whole; and this in spite of the increasing unpopularity of 'general' histories in more exalted academic places. Without general histories there will be little or no communication between professional historians and the rest of society, and a fatal inability to set specialized studies within a proper context. Against the valid assertion that history's generalizations are always untrue, must be set the equally valid assertion that without generalization there is no history. Those who, in Sir Eric Ashby's sharp words, devote their time to 'crawling along the frontiers of knowledge with a hand-lens' must not be allowed to object to those who try to take in rather more of the scenery and make it possible for interested parties to study the general lie of the land.

Even this book, however, does not seek to cover so many topics that, as can so easily happen in a 'general' history, none of them is treated adequately. Not all aspects of the reign have received the same depth of treatment. The book is very much a history of England; it makes no claim to be a history of 'Britain'. In those parts of the book concerned with economic problems, the emphasis is placed on railways because of the tendency of those without specialized knowledge of economic history to think so much in terms of the early developments in the textile industries as to regard 'the industrial revolution' as a phenomenon chiefly characteristic of the pre-Victorian period. The 'Great Depression' has been examined with some attention because, owing to the controversy which has surrounded it, it is a topic about which it is exceptionally hard for those who are not economists or economic historians to find any sure ground. On the other hand, those who view history primarily as social scientists will, it is hoped, find the book's attention to political, diplomatic and imperial developments helpful. Many books on the Victorians have also tended to skimp the years after 1875. This book tries to bring out their importance. Since, moreover, one of the distinguishing features of Victoria's reign was the ever-increasing scope of Empire, an endeavour has also been made to incorporate a closer examination of British Imperialism throughout the years from 1837 to 1901 than is sometimes provided and to link this topic more closely and realistically with what is usually somewhat narrowly interpreted as foreign policy.

Any serious attempt to look closely at Victorian England results in an increasing awareness of the extent to which it was an association, and at times a marked dissociation, of very different ways of life. Ideally, one would wish to produce an integrated, coherent picture of Victorian society in the round; but the suspicion is unavoidable that the result would be to impose a pattern which, because it was a pattern, was a falsification. The rather disparately 'topical' character of the book is therefore the result of what has seemed a necessary precaution against attempting to achieve what one suspects to be unattainable. Even within these self-imposed limits, a book such as this cannot but be characterized by errors, some avoidable and some unavoidable, as well as being open to the charge of idiosyncrasies of emphasis. For these shortcomings one must apologize in advance and hope that, in spite of them, it will achieve its real purpose of encouraging the reader to go on to other and doubtless better books about the Victorians.

Woking, 1972   L.C.B.S.

1 · *People of the Book*

And none, O Lord, have perfect rest,
For none are wholly free from sin;
And they, who fain would serve Thee best,
Are conscious most of wrong within.

Hymns, Ancient and Modern

Nobody is gay now; they are so religious.

LORD MELBOURNE to Queen Victoria, 1837

The word 'Victorian', like all such terms, is misleading. Victorianism neither began in 1837 nor ended in 1901. A man of sixty in 1867, no less than a man who reached that age as late as 1927, could certainly be described as a Victorian. Yet the Victorianism of the first would have been shaped almost wholly by the pre-Victorian experience of the thirty years he had lived before the Queen's accession in 1837; and the second would almost certainly carry with him, into the fourth decade of the twentieth century, ideas and attitudes acquired in the last thirty-four years of the Queen's reign. Victorian ideas and attitudes were in many ways symbolized by Darwin, Tennyson and Gladstone; yet all three were already twenty-eight years of age when Victoria became queen. That great 'Victorian' headmaster, Arnold of Rugby, was a subject of the Queen for only the last five years of his life; and Jeremy Bentham, by 1837, had been dead for five years. In 1837, Dickens, Browning and Samuel Smiles were all twenty-five, John Bright twenty-six, John Stuart Mill thirty-one, John Henry Newman thirty-six and Palmerston as much as fifty-three. When the Queen died, Bernard Shaw had another fifty years to live, H. G. Wells another forty and Florence Nightingale another nine. Stanley

Baldwin was already a man of thirty-four, Neville Chamberlain thirty-two, Bertrand Russell twenty-nine; and Beatrice Webb had completed only half her life-span. Incongruously, two of the few persons of influence whose entire lives were encompassed within the years of Victoria's reign were Parnell and Oscar Wilde. The Victorian age cannot thus be thought of as wholly contained within the sixty-four years of the Queen's reign, since men's ideas and attitudes, once acquired, and their institutions, once established, change more slowly than history books sometimes suggest. Victorianism owed many of its chiefly-remembered characteristics to developments which took place in the years between 1780 and 1837; and the late-Victorian era is much of a piece with the first half of the twentieth century, so that there are respects in which England remained Victorian, and was governed and administered by Victorians, throughout the century that separated the Great Exhibition of 1851 and the Festival of Britain in 1951.

The Victorian age is not merely part of a continuity greater than itself; it contains within it many discontinuities. Under careful examination the appearance of a steady progress from oligarchic to democratic suffrage tends to dissolve. The commercial and industrial predominance with which the reign began, and for which it is celebrated, was waning, and seen to be waning, well before 1901. Once in almost every decade the Victorians endured major or minor recessions, and in the last twenty years of the period were unshakeably convinced that they were suffering from a Great Depression. The sense of secure affluence and inevitable progress, with which the Victorians are popularly credited, was arrived at by more thoughtful minds only after a most careful counting of blessings. The result might well be summed up in nothing more arrogant than a measured belief that, in spite of everything, there had been 'improvement'. Nor was it uniformly an Age of Imperialism. The onward march of Empire was something of an unpremeditated scramble in the stormy late afternoon of the Victorian era. The Pax Britannica based on naval power was the long-lasting afterglow of Trafalgar; but as early as the 1860s it is noticeable how little effect the world's greatest naval power could have on the startling changes that then took place on the shores of the Baltic and the Mediterranean and on the other side of the Atlantic. By the end of the reign, officialdom was as pensive about naval defence as about economic prospects.

If, however, one looks for the most enduring and distinctive characteristic of the Victorian age, one finds it in its high sense of moral responsibility. A consideration of this is more important to an understanding of the Victorians than any other factor. For, whether they were being humanitarian or utilitarian; benevolent or heartless; sentimental or pornographic; religious or irreligious; evangelical or high church; Malthusians or Fabians; Little Englanders or Imperialists; whether sternly administering a ruthless Poor Law or congratulating themselves, as they did throughout the century, for having liberated negro slaves; the Victorians were almost always acting with reference to their all-pervading belief in the moral imperatives of personal responsibility, of duty, and of living for something other than the satisfaction of the immediate needs of the self. It mattered little whether a man did his duty because it was owed to God or because he believed it to be owed solely to his fellow-men in a universe from which God had been banished. The religious revival which the Victorians inherited from Wesleyanism, and from the evangelical movement within the Established Church, implanted the moral imperative so strongly within the nation's conscience that it was little affected by the relative decline in religious observance and belief of the second half of the reign. It survived long enough to be exemplified in such varied post-Victorians as George Lansbury and Lord Reith.

That evangelical religion tended to inculcate an obsessive belief in work, in seriousness of behaviour, in respectability and the idea of self-help, inevitably led to the quasi-Marxist view of it as a carefully cultivated 'ideology' designed to induce in the masses a docile acceptance of the tyranny of the capitalist entrepreneur. That such virtues, with their concomitant encouragement of frugality among the poor and abstention from luxurious display in the rich, were well suited to a nation engaged in the task of industrializing an underdeveloped economy almost wholly out of its own resources is attested by the sedulous cultivation of a similar, if godless, puritanism in the U.S.S.R. after 1917. They could provide justification for long hours of work and low standards of personal comfort among the labouring poor and, among the rich, a readiness, by foregoing present pleasures, to invest their wealth for the future of their families and of society. Given the uncertainties of commercial and manufacturing activity in the unstable and constantly changing circumstances of international trade, there was no hope of progress (or, for the poor, of survival) unless lives were conducted with a conscious and prudent regularity. The sexually self-indulgent were prodigal of time and money, two factors essential to industrial and commercial enterprise; so also were those who ignored the insistent evangelical calls to temperance in the matter of alcohol. Those who would not, or could not, practise self-help caused themselves and their families to become a charge on others; and the belief that this would weaken their moral fibre still further shows that the workhouse test imposed by the Poor Law Amendment Act of 1834 served the fundamental moral purpose of deterring the feckless and protecting the respectable.

Since none of these ideals of behaviour was new, being an integral part of the traditional Puritan ethic, there is little need to disagree with the Marxist view that they became a predominant creed in the Victorian period because they were socially useful. Indeed, few devout Christians would have seen anything amiss in this. Arnold of Rugby was strongly of the opinion that the Church was a society 'for the putting down of moral evil' and 'for the moral improvement of mankind' and that what was wrong with the Established Church in the early years of the nineteenth century was that it had lost sight of the 'social character' of religion.[1] The principal burden of Victorian hostility towards the Roman Church was the moral and social backwardness of the countries in which it was predominant. Attending evening prayer in a London parish church, the

[1] Quoted Basil Willey, *Nineteenth-Century Studies* (Harmondsworth, Penguin, 1969), p. 64.

Frenchman, Hippolyte Taine, felt he had attended 'an ethical meeting at which the chairman does his talking from the pulpit instead of the platform'. For the Englishman, Taine also wrote,

> The Church . . . is the moral health department, an office for the good administration of souls. For all these reasons, respect for Christianity is accepted by public opinion as a duty, and even an aspect of ordinary seemliness of behaviour. An ordinary Englishman would be very reluctant to admit that an unbeliever could be a good Englishman and a decent, respectable man.[1]

The fact that a moral code appropriate to the economic and social needs of the time emerged from a religious revival in the late eighteenth century is due to the simple fact that the thinking and feeling of all but an intellectual minority could be formulated in no idiom other than the religious at that time. The non-Christian ideas of the eighteenth-century Enlightenment were at best only for the few and were soon discredited on the grounds that they had 'led to' the 'horrors' of the French Revolution; and the formalism of eighteenth-century Anglicanism, which equated fervour with something deplorable called 'enthusiasm', may be said to have left English society with no coherent set of beliefs to bind it together. And as rapid industrial growth and the population explosion of the time began to impose their pains and stresses, first Methodism and then evangelicalism were bound to attract troubled minds in all ranks of a fractured society, just as Jacobinism, secularism and trade unionism were to attract other troubled minds. At its worst, and naturally the Victorians remembered only the worst about their predecessors' behaviour, the eighteenth century could be represented as a time when parsons need never preach, schoolmasters never teach, constituencies have no constituents and corporate bodies fulfil few if any of the functions for which they were set up. The royal family was either dull or disreputable. The aristocracy was usually rakish or cultivated, but in either case extravagant and intellectually

[1] Taine, *Notes on England*, trans. Edward Hyams (London, 1957), pp. 157 and 193.

sceptical. Thus, when, in 1831, the country was faced with the onset of cholera for the first time[1] the M.P. who suggested that the matter called for 'a general fast', as an act of national penitence, was not one of the responsible members of the House but a known eccentric. His proposal was greeted at first with incomprehension and ribaldry. On the day finally appointed, the congregations at St Paul's, Westminster Abbey and the Chapel Royal were small and inattentive. At the lower end of the scale, the pressure of population on an economy that was expanding fast, but not fast enough, and the wholly new regimentation imposed on those who came into the factories, were already breaking up the ordered life of a predominantly rural community in which everybody knew his place.

In such conditions, only a minority will join others in schemes, revolutionary or otherwise, to shape society anew for the future. Most will seek for personal salvation in the here and now. It is too often forgotten that in comparison with evangelical religion it was Jacobin and later Socialist preaching which promised pie in the sky (or at best denied it to all mankind until the Dawn of the Revolution). The message of the Methodists and the evangelicals was that whoever acknowledged Jesus as his personal saviour secured salvation at once. Nor must it be assumed that such vitalizing promises of instant salvation were made only or even principally in the pre- and early-Victorian era. There were great revival movements in the 1860s. Moody and Sankey, the American revivalists, conducted successful campaigns in England in 1875 and 1884; and it was between these two dates that William Booth's Mission was formally constituted as the Salvation Army. The capacity of religious revivalism to affect men's lives persisted throughout the Queen's reign.

The most significant element in the Methodist and evangelical movements was their freedom from the old Calvinist doctrine that salvation was only for 'the elect'. After Wesley, salvation was for all, and it was this universality that consorted so well with the needs of a time when persons of all classes were no longer certain about their standing in society and all men

[1] See p. 48.

felt under attack, the rich because of their wealth, the poor because of their poverty. And this universality made revived Christianity a social religion as well as a religion of personal salvation, embracing the causes of negro slaves, child chimney-sweeps and factory women and children and, at the century's end, giving much of its earnest quality to the nascent Labour movement. Hardly less significant for an explanation of the widespread character of the religious revival was that, whereas Methodism found itself outside the Established Church, the evangelical movement was a revival within it. Thanks to this, and to the important social and political connections of William Wilberforce, its brightest luminary, the evangelical movement spread revived Christianity upwards from the middle class to the upper classes. Methodism in isolation would not have had such consequences, since it was socially tainted by its early appeal to the lower orders. Thus, when Wilberforce himself first displayed signs of religious zeal his grandfather threatened, if the result were his adoption of Methodism, to cut him out of his will. In consequence, by the time Victoria became queen, the raffishness of her royal uncles, the sons of George III, was coming to be seen as a survival from the bad old days. The high-minded seriousness that characterized so many of the aristocracy henceforth, and which marked Peel and Gladstone and, later, Lord Salisbury, as essential Victorians, explains the rather pathetic, jokey cynicism of the ageing Lord Melbourne when confronted in the first years of Victoria's reign with the decline of gaiety and the rise of religion; it explains the fact that Palmerston's popularity in mid-century depended almost entirely on his being 'a character' and thus in many respects out of character with the times; and it points up the evident singularity of Disraeli, whose character 'typical' Victorians quite failed to understand, having instead to transform him into a creature of myth and legend.

Revived Christianity also provided a popular culture and a deep emotional experience. The Victorian age is perhaps most faithfully reflected in the pages of *Hymns, Ancient and Modern*, of which the first edition appeared in 1861. The words of Wesley's 'Jesu Lover of My Soul' (Let Me To Thy Bosom

Fly) ruthlessly exploit and express the depths of burdened anguish:

> Hide me, O my Saviour, hide,
> Till the storm of life is past;
> Safe into the haven guide,
> O receive my soul at last. . . .
>
> Other refuge have I none;
> Hangs my helpless soul on Thee. . . .

The same guilt-laden sense of alienation that was not peculiar to its author, though he had his treble share of it, is expressed in John Henry Newman's 'Lead Kindly Light', a hymn of intense popularity till well into the twentieth century:

> The night is dark and I am far from home,
> Lead Thou me on.

And the domestication of the ineffable down to the commonest level of daily experience could hardly go further than Mrs Alexander's 'Once in Royal David's City', which succeeded in transforming the Lord of All Things, once the daunting Pantocrator of Byzantine mosaic, into anybody's curly-headed baby being bathed in a zinc bath by the nursery fire:

> He was little, weak, and helpless,
> Tears and smiles like us He knew;
> And He feeleth for our sadness,
> And He shareth in our gladness.[1]

The self-indulgent sentimentality to which this points and which is characteristic of so many Victorian minds was, in its intention, wholly to the good. A deliberate over-valuing of the humble and the domestic, the frail and the defenceless, was a positive first challenge to the under-valuing of them that the rough and acquisitive nature of an insufficiently improved society continued to encourage. It represented an enlargement of the human sympathy by Dickens that he could persuade thousands to weep over the deathbed of Little Nell or the

---

[1] It is, of course, not Mrs Alexander's fault that the hymns she wrote for children proved so popular with adults.

sufferings of Bill Sikes's Nancy. For too many members of
society, females of the poorer classes were still only objects to
be desired, enjoyed, employed or discarded, at the whim of the
more fortunate. Popular literature of the time is liberally
sprinkled with gruelling accounts of grieved parents weeping
over tiny graves. Tennyson, hardly less than Dickens, wallowed
in the sentiments inspired by the early death of a humble child:

> You'll bury me, my mother, just beneath the
>   hawthorn shade,
> And you'll come sometimes and see me where
>   I am lowly laid. . . .
>
> Don't let Effie come to see me till my grave
>   is growing green:
> She'll be a better child to you than I have
>   ever been. . . .

Yet, with infant mortality at the rate it was, and while
medical science and social hygiene were too primitive to put it
right, for such routine deaths to be publicly presented as events
of grievous concern to all who could read was at any rate the
beginning of a civilizing process. By wringing people's hearts
it got something done in the end.

In the same way, the middle-class morality which the
Victorians learned from the religious revival was an essential
defence, in an imperfectly organized and newly urbanized (and
therefore still disorientated and badly managed) society against
the historic moral laxness of the traditional aristocracy and the
more frightening lack of civilized standards among the new
urban masses. If women did not go out unaccompanied or
unchaperoned it was not solely because they were prudes but
because they might otherwise be robbed, accosted or assaulted
by drunks. The spectacle of the multitudes who occupied the
sprawling underworlds of London and many other towns
excited the hostile comment of foreign observers throughout
the century. In consequence, the narrowly respectable and
righteous were making a reasonably correct sociological
assessment in regarding themselves as newly-arrived Children
of Israel in a land otherwise given over to lewdness. Obsessed,

as the respectable were, with the dogmas of self-help and personal responsibility, they were convinced that the weaker vessels among them would inevitably sink into depravity if they departed in the slightest from the rules of respectability. Observance of these rules was the outward and visible sign that they continued in a state of grace. Such signs were the frequent reading of the Bible, the institution of family prayers (little practised at the beginning of the century and in decline at its end), a strict observance of the Sabbath and, in sterner households, a refusal to play cards, to touch strong drink or to mention in the presence of females such matters as miscarriages or the terms of even acts of Parliament where they were concerned with the state of the sewers. The price of this devotion to the doctrine of omnipresent temptation was a vigilance so extreme that when the Crystal Palace was moved to its permanent site at Sydenham it was laid down that it should remain closed on Sundays and that all its nude statues should first be supplied with fig leaves. The more sensitive among the righteous were hardly less vigilant against their own sinful desires than those of others, so that many Victorian worthies otherwise distinguished by their undoubted intellectual stature seem, to a later age, neurotically and ridiculously guilt-ridden. Lesser spirits were pharisaical, thanking God they were not as other men. Yet, if some people had not taken a pride, even a pharisaical pride, in being better than their half-barbarous fellows or their morally lax forbears, life in Victorian England would have been worse than it was.

Like all moral codes, the Victorian, with its demand for high seriousness and strict conformity to a set of social rules based on religious sanctions, was honoured as much in the breach as in the observance. Though marital infidelity among the more stable elements at all levels of society was unusual, kept women, prostitutes, and irregular unions among the poorer classes were all features of the Victorian scene and the code had to be protected by strenuous, and often highly successful, efforts to pretend that such phenomena did not exist. Sexual attitudes were further contorted by the manner in which women were called upon to be their principal custodians. It was ultimately their responsibility to maintain sexual moral standards by being unapproachable before marriage and unresistingly available to their male partner on demand thereafter. They were expected to be as physically unaroused when behaving as chaste wives as when being chaste spinsters. In neither capacity were they to encourage, let alone enjoy, the regrettable male impulse to indulge in 'the baser passions', for this would certainly impair the vigour and assiduity with which the man attended to his man's prime duties as worker or employer. Worse still, such encouragement would multiply for wives, in an age almost wholly unacquainted with contraception, the frightful risks of pregnancy. Thus women tended to shrink from sex, aggravating still further the serious-minded male's sense of guilt. It may be suspected that the amount of private misery resulting from conformity to the Victorian sexual code was not greatly less than that which resulted from departing from it.

In time, it came to be the code above all that mattered. On this, all but the most hardy minds were agreed. If it were departed from, at all costs scandal must be avoided; for, if scandal there were, the guilty ones must be punished. And since that punishment was social ostracism, avoidance of scandal, rather than abandonment of the conduct that gave rise to it, was of primary concern. This was not so much hypocrisy as a combination of common sense and common charity. While nobody knew officially that Kitty O'Shea was Parnell's mistress (though everybody seems to have known as a matter of fact, except for Gladstone), both the code and Parnell's career were protected. Once Captain O'Shea began divorce proceedings and the matter became public knowledge, Parnell lost his career at once and was dead in less than two years; but even so, he lost his political career less for his breach of the code than for flaunting it by refusing the temporary retirement from politics that his friends declared would enable the matter to be forgotten.

Yet stern devotion to the moral code was so much a part of Victorian thinking that it survived and was indeed often intensified by abandonment of the dogmas of what was called Revealed Religion. John Stuart Mill, George Eliot and T. H.

Huxley, to name but three, though discarding a supernatural religion, attributed hardly less supernatural validity to Morality itself. They claimed indeed that their Morality was purer and more exalted than Christian morality. By the middle of the century it was becoming increasingly difficult for sensitive, intelligent minds to accept that the sole basis of right behaviour was literal belief in a series of miraculous happenings which were alleged to have happened two thousand years beforehand. Apart from this, the good behaviour of Christians was based on fear, or love, of God. It was undertaken out of a dread of eternal punishment or in the hope of eternal bliss; but the non-believer who behaved rightly did so in the confident expectation of neither reward nor punishment. This was held to be a higher morality, one purged not only of superstition but of the slightest element of even spiritual self-interest. Unbelievers also felt impelled towards strict ethical standards by the very universality of the assumption that morality depended upon faith. If lack of religion were to result in loss of moral standards, then their unbelief stood condemned; and so far from abandonment of religion leading to licentiousness, the unbelievers of the nineteenth century were unrivalled for the aridity of their moral attitudes.

Thus, the best of the Victorians accepted a moral code of duty, high seriousness and dedication to work which, though derived from religion, was strong enough to survive a loss of religion. And it was this, together with other more tangible factors deriving from the unique economic circumstances of the time, that gave the Victorians what has since seemed their quite astonishing energy. For some, the consciousness of obligation to God or to their fellow-creatures provided the driving force, as did an almost obsessive idea that Time was a precious gift from On High for the fruitful stewardship of which every man would be one day called to account. For many, it was a sense of guilt that kept them endlessly active, impelling them to 'sublimate' their sensual desires in work, or good works; or an impassioned desire to have, at the Last Judgment, a sufficient store of good or great things done to outweigh in the balance the sinfulness with which they were sure they were filled. Gladstone's daemonic energy seems to have ben derived from such factors. Others were driven on by the less subtle consideration that to rise in the world, to achieve respectability and social esteem, would provide tangible evidence in this life that their ways were pleasing to the Lord. The code channelled their lives into a narrow stream along which, in consequence, their energy flowed with dynamic force. The general acceptance of the primacy of doing one's duty as a responsible being left their minds wholly free to concentrate on action. Those who were troubled by doubt were, for the most part and in the long run, troubled only by theological doubt; and most of them worked through that doubt only to discover that the old moral imperatives were now stronger rather than weaker. And so, Tennyson could write in *In Memoriam*,

> There lives more faith in honest doubt,
> Believe me, than in half the creeds

and, in *Locksley Hall*,

> Yet I doubt not through the ages one increasing
>   purpose runs,
> And the thoughts of man are widened with the
>   process of the suns.

Men whom theological doubt could not turn from their deeper faith and who felt themselves the conscious agents of an increasing cosmic purpose could hardly help but agree with Macaulay that they belonged to 'the most enlightened generation that ever existed'. They could thus feel self-confident without becoming self-indulgent, could strive without relaxing into self-satisfaction. They could believe that all things were possible to them without loss of humility, or forgetfulness of the essential fallibility of all things human. They could find in social criticism an excuse neither for opting out nor for cynicism; instead, it was a call to yet more strenuous effort to redeem the precious Time that had been so providentially granted them.

Yet Victorian religion was subject to a major limitation.

Though it spread upwards in society it reached no further down than the uppermost sections of the labouring class. The most famous piece of evidence is the count taken on the last Sunday of March 1851, when the most conservative estimate of the number of adults who attended no place of worship at all on that day was 5·25 millions out of a total population in England and Wales of just under 18 millions. Apart from this, social and religious workers among the poorer districts were reporting all through the century their grieved astonishment at the extent not only of indifference towards, but also of sheer ignorance of, the Bible and the rudiments of Christian belief. Yet this was the foreseeable fate of a religion that came too readily to equate itself with respectability. The distinction which the most earnest of religious persons drew between the 'deserving' and the 'undeserving' poor likewise tended to set limits not only to formal acts of charity but also to a more genuinely Christian concern for the labouring poor. The association of Christianity with respectability was further reinforced in the Victorian period by the steady improvement in the legal and social status of the Dissenters, who increasingly lost touch both with political radicalism and with the working class as a result. Also contributory was the fact that the Bibliolatry of Victorian religion made it appropriate to the literate, but less so to the semi-literate and the illiterate. Bible Christianity, by tending to identify serious religion with the close study of an essentially obscure holy text, could easily degenerate into an arid pedantry that was only pseudo-religious. The People of the Book, as they liked to call themselves, tended to become bookish in the dreary sense and (as Dickens was eager to demonstrate) joyless and glum. It needed insistent injections of revivalism if it was to be revitalized; but though mid- and late-Victorian revivals had dramatic immediate effects they were limited geographically and not usually long-lasting. The more enduring success of the Salvation Army was due both to its deliberate eschewing of the respectable and to its romantic, symbolic and musical elements. This also accounts for the persistence of the ritualist revival in the 'Anglo-Catholic' wing of the Established Church, whose medievalism, deriving in the main from John Henry

Newman and the Oxford Movement, was often successful in
slum parishes and often identified with social causes. In the
main, however, the Established Church and the traditional
Dissenting bodies, like most typical Victorian modes and
institutions, failed to embrace the 'dark, uninstructed masses'.
Charles Kingsley put his finger on one of the principal reasons:
'It is our fault. We have used the Bible as if it was a mere
special constable's handbook – an opium dose for keeping
beasts of burden patient while they were being overloaded.'[1]

This failure was not merely the result of the cult of respectability. It resulted from the fact that the churches, like all other
voluntary organizations in Victorian England, could not keep
pace with the continuous growth of population, the increasing
expansion of towns, and the ceaseless shifts of population that
took place. The traditional religious bodies built churches,
chapels, schools and Sunday schools, and established missions
in the slums, all through the century; but they were never able
to catch up. In this, as in their other social concerns, the
Victorians were defeated by the sheer size of the problems
confronting them; but historical accuracy compels recognition
of the fact that they never gave up trying.

There are indeed fairly solid reasons for the view that the
religious vitality of the Victorians decreased hardly at all as the
years passed by. In the pre-Victorian period the Methodists
and the Old Dissenters made the running because the laxity and
inefficiency of the Anglican Church and its identification with
the landed gentry alienated it from the new urban population
called into existence by industrial change. It was always easier
to start a new Dissenting place of worship than to set up a new
Anglican parish or to expand the operation of an existing one
in an age of non-resident priests, pluralities, and underpaid
curates. Overwhelmingly, the typical parson was a country
parson, a leader, with the squire, of a village society. But from
1840 onwards religious expansion developed on all fronts. The
Church reformed its organization and thus made possible the
translation into practical effect of the two-headed inspiration
that came from the evangelical and Tractarian movements,

[1] *Politics for the People* (London, 1848).

While the evangelical movement tended to stimulate personal piety first and foremost, the Tractarian movement made for a keener awareness of the Church as part of a living tradition, for a more dignified ceremonial, for a proper regard for liturgy and for a religious consciousness less narrowly verbal than was normal to the tradition established in the eighteenth century. To these new elements in the Established Church and the continuing vitality of Dissent, both New and Old, was added the revived life of the Roman Catholic Church. This derived from the Catholic Emancipation Act of 1829, the great influx of Irish into Liverpool and London, the reestablishment of the Roman hierarchy in 1850 and the great influence of the two ex-Tractarian Anglicans, Cardinal Manning, who succeeded the incompetent Wiseman as Roman Catholic archbishop of Westminster, and J. H. Newman. Manning identified himself closely with the social problems of the working class in the 1870s and 1880s; and Newman, though at first execrated for his apostasy, came to be regarded at the end of his life with respect both for the moderation of his Catholicism and the generosity of his attitude to the Anglicans from whom he had become separated.

The figures reveal quite remarkable religious activity in the second half of the century. Between 1841 and 1876 the Anglicans built 1,727 new churches in England and Wales and restored over 7,000 old churches. The Congregationalists increased the number of their places of worship from 2,236 in 1861 to 4,579 in 1901; the Baptists increased the number of theirs from 1,150 to 6,313; the Roman Catholics increased theirs in the same period from 798 to 1,536.[1] The result was that the 'empty pews' of which complaints were made at the end of the Queen's reign testified as much to the zeal of the Victorians as church builders as to the spread of indifferentism. And although Anglicanism declined in relation to the growth of the population, the number of baptisms, confirmations and communions mounted steadily all through the century; a Roman Catholic writer in 1884 attributed the relatively slow growth of Roman Catholicism to 'the great revival in the church life of the Church

[1] O. Chadwick, *The Victorian Church* (London, Black, 1969), Vol. II, p. 241.

of England'. The influence of Gladstone similarly ensured that the revival of the first part of the century continued to bear fruit in the seventies and eighties; a devout Tractarian himself, he ensured the preferment to many positions of eminence in the Church of men who were products of the Oxford Movement.[1]

Nor was the indifference of the working class ever as total as is sometimes claimed; the term 'working class' is, like the term 'middle class', in any case too broad to make precise statement possible. For, although the cult of respectability doubtless kept the poorest and roughest out, it also let them in as soon as they should become less poor and less rough; it was no bad thing, perhaps, that once a woman could afford a bonnet rather than a shawl, or a man a collar and tie, the doors of a respectable church were instantly opened to them. Indeed, it can be shown that to proceed from agnosticism to non-conformity and thence to Anglicanism was a not unusual *curriculum vitae* of the humble who succeeded in the world; a great deal of the irreligion of the Victorian age was the expression of social and political, rather than theological or intellectual, dissent. And over against the lack of church attendance have to be set the extraordinary statistics of Sunday school attendance. In 1818 about 4 per cent of the population attended Sunday school; in 1888 about three children out of four attended Sunday school in England and Wales, almost all of them from the working class.[2] Sunday schools remained strong in the towns, even after the passing of the 1870 education act, and in Lancashire there was a strong tradition of prolonging Sunday school into adult years, a practice which long continued among Congregationalists. The more successful Sunday schools were often cheerfully inter-denominational and must have been theologically naïve in the extreme. Yet the combined effect of the Sunday school movement and the

[1] Unlike Palmerston and Disraeli, who promoted evangelicals as a safe-guard against creeping 'Romanism'.

[2] See Chadwick, op. cit., pp. 256–62, and especially the judgement, 'Though Victorian working men did not go to church often, they or their wives sent their children in multitudes.' That their motives for doing so were not wholly religious but for the purpose of securing a little Sunday afternoon privacy for themselves does not affect the issue.

spread of compulsory education by the end of the century probably meant that working-class children knew their Bible better in 1901 than their predecessors in 1837.

Unquestionably, a larger proportion of the population stayed away from church in 1901 than had done so in 1837. How far this reflected a decline in genuine religious feeling is impossible to judge, since religious feeling is not quantifiable. The difference may mean no more than that in 1837 most people lived in villages whereas in 1901 most of them lived in towns. Absence from a village church in 1831 would be a noticeable act of self-alienation from a small community; absence from a town church in 1901 was an anonymous act performed in company with hundreds of others equally anonymous, and was therefore devoid of social significance. Furthermore, in 1837 Sunday's difference from weekdays lay wholly in the fact that it was the day for going to church (which was usually locked up on every other day). By 1901 it was the day also for cycling, golf, the excursion train and the Sunday newspaper. In 1837, church and chapel were willy-nilly for all and sundry; by 1901 they were coming more and more to be principally for the devout or the would-be devout. They were no longer central to life, since so many of the other functions of church and chapel had by then been secularized. But there can be little doubt that those who did attend church or chapel in 1901 got more out of doing so than they would have done in 1837; and in all denominations they enjoyed a more ordered liturgy, better music and a wealth of heart-warming hymns.

In the long run, what may have been more important for the churches than the relative decline in attendance by 1901 was the great gap that the second half of the century had opened between the theology of the people and the theology of its theologians. The theology of the people by 1901 was very largely (though minus much of its hell-fire element) what official theology had been in 1837. It still depended on a conscious or unconscious belief in the inerrancy of the King James Bible and was nourished almost wholly on 'Bible stories' literally, if elaborately, interpreted. It was a theology of sentimental escapism (Rock of Ages, cleft for me./Let me hide myself in Thee) and of rewards and penalties in the hereafter. It defined 'works' in practice as helping at bazaars and fêtes (both Victorian novelties) or teaching in the Sunday school. It tended therefore to be bibliocentric and congregationally-minded, both in the narrowest sense. It thus lacked contact with the intellectual life, not only of the secular world, but of the Christian Church as it had been developing since 1837.

It was because the theology of the people was in no sense intellectual that the intellectual difficulties created by what was loosely called 'science' did less to weaken the hold of religion over the people than is sometimes claimed. The first intellectual blow to traditional notions was administered by the geologists. Their studies demolished both the story that the world had been created in six days, and the accepted calculation that the world's history had begun late one October afternoon in the year 4004 B.C. The second blow was the theory of evolution, as it emerged from Darwin's *Origin of Species* (1859) and his *Descent of Man* (1871). This, it was thought, discredited the central Christian teaching that man was a special creation wholly distinct from the animals. More serious blows were administered by biblical criticism, from which it emerged that the Bible on which the whole of Anglo-Saxon Christianity was based was an inaccurate text; while historical study, as well as the development of the natural sciences, called in question the literal truth of both Old and New Testaments. This was a serious matter to men accustomed to believe that Jonah had in very truth been swallowed by a whale and lived to tell the tale, and who speculated thoughtfully upon the exact dimensions of Noah's Ark. Moreover, as soon as it was alleged that some parts of the Bible were legendary, there seemed no logical objection to dismissing all of it as legendary. If only some miracles were true, how many were true, and which ones? If Adam and Eve were legendary, then so was the Virgin Birth; and if the Virgin Birth, why not the Resurrection?

It was a striking achievement of the Church to survive this intellectual crisis and emerge in such relatively good order. A large number of reputable clerics soon accepted the intellectual impossibility of continuing to base Christianity on the inerrancy of the received biblical text. Between 1879 and the end of the century it became increasingly easy to find bishops willing to ordain men who openly avowed their disbelief in the verbal inspiration of the Bible. It was a remarkable reassertion of the traditions of latitudinarianism and comprehensiveness that the Church had established in the eighteenth century and against which the Tractarians had inveighed so fiercely in the 1830s and 1840s.[1]

Yet the transition was undertaken only by means of a conspiracy of silence. The clergy were roughly of two sorts: those who preached old beliefs because they still adhered to them, and those who avoided preaching the new ones for fear of unsettling the minds of their faithful congregations. The occupants of the pews wanted to be assured that their sins were forgiven, not to be purged of theological error; and it was beyond the capacity of the clergy to teach, or of their congregations to understand, the sophisticated difference between the simple old faith that the Bible *was* the word of God and the confusing new idea that the Word of God was *in* the Bible but that it was necessary to look very cautiously in order to find it there. In consequence, as the century came to an end, the Church appeared, to faithful and faithless alike, as the custodian of a set of beliefs which science and scholarship had long ago

[1] There were, of course, repeated crises. There was a ten-year storm following the publication in 1860 of *Essays and Reviews*, in which certain leaders of Anglican opinion, including the future archbishop, Frederick Temple, sought to encourage biblical criticism among Christians. There was the scandal caused by Bishop Colenso of Natal. In 1863 he was deprived of his see by the South African bishops for heretical attacks on the factual accuracy of the Pentateuch. In 1865, the judicial committee of the privy council declared his deprivation invalid. The South African bishops excommunicated him in 1866. The Church of England itself skilfully evaded any official pronouncement on the doctrinal issues. In 1889 there was more trouble over a collection of essays, *Lux Mundi*, edited by Charles Gore, later bishop of Worcester, Birmingham and Oxford, which sought, among much else, to show that disbelief in the literal truth of parts of the Bible was not incompatible with a conviction of the inspired nature of its total message.

exploded. In keeping faith with the simple-minded, it lost contact with the intelligent.[1]

By 1901 the Church was also being outpaced and outflanked as a social force. Organized working-class protest had always been ready to claim a religious sanction for the various ways in which it cried, Woe unto you, ye rich. Both Tractarianism and the Romanism of Manning were deeply concerned with the condition of the working class. But the Christian Socialism preached by F. D. Maurice and Charles Kingsley in the aftermath of the failure of Chartism proved hardly less effective than Disraeli's notions of Young England and Tory Democracy.[2] Through their manifold social and charitable work, the churches did much to succour the actual victims of an imperfect society; they had almost nothing to contribute to the task of reshaping the society from whose evils the objects of their charity suffered.[3] Lord Shaftesbury typifies this lack: indefatigably the friend of the poor he yet had neither time for, nor patience with, organized efforts to change society's structure. And so, by 1901, the social conscience was, like education and rural local government, becoming secularized. The socialists who emerged from the Victorian period into the Edwardian operated without benefit of clergy. Many were Nonconformist lay preachers; only one notable one, George Lansbury, was an Anglican. When fifty years later, Aneurin Bevan said of the Labour party that it was a moral crusade or it was nothing, the phrase – in so far as it meant anything at all to his hearers – was a measure of the extent to which the twentieth century had secularized – and probably emasculated – something that the Victorians would have regarded as wholly and necessarily religious.

[1] Thus, Bertrand Russell seemed to retain, to the end of his long life, the idea that the whole of Christian thinking was contained within the horrific superstitions beloved of his nanny, and Bernard Shaw could present as a sort of *summa theologica* the primitive forms of Christian belief he attacked in the preface to *Androcles and the Lion*.

[2] Christian Socialist influence did however contribute a good deal to the changed attitude of government to friendly societies and trade unions in the 1850s and 1860s.

[3] Nor did congregations greatly enjoy sermons about social problems.

2 · Age of Steam

From west to east, and from north to south, the mechanical principle, the philosophy of the nineteenth century, will spread and extend itself. The world has received a new impulse. The genius of the age, like a mighty river of the new world, flows onward, full, rapid, irresistible.

HENRY BOOTH, treasurer of the Liverpool and Manchester Railway, 1830

The term manufacture is no longer confined to its original signification – the production of human manipulation – but is now generally applied to articles made by machinery, from raw materials, supplied by a beneficent Providence, for adaptation by the industry and ingenuity of man for the wants and enjoyments of civilized society.

LEWIS D. B. GORDON, Regius Professor of Mechanics, University of Glasgow, 1851

The breakthrough towards an industrialized society had already occurred before the Victorian period began. But although, taking the long-term view, the transformation proceeded with ever-increasing momentum throughout the century, this was by no means how contemporaries always saw it. In the six years after the wars with Napoleon there were serious doubts that the expansion of the previous thirty years could be maintained. Though the years from 1831 to 1836 were a time of considerable growth this was not reflected in any marked increase in real wages, while from 1836 to 1842 there were bad harvests and a depression in the cotton industry; and the economy proved incapable of absorbing a labour force greatly enlarged as a result of the marked and apparently unexplained increase in the birth rate during the century's second decade. The economic advance that took place from the mid-forties onward was largely a consequence of the development of the railways and then of steamships, and was sustained by a great increase of productivity in agriculture. Between 1816 and 1842 exports had risen at an average annual rate of 7 per cent; but from 1842 to 1873 the rate was 11 per cent, while the annual value of exports rose from just above £50 million in the former year to well over £200 million in the 1870s.

The striking feature of such figures is that such rates of growth, though frequently exceeded elsewhere in later years, had never before occurred in any human society. The only precedents were contained within the history of the United Kingdom itself, in the years from 1750 to 1840; and it could hardly have been envisaged that the growth that took place in that period would be so greatly outpaced in the middle of the nineteenth century. In consequence, however important it is to recall that by later standards the industrialization of England proceeded at a quite modest pace in the eighteenth and nineteenth centuries, it is still nevertheless true that to refuse to speak of an industrial revolution in this connection is to be pedantic. What happened in pre-Victorian and Victorian England had never happened before; and once it had happened in England, there was hardly a people on earth who, a century later, had not caused it to happen to themselves or who were not strenuously trying to make it happen.

The achievements of Victorian England marked the beginning of the end of the long period of human history during which the normal mode of human existence had been based on agriculture; when the growth of population had been inhibited by its capacity to outrun the productivity of land; when the only sources of power were wind, moving water and human and animal muscle; when urban life was always the exception and the village or the landed estate the norm within which most of the population of even the most civilized societies had for centuries been accustomed to live; when commerce and communication between continent and continent were slow and laborious in some cases and all but impossible in others. It was a world of small, separated and usually under-nourished communities linked with one another and the wider world, if at all, by horse, pack animal, caravan or wooden sailing ship. It was thus, more frequently than is often realized, subject to famine, since this could occur as a result of purely local shortage. The wry consequence was that one of the few traditional means by which the ordinary man could enjoy high wages was by being one of a minority fortunate enough to survive famine or plague. Otherwise, poverty was neither exceptional nor cyclic; by any acceptable twentieth-century standard it was normal.

Evidently, England had been moving away from this state of affairs at least since 1700. Hardly less evidently, it had not escaped entirely in the nineteenth century; and it is in this respect that the term industrial revolution must be used with caution. All the same, the remarkable thing about pre- and early-Victorian England is not that many people were desperately poor and ill-housed and, at various times and places, without work; what was remarkable was that, thanks to the first stages of the industrial transformation, the population did not starve. What could happen to a country where an increasing population relied for subsistence solely on the land was made plain by the melancholy history of nineteenth-century Ireland. Until the decade ending in 1830, the rate of population growth in Ireland was not dissimilar to that in England. By the 1840s, pressure on the land was outrunning even the capacity of the genial potato to sustain life; and the potato blight from 1846–9, allied with sheer ignorance of agricultural science and the moral callousness of the New Poor Law, itself derived from intellectual attitudes which events had outdated, sufficed to produce on a grand scale the circumstances, in mid-nineteenth-century Europe, of a medieval famine. In 1841, Ireland's population was over 8 million. The next decade showed a 20 per cent decline, compared with a 14·2 per cent increase in every decade from 1800 to 1830.

The notable manifestations of the first stages of pre-Victorian industrialization were the rapid expansion of the cotton industry, important improvements in transport by road and canal, the birth of the chemical industry, and the first successful industrial employment of steam power. This accelerated, and depended upon, the growth of the mining, iron, engineering and machine tool industries as well as upon increases in agricultural productivity. Inseparable from these innovations, in part their cause and in every respect their consequence, was a rapid growth of overseas trade. The long-term social effects were the beginnings of the factory system of production as a norm and the resultant concentration of the new working population in urban areas close to coalfields and iron deposits. That this meant, most notably in the first quarter of the century, a frightening congestion of population in the northwest was due also to its proximity to the great port of Liverpool and to the lack, before the coming of the railway, of facilities for the rapid transportation of bulky goods. This is reflected in the growth-rate of the urban areas of Liverpool, Manchester and Glasgow.

The decisive technological developments behind the expansion of the economy after 1840 were railways and steam navigation, with the railways as the principal pacemaker. Effective railway history had begun with the opening of the Liverpool to Manchester line in 1830, using locomotives designed by George Stephenson. There was steady growth during the 1830s from the route mileage figure of 97 in 1830 to one of 969 in 1839. But by 1841, the figure had already risen to 1,775; by 1851 it was 6,266 and, by 1861, 9,446. Thereafter, the figure continued to rise until it had been doubled once more by 1901. Nevertheless, the route mileage in operation by the mid 1860s was about the same as that still in operation a century later.

Between 1838 and 1841, main trunk lines linked London with Birmingham, Brighton, Bristol, Manchester, Liverpool, Southampton and York. The economic effects were widespread and almost instantaneous. Half the total investment finance of the country went into railway projects in the mid-1840s. A greatly increased demand for coal, iron and building materials was generated. Hundreds of millions of bricks were needed for tunnel linings and viaducts, tons of gunpowder for blasting through rock, tons of candles for lighting the workings and, at the height of the boom, a labour force of over a quarter of a million men.

The construction of the railways stimulated the imaginations of nineteenth-century Englishmen to such an extent, however, that to treat it as a purely economic factor is to underestimate it. It affected almost everyone concerned with a sense of grandeur. The mere spectacle of such speeds, to a species hitherto accustomed to travel at an absolute maximum of 15 m.p.h., and then only exceptionally, was intoxicating. The first issue of Bradshaw's railway timetable showed, as early as 1839, average speeds on trunk lines in excess of 30 m.p.h. A relatively small proportion of the population could gawp in admiration at the new blast furnaces. But the steam locomotive carried the message of the power revolution to every man. Already by 1851, the railways carried 79 million passengers; by 1861 they carried 163 million and, by 1871, 359 million. In the first year of Victoria's reign, the first London railway, running from London Bridge to Deptford, had a fifteen-minute service all day, including Sunday; and on Whit Monday 1839 it ran a six-minute service and carried 35,000 passengers.

The message was the headiest possible: nature had been conquered. Coal and iron, wrung from the bowels of the earth could, through the miraculous ingenuity of machines devised by human beings, be so operated upon that the end-product would confer on the population at large the power to abolish space and time. Parts of the country that had once been separated from one another by weeks and days were now separated only by hours. By the 1840s, the 112-mile journey from London to Birmingham could be completed in 5½ hours; by the 1850s, the 191 miles to York could, at best, be covered in rather less than that time. Already, Brighton was nearer to London Bridge than, in the absence of anything but horse transport between the two termini, London Bridge was to Paddington. And if the 1844 Railway Act, compelling at least one train a day to call at each station on the line and at third-class fares of a penny a mile, was often complied with in ways which inflicted maximum inconvenience, the less wealthy classes may be said to have benefited most from the railways since all previous forms of transport had been normally too costly. From 1844 onwards, they benefited from cheap excursion trains, from the low fares resultant upon cut-throat competition and from the introduction after 1860 of cheap workmen's tickets. Longer-term consequences were the encouragement of the outward spread of towns. Neither all employers nor all workers now had to live within walking distance of their place of employment, so that urbanization soon developed into suburbanization. The railway permitted house building in less built-up areas where land was cheaper.

Most impressive was the sheer magnitude of the engineering work involved: the viaducts, cuttings, bridges and embankments so amazed contemporaries that they affirmed that this was the greatest building operation since the Pyramids. It can still astonish: the viaducts constructed brick upon brick, the cuttings and embankments fashioned with benefit of little mechanical aid more complicated than a pulley, and solely by exercise of human muscles assisted by those of the horse; the tunnels burrowed out shovelful by shovelful, once gunpowder had served to blast its untidy explosions. A touch of madness, a slightly demented obsession with the gigantic, seemed to obsess nearly everyone involved. The engineers and the contractors were particularly encouraged to discount practicalities by the fact that much of what they had achieved had been the product of guts and hunch.[1] Although their more enduring achievements testify to very great skill, the professions of engineer and surveyor were as yet barely recognized. Though the Institution of Civil Engineers was founded in 1818, the Mechanical Engineering Institution was not founded till 1847 (George Stephenson was its first president) and the Surveyors' Institution not until 1868.

Thus, the early railway engineers and contractors were not

---

[1] But see A. E. Musson and E. Robinson, *Science and Technology in the Industrial Revolution* (Manchester, Manchester U.P., 1969), for a warning against taking this view too literally.

carefully-trained inheritors of an historic academic tradition, but pioneers tackling problems that had not been tackled before. And some of them were rather ready to view their problems as obstacles that could invariably be overcome provided they responded to the challenge with appropriately heroic determination. Indeed, every line that was eventually opened was a triumph won only at the expense of persistent struggle. That, in order properly to survey the projected line from London to Birmingham (opened in 1837), Stephenson is said to have walked the whole distance between the two cities twenty times, is one measure of the difficulty of obtaining basic technical data. The extreme case of the construction of the Woodhead tunnel through the Pennines to link Manchester and Sheffield between 1839 and 1845 and again from 1847 and 1852 demonstrates most of the practical and human problems. By 1841, the original engineer of the tunnel was £80,000 the poorer on account of his involvement in the promoting company's shaky finances. His first estimate of the cost was £60,000; the final cost was over £200,000, and recurrent halts in the work were necessitated when the company periodically ran out of cash. Woodhead itself was an isolated place, 1,000 feet above sea level, nine miles from the nearest small town; men worked in shafts about 500 feet deep, but of only 10 feet diameter, while the single-line tunnel itself was only 18 feet across, was knee-high in mud, and had water (which the men sometimes drank) constantly running down the sides. The men's clothing was generally soaking wet and the interior dense with gunpowder smoke. The casualty list of the dead or maimed represented a higher proportion of those involved than the reported casualty lists of the main battles of the Peninsular War; and matters were sufficiently notorious to be the subject of investigation by the Commons Select Committee. The driving of the second tunnel between 1847 and 1852 was marked by the ravages of the cholera epidemic of 1849.

The legal and financial hazards were no less considerable. Every line required the passage of a private act of Parliament, necessitating the preparation of the most elaborate plans. This often raised the problem of how land could be surveyed in the absence of the agreement of its owner. Landowners either opposed railways on principle or in the hope of squeezing higher compensation out of the promoters. Others, heirs to the improving landlords of the eighteenth century, with an aesthetic as well as a proprietorial attitude to the deliberately landscaped prospect to be viewed from their great houses, demanded expensive diversions or unnecessary cuttings, so that the railway be effectively hidden from their sight. The authorities of Eton College and of Cambridge University both compelled the railway to pass at an inconvenient distance from their hallowed precincts. All these various negotiations consumed so much money and time (the drafting and presentation of a private act of Parliament was a task for expert and expensive lawyers) that it is not surprising that there was a large number of projected lines which failed to secure approval or which having secured it, had not been proceeded with. Much had to be done to secure promises of capital investment, the return on which lay in a highly problematic future or which might never materialize. M.P.s had to be lobbied and influenced; numerous M.P.s were alleged to be in the pockets of the railway promoters, the most ambitious of whom, George Hudson, was said to have spent half a million in persuading M.P.s to serve his interests.

The degree and variety of energy needed before any construction could actually begin meant that the engineers and in particular the men in their drawing offices, were at times working twenty-four hours a day. Stephenson was said to have once dictated memoranda continuously for twelve hours during one busy fortnight, stopping only because his secretary collapsed. One of his leading draughtsmen spent only one night in bed during the same fortnight. Another engineer, Vignoles, reported once working on urgent plans for three days and three nights continuously. He was 'completely knocked up'. Brunel, when the bills for establishing the Great Western Railway were being promoted, 'scarcely ever went to bed', but, of robuster temperament than Vignoles, appeared to thrive on catnaps in an armchair.

It is understandable that men capable of such feats of mental endurance and of organizing to a successful conclusion the work of contractors and sub-contractors, with their vast armies of tough, terrifying navvies, should develop Napoleonic tendencies. After all, the only aspect of the Crimean campaign that was efficiently organized was the construction of the railway from Balaclava to Sebastopol by several hundred navvies strictly protected from the harassments of military discipline and under the ultimate control of the celebrated railway contractor, Sir Michael Peto. It is not surprising therefore to find Brunel obstinately clinging to his seven-foot gauge for the G.W.R., to his idea of an atmospheric railway, and finally working himself to death over the construction of the gigantic vessel, *Great Eastern*. Later in the century there were the farflung dreams of Sir Edward Watkin who, apart from starting (and abandoning) the construction at Wembley of a rival to the Eiffel Tower, grandiloquently desired to transform London's Metropolitan line (once it had reached out graspingly as far as Aylesbury) into the main line of a great trunk route joining Manchester with Paris, via Dover and a Channel tunnel. All that emerged from this was the establishment, instead, of London's last and thirteenth main-line terminus, at Marylebone, in 1899.

In the realms of finance and promotion, the most celebrated example of the tendency to excess that the railway created was the career of the so-called Railway King, George Hudson. A York linen draper, he set up as a banker on the proceeds of a legacy and began to play the market in railway shares. He promoted a number of new companies and the amalgamation of existing ones. In this he performed the valuable function of causing railways to be thought of as national or regional rather than purely local ventures, a task which in other countries was to be undertaken by the state. By 1848, Hudson was in financial control of 1,450 out of the 5,000 lines of track then in existence; he was M.P. for Sunderland and thrice Lord Mayor of York. In 1845, at the height of the railway mania he symbolized, 600 separate railways were projected; if all had been constructed, the cost would have been £563 million. In the furtherance of his schemes, Hudson cornered essential materials and sold them to his railway companies, issued fraudulent balance sheets and, when the bubble burst, lost his fortune and his reputation at once.

A large number of the railway building projects of the 1840s and later were unsound. Yet, proof against all the trials and difficulties, the gullibility of a naïve investing public kept it unshakeably loyal to railway stocks and shares. The result was that the cost of building railways in Britain was exceptionally high. The optimism of the unregulated competitive spirit frequently meant also that the engineers were given their heads regardless of economic considerations, and there was loss of efficiency through lack of coordination and of standardization of equipment. Less than half the lines projected were in fact built, and many of those that were built brought little or no return to investors. This did not prevent railway preference shares being, next to gilt-edged, the favourite stock of the middle-class investors throughout the century.

In the early years there were frequent accidents and breakdowns, providing much stimulus for articles and drawings in *Punch* in the early 1840s. There were generally low standards of safety until the Railway Act of 1844 established minimum standards and an inspectorate to enforce them. But these obstacles were easily brushed aside; an industrializing society was already learning to accept faulty engineering design as one of the facts of life, as 'teething troubles', fundamentally irrelevant to the onward march of triumphant technological progress. Hence, it was common form to greet the arrival of the first train on any line with elaborate public ceremonial, a band playing 'See the Conquering Hero Comes' and a grand banquet accompanied by rotund, congratulatory speeches from local or national bigwigs. Symbolic of the Victorian attitude to the railway were the vast, imposing Doric arch at the entrance to Euston Station which, when built in 1839, appears, in a contemporary lithograph, so out of scale with its surroundings as to suggest Shelley's celebrated poem about Ozymandias, King of Kings; and the bizarre pseudo-Gothic extravagance of St Pancras. This architectural magniloquence, repeated so often in Victorian railway building, demonstrates that, to the Victorians, a great railway station, or a tunnel through the great rocks, was a cultural monument and must therefore be made to look like one; if only to prove to traditionally-minded critics that the men of the railway age were not mere soulless materialists. As is usual in aesthetic arguments, both sides were at fault in not seeing that the products of nineteenth-century civil and mechanical engineering had an aesthetic of their own. Hence the artifacts that were not dressed up in borrowed cultural finery are probably those most worth preserving.

The English did not merely build railways for themselves; their capital and their technology and the fierce, efficient energy of the British navvy were all soon engaged in railway-building abroad. Lines were built in Belgium and France in the 1830s and 1840s. In mid-century, loans running into millions were raised in London for railway-building in the United States, Russia, Italy, India, Australia and in South America. Except in the case of the United States, all the rolling stock, the coal, the iron and the engineers were exported along with the capital. The result was that railways opened up the Americas, the Antipodes and then South Africa, cheapening the cost and increasing the flow of raw materials into Britain.

Steamships contributed to similar ends. In the pre-Victorian era, the steamship, relying on the paddle wheel, was largely confined to inland waterways and the transport of passengers to seaside holiday resorts, a function still performed vestigially by paddle steamers in the first half of the twentieth century. Steamships carried sail in case of breakdown, and to compensate for the slow speed and wasteful inefficiency of their low-pressure engines. On the first Atlantic crossing by steamship, by the *Savannah* from the United States in 1818, the engines were used for only 80 hours of the trip, but nevertheless consumed the whole of the vessel's coal supply. The fitting of a condenser to obviate the use of salt water in the boilers was the next advance, and from 1838 progress was more rapid. In that year the British and American Steam Navigation Company's *Sirius*, of 708 tons, crossed from London to New York via Cork with 100 passengers; and the *Great Western* of 1,440 tons did the crossing from Bristol in 15 days. Built by Brunel, the

Great Western had been conceived as the means by which the Great Western Railway might in effect provide a passenger service from Paddington to New York. In 1840, Samuel Cunard founded the Cunard line, building four sister ships for the transatlantic service. From the time of the foundation of the General Steam Navigation Company in 1824, a steamship service to India was being developed. The East India Company maintained a steamship service for mails and passengers from Bombay to Suez; after transport overland to Alexandria, the link with England was by sailing ship until this part of the journey was taken over by the Peninsula and Orient Line's steamships in 1839. From that year, the Royal Mail Steam Packet Company, starting with ships of a tonnage of up to 1,900, began a service to the Caribbean, later extended to South America.

Unusually in the history of the time, these first steps towards Britain's maritime supremacy owed much to state assistance, since the early steamship lines were financially profitable largely because they were subsidized by government contracts for the carrying of mail. These subsidies amounted to as much as £1 million in 1860. In spite of this, steamships accounted for only one-sixth of the total British tonnage as late as 1865.

The change from wooden to iron ships and from paddle-wheel to screw propeller was also slow. This was partly because the Admiralty was certain that iron ships were more vulnerable than wooden ones and insisted on paddle wheels as a condition of granting mail contracts. Brunel designed the *Great Britain* in 1839 as an iron ship with screw machinery. The Cunard line did not change to iron till the 1850s nor adopt the screw propeller till the 1860s; the P & O Line changed over somewhat later. The eventual triumph of steam depended largely on the development of the compound engine, invented on the Clyde in the 1850s, which was to lead to the reduction of fuel consumption by efficient engines by one half. This helped to reduce the advantage that sail still had on the longest trans-oceanic journeys owing to the delays and difficulties of coaling steamships on such journeys.

The greatest period of growth in shipbuilding did not in fact occur until after 1850. The impetus was due in part to the repeal in 1849 of the Navigation Laws which, in accordance with free trade principles, removed all restrictions on the carriage of goods to and from British ports by foreign vessels. This exposed British shipping to the fear of considerable competition from the United States. Relevant also was the discovery of gold in Australia, which did much to provoke the technological improvements required to ensure swift transport to the Antipodes. Growth was further assisted in the 1860s by the absorption of the United States in the Civil War. Hence, whereas in the 1840s 131,000 tons of shipping had been built, in the 1860s the tonnage built was 314,000; and by the 1880s the United Kingdom had more registered tonnage than all the rest of the world put together.

The combined effects of railway and steamship development were greatly to increase Britain's competitiveness in the world's markets. The reduction in the time taken to transport raw materials and finished products overseas greatly reduced costs. The earnings of British shipping, associated, as always, with insurance and finance, helped to produce the invisible earnings which made possible the regular excess of imports over exports and provided much of the capital used for overseas investment.

The dominant position thus acquired in world trade was unique. A quarter of the world's trade passed through British ports; Britain produced 40 per cent of all the manufactured goods bought by the world's traders. Britain's initial advantage as an industrial pioneer had thus been immensely strengthened by railway and steamship development. And since 93 per cent of all British exports in the 1850s were manufactured goods (two-thirds of them textiles), the British were clothing the world, equipping it with railways and machinery, and at the same time exporting the capital the world needed to finance industrial development, as well as the coal from which it would derive its motive power. The establishment of a free trade policy provided both a practical and theoretical encouragement of the process. It was taken for granted that the specialization by which the world exported raw materials and the interest on Britain's investments, while the British exported manufactures and capital in return, was part of the natural order of things. Until the last quarter of the century, less than 10 per cent of Britain's imports were of manufactured goods; the overwhelming majority of imports were of raw materials and food and livestock; and it is noteworthy that it was in the 1850s that the percentages of total imports represented by grain and textile raw materials were both at their highest.

Several long-term consequences flowed from the success of the British in achieving this economic overlordship in the world by the middle of the century. First, the U.K. came to possess an economy which, in the light of later events, could be described as so specialized as to be top-heavy, and liable, by its very success, to induce a certain degree of inertia and inflexibility. Its economic strength depended absolutely on those basic industries which had swept all before them in the virtually monopolistic circumstances of the century before about 1870: the textile industry, coalmining, shipbuilding and heavy engineering. It was an economic supremacy that might not have been achieved without free trade; but it was a supremacy that free trade would in the long run bring to an end in default of a prudent and timely diversion of capital resources and of the labour force to newer industries. It was in no way inevitable that the British would harm themselves by industrializing the rest of the world by the free export of machinery and capital; indeed, Britain's greatest industrial rivals, the United States and Germany, were, by the end of the century, fast becoming her best customers. But what may perhaps be considered harmful was the overlong concentration of the economy on basic industries that could not be basic for ever. There were anxieties on this score well before the end of the Queen's reign, silenced after it ended by the phenomenon of continuing absolute growth in the early years of the twentieth century. But the problems facing the British after 1918 were rendered peculiarly difficult by the nineteenth century's single-hearted commitment to the industries most appropriate to the economic opportunities of a unique period of industrial pioneering. Nothing could stop other nations from developing their own textile industries, exploiting their far greater resources in population and raw materials, building their own ships, mining their own coal; there was thus the hidden danger that parts of what was originally the world's first (and therefore only) workshop might come in time to look like a museum of industrial archaeology. The scale, the prestige and the manifestly central part played by the basic industries in the dramatic history of the first three-quarters of the nineteenth century were to weigh like lead on the English for most of the twentieth century. The admiration now provoked by the solid, permanent quality of all that the Victorians constructed and by the splendid energy they derived from their supreme confidence in the future must not blind us to the fact that their confidence was to some extent misplaced and that some at least of what they built was built to last too long: a criticism that can be applied to their housing, their railways, their shipyards, their coalmines and their textile mills.

The great export of capital overseas was another feature of the nineteenth-century economy which could perhaps be regarded as a somewhat distorting factor. Without the earnings of overseas investments and the cognate earnings of other 'invisibles' such as insurance and banking, the British could never have made a profit in the world of international commerce, since the cost of imports exceeded the earnings of manu-factured exports throughout the century. Yet the concentration of surplus capital on investment abroad, when considered in conjunction with the concentration of physical resources on the basic industries, may be held to have overlong postponed the adoption of a policy of investment, both social and entrepre-neurial, at home. Continuous expansion of the traditional industries and the export of capital were undertaken because it was believed that this would maximize profit for the investor (a belief that later developments sometimes falsified) and extend the overseas markets for traditional British manufactures and capital goods. The effect was to starve the nation of social improvement (in relation to the scale of the need for it) and to reinforce the Victorians' obstinate resistance to investment in public health, housing and education. The Victorian technique of postponing as long as they could the adoption of collective social policies and of relying hopefully on the not very effective anodyne of private charity as the chief means of dealing with poverty left a burdensome legacy to succeeding generations. It might have been better for the late Victorians and their descendants if, for instance, Joseph Chamberlain had sought to instruct his generation not that the Empire was 'an undeveloped estate' but that much of the United Kingdom had been turned into a slum.

3 · Disease and Drudgery

Is the condition of the English working people
wrong; so wrong that rational working men
cannot, will not, and even should not rest quiet
under it?

CARLYLE

There is no community in England; there is
aggregation, but aggregation under circumstances which make it rather a dissociating than
a uniting principle. . . . In cities that condition
is aggravated. A density of population implies a
severer struggle for existence. . . . In great cities
men are brought together by the desire of gain.
They are not in a state of cooperation, but of
isolation, as to the making of fortunes; and for
all the rest they are careless of neighbours.
Christianity teaches us to love our neighbour as
ourself; modern society acknowledges no
neighbours.

DISRAELI, *Sybil*

It is misleading to emphasize too much the effects that
industrialization had had upon ways of life even by 1851. At
that date, agriculture still employed 1·79 million persons and
about 25 per cent of adult male workers, though the percentage
had been dropping and would continue to do so. Domestic
service constituted the second largest source of employment,
with about one million workers, and the building trades
employed about 0·75 million. The cotton industry ranked fourth,
employing just over half a million; but there were still fewer
coalminers (216,000) than boot and shoemakers (274,000). It is

figures such as these which impose restraint on the use of the term industrial 'revolution'; for, of these major occupations, only coal and cotton were based on the new industrial technology and only cotton was organized on the factory system. The agricultural worker, the domestic servant, the building workers and the boot and shoemakers were affected, like everyone else, by the industrial transformation; but the new technology had hardly impinged at all on their daily work.

For this reason alone it is dangerous to generalize about conditions among 'the working class' in the nineteenth century. Judgements based on the assumption that the majority of 'workers' were to be found in factory or mine are as fallible as those based on the assumption that, because deep coal-mining and power-driven factories were novelties born of the industrial revolution, so also were grinding poverty, gruelling hours of work and filthy living conditions. It is also important to bear in mind that, generally speaking, the only members of society who have ever tended to speak well of industrial entrepreneurs have been other industrial entrepreneurs. By definition almost, 'mills' have all been 'dark' and 'satanic' ever since Blake coined the phrase;[1] and businessmen are almost always, *ipso facto*, hard-faced at worst and hard-headed at best. In the nineteenth century they were resented by the traditional aristocracy; despised by Romantic writers as materialistic and uncultured; and condemned by radicals as wreckers of the old rural way of life. It was so difficult to distinguish between aristocratic and working-class propaganda in this respect that Disraeli was later able to create a myth for the Conservatives by putting the two together and calling the result 'Tory Democracy', while Marx united Romantic and working-class protest with the Jewish Messianic tradition to make them powerful elements in his 'scientific' socialism. Much of what has been written about the industrial revolution presupposes that it was preceded by an age of rosy-cheeked children romping round picturesque cottage doors waiting to greet father's return from the smiling fields of Merrie England in time for a

[1] Referring, in fact, to the universities, it is said.

supper of Roast Beef washed down with a clear sweet draught of Fine Olde Englishe Ale.

That standards of life among the labouring poor in the towns were abysmally low can be confidently affirmed; but almost any other general contention is probably impossible before about 1860. In the second half of the nineteenth century it can be agreed that expansion was so great that almost everyone benefited from it; but even so it could easily be argued that the gap between rich and poor had widened by 1900, as is perhaps evidenced by the fact that the Condition of England question was hardly less of a preoccupation at the end of the Queen's reign than at its beginning. The most that can perhaps be asserted about the earlier period is that, among the artisan class, real wages rose modestly between 1815 and 1860 in the towns; but this disregards the incidence of unemployment, the alternation of boom and slump, the fact that some workers did much better than others and that town life almost certainly involved an exceptionally degrading lack of amenity. In view of the continuous increase of population throughout this time, even a modest rise in real wages must be considered a notable achievement. Clearly, contemporaries thought it unlikely that it could be maintained. All but the most hardy optimists took serious note of the theory of Malthus that population growth tended always to outrun productive capacity and that, unless the labouring classes controlled their passions, mass starvation must surely be the ultimate consequence. It did not seem possible that there could be any enduring departure from the situation as it had been before the industrial revolution, when it was estimated that half the then much smaller population was dependent on charity or poor relief.

Against this background, the long hours and low wages of urban unemployment represented something of an improvement. The ability to supplement those low wages by the earnings of wives and children was also both an economic advantage and a means of preserving, in factory and mine, the basic unity of the family. But the increasing use of power-driven machinery and the growing complexity of industrial operation imposed upon factory workers a tempo of work quite unlike that to which free men had hitherto been accustomed. Factory work did not slacken with the seasons; it was work for all seasons. The working day ceased to be longer or shorter according to the hours of daylight. Ideally, it proceeded at a uniform pace, reaching neither a frenzied climax like that of harvest-time nor descending into periods of near-unemployment as farmwork tended to do when the land was unworkable in winter. Indeed, if factory output showed signs of the cyclical peaks and depths of rural work it was a sign of malfunctioning and steps would be taken to correct it. In the one case, more hands and more equipment would be acquired; in the other, corrective action might now be as drastic as the bankruptcy of the owner and the total destitution of his former employees. Cultivation of the land continued to be organized on the assumption that a measure of underemployment both of labour and capital resources was an essential part of the process. The new industries could not carry the burden of a single idle machine or a single idle hand.

This was because circumstances made the times intensely competitive. Few early entrepreneurs had large capital resources, and most were alarmingly dependent on short-term credit. They were convinced, and not without reason, that, since so much of their little capital was so precariously invested in their machinery and buildings, they could get a profitable return only by working their machines, and therefore their employees, for as long as possible and by cutting their wages bill to an irreducible minimum. In a sense this is always likely to happen in a society which is undergoing the initial phase of industrialization; the creation of new industries is always an exercise in the concentration of resources upon long-term ends and in the wholesale regimentation of the labour force for the performance of unfamiliar tasks without hope of immediate personal reward. No country was again to perform this feat out of its own native resources in finance and skills; and only the countries of Western Europe and the United States were able to effect the change within the framework of at any rate a

formally free society.[1] Almost all twentieth-century trans-
formations of formerly rural societies have been accompanied
by draconian governmental 'planning' and frenzied governmental propaganda, together with much foreign aid, financial
and technical.

The entire industrializing process in Britain was an improvisa-
tion, undertaken without benefit of sophisticated techniques of
business organization or supporting professional skills, let
alone planned government action. Undertakings were conducted with only the crudest notions of forward planning and
control, without understanding of the problems of labour
management, and without either an established accountancy
profession or a wide-ranging system of insurance. The pressure
to extract the maximum from the labour force was probably
inescapable if an entrepreneur was to succeed at all in circumstances of intense and uncontrolled competition; and the
workers put up with it because it was better than starvation for
themselves and their families. It may well be significant that the
really dramatic movements of protest before 1840 were so
sporadic and short-lived. The relatively isolated outbursts of
machine-wrecking, the virtual extinction of the skilled hand-
loom weaver with hardly a demonstration from them large
enough to figure in the history books, and the localized unrest
of the half-decade after Waterloo were probably less violent in
total than the agricultural labourers' revolt in the southern
counties in 1830–2, which arose less out of the evils of the new
industrialism than out of the absence in southern England of
any opportunity to participate in them.

Yet, and the persistent longing for a return to rural ways
which is expressed in the popular ballads of the century is a
reminder of this, almost the whole urban labour force of at
least the first half of the nineteenth century was composed of

---

[1] The implication that low (and between 1820 and 1840 declining) real
wages were inescapable in the earlier phase of industrial transformation
can, of course, be challenged. The determining factor was probably the
population expansion that made labour so cheap a commodity. For an
analysis of the arguments on this issue see Harold Perkin, *Origins of
Modern English Society, 1780–1880* (London, Routledge, 1969), pp. 134–49.

adult men and women who, having been born in rural England, felt themselves to have been deprived of their natural way of life by the processes of industrial change. The century's nostalgia for the rustic past was doubtless reactionary, illusory and sentimental, but its persistence reveals much about men's deeper feelings and discontents. No less revealing in the realms of more imaginative self-expression is the discovery of Nature by the Romantic movement at the precise moment when it was ceasing to be the universal background of human experience. The association between mining and penal servitude is of long standing, historically speaking; the difference between a factory and a prison was, and perhaps still is, more apparent than real; and, characteristically, human beings, though gregarious and exceptionally adaptable, have never by tradition been universally urban.

The urban life to which the new industrial worker was condemned was perhaps as offensive as the mechanical rhythms of work. Urban wages were higher than agricultural wages and less liable to seasonal fluctuations; but, owning nothing but their labour, urban workers were dependent entirely on wages for their food and shelter, usually lacking even the smallest of gardens and, unlike the farm worker, receiving no payment in kind. Unaccustomed to (relatively) high and regular wages, and having but limited leisure and little opportunity for other pursuits, they tended to spend heavily on drink and put nothing by for periods of unemployment or illness, both of which could therefore quickly reduce them to a destitution perhaps more complete than they might have endured in the countryside.

The concentration on maximization of profit which the early industrializing process tended to necessitate was most notably manifest in bad housing and urban squalor. The new towns grew merely because where there were factories, workers needed shelter as near to them as possible. Urban government barely existed in such places or, where it did exist, had abandoned its powers of regulation as part of the general decay of corporate activity in eighteenth-century England. The growth of the textile towns of Lancashire and Yorkshire by 1830 and of the north-east towns immediately after the coming of the railways was at a pace greatly in excess of the growth rate of the population as a whole. The combined result of small wages and a rapidly increasing population was to reduce the size of the family living-space, sometimes to one room or merely a part of a room. The only way working-class accommodation could be made to yield a profit was by overcrowding. Any improvement in housing conditions would mean increased rents, which workers could not afford, just as the eventual arrival of sanitary services might reduce the family's income from the sale of its night soil, and be delayed in any case because of the increased cost to the ratepayers. More space per family would increase the distance between home and work and thus lengthen the effective working day, which was already too long. Moreover, at a very early stage of urban development, the outward expansion of areas of working-class housing was checked by the pre-emption of outer areas by the middle class. Housing of workers beyond the earliest middle-class zones had to wait upon increased wages and the coming of the railway and the tram.

The building trade itself was in the hands of small jobbing men, and the long-term borrowing which large-scale planned home building required was beyond them. The worst sort of working-class property seems to have been built mostly by small men and mostly owned by very minor 'capitalists'. Significantly, it was the wealthy philanthropist and capitalist who first tried to assume responsibility in the matter. The Society for Improving the Condition of the Working Classes was founded in 1844 and, a year later, the Metropolitan Association for Improving the Dwellings of the Industrious Classes. The American millionaire, George Peabody, and the wealthy Baroness Burdett-Coutts devoted large sums to the construction of tenement buildings. But these philanthropic activities had only a peripheral effect.

The squalor and degradation of the new towns in England until at least mid-century were in some measure a consequence of the general climate of opinion at the time. Politically, the English were long accustomed to regard themselves as 'free' by comparison with continental Europeans. Economic thinking was dominated by the broader implications of free trade theories and of *laissez-faire* principles. Religious thinking placed a heavy emphasis on the doctrine of self-help and individual responsibility and this created an obsessed fear that to do anything systematic for the poor would encourage them to look to the rich for salvation and still further undermine their evident incapacity to save themselves. Socially, the English lacked any deep-rooted tradition of civic grandeur derived from either public or private enterprise. The industrial revolution came upon a society whose conspicuous spending had been mainly lavished on great country houses, many of which in any other countries would have been described, not as 'houses', but more straightforwardly as 'palaces'; and on the landscaped gardens that domesticated and civilized the rural scene. The London squares and the elegance of Bath and parts of Bristol were designed for purposes hardly less private and domestic. A nation ruled by a wealthy landed aristocracy that looked down on monarchy and, whatever economic and political concessions it conceded to the commercial and industrial classes, was determined to retain the substance of political and social power, could have but little experience of civic pride. The new industrial towns could only aspire in this direction after almost irreparable damage had already been done and when to fail to act with a sense of civic responsibility would have been seen as a failure to compete with other commercial and industrial centres and as (at last) a bar to greater efficiency and also (at last) as a peril to public health.

The predicament into which urban life had thrust the population was dramatized by cholera. From its first appearance in Sunderland in 1831, until well into the 1860s, cholera was frequently epidemic; in 1848-9 it killed at least 130,000 people. Its causes were thought by some (the contagionists) to be spread by physical contact and by others (the miasmatists) by the release, owing to unascertainable atmospheric conditions, of an infection lurking mysteriously in stagnant water or dirt. The miasmatists appeared to have the upper hand in the controversy and devices to purify the air ranged from the suggested firing of cannon at hourly intervals in public places to the frequent burning of tar barrels in the streets. As was so often true in Victorian England, the facts of the matter were discovered by relatively obscure men working, unlike most Victorian bigwigs, medical or otherwise, in personal contact with the masses. John Snow, a modest medical practitioner of Soho, London, published in 1849 his opinion that cholera was spread by the pollution of drinking water by sewage. In 1855, he investigated a London cholera epidemic which killed more than 500 people in just over a week and found that almost all the victims had drunk water from one particular source, an infected pump in Broad Street, Soho.[1] The epidemic stopped as soon as the Broad Street pump was put out of action. These findings were confirmed by those of the registrar general's statistician, William Farr, who traced the source of an outbreak in 1866 to one particular East End reservoir. It had been accidentally contaminated by sewage from premises occupied by a cholera victim.

Snow's original publication received little official attention, the miasmatists being bent on campaigning vigorously against filth in general as a cause of 'poisoned air'. Two of the three persons most celebrated for their interest in health in Victorian times, Edwin Chadwick and Florence Nightingale, remained miasmatists all their lives. The third, and in most respects the greatest of the three, Sir John Simon, preferred to remain a miasmatist until more exact scientific and medical investigation had substantiated Snow's empirical observations. Nevertheless, the realization of the miasmatists that cholera was at its worst in insanitary places led to widespread national protests against the evils of the open sewers, the defective drains, the foul ditches and the refuse-littered streets of the towns of the 1840s. Even where piped water and sewers did exist they could offer little guarantee against seepage from sewers to water supply, given the use of wooden pipes and brick sewers. What was needed was the glazed earthenware drainpipe and a resolute decision that the filth be cleared away.

[1] Modern Broadwick Street, and opposite the northern end of what is now Lexington Street.

Such resolution was forthcoming from Edwin Chadwick, secretary to the poor law commissioners, who, in 1842, in association with Dr Kay (Sir James Kay-Shuttleworth) and Dr Southwood Smith, published for the commissioners a Report on the Sanitary Condition of the Labouring Population. With typically Victorian tirelessness, Chadwick and his associates produced pages of charts and statistics to justify his demand for unified sanitary control in every town, for piped water in every home and for the paving of every urban street – and for narrow-bore earthenware pipes. There followed a royal commission, set up by Peel's government in 1843, on sanitary conditions in fifty major towns. It revealed that only six of them had a satisfactory water supply.[1] Even so, a Public Health Bill was rejected in 1847 and became an act in 1848 only because another cholera outbreak began. The act set up a General Board of Health composed of the first commissioner of works (a member of the government of the day) together with Ashley (Lord Shaftesbury) and Chadwick, though a fourth member, Dr Southwood Smith, was added shortly afterwards. Henceforward, sanitary powers could be acquired by local authorities on the petition of 10 per cent of the ratepayers, instead of, as previously, by way of the expensive procedure of private acts of Parliament. Additionally, the board itself could enforce the adoption of sanitary powers on any area where the death rate exceeded 23 per thousand. In such areas outside the corporate towns a Local Board of Health would be set up, with the General Board having the power to approve the appointment and dismissal of officials. The opposition to the act concentrated on the objectionable character of its interference with local government and on the scant respect it had for the

[1] In one part of Manchester in 1837, the economist Nassau Senior found 'a whole street following the course of a ditch, because in this way deeper cellars could be secured without the cost of digging, cellars not for storing wares or rubbish, but for dwellings for human beings. *Not one house of this street escaped the cholera.* In general the streets of these suburbs are unpaved, with a dung-heap or ditch in the middle; the houses are built back to back, without ventilation or drainage, and whole families are limited to a corner of a cellar or garret.' (See Engels, *Condition of the Working Class in England in 1844*, London, Allen & Unwin, 1920, pp. 63–4.)

medical profession, since Southwood Smith was the least important of the board's members.

Chadwick's much-criticized zeal was nevertheless not merely the driving idiosyncrasy of a fanatical devotee of social efficiency. It was in tune with the desires of many sensible professional men and local worthies reacting angrily but intelligently against the chaos of the new industrial townscape. The systematic study of sanitation had already been pioneered in Manchester and Liverpool, which secured sanitary powers for themselves, in advance of Chadwick's Act, in 1845 and 1846. In 1847, Liverpool became the first town to appoint a medical officer of health, Dr W. H. Duncan; and Kay-Shuttleworth had been working on sanitary problems in Manchester since 1831. Consciousness of the sanitary idea was sufficiently widespread to lead to the formation of a Health of Towns Association with branches in such widely separated towns as Halifax, Walsall and Worcester. Most significant of all had been the tardy decision of the City of London to become the second city in the country to appoint a medical officer of health in 1848, chiefly in order to anticipate any attempt to interfere in its affairs by the General Board. Its choice was John Simon. Already well-known as a surgeon, he was also making a great reputation for himself as a pathologist at St Thomas's Hospital. As the first lecturer in pathology ever to be appointed to a teaching hospital, he was to bring to the cause of public health what it had so far lacked, the understanding and authority of a medical man with a sound scientific background.

It is perhaps characteristic of the period that the impetus towards sanitary regulation in the interests of the local community as a whole should have been provided mainly by professional men with practical experience of what conditions were really like and with the zeal and patience to study their effects in detail. Their motives were neither political nor, necessarily, humanitarian. Chadwick's aim was the characteristically Victorian one of cutting down the cost of the Poor Law; Southwood Smith, having worked in the London Fever Hospital, had a more humane approach; Shaftesbury's approach was wholly humanitarian; while Simon regarded the improvement of public health as 'a great Christian duty' and numbered among his many friends Charles Kingsley and other Christian Socialists, as well as John Ruskin. In general, however, most 'sanitarians' saw town life as in a highly dangerous mess, sought for the means to clear it up and hoped that by presenting the facts they could both awaken the public conscience and stir up the politicians.

What chiefly caused Chadwick to founder, apart from his unconciliatory and bureaucratic attitude, was his devotion to the principle of centralized government control over public health. His opponents objected not merely to the expense that his sanitary enthusiasm might impose upon them; they saw him as an instrument of tyrannical administrative interference by government. Local 'liberty' had been imperilled by the setting up of poor law commissioners, led by Chadwick, to superintend the work of the boards of guardians; now, this same Chadwick was attacking the same principle of local independence through the General Board of Health. That, for example, the local authority on whom the General Board imposed the terms of the act compulsorily still retained full discretion as to whether it exercised the powers it had been given was completely overlooked by Chadwick's enemies. *The Times* thought accepting the risk of catching cholera preferable to being 'bullied into health'. But although the appeal was to the principle of civic liberty against government tyranny, sanitary policy was resisted in so many places chiefly because to insist on a regular supply of piped water, the installation of taps and water closets, interfered with property rights and cost money. The inalienable right of every man to do what he liked with his property and to have as little as possible of his money taken from him in rates and taxes was considered a fundamental. No man, however distressful his living conditions, should expect to have them improved out of the public purse. It is perhaps fortunate that medical opinion was convinced that cholera was caused by infection passing through the air from areas of filth and poverty, since this caused such areas to be regarded as a threat to the respectable members of society and therefore one which they could be persuaded to attend to.[1]

In 1854, however, when the General Board's five-year span of existence under the 1848 act came under review, it had already incurred such hostility that Chadwick, Shaftesbury and Southwood Smith had all resigned from it, and it was reconstructed under a new president, Sir Benjamin Hall. Though previously a strong opponent of centralization, Hall was impelled by a new cholera outbreak in 1854 to be even more interfering than Chadwick had been; not for the first or the last time, personal acquaintance with the real magnitude of the problem induced an abandonment of entrenched attitudes favourable to so-called 'liberty'. Hall harried the metropolitan boards of guardians and criticized the water companies for the irregularity of their supply. More important still, by the Public Health Act of 1855, Hall secured the services of Sir John Simon to a newly created post as medical officer to the General Board. Simon's translation from the City of London to the General Board had the approval of the medical profession and of those who saw his work in the City as a vindication of the principles of municipal freedom, since, despite much obstruction and the frustration of his larger aims, he had done much to improve public health in the previously exceptionally insanitary area of the City.

Nevertheless, although the reconstructed board did much routine work, it failed to secure either additional power or even a guarantee of permanence from the politicians of the 1850s. Palmerston was intermittently sympathetic but his mind was on other things; the advent of the Tories under Derby and Disraeli in 1858 almost led to the extinction of the board altogether and it was saved only by the return of Palmerston to office in 1859 when a further important Public Health Act was passed, though against considerable opposition and by a narrow majority. An act of the same name, passed by the

---

[1] 'Householders of all classes should be warned that their first means of safety lies in the removal of dung-heaps and solid and liquid filth of every description from beneath or about their houses and premises.' From the *Report* of the General Board of Health, 1849.

Tories in 1858, had made Simon medical officer to the Privy
Council, to whom the old General Board's right to make
regulations to combat dangerous epidemics had also been
transferred; but the 1858 act had been given only one year's
validity. The 1859 act gave the Privy Council, through its now
almost independent medical officer, the power to make whatever inquiries were thought fit into public health in any area,
and empowered the medical officer to make reports to the Privy
Council on any matters affecting public health, thus ensuring a
maximum of publicity for the medical officer's views. The act
was so ambiguously phrased that its effectiveness would depend
almost solely on what the medical officer chose to make of it.
And Simon, though a determined man, himself spoke of his
functions as primarily scientific, investigatory and educational
and only partly administrative. As a result of this caution he
continued to enjoy, because of his knowledge, his tact and his
ability to produce terse, impressive reports, all that high public
standing that had been denied to the unfortunate Chadwick.
Among the few who remained unmovably hostile to Simon
were Florence Nightingale and (understandably) Chadwick.

Throughout the first half of the sixties, Simon and his medical
staff plugged away at the task of investigating and reporting
upon the innumerable deficiencies in the nation's health. They
noted the connection between ill-ventilated working conditions
and the incidence of bronchitis and tuberculosis among persons
employed in such conditions. They reported much serious
malnutrition among Lancashire workers during the cotton
famine of 1861–2 which resulted from the American Civil War
and, further, that standards of nutrition were as bad, if not
worse, among all who worked in sweated trades. They came to
the grim conclusion that local authorities lacked any real power
to tackle the health problems created among the poor by bad
housing conditions; and, worse still, new epidemics of typhus
and smallpox, and the certainty in 1865 of a further cholera
outbreak, led Simon and his collaborators to declare that there
was no statute in existence which aimed at preventing the
spread of contagious diseases.

Partly as a result of this work by Simon's medical department there was a splutter of miscellaneous legislation relating directly or indirectly to public health. In 1864 a Factory Act legislated against dirty and ill-ventilated factory premises; and in 1867 inspection of merchant seamen with a view to preventing scurvy was introduced. The major act, however, was the Public Health Act of 1866, passed mainly by its Whig sponsors with only grudging support from the Tories, during the Derby–Disraeli Tory ministry of that year; once again, it was probably only the fact that cholera was once more raging that enabled the act to be passed at all.

The Public Health Act of 1866 extended the range of the local authorities who were empowered to compel adequate house drainage and proper water supplies within their areas. It extended the definition of 'nuisance' to compel local authorities to act against overcrowded housing conditions and against all ill-ventilated or overcrowded workplaces; and failure to act could be followed by intervention by the Home Office. Local authorities were given the power to enforce sanitary works in any house or lodgings, and not merely in the poorest ones. Comprehensive in form, the act certainly stimulated the more progressive authorities; but its permissive enactments were not widely applied and the act did nothing to reduce the confused muddle of local authorities which possessed sanitary powers. As late as 1869, large parts of Birmingham and Manchester still lacked water sewerage and the London water supply was officially described as of a quality that displayed a 'criminal indifference to the public safety'. The infant mortality rate, the death rates from smallpox, typhus and puerperal fever showed almost no diminution, and in the case of puerperal fever the rate continued to increase.

Thus, by the end of the 1860s, the framework of a public health policy existed, and, thanks largely to Simon, the facts which rendered such a policy a necessity had been fully uncovered. But vested interests among property owners, water companies and squabbling local authorities, coupled with the occasional nature of Palmerston's concern with sanitary matters, the fairly steady hostility of the Tories – particularly, in this period, Disraeli – had all prevented more than modest improvement in relation to need. The best that could be said, perhaps, was that the cholera epidemic of 1866 was the last and the least disastrous. Yet the advances that were to be made in the last three decades of the reign were wholly dependent upon the largely frustrated efforts and tireless propaganda, first, of Chadwick, and then, more effectively and for a longer period, of Simon. All that was needed was consolidation and proper enforcement of existing legislation through a less chaotic system of local government.

If it was hard to convince the respectable classes of the social and economic value of sanitary reform it was harder still to convince them of the need to improve working conditions. It was regarded as axiomatic that any improvement of working conditions would inevitably be wholly at the expense of the employing and taxpaying sections of the community. In the main, therefore, better working conditions for adult male workers had to wait upon the effects of long-term economic change, on the slow general rise in living standards and on the development of responsible trade unions. No statutory limitation on the working hours of men was enacted in the Victorian period: what legislation there was applied specifically only to women and children and none of it applied to workplaces falling outside the legal definition of a factory or mine.

The employment of women and children was, to begin with, no more than the transfer to factory and mine of the tradition of family employment in the putting-out system of the pre-factory era and in agriculture. As was rediscovered in the second half of the twentieth century, the large-scale employment of women always raises the problem of child-minding. The young married schoolteacher who takes her under-five toddler into her classroom with her is doing what factory-employed couples did in the early nineteenth century as an exercise of elementary parental duty. What else could such parents have done with their children? Hence, the earliest Factory Act, that introduced by Sir Robert Peel's father in 1802, applied only to the wretched pauper children, transported (by the barge-load sometimes) by overseers of the poor, to be 'apprenticed' in the new factories; the point was that pauper children had no parents to exercise custodianship over them. In 1819 Sir Robert Peel put through an act intended to apply to all children. This was largely the outcome of the representations of Robert Owen, the Lanarkshire mill owner who enraged contemporaries by treating his employees as human beings and still making a profit, and then enraged them still further by demanding state action to impose his standards on other employers. Peel's act was much less than Owen had wanted: it applied solely to cotton mills, prohibited the employment of children under nine, and imposed a maximum twelve-hour day on children between the ages of nine and sixteen. The act had little effect since its enforcement was in the hands of the local justices, many of whom shared the attitude to child labour of the mill owner who justified a fourteen-hour day for children by declaring, 'Nothing is more favourable to morals than habits of early subordination, industry and regularity.'

Nevertheless, agitation for more effective legislation increased. It began for the first time to come from the workers themselves, since technological developments more and more required factory discipline to be put in the hands of foremen and managers instead of the child workers' own parents. The result was the 1833 act, which forbade the employment of children under nine in textile factories other than silk, and limited the working hours of all children and young persons between the ages of nine and eighteen. The creation by this act of a factory inspectorate has caused it to be labelled the first 'effective' factory act. Since, initially, only four inspectors were appointed for England and Scotland, and there was no registration of births until 1837, it can hardly be said to have become 'effective' before the mid-forties.[1] On the other hand, the reports of the factory inspectorate from 1835 onwards provided for the first time a steady flow of accurate information about factory conditions, which, in the depressed circumstances of the first years of the Queen's reign, tended to get worse. The inspectors produced a sorry picture of unprotected dangerous machinery, bad ventilation, and persistent efforts to get more out of the workers by increasing the speed of the machinery.

[1] See also p. 68.

c

Observers also began to point to the spread of tuberculosis in the factory towns and to the effects upon working mothers, making them too exhausted to look after their children. The result was that the 1844 Factory Act, as well as requiring dangerous machinery to be fenced, limited the working day of children to 6½ hours and the working week of women to sixty-five hours. To indicate that there were limits to the subordination of economic necessity to sentimentality, the act, for the first time since 1819, legalized the factory employment of eight-year-olds.

Emphasis was then concentrated on the campaign for a ten-hour day, which had been conducted by Lord Shaftesbury and others since 1831, who had hoped to have their aims realized first by the 1833 act and then by the 1844 act. The overt demand was for a ten-hour day for women and children, since statutory limitation of the hours of work of men would stand little chance of parliamentary approval. It would represent 'an interference with the freedom of the subject which no other legislature in Christendom would have countenanced for a moment'[1] and bring instant ruin to British industry, since the economists of the time had proved to their own satisfaction that employers' profits were earned solely in the last hour of the day. The only way round these objections, therefore, was to appeal exclusively to humanitarian feelings, though Macaulay showed better sense when he said he could not believe that 'what makes a population stronger and healthier and wiser and better can ultimately make it poorer'. The Ten Hours Act for Women and Young Persons was passed in 1847, and the regulation of the hours of these workers compelled owners in practice to apply the same rules to men.[2] Parliamentary draughtsmanship had, however, provided employers with a useful loophole: the act had not said that women and children should work only for ten continuous hours. Accordingly the working day was prolonged to suit employers' convenience by

[1] Dr Andrew Ure, *The Philosophy of Manufactures* (1835, 3rd edn, London, H. Bohn, 1861), p. 297.
[2] In Lancashire, in 1847, out of 277,028 cotton workers only 47,944 were adult males.

calling in the women and young persons in relays at different times during the day and this likewise lengthened the male working day. Amendments had to be passed in 1850 and 1853 but, to get them through, Shaftesbury had to concede the lengthening of hours of work from ten to ten and a half.

There was less long-drawn-out resistance to the reform of the mines since, whereas the employment of women and children was increasing in textiles, their employment in mines was becoming less economic. Much of the celerity with which the Mines Act of 1842 was passed must, however, be attributed to the horrific revelations contained in the (illustrated) report in 1842 of a commission set up by the Commons on the insistence of Shaftesbury. Due allowances must doubtless be made for the predisposition of the commissioners and their inquisitors to believe what they were told, and for the artistry with which young children can wring the hearts of innocent adults when they think it will suit their purpose; but even if the horror stories contained in the report were not all necessarily typical it can hardly be maintained that the employment of women and small children in the coalmines of the 1840s was defensible on any grounds. The sexual element in the report reinforced its propagandist effect. The Blue Book's picture of a female, stripped to the waist, crawling on all fours and dragging a truck, and of pubescent ill-clad boy and girl sitting face to face and clasping each other as they are wound down the shaft into the depths must have had something of the effect of 'a shocking revelation' to the sex-frightened middle classes. Nothing could stir them to action more quickly than a chance to improve the sexual morality of the labouring poor; and the employment in mines of females as well as of boys under ten was forbidden within a few months of the report's appearance.

After the basic (and far from effective) legislation of the 1840s, there were acts in 1850, 1855 and 1860 to enforce safety regulations in mines, and by the act of 1860 the employment of boys under twelve was prohibited. From 1864 onwards, regulation of working conditions was applied to the metal trades, printing, papermaking and blast furnacing; and the Factory Act of 1878 consolidated the factory legislation of the period much as the Public Health Act of 1875 had consolidated sanitary legislation. The role of the factory inspectorate in these developments can hardly be exaggerated.

Whereas the sanitary movement owed most to professional men concerned with social and municipal efficiency, factory reform was chiefly the work of men, most notably Shaftesbury, working in the humanitarian tradition. This in part reflects the fact that, for all its limitations, there was a long-standing medical profession for the Victorian era to inherit from the past, but no managerial tradition. All that was inherited from the past in this respect was the law of master and servant, operating within the social context of widespread pauperism and of the well-attested habit of servants in any fair-sized establishment of cheating and sponging on their masters. Carrying this, the only managerial experience that their culture offered, into the harsh competitive world, afflicted as it was from 1837 to 1842 with a severe depression, it is not surprising that the bulk of the entrepreneurs and many of the politicians should bitterly resent state intervention between masters and men, and that they could see economic advantage in no labour situation other than one based on the largest number of working hours for the lowest possible wages. The conflict thereby created between the supposedly irreconcilable claims of economic advance and humanitarian sentiment has been a constant and dislocating factor in social and economic life ever since. Worse still, the revelations of early industrial conditions in the first years of Victoria's reign came to be regarded as the universal norm of industrialism and capitalism. Much Socialist thinking came to be based on the unhistorical assumption that the evils of the system as revealed in the early 1840s provided the basis for a set of immutable laws about the development of society in the future.

The important thing, however, is that the evils were revealed and not hushed up; and that, once revealed, they were changed. It is permissible to chafe at the tardiness with which they were changed; but it has to be recognized that these conditions were seen by society at large as an affront to its conscience and its sense of fitness, and became a spur to improving action. It is important also to recall that only a small proportion of the population consisted of cottonmill owners and mine owners. Socially and politically, it could be argued, they were as yet in a fairly vulnerable position; and political capital could be made out of their real and alleged iniquities. Shaftesbury himself was a Tory and a determined anti-Socialist, anti-Chartist, anti-democrat; and landlords who exploited the agricultural tenantry were not always unwilling to support acts to stop manufacturers exploiting their 'hands' at a time when the manufacturing interest was mounting an attack on the land-lords by demanding an end of the Corn Laws that were alleged to be protecting them.

4 · *Lord John and Sir Robert*

1832–46

A body of men, connected with high rank and property, bound together by hereditary feelings, party ties, as well as higher motives, who in bad times keep alive the sacred flame of freedom, and when the people are roused, stand between the constitution and revolution, and go with the people, but not to extremities.

SIR FRANCIS BARING on the Whigs

'A sound Conservative government,' said Taper, musingly, 'I understand: Tory men and Whig measures.'

DISRAELI, *Coningsby*

The closer the view that is taken of the political developments of the thirties and forties of the nineteenth century, the more the attention is drawn to what did not happen, and what did not change during those two decades. It is easy to assume that, whereas in continental Europe what is rather loosely called 'Reaction' was triumphant, England provided, by contrast, the shining and singular spectacle of 'Reform'. This distinction is rendered more plausible by over-complacent contrasts between the dramatic tottering of thrones in Europe in 1848 and the sad death of Chartism in that year in a pathetic drizzle of English rain and feeble Victorian puns. Yet there are parallels between the English and continental stories as well as contrasts. Continental governments rode out the squalls of 1820 as Liverpool's Tory governments outrode Spa Fields, the Blanketeers, Peterloo and Cato Street. In England, the Whigs 'betrayed' many of the supporters of the Reform Bill of 1832 hardly less than Louis Philippe 'betrayed' the French revolutionaries of 1830. The aftermath of 1846 and 1848 in England was a twenty-year suspension of social and political conflict not wholly unlike that over which Louis Napoleon presided for the two decades after 1851. And though Chartism failed with a whimper and the 1848 Revolutions failed with a bang, they both still failed; and governments emerged from them stronger than ever. Throughout the 1850s, both in England and on the Continent, governments were less disturbed by the rumblings of a discontented populace than for almost a century past. A good case can be made for regarding the nineteenth century in political matters as a counter-revolutionary century.[1] Those who agitated for radical or socialist revolution were everywhere defeated; their positive achievements were negligible. The presiding genius of the age was neither Bentham nor Marx but Burke.

In retrospect, all the reforms in English history, at least until 1848, appear to have had, as their prime first cause, the Reform Act of 1832. As the first great constitutional landmark since the Glorious Revolution of 1688 it is thought of as having swept away the old eighteenth-century parliamentary system. Since it restored the Whigs to power, it led automatically to the 'Whig Reforms' and thereafter to the great economic revolution implied by the Repeal of the Corn Laws which, though introduced by a Conservative prime minister, was passed with Whig votes. Since in due course those same Whigs (usually by imperfectly explained processes) became Liberals under Gladstone, the whole of the half century after 1832 seems to acquire a Whig-Liberal-Reforming character as an inevitable consequence of the Reform Act.

It is however possible to take a less cosy view of the period and to describe it as one in which the political leaders, whatever label was attached to them, were united in a common cause,

---

[1] This is notably true in Germany and Italy. Bismarck and Cavour were both counter-revolutionaries. The only nineteenth-century radical to leave his mark on his country's history was Garibaldi; but he had to turn Royalist in order to do so.

namely the preservation of the traditional structure of eight-eenth-century society and politics (or as they would have said, Church and State). What divided them was controversy as to the means by which this could best be achieved; on the grand strategy they were of one mind. The more sensible Conserva-tives believed that the existing structure should be changed only if and when certain parts of it looked likely to provoke open revolt. The Whigs believed that, when signs of revolt appeared, they should capture the leadership of the movement in order to ensure that it did no real damage. Between these two views there was a distinction that made for only minor differences. In consequence political decision-making was usually based on the circumstances of the moment. The Tory decision to oppose parliamentary reform in 1830 was largely fortuitous, the Whig decision to support it a nervously calculated risk taken by men who hoped they were guessing right; and the Whig decision to come out wholeheartedly in favour of Corn Law Repeal in 1848 was more, rather than less, belated than Peel's decision to introduce it.

What threatened the fabric of the established order in the 1830s was an accumulation of radical aims derived from the politics of the second half of the eighteenth century, made all the more formidable by having been held in check by the law-and-order policy of what was considered to have been fifty years of Tory misrule, a policy undertaken in fearful reaction against the 'excesses' of the French Revolution. It had some-thing to do with memories of Wilkes and Fox and Tom Paine and relatively little with the industrial revolution, save that its operations received the full support of the employing classes. It could also perhaps be regarded as the re-emergence of a political underground whose subterranean origins may have gone as far back as the revolutionary days of the 1640s and early 1650s. It was opposed to the power of the Lords, as representa-tive of a hated landed aristocracy. It was opposed to the Church of England as a privileged system which compelled Dissenters to pay church rates, excluded them from taking degrees at England's only two universities, prevented them from marrying or from registering their children's births except in a parish church; which made it impossible for them to bury their dead with any religious rites save those of the Church of England prayer book, and which enjoyed the political privilege of having its bishops in the Lords, where they had abused their power by obstructing parliamentary reform. Radicals were wholly opposed to the electoral system since it made the Commons absurdly unrepresentative and largely subservient to the Lords. It was wholly opposed to the landed interest as such, and convinced that its selfish and ruthless character accounted for the widespread rural distress, particularly in the southern counties. And it was reinforced in the 1820s and 1830s by Irish discontent, dramatized by the colourful personality of Daniel O'Connell 'the Liberator'; and though Ireland's cause was never England's, Ireland itself was a kind of Chamber of Horrors displaying the faults of the ruling system of England at their gruesome worst. In consequence, the struggle for the Reform Bill was thought of as part of a programme that included the disestablishment and disendowment of the Church, a drastic reform of the Lords, secret ballot, frequent elections, a wide suffrage, the repeal of the union between England and Ireland, and the abolition of slavery.

The Whigs, by their espousal of the cause of parliamentary reform, had got into power by putting themselves at the head of this movement; and thereafter had the perilous task of maintaining themselves in office while satisfying few if any of its further demands, even though the radical cause had a good many vocal and often uncontrollable advocates on the government's own side in the first House of Commons elected after the Reform Act. Any attempt to meet the programme would involve the resignation of several cabinet ministers or, failing that, a head-on struggle with the Lords, which Grey and Melbourne, his successor, were at all costs resolved to avoid. It was fortunate for both the dominant parties in Parliament that radicalism was never more than a collective noun to describe an assortment of 'clever and crotchety' characters among whom no effective leader ever emerged.

The history of the Whig governments of Grey and

Melbourne after the passing of the Great Reform Bill was nevertheless tinged with farce. Grey had virtually been drafted to preside over the Reform Bill struggle on the strength of an advocacy of parliamentary reform over thirty years before, which he now looked upon as a youthful indiscretion. To find himself, in his late sixties, assuming responsibility for a Reform Bill which became law only as the combined result of mob violence and a threat to coerce the Lords by the creation of peers was painful to him. His capacity to control a wayward Cabinet, only some of whom were real Whigs (Whigs were so exclusive an aristocratic connection that there was never enough of them to go round), and a following of incalculable so-called liberals and radicals, was limited. Barely two years after the Reform Act he resigned, grumpily accusing his colleagues of conspiracy behind his back.

By that time, four of his leading Whig supporters had left him, being provoked into doing so by a sudden alarming announcement by the party's leading man in the Commons, Lord John Russell, that any of them who opposed the expropriation of the Church in Ireland was guilty of 'bigotry and prejudice'. After only four months in office, Lord Melbourne, his successor, was dismissed by William IV, allegedly on the not unreasonable grounds that by that time the government had become too weak to govern, but in reality because he thought that effective power in the government was about to pass into the hands of Lord John Russell, who seemed likely to transform a conservative-minded Whig government into a Radical one, bent on the despoliation of the Church. The Tory leader, Peel, was sent for in December 1834, and an election resulted which gained the Tories a hundred seats.

But since Peel still had no majority, Melbourne came back as prime minister in April 1835 embarrassed, not only by an increase in the number of Radicals on whom he would have to rely, but also by the cantankerousness of a frustrated King who had tried and failed to get rid of him.

William IV's death in 1837 produced another election, which still further reduced the government's majority in the Commons, but produced also a new sovereign whose favours ensured its continuance in office. The eighteen-year-old Victoria conceived an instant schoolgirlish crush on Melbourne which he took care to nourish because it kept him in power (which in his easy, dilatory way he greatly enjoyed) and because he so obviously found the Queen's attachment to him both piquant and poignant; he was fifty years the Queen's senior. Unable to find an efficient chancellor of the exchequer, the government staggered on, its financial incompetence increasingly manifest, till in 1839 Melbourne decided the time had come to resign. But before assuming office, Peel, in view of the Queen's known partisanship for the Whigs, asked for changes to be made in the Household. The Queen would not consent to dismiss the Whig ladies of the bedchamber and informed Peel (in terms devised by Melbourne) that such a procedure was 'contrary to usage and repugnant to her feelings'. Peel therefore declined the Queen's commission and 'dear Lord M.' was back yet again. It was an issue on which only Peel had a good case and the survival of the Whigs by petticoat favour for two more years was a bathetic conclusion to a story that had begun with the heroics (even if they were largely mock-heroics) of the struggle for the Great Reform Bill.

Desperate for an electioneering dodge by 1841, the Whigs began to toy in a prevaricating fashion with vote by ballot and a repeal of the Corn Laws, in the hope of once again riding back to power on the radical band-wagon. But public confidence had deserted them, and they were defeated in the Commons by 91 votes immediately after the 1841 election. This time there was no trouble for Peel over the ladies of the bed-chamber. Since 1840, the Queen had found a new love in Prince Albert, whom she had married that year; and Albert was solemnly resolved that his Beloved and he should be 'apart from politics and party'. Thanks to his good offices, a formula was found comfortably in advance, and Sir Robert Peel moved smoothly to the centre of a stage he had already been coming to dominate even though he had been improperly kept too long in the wings by an eventually repentant sovereign.

The statute book contains much that stands to the credit of the Grey and Melbourne governments, and both Gladstone and Disraeli later expressed their approval of the Whigs' legislation. Yet much that the Whigs did was so manifestly done as a nervously grudging concession to radical pressure and modified so often for fear of the Lords, that the credit they earned was largely in the form of a post-dated cheque to be honoured only in the perspectives of history. O'Connell called them 'base, bloody and brutal' (though what O'Connell said was not necessarily evidence about either the Whigs or about O'Connell's attitude to them); Disraeli said Melbourne was a saunterer and a lounger, presiding over 'reckless aristocrats stricken with palsy'; Cobden accused them of 'truckling subservience' to the Tories; others accused them of being in office for nothing but money and 'the vanity of power' and of being 'a party dying of inertia'. And the enactment in which the Whigs took the greatest pride and the one which the Tories did little to obstruct (though Disraeli, with his eye on the future, attacked it violently in the House in 1839) was the Poor Law Amendment Act of 1834. This was certainly in conformity with the need of the time for the replacement of uncontrolled muddle by accountability and efficient administration and was a serious attempt to deal with the major social problem which the country then faced, given that more people were then affected by rural poverty than by urban. But the attempt (it proved ultimately unsuccessful) to end all outdoor relief, together with the imposition of the bureaucratic apparatus of the guardians and the poor law commissioners, demonstrated unequivocally the essential inhumanity of the utilitarian school of thought.

The Whigs abolished slavery and passed the Factory Act of 1833.[1] Yet the proposal to abolish slavery was omitted from the King's Speech when it was first drafted and the Factory Act was, and was seen to be, a device mainly to ensure the failure of the adult ten-hour campaign. Moreover, the government insisted that the hours of work of 'young persons' between twelve and eighteen should be limited to ten hours a day and not to eight as Shaftesbury had proposed; an amendment which led Cobbett to observe savagely that this appeared to mean that Britain's greatness depended neither on her navy, her com-

[1] See p. 57.

merce nor her Empire but on the extraction from several thousand little girls of another two hours' work a day. The establishment of the annual government education grant in 1833 and the appointment in 1839 of a Privy Council committee to supervise its administration and the training and inspection of teachers amounted, financially, to a drop in the ocean and was an abandonment of the government's original plans to bring the scheme wholly under government control and to give more equitable treatment to the nonconformists.[1]

The Municipal Corporations Act of 1835 was perhaps the nearest the Whigs ever got to passing whole-hog Radical legislation. On the evidence provided by a commission of inquiry packed with Radicals, two hundred old corporations were replaced by 178 municipal boroughs, each with a council elected by household suffrage; and Peel and Wellington so far lent their support that they disciplined the Lords into doing nothing more to emasculate the act than to insist on the creation of borough aldermen who would hold office for six years instead of the councillors' three, thus minimizing the dreadful consequences of frequent appeals to the democracy. More effectively anti-democratic in practice was the provision that householders could vote only if they had paid rates for three years. This could result (as in Liverpool) in the number of electors for local elections being actually smaller than that for parliamentary elections.

The expectation that the Whigs would go on, from the start their predecessors had made, to destroy the privileged position of the Church of England was greatly disappointed. On the credit side was the fact that the process which the Tories had begun, by repealing the Test and Corporation Acts in 1828 and by passing the Catholic Emancipation Act in 1829, was continued by the Whigs, and 'the absolute right of dissenting or Roman Catholic citizens to hold public office was everywhere established under Lord Melbourne's government'.[2] But it had always needed something like a political conjuring trick for the Whigs to combine their appeal to the Dissenters (in the

[1] See p. 190.
[2] O. Chadwick, *The Victorian Church* (London, Black, 1966), Vol. I, p. 112.

interests of civil liberty) with their claim to be the true heirs of those who had saved the Established Protestant Church from Romish tyranny in 1688; since, though Whigs were temperamentally anti-Papist to a degree, the Dissenters were hostile to the Established Church. The Reform Act, coming so soon after the acts of 1828 and 1829, convinced both Dissenters and churchmen that the Establishment was doomed. Among churchmen it set Newman on the path that eventually led to Rome, produced Keble's Oxford sermon on 'National Apostasy', and gravely alarmed the youthful Gladstone.

All that the Whigs succeeded in doing was to inflict minor wounds which, though giving rise to agonized cries of 'the Church in danger', aroused even louder accusations of betrayal from the Dissenters. The Whigs heeded the former rather than the latter and Dissenting support for them had withered well before 1841. By that time the Whigs had met Dissenters' demands for the civil registration of births, deaths and marriages and had allowed them to marry in their own chapels (though only provided a registrar was present). They legislated for certain valuable administrative reforms in the finances of the Church and established the Ecclesiastical Commission largely owing to the initiative of Peel; and a charter was granted to 'the godless college in Gower Street' (University College) which in effect was the first step in the creation of London University. This, though dodging the issue of religious tests at Oxford and Cambridge, did hold out prospects of England at last having one university which imposed no religious tests.[1] The Whigs failed to abolish church rates in the face of dissension in their own ranks and mounting opposition in the Lords; and for the same reason shied away from tackling the grossly anomalous position of the Church in Ireland which, in addition to being grossly over-endowed, imposed its tithe on a miserable Roman Catholic peasantry.

Throughout, the government appeared to have been blown hither and thither by the winds of expediency, to have lacked the courage of its convictions or to have had too few opinions to be courageous about. Its measures were half-measures to the

[1] Though it could not, initially, award degrees.

extent that justifies applying to the struggle that brought them to power the description applied by Victor Hugo to the July Revolution in Paris in 1830 – a revolution that was stopped half-way. To all this must be added the financial incompetence of the Whigs as the years from 1837 onwards brought bad harvests, a decline in trade and ever-mounting government deficits. In these circumstances, to accede in 1839 to the Radical demand for the penny post merely made matters worse by making the deficit of 1841 larger than ever. By that year, the Whigs had been deserted by much of the army they had set out to command in 1831. In the manufacturing towns, respectable Radical feeling was already transferring its energies to the Anti-Corn Law League and the less respectable had already turned their attention to Chartism. The Whigs had certainly cooled the ardour of the political forces they had led to victory in 1832; but by 1841 they seemed once more to be what they had been before 1830 – a noble band of captains without an army to follow them.

That the old order survived the Reform Bill was due at least as much to the caution which Peel imposed upon the Tories as to the caution the Whigs imposed upon the Liberals. Though a minority in the Commons after 1832, the Tories were still in the majority in the Lords and hardly less reconciled to finding themselves in opposition after long years in office than their descendants were to be in 1906. But just as the Whigs had to try to reconcile their professional championship of liberty with their determination to preserve aristocratic predominance, Peel saw that the Tories had to reconcile their long-standing championship of law and order with the patent fact that, if change was indiscriminately resisted, law and order would break down.

The message had been signalled clearly enough in 1829 when the threat of civil war in Ireland had compelled them to abandon their last-ditch resistance to Catholic emancipation; and it was the refusal of the Tories to accept this so-called 'betrayal' that had split the government, brought it down, let in the Whigs and, with them, the Great Reform Bill. The struggle for the bill repeated the message. Tory resistance to the bill in the Lords had had to be abandoned in face of the threat to law and order created by the widespread mob violence of 1831. It was hard indeed for the party of Peterloo and the Six Acts to see this mob violence used by its parliamentary rivals as a political weapon to force a constitutional revolution on to the statute book and to threaten the Lords as an institution. Yet, as a party that claimed to believe in strong government, the Tories could hardly indulge in factious and obstructive opposition after 1832; and indeed had little need to do so. They had merely to be patient enough and the Whigs would undo themselves. Nowhere in nineteenth-century Europe did it prove difficult to rally the majority of property owners, urban as well as rural, to the side of whoever claimed to be able to save Church and State from godless radicalism; and godless radicalism was precisely what the Whig leaders had unleashed and seemed able to withstand only by staggering from expedient to expedient. Gladstone was not alone in seeing 'an element of anti-Christ in the Reform Bill'.

The turning point was William IV's dismissal of Melbourne in 1834 in an endeavour to save the state from a government likely to be dominated by the fidgety radicalism of Lord John Russell. By making Peel prime minister, if only for a few months, this move established him for the first time as Tory leader and enabled him, in the Tamworth Manifesto, to proclaim with authority and to the electorate at large, what he had already declared in the Commons a year earlier: that he regarded the Reform Bill as the final settlement of a dispute that was now closed and that he favoured reforming whatever it seemed essential to reform 'gradually, dispassionately and deliberately'. Yet, as well as appealing in this way to those who might otherwise convince themselves that only by adherence to the Whigs could they hope for reform, both Peel and his principal lieutenants continued throughout the thirties to stress their commitment to Conservatism, that is to the preservation of the existing constitutional powers of King, Lords and Commons and of an Established Church committed to reformed Protestantism.

To readers living in the late twentieth century this definition of Conservatism tends to appear either meaningless or irrelevant. Posterity sees the problem of the second quarter of the nineteenth century as that of adjusting social and political institutions to the needs of a state undergoing an *industrial* revolution. But a large part of the thinking nation at the time saw the problem as that of resisting a *social* revolution. The way to cope with the threat was not to reconstruct society for the benefit of vulgar, rapacious factory owners or the dark, uninstructed urban masses, but to defend the existing society; and the only way to define existing society was to rehearse the character of Church and State as they were held to have been fixed at the time of the Glorious Revolution. And the only way to defend that society was to preserve the social and political power of the nobility, the clergy and the gentry.

The Whig leadership had exactly the same aims, certainly once Melbourne became prime minister. But the Whigs could hardly say so, given that they had come into office as proponents of contrary ideas. They were thus committed to an unavailing search for some means of perpetuating their role as leaders of Liberalism and Radicalism, after Liberals and Radicals had lost faith in them. This, combined with their financial incompetence and the depression from 1836 onwards, enabled the Tories to appear not only as champions of order but of sounder government finance and of economic revival.

Once in power, however, the Conservatives faced a mirror image of the dilemma that had faced their Whig predecessors. Political facts and their own principles stopped the Whigs from carrying out a purely radical programme; political and economic facts prevented Peel from carrying out a purely conservative programme. From a political point of view, Peel's government ended much more disastrously than Melbourne's, in a split that denied his party effective power for almost thirty years.

Until 1845, the only cause for complaint his followers had against Peel was the strict discipline he imposed on them. But in that year he suffered, as was the normal fate of British politicians, from the excess of prejudice that invariably resulted from an attempt to do anything sensible for Ireland. Maynooth

College, an institution for training Irish priests, had been receiving a government subsidy of £9,000 a year since the Act of Union; Peel wished to increase the grant to £26,000. At a time when the Tractarian Movement was inducing in the English mind the frightful suspicion that the Established Church was flirting with Romish doctrines, the spectacle of a Conservative prime minister subsidizing Papistical education in priest-ridden, superstitious Ireland so strained the loyalty of Peel's following that half of them voted against the Maynooth proposal; the majority it secured depended on the votes of Whigs. It was a moment in Tory fortunes that paralleled the defection of four senior ministers from Grey's government over religious issues in Ireland in 1834 and Grey's own resignation shortly afterwards.[1] When the issue of Corn Law Repeal arose a year later, almost all those who voted against Peel on that issue had also voted against him over Maynooth.

If Chartism was an economic and social movement wearing the guise of a political campaign, the agitation against the Corn Laws was a social and political movement in the guise of an economic one; and there is a sense in which to debate whether the Corn Laws had really protected agriculture or whether their repeal did or did not help or hinder either manufacturing industry or agriculture is indeed to debate technicalities.[2] Like Chartism, the Anti-Corn Law League was an attempt to continue the Reform Bill struggle by other means. It was seen by its supporters and its opponents alike as a renewal of that attack on the established order which the Whigs had aborted in the 1830s. Repealers and Protectionists alike saw the Corn Law question in terms of an attack on Crown, Aristocracy and Church; and on Parliament too, since the League was held to be trying to submit it to improper if not revolutionary pressure. That it was conflict between the old unreformed England and the new can be attested by the fact that many of those landowners who were already involved in the new urban and

---

[1] See p. 66.
[2] As regards lower prices, the free trade battle over corn 'was a political mountain that brought forth an economic mouse'. (P. Mathias, *The First Industrial Nation, 1700–1914*, London, Methuen, 1969, p. 302.)

manufacturing England, by virtue of being substantial urban landowners or owners of coal- or iron-bearing land, tended to be far less zealous for Protection than those to whom one could, borrowing a phrase used in a controversy about an earlier century, describe as 'pure' gentry – those with little liquid capital, relying wholly on their land, and haunted by the conviction that one bad year would be their permanent ruin.

It was his astute realization of all this that had caused Lord John Russell to try to dangle the prospect of a drastic lowering of the corn duty before the electorate in 1841. Peel woke up, as it were, to discover that the Whigs had inscribed 'Protection' on his Conservative banners overnight; and all who read it instantly ran to him. Peel, however, regarded himself as un-committed; though a free trader, in practice he took the pragmatic view that the landed interest was a special one it was not practical politics to interfere with. The notion that he had been elected with the prime duty of protecting the landed interest against the Anti-Corn Law League was one that was wished on him by Russell and his backbenchers; it was not a role he had either chosen or proclaimed for himself. By the autumn of 1845 he was becoming so convinced of the validity of the League's arguments that he had already made up his mind to come out in due course in favour of Repeal. The distress caused by the Irish famine and the failure of the English harvest provoked him to try to act more speedily, though it is hard to see what practical relevance to the current distress either in England or Ireland could have been achieved (or was achieved) by Repeal.

And then, cutting across Peel's discussions with his cabinet colleagues, came yet another of John Russell's *coups de théâtre*. He issued an open letter from Edinburgh announcing his discovery that the Corn Laws blighted commerce and divided the classes, caused poverty, disease, death and crime, and ought accordingly to be repealed. It was a clear bid by Russell to recover for the Whigs the leadership of the Liberals and Radicals that had been lost in the late thirties. Unwilling to be transformed into a prime minister who would be accused of giving way on a major issue at the behest of the Opposition, Peel, in default of adequate cabinet support for Repeal, resigned, being fully prepared to support Repeal if it were introduced by a government led by Russell. But Russell found the Whig chieftains as divided over the distribution of offices in any new government[1] as they were over the desirability of repealing the Corn Laws.

For the moment, Russell's *coup* had misfired; unable to form an administration, he therefore, in Disraeli's words, returned the 'poisoned chalice' to Peel. And poisoned it was. Peel would have to repeal the Corn Laws with Whig votes and wreck the Conservative party in the process. When Peel's bill to provide for a reduction of the duties on wheat, oats and barley to a nominal shilling a quarter was put to the Commons, two-thirds of those who voted for it were on the Whig side and almost all its opponents sat on his own benches. In the Lords, the Whig magnates consoled themselves with the consideration that Repeal would be more damaging to Tory politicians and Tory landlords than to their own great wealth, and voted overwhelmingly in the bill's favour. Immediately thereafter the Protectionist Tories joined with the Whigs, the Radicals and the Irish, in what Wellington not altogether unjustly described as 'a blackguard combination', to defeat the government's Irish Coercion Bill. Peel resigned office at once and – with little advantage either to the country or themselves – the Whigs came back to suffer the pains of office under the incompetent leadership of Russell.

The Repeal of the Corn Laws had all the elements of a political melodrama composed by Disraeli – and perhaps in a sense that is what it was. At the centre of the action was Peel, a great man brought down by events, his character marred by failures of foresight and imagination but redeemed by an open and manly repentance uttered movingly over the broken body of the party to which he had devoted his life. The thundering oratory of Cobden and Bright and the swelling organ-voice of

---

[1] 'Sir Robert said, "He (Lord John) will have difficulties and perhaps did not consider what he was doing when he wrote that letter; but *I will support him.*"' (Memorandum by Prince Albert, 7 December 1845.)

the Anti-Corn Law League; the legerdemain by which Russell sought, with the wave of his magic wand, to present the Whigs as Repeal's coroneted fairy godfathers; the gruesome conjuring up of the spectres of famine and death from the potato patches of Ireland; and finally Disraeli's unscrupulous invective in the rôle of Demon King fiendishly exulting in the Great Man's Fall – all these very Victorian elements in the story of 1845–6 made sober analysis almost impossible. Yet what happened then was that Peel revealed himself finally as the one man on the political scene who proved willing, when the facts demanded it, to bring the actual conduct of public affairs into line with the realities of a rapidly changing society. And Whig noblemen and Tory gentlemen joined together in a successful counter-revolutionary conspiracy against him.

Here indeed (unless one preferred to seek it wholly among the Whigs) was the 'organized hypocrisy' that Disraeli professed to find in Peel's brand of Conservatism. The men whose spokesman Disraeli so enthusiastically made himself were men who were persuaded that to repeal the Corn Laws at the behest of a manufacturers' agitation (or out of the needs of Irish misery) was a threat to their survival as a class. Peel was convinced that it was not; and that even if it were, no political party after the Reform Bill could survive if its sole basis was the preservation of the interests of one particular class. He saw what the Protectionists themselves were to discover within four years of Peel's fall: that, as a Protectionist party, the Tories were doomed to be a permanent political minority. In the larger sense, therefore, the old idea of Peel as a man with insight but no foresight has little to commend it. Over Repeal, the only factor he did not foresee was Russell's Edinburgh Letter; but to divine what clever political prank Lord John might get up to next would have required second sight rather than foresight.

More illuminating is Walter Bagehot's patronizing view[1] that Peel was the best type of statesman to be hoped for under a 'constitutional' system because under such a system 'you have excluded the profound thinker; you must be content with

[1] *Biographical Studies*, essay I, 'The Character of Sir Robert Peel' (London, Longmans, 1895), p. 42.

what you can obtain – the business gentleman'. The England
of the forties needed nothing more urgently than a political
leadership prepared to be guided by facts, on which the men
of 'principle' whom Bagehot rated more highly have frequently
only the most tenuous hold. Peel's grasp of fact between 1841
and 1846 was perhaps unrivalled by any prime minister of the
century. The national economy required an immediate restoration of government finances and a vigorous encouragement of
economic expansion at a time of distress and mounting social
discontent. This could only be done by a 'business gentleman'
with a respect for facts and figures.

More even than the thirties, the forties was a decade of blue
books, commissions and inquiries. It was during Peel's
administration that Chadwick's sanitary report was published,
leading to the Public Health Act of 1848 after Peel's fall, as
also was the report leading to the Mines Act of 1842; both
reports were best sellers. The Factory Act, like the Mines Act,
showed, for all the government's hard-faced caution about
them, that social reform was as likely to come from a Tory as
from a Whig government. The Bank Charter Act of 1844
provided the sub-structure of a stable financial system for the
rest of the century: it made the note-issuing department of the
Bank of England independent of its banking department,
required all note issues in excess of £14 million to be covered by
bullion, and it took steps to extinguish the note-issuing power
of country banks. Aimed at preventing financial instability by
the over-issue of notes it can be regarded as perhaps unduly
restrictive, since the banking department could in difficult
times be denuded of gold at a time when the note-issuing
department was stocked with useless reserves. This happened
in 1847, 1857 and 1866 and the operation of the act had to be
suspended on each occasion. Nevertheless the act did ensure
that, though a private institution, the Bank took on much of the
character of a central state bank. Another step taken to prevent
excessive speculation was the Companies Act of 1844 which
required incorporated companies to be registered and to
publish prospectuses and accounts. The Railway Act, also in
1844, and piloted through by Gladstone, instituted the 'parlia-

mentary train',[1] gave the government control over rates of carriage, and even adumbrated the possibility of the state purchasing lines constructed in the future. All these acts were the outcome of detailed investigations by parliamentary committees.

Most celebrated of Peel's achievements were his fiscal reforms. The freeing of trade from a multiplicity of taxes had begun in the 1820s but had not advanced under the Whigs; it was now undertaken in drastic manner.[2] His budgets of 1842 and 1845 achieved such widespread tariff reductions that, by the latter year, all taxes on exports had been abolished, most raw materials could be imported free and the duty on manufactured goods was only 10 per cent. There was now no duty on imported cotton, and duties on timber and sugar were also greatly reduced. To provide for compensatory revenue and to facilitate the widely-diffused benefits of free trade, income tax was reintroduced in 1842 at 7d in the £ on incomes over £150. The Whig deficit of £2 million was converted into a large surplus and there was a vigorous trade revival; and that Peel's reforms contributed greatly to the steady dissipation of the discontent with which the forties began remains one of the few propositions about nineteenth-century history about which there seems to be little argument.

Of course, all this was very dull and difficult to present to all but the most sophisticated minds as being particularly 'conservative', since it is always hard to convince the conservative-minded that the best way to conserve society is to take the sting out of political dissent by removing its causes – in the case of the 1840s, economic distress. Bagehot complained that all Peel seemed to do was 'repeal' things, arguing that this showed Peel

[1] See p. 29.

[2] The multiplicity of the taxes on commodities at the start of the century was memorably described by Sidney Smith: 'The schoolboy whips his taxed top – the beardless youth manages his taxed horse, with a taxed bridle, on a taxed road; – and the dying Englishman, pouring his medicine, which has paid 7 per cent, into a spoon which has paid 15 per cent – flings himself back upon his chintz bed, which has paid 22 per cent – and expires in the arms of an apothecary who has paid a licence of a hundred pounds for the privilege of putting him to death.'

lacked a creative mind. Even Gladstone thought the Whigs had produced more valuable 'general legislation' than Peel. Worse still, Peel himself was a 'dull' man, 'fitted to work and explain; he was not able to charm and amuse'. Shaftesbury thought him an iceberg with a faint thaw on the tip; O'Connell said his smile was like the gleam on the silver plate of a coffin lid; and when, in 1850, Peel was fatally thrown from a horse in Hyde Park it was perhaps because someone standing by refrained from cautioning him that the horse was refractory out of fear of the glacial response with which Peel might treat his friendly warning. Disraeli had no difficulty in disliking and attacking this aloof, frigid man. As the Repeal crisis loomed, Disraeli wrote, 'things must be done by parties, not by persons using parties as tools – especially men without imagination or any inspiring qualities or who, rather, offer you duplicity instead of inspiration'.[1]

Not only was Peel 'dull'; he was indeed a 'business gentleman'. He treated his backbenchers as lobby fodder. He overawed his cabinet colleagues by his detailed mastery of their departments as well as of his own work and by his outstanding competence in the transaction of government business. Gladstone reported it as a novelty that when Peel fixed a cabinet meeting for a certain hour he expected everybody to be there at the time appointed. This was indeed to be a 'business gentleman', given that his Cabinet contained eight peers, two heirs to earldoms, three baronets, one knight and only one plain mister.[2] And it was a business gentleman's mind which saw, in 1845, that the logic of free trade policy since 1841 had made resistance to Corn Law Repeal no longer a matter of principle. Already, the landed interest had seen duties on imported cattle, meat, butter and cheese reduced, and the sliding scale on corn cut down. But Bagehot thought it all proved that 'a want of principle' was a characteristic of 'constitutional' statesmen; and J. H. Newman declared, in his characteristically dejected style, that it was 'pitiable' that Peel could not understand that a political party without an idea had

[1] Robert Blake, *Disraeli* (London, Eyre & Spottiswoode, 1966), p. 223.
[2] *ibid.*, p. 166.

no unity. Yet, apart from Peel, the Tories had no principle at all, except that of stopping the nineteenth century because they wanted to get off. Cobden must surely be seen to have the best of the argument when he said in 1850 that now that Peel was dead, the 'idea of the Age has no other representative among statesmen'.

5 · *Patriotism Prevails*
1846–65

These Chartisms, Radicalisms, Reform Bill,
Tithe Bill, and infinite other discrepancy, and
acrid argument and jargon that there is yet to be,
are *our* French Revolution: God grant that we,
with our better methods, may be able to transact
it by argument alone.

CARLYLE

We don't want no alteration
Of the present Legislation,
'Twon't affect our sittiwation –
Too full of beer.

Punch, 1859

The economic difficulties of 1837–42, when harvests were bad
and there was a serious recession in manufacturing industry and
much unemployment in Lancashire and the Midlands, produced
the two great extra-parliamentary movements of the Victorian
period, Chartism and the Anti-Corn Law League. Although the
Chartists failed and the League may be said to have succeeded;
and although they differed in that Chartism was almost wholly
a working-class movement and the League a wholly middle-
class movement, they were alike in that they both testified to a
widespread feeling that the Reform Act and the Whig reforms
thereafter amounted to no more than an unfinished business.
The two movements were also similar in their final outcome.
Though Chartists sometimes acted violently whereas the League
only talked violently, it could be seen in the end that Chartism

offered no serious threat to the existing social order and the League no serious threat to the existing political order.

The original source of the Six Points[1] which became the substance of the People's Charter was a group of respectable working-class Radicals who, in 1836, formed the London Working Men's Association. The Six Points attracted so much attention that local groups to agitate for their acceptance by Parliament came into being and the influential Radical body, the Birmingham Political Union, led by the Radical banker, Thomas Attwood, M.P., gave its approval. It was in Birmingham in 1838 that the Chartist Movement was formally launched, with the aim of petitioning Parliament to pass a bill containing the Six Points. There was widespread enthusiasm in the North and Midlands. A Convention would be elected to present the petition to Parliament; and if the petition were rejected there would be a month-long general strike, called a 'Sacred Month'.

From the beginning, the movement was dogged by the lack of efficient organization and agreed leadership. Lovett of the L.W.M.A. and Attwood of the Birmingham Political Union were alarmed at the frequent references to the use of 'physical force' in the speeches and writings of the demagogic Irishman, Feargus O'Connor, who had founded a Radical paper, *The Northern Star*, to propagate his Chartist ideas. As a follower of the Irish 'Liberator', Daniel O'Connell, O'Connor was applying to the English agitation the lesson which appeared to have been learned from Irish agitation for Catholic emancipation in the 1820s: namely that the English would do nothing unless they were threatened with violence, but that if they could be persuaded that the threat was serious enough, they would give way. This tactic had the divisive effect of frightening essentially respectable English Radicals, like Lovett and Attwood, while encouraging unsophisticated working men up and down the country to believe that O'Connor's talk of

---

[1] The six points of the People's Charter were demands for: universal (male) suffrage; secret ballot; equal electoral districts; payment of M.P.s; abolition of property qualifications for M.P.s; annual parliamentary elections.

violence was meant seriously. The first signs of this were apparent in 1839; already before the petition had got to Parliament, there had been clashes between police and workers in the Bull Ring, Birmingham.

Naturally enough, Parliament rejected the first Chartist petition in that year, and this faced the Chartists with the fact that they had no money, no organization and too few supporters to carry out their threat of a Sacred Month. To make the point very obvious, the army commander in Manchester, General Napier, carefully explained to the Chartist leaders the precise resources in men and material at his command and what would be the consequences of an attempt at insurrection. There was, in consequence, no Sacred Month; but there was a pathetic attempt by several thousand Chartists to seize control of Newport, Monmouthshire, which was put down by the exertions of twenty-eight soldiers. The leaders, John Frost, Zephaniah Williams and William Jones, were sentenced to death, though their sentences were shortly afterwards commuted to transportation. By 1840, almost all the Chartist leaders were in prison, though most of the sentences were short.

It is testimony to the strength of the feeling behind the movement that, in spite of these setbacks, a second petition, six miles long and with over three million signatures, was presented to Parliament – and rejected – in 1842. Once again, rejection produced ineffective violence. There were strikes from the Midlands to Scotland and the hope that they would be transformed into a general insurrection. After prevaricating for a time, O'Connor swung round to denouncing the strikes, as he had tried to prevent the rising in Newport. Condemned by him, the strikes fizzled out amid hundreds of arrests and 79 sentences of transportation.

The spectacle of tottering thrones all over Europe in 1848, coming as it did at a time of economic hardship, revived the movement yet again. The presentation of a petition with, it was thought, up to six million signatures would be made by an immense procession converging on Westminster after a monster meeting on Kennington Common. The Duke of Wellington took over the defence of London, which was packed with troops and also with special constables, the most eminent of whom was the future Napoleon III; and for good measure 1,500 Chelsea pensioners were assigned to the defence of Battersea. But once again, O'Connor stopped short of translating violent words into violent action. He agreed with the police not to hold the march, but to dispatch the petition to the Commons by cab. The six million signatures proved to be slightly under two million. This time there was a perhaps more widespread, more desperate and more inefficient splutter of insurrectionary attempts; and more prison sentences and sentences to transportation. The movement did not revive again, doubtless because times were getting better; only a few of its leaders (O'Connor went mad in 1852) continued their propaganda. But O'Connor's funeral in 1855 was the last sizeable Chartist gathering in history.

The importance of Chartism is not that it failed but that it existed and was, in due time, remembered. The volume of support for it almost certainly did much to impress upon the nation's rulers that, if the principle of government by consent were to survive, the working classes would have to be reckoned with. The rejection of the Charter expressed clearly enough the government's view that there should be no formal resort to working-class consent through the adoption of universal suffrage; but the awareness that social order could not be guaranteed if working-class needs were ignored was sharpened by the widespread extent of the support for Chartism. And it seems that governments handled the Chartists with an unexpected combination of firmness and moderation. A quiet, efficient dispatch of troops and police by rail to disturbed areas, the absence of provocative acts against the agitators and the lack, by previous standards, of excessive vindictiveness towards those found guilty under the law, argued a greater sense of social realities than did the savage suppression of the agricultural labourers' revolt of 1830. Governments may also have learned to handle working-class unrest with less panic-stricken severity as a result of the completeness of the Chartist defeat, and above all by the realization that, when put to the test, the Chartists had not, in any organized sense, used very much physical force after all.

Both government and people derived from the Chartist collapse that kind of reassurance as to the basic stability of society that was derived from the country's peaceful emergence from the General Strike of 1926.

For the labouring poor of the North and Midlands, Chartism, for all its confusion, offered a unique opportunity for the making of a protest which, if not concerted, was at least widespread, and which was to be recalled with emotion and with pride. For the changes of the next fifty years were to prove that the Chartists, though ahead of history, were in almost all respects prophetic of it. And Chartism also taught a more immediate lesson: that to threaten governments with the use of force when the means to apply such force did not exist was to court certain defeat. Somehow, working men must learn to work within society and not against it.

Inevitably, the Anti-Corn Law League made a more positive impression than Chartism since it represented the aims of the already powerful and self-reliant manufacturing interest of the Lancashire cotton industry, and was based on Manchester, already a proud provincial capital. Founded there in 1839, it secured the advocacy of the Manchester manufacturer, Richard Cobden, and John Bright, a Quaker industrialist from Rochdale. They were successful in limiting their aims to the specific one of repealing the Corn Laws while representing this objective as part of a social and moral crusade. Advocacy of free trade was justified on the grounds that it would give the manufacturing interest more outlet for its products, and thus increase employment; it would lower the price of bread, and thus further improve the condition of the labouring poor; it would actually stimulate agriculture through the removal of artificial protection and through the increased demand for its products in the towns that would result from the increased prosperity of manufacture; and it would prelude the establishment of international harmony because reciprocal free trade agreements would cause a great and beneficial expansion of trade between nation and nation. Thus, an economic policy advanced primarily in the interests of Lancashire cotton was presented as the interest of the nation as a whole and even of the world at large. And the only obstacles in the way of this great cause were said to be the landed aristocracy, which was represented as parasitically drawing rents while doing no work, and the Church of England, which also had a vested interest in the land by virtue of its income from tithe. Thus the League drew great strength from the frustrations of the Dissenters at the failure of the Whigs to abolish church rates; and Bright in particular larded his speeches with biblical references, asserting on one occasion, 'As a nation of Bible Christians we ought to realize that trade should be as free as the winds of heaven.'[1] In this way, the aims of the League, though apparently narrower than those of the Chartists, were in fact more comprehensive: they were an endeavour to make effective that transfer of power from aristocracy and Church to the manufacturing and dissenting interests which the Reform Bill struggle had sought to achieve and which the Whigs had prevented.

Yet in certain important respects, the League was hardly more successful than the Chartists. The proposition that it was the League's propaganda that converted Peel can hardly be sustained. He was converted intellectually by the logic of his own policies; and the determining factors in the decision of 1846 were the emotions caused by English hunger and Irish famine and the astute stratagem of Russell's Edinburgh Letter. And once Repeal had been effected, the League proved unable to exploit its apparent triumph. As a great movement to force a change in the balance of social and political power it may be said to have won a battle, but to have lost the war. The middle class, the manufacturing interest and the Dissenters won as little direct control over government from Corn Law Repeal as they had from the Reform Act.

The overthrow of Peel, which Russell so largely engineered, enabled the Whigs to emerge for a second time as the parlia-

---

[1] Asa Briggs, *Victorian People* (Harmondsworth, Penguin, 1965), p. 215. Hence Tennyson's gibe (*Maud*, X, iii):

> This broad-brimmed hawker of holy things
> Whose ear is crammed with his cotton, and rings
> Even in dreams to the chink of his pence.

mentary leaders of an extra-parliamentary movement. They would not have been able to do so but for the obtuseness of the Protectionist Tories; and Russell's government of 1846–52 functioned in the Commons with Peel and the Peelites exercising over them the same watchful superintendence that Peel had exercised over Melbourne. It was because of the essentially aristocratic character of Whig leadership and the 'betrayal' of Radical causes in the 1830s that Cobden had written in 1843 of his suspicion that the Whigs would use the League's agitation as a means of making 'a sham fight against the Tories at our expense. Depend on it [he wrote] the Whigs are plotting how they can use us and throw us aside. The more we show our honesty in refusing to be made the tools of a party the more we shall have the confidence of the moderate and honest Tories.'[1] It explains, too, why Bright sought to continue the radical policies of the League by other means after Repeal had been achieved. The League, to him, was 'the foe of aristocratic injustice' and the state Church was 'the creature and tool of the aristocracy'. He declared in 1849 that the League had proved 'that the landed aristocracy had reached its height and henceforth it would find a rival to which eventually it must become subjected. We have been living through a revolution without knowing it.'[2] And Peel pointed up the role of the Whigs as opportunist interlopers in the Repeal issue when he went out of his way, in his resignation speech in 1846, to pay particular tribute to the work of Cobden in bringing about what had, in the upshot, been put through the Commons by the incoming Whigs.

In choosing to repeal the Corn Laws himself, instead of, for instance, asking for a dissolution and making an election issue of it, Peel contributed a great deal towards frustrating the Radicals' wider aims. The passage of Repeal, through both Houses, in a real sense gave the lie to the League's wider accusations against the existing constitution and thus helped in fact to preserve it. Peel declared as much to his Tamworth

[1] Donald Southgate, *The Passing of the Whigs 1832–1886* (London, Macmillan, 1962), p. 126.
[2] See Asa Briggs, *op. cit.*, p. 216.

constituents in 1847. The passing of Repeal, he said, 'tended to fortify the established institutions of this country, to inspire confidence in the equity and benevolence of the legislature, to maintain the just authority of an hereditary nobility, and to discourage the desire for democratic change in the constitution of the House of Commons'.[1] A more precise exposition of Peel's view that the concession of essential reforms was the soundest form of Conservatism could hardly be desired. The 'revolution' Bright accuses his contemporaries of being unaware of failed to take place; but, ironically, it was the Repeal of the Corn Laws that prevented that revolution.

The return of the Whigs under Russell was indeed evidence of why the country was not aware of Bright's 'revolution'. The composition of Russell's government indicated that the great landed aristocrats and their sons were as much rulers of England as ever. The government was recruited almost entirely from the close cousinage of the few great Whig families; as late as 1859, Russell and the Whigs were described as 'incurable in their superstition about ducal houses'. The politics of the years between 1846 and 1867 appear, against the background of the social and economic realities of the time, and even in relation to the many valuable reforms that took place during them, quite exceptionally irrelevant. Russell, prime minister from 1846–52, became increasingly tiresome to his followers. A brief Protectionist Tory ministry under Derby lasted for only a few months in 1852. Thereupon, the Whigs, who would no longer endure Russell's leadership, formed a shambling coalition with the Peelites. This government, under the venerable Lord Aberdeen, lasted from 1852 until, having mismanaged its way into the Crimean War and then mismanaged the conduct of it, it was replaced in 1855 by a government headed by Lord Palmerston. Palmerston's accession to the premiership was one of the century's more unlikely political happenings; being exceeded in its improbability only by the circumstances that, with a brief sixteen-month interval from 1858–9 when Derby was in again, he remained prime minister until he at last

[1] Quoted J. D. Chambers and G. E. Mingay, *The Agricultural Revolution, 1750–1880* (London, Batsford, 1966), p. 157.

D

died in 1865 at the age of eighty-one. Russell succeeded him, introduced a reform bill, and was thrown out by the Tories and his own party, to be succeeded in 1866 by Derby, whose Tory government passed the Second Reform Bill with Whig votes in 1867. In 1868 Derby died and Disraeli became prime minister for the first time. Only when, at the end of 1868, the first election under the new Reform Act produced a Liberal majority and Gladstone began his first premiership, did political life and political rivalries once again appear to relate to great national issues.

Of all the aspects of these twenty years that most needs explanation, the most surprising is the combination of an almost complete absence of coherent political leadership with an almost total cessation of the anti-aristocratic Radicalism that, in the 1830s and 1840s, had looked like sweeping the country towards a drastic shift of political power. The political scene was wholly confused. The Whigs were few in number, fully aware that they stood vulnerably for a past that was disappearing, yet dissatisfied and disunited under Russell. The Radical M.P.s (notably Cobden and Bright) were now on the whole much respected as individuals but were not in general considered socially suitable to be offered office. The Peelites were unreconciled to the Protectionist Tories and scornful of the Whigs; and as ministers under Aberdeen they were not, Gladstone apart, very competent. The Protectionist Tories ceased to advocate Protection from 1852 but remained an apparently permanent minority in the Commons and in the country. Derby's leadership of them was the least absorbing interest of a life more usually devoted to the card-table, to Newmarket, or to the study of Homer; and Disraeli, so far from educating his party at this time, had great difficulty in overcoming its strong suspicion that he was an unscrupulous charlatan. Palmerston's ascendancy was an eccentricity based on two factors: by 1855 Parliament found itself with a complete absence of alternative candidates for the premiership and Palmerston had acquired, and took great pains to keep, the reputation of a hearty English patriot. Yet it still does not fail to surprise: for a whole decade, the most politically mature nation on earth subscribed willingly

to the leadership of a cheery old card who refused to entertain
the idea of parliamentary reform twenty-five to thirty years
after the drawing up of the People's Charter and who anticipated with most pleasure those parliamentary sessions in which
there was likely to be almost no legislation.

The phrase most frequently invoked to explain the quietness
of the quiet years is 'mid-Victorian prosperity'. This implies
that during those years the rich got richer and the poor became
less poor. The belief was certainly widespread at the time, but
this prosperity was based on rising money incomes rather than
on rising real incomes, and was accompanied by a widening gap
between rich and poor, and a widening gap between the wages
of the skilled worker and those of the unskilled. All the
evidence is that great squalor and horrifying poverty continued
to be widespread; and the relevant economic difference between
the fifties and sixties and the years before may well be no more
than that, although there were severe setbacks to trade and
industry between 1855 and 1857, recovery was much more
rapid than from similar crises earlier in the century, and that
there was no serious economic crisis until 1866–7, when the
twenty years of political quietude were broken, though only
temporarily, by the agitation for the Second Reform Bill.
The least vulnerable suggestion is probably that the rising
wealth of the middle classes, and the rising wages of the more
highly-skilled working men, provide at least some explanation
of why the middle classes appeared so reconciled to their
exclusion from the business of government, and why the skilled
workers concentrated their attention on evolving organizations
which, though exclusively working-class organizations, were
without political programmes.

The contemporary explanation was provided by Bagehot and
by others before him: England was, they decided, a 'deferential'
society which was accustomed to, and in a sense demanded,
aristocratic leadership. That this should occasion surprise is a
tribute to the extreme effectiveness of radical propaganda in
convincing both observers and posterity that Manchester's
view of the aristocracy as idlers who contributed nothing to
society had been universally accepted. What Manchester

thought might well be what London and everybody else would come to think eventually: but men's minds did not change as quickly as that. Even the proposition that the aristocracy had ruled by prescriptive right before 1832, but only by consent once the Reform Bill was passed, can be viewed as an over-statement, since the Whigs had based their power on a theory of consent long before 1832 and had, in 1688, mobilized and led interests that were not exclusively aristocratic.[1] That society in general should defer to such an aristocracy was inherent in the continuing social and political influence of the aristocracy in the localities as well as in central government, and in the circum-stance that the whole basis of secular life (and even more so the life of the Established Church) was, and remained, patronage, and not, as it was slowly coming to be by the end of the nineteenth century, 'merit' as defined by approved professional qualification. In many spheres of life, the surest prerequisite of success was still aristocratic patronage; and, while ducal hands continued to feed them, men were loth to start biting them, whatever they were instructed to do to the contrary from the sturdily independent North.

Moreover, the commitment of the traditional constitution to the idea of representative institutions, to the theory of consent, as well as to the notion that the function of govern-ment was to hold a balance between diverse 'interests', stamped in advance as unacceptably revolutionary any attempt to base government exclusively on the interests of manufacturers[2] or, by way of universal suffrage, on the interests of the unproper-tied masses. By contrast, an aristocratic statesman would appear to be above 'interest' and, by prescription, a guardian of the authentic traditions of the constitution. The vehemence with which Bright sought, during the Corn Law agitation, to represent the aristocracy itself as a selfish and partial 'interest' suggests how relatively novel – and revolutionary – such a conception was.

---

[1] *Punch* described Lord John Russell as forever about to land at Torbay to save the cause of English freedom.
[2] This was the burden of the complaints of the Protectionist Tories against the repeal of the Corn Laws.

On a practical level, too, the 1832 Reform Act itself perpetuated aristocratic influence. Most parliamentary seats were still allotted to the counties and the small boroughs, where aristocratic influence was much stronger than in the newly-enfranchised large towns. Only men with large unearned incomes could enter Parliament early; thus, professional or business men were either excluded altogether or until much later in life than members or protégés of the landed aristocracy. That this situation was for so long accepted testifies to the persistence of the view that this was part of the natural order of things.

Another factor making for the acceptance of continuing aristocratic control was the rapidly growing sense of identity between those who derived their wealth from manufacture and those who derived it from land. Until the last quarter of the century, when land lost much of its attraction for men of wealth, the crown of a successful lifetime devoted to manufacture was the purchase of a landed estate. Eighteenth-century English society had been a relatively open society, and from the earliest days of the industrial revolution there had been a measure of common interest between, for instance, those coal-mine owners who were dukes and those who were not. The bad-tempered young man in Tennyson's *Maud* provides this hostile mid-century account of the transformation of coal owner into landed aristocrat:

> This new-made lord, whose splendour plucks
> The slavish hat from the villager's head

had for grandfather one who

> crept from a gutted mine
> Master of half a servile shire,
> And left his coal, all turn'd into gold
> To a grandson, first of his noble line,
> Rich in the grace all women desire,
> Strong in the power that all men adore,
> And simper and set their voices lower,
> And soften as if to a girl, and hold
> Awe-stricken breaths at a work divine,
> Seeing his gewgaw castle shine,

New as his title, built last year,
There amid perky larches and pine,
And over the sullen-purple moor
(Look at it) pricking a cockney ear.

Thus aristocratic control of government and society was both something which eventually the industrialist might hope to share and which was also a safeguard for the preservation of the new men's property and profit. While it continued, the middle class could, according to circumstance, secure its own aims by threatening to rouse the working class against idle aristocratic rule, and then protect itself against working-class encroachment by appealing to an aristocratic government to join with the middle class in the defence of the propertied interest as a whole. The 'age of equipoise' of the fifties and sixties was in essence an alliance of the propertied classes not greatly unlike that which, across the Channel, accepted and sustained the Second Empire, which was as much of a pause for social consolidation in France as was the age of Aberdeen and Palmerston in England, and of almost exactly the same duration. Thus, for all his thunderings against the aristocracy in the 1840s, Bright's continuing radicalism thereafter did not prevent him from asserting that he was 'the perfect Conservative' and a true defender of 'the ancient and noble' constitution of England and an opponent of universal suffrage.[1]

That England achieved this respite without revolution was due both to the absence of a revolutionary tradition (except in the highly ennobled sense that the Whigs revered the Glorious Revolution) and to the political realism of both Peel and (for all his unpredictability and personal tiresomeness) Lord John Russell. Peel's business-gentleman's insistence that Tories face facts and see that their political survival depended on standing for something broader than the interests of a class within a class worked hand in hand with Russell's belief that though the Whig aristocracy had a prescriptive right to rule, it should do so as a leadership responsible to causes that were not necessarily

---

[1] Did Disraeli, in establishing household suffrage in 1867 (the year Napoleon III legalized trade unions), take note of the conservative results of universal suffrage in France?

aristocratic. Both preserved aristocratic rule; but, equally, they preserved social stability and civil peace.

The sense that they lived in an open society was greatly fostered among mid-century Englishmen by the popular success of the writings of the great apostle of self-help, Samuel Smiles. When in 1859 he published his book called *Self-Help* and, from 1861–5, his *Lives of the Engineers*, he enthroned the myth of the self-made man in the general consciousness just at the time when the phenomenon was ceasing to be typical. Yet it served to perpetuate in the thinking of mid-Victorian society propositions that belonged most properly to the early industrial revolution of the pre-Victorian period. The widespread popularity of Smiles's invigorating belief that by thrift and hard work any moral person could rise to eminence must be accounted one of the explanations of the social calm of the mid-century years. If, by a resolute acceptance of life as a competitive struggle, a man who braced himself for the effort might obtain the great prizes of prosperity and an assured competence, it was of little account if government remained in the hands of great ducal families.

The quiescence of the working classes after the expiry of Chartism may be ascribed to the diffusion of prosperity among their natural leaders, namely the middle class, the skilled artisans and shopkeepers. The revolutionary class-conscious proletarian has always been more of a myth than a fact, and historians may eventually agree to cast him into the limbo of obsolete concepts along with the contract theory of society or the idea of the noble savage. Many of the class-conscious working-class revolutionaries known to history have been frustrated would-be bourgeois intellectuals. To be a revolutionary, a man must detach himself from the life of the mass of workers and indulge in such essential bourgeois activities as the reading of books, the interchange of general ideas, the exercise of oratory, the organization of committees, the framing of manifestos. These are activities quite outside the patterns of working-class life; they impose a standard of austere, dedicated personal behaviour wholly different from the generous, feckless, uncompetitive, residually tribal and resolutely pragmatic attitudes of the working men of real life. Most real-life working men who have engaged in such activities have ended up as down-to-earth conservatives, usually seeking to compensate for their surviving working-class characteristics by a public display of their 'sturdy patriotism'.

Of course, there was always a minority of dedicated, self-educated and continuously self-educating men, often highly-skilled craftsmen, who retained their radical or socialist ideas and their inner toughness and working-class consciousness all their lives. It is due to these men that the memories of Peterloo and the aspirations of Chartism were kept alive throughout the Victorian period, on into the early days of the Independent and the parliamentary Labour parties. Such men, were, however, few in number – the steadfastness and dedication required made sure of that – so that they led obscure lives and were remembered, perhaps, only in small working men's clubs as attending lectures on Shelley, or Free Thought, or Carlyle or the Paris Commune and as reminiscing about Bronterre O'Brien and the other Chartists, reverencing Charles Bradlaugh and supporting the National Secularist League, and buying low-priced books on astronomy or practical chemistry. But if one looks at the majority of those whom one must, so unhelpfully, label 'the working class', it would seem that the most usual ideas at work derived from the gospels of self-help and of Christianity rather than from a doctrine of class conflict. This was also in part because there was no such 'thing' as 'a working class'. There was only a countless number of different occupations, an infinite gradation of skills and un-skills and a wholly disuniting range of incomes and, indeed, social traditions. The printers, the joiners, the cutlers, the building and engineering craftsmen, constituted an aristocracy within the working class which would have little in common, for example, with the cheap furniture-makers living in squalor in Bethnal Green. It may be taken for granted that the labour aristocrats adopted many of the *mores* of the middle class in their private lives as soon as they could afford it, leaving the melioration of the condition of the really poor and destitute to middle-class and aristocratic philanthropy.

If they included church- or chapel-going in their pattern of respectable habits they would hear a theoretically classless gospel and certainly one whose message was concerned with personal salvation and with proclaiming that the Lord was on the side of the godly, sober and prosperous in this world no less than in the next. The view put forward by Halévy that Methodism saved England from revolution has been questioned – though the Toryism of Wesleyan Methodism is less in dispute – but it is probably a mistake to undervalue the influence of the religious denominations in general in the preservation of a large measure of social cohesion. Apart from those (probably the majority) who did not want to hear about political or social problems from the pulpit, the existence of nonconformity made it possible to be against the established order and its Established Church without also being irreligious. The emphasis on personal salvation that was common to all Christian communities delayed, and perhaps delayed indefinitely, the development of an ideology based on the idea of collective salvation through 'class'; and however much the Dissenters raged against the Establishment and its aristocratic allies, they did so not for the sake of a class but for an interest – and an interest whose leaders were for the most part distinguished both for their attachment to respectability and their dislike of violence. The most radical of the sects appear to have been the Primitive Methodists, but even they seem to have contributed to working-class activity mainly their moral earnestness and their flair for organization. And if the Church of England was, by and large, the least radical, the influence of the evangelicals upon factory reform and of the Christian Socialists upon the legalization of friendly societies and trade unions helped to broaden its appeal, so that at no time was the working class forced into an anti-clerical, atheistic and wholly class-conscious ideology such as later hagiographers of 'the working-class struggle' would have desired.

The most characteristic organization of the nineteenth-century working class was in fact a-political and non-religious. This was the friendly society. In 1803 the friendly societies had had a membership of 704,000. By 1872 it was as much as four million:

the largest friendly society, the Manchester Unity Independent Order of Odd Fellows, had just under a quarter of a million members in 1845 and nearly half a million thirty years later, heavily concentrated in Lancashire and Yorkshire. It was reckoned that 'nearly half the adult male population' belonged to a friendly society and in 1872 there were four times more members of friendly societies than there were trade unionists and twelve times more than there were members of the Co-operative Society. Perhaps because (originally with the combination laws in mind) they forbade political and religious discussion in their proceedings, and perhaps because of their peculiar strength in the industrial counties, friendly societies tend to appear in general histories of the period merely as what trade unions claimed to be in the 1850s and 1860s (trade unions did in fact operate as friendly societies as well as purely industrial organizations). Yet the figures indicate their numerical importance and their activities attest their social significance.

They were largely concerned with the inculcation of the bourgeois gospel of respectability and self-help and mutual improvement, mollified by the principles of brotherly charity. The simplest friendly society took the form of a burial club, to ensure – but the matter is symbolic indeed – that a man's family could afford to give him a respectable burial and not find themselves forced to the ultimate shame of a pauper funeral and a pauper's grave. As they developed, they provided, in proportion to a pre-determined scale of contributions, unemployment and sick pay, free medical treatment (from a doctor who agreed to treat 'lodge' members in return for a capitation fee), and widows' and orphans' pensions. They also provided distress grants to brothers in need and in the case of the larger societies not only conviviality but mutual improvement. Their secret rituals and passwords, their jewels, collars and aprons, offered a working-class parallel to bourgeois freemasonry, and their ceremonies were accompanied by 'lectures' in set form, on such themes as prudence, thrift, sobriety, hard work, domestic harmony and benevolence, all of them being understood as characteristics most likely to keep human beings in line with the general attributes and intentions of a Divine

Providence. Thus the most widely used working-class organization was one devoted to totally bourgeois activities such as insurance, thrift, abstemiousness and a thoughtful care for the morrow. It did nothing to promote aggressive 'class-consciousness' and everything to promote respectability; and the experience it gave to better-off workers of the techniques of financial management and administration was of great value in helping to integrate them into society as a whole.

In similar fashion, trade unions turned from thoughts of revolutionary struggle to transform themselves into organizations working for the advancement of an 'interest' within society. The so-called New Model Unions, with their paid officials, high subscriptions of a shilling a week or more, and their national organizations, were the craft unions of building and woodworkers, together with unions of cotton spinners, metalworkers, miners and engineers. Their membership was less than a million in mid-century and they represented less than 15 per cent of all industrial wage earners. In general, they were tough but skilful negotiators, concerned either to limit recruitment to their trade (in the case of the craft unions) or to insist on agreed rates for piece-work in the case of textile workers and miners. When they used the strike weapon they did so for the specific purpose of defending the interest of their own jobs and eschewed the revolutionary notions of Robert Owen and the Grand National Consolidated Trades Union of 1834 which had failed so conspicuously. The result was that, in the end, they came to be seen for what they were: not anti-social conspiracies but bodies pursuing the legitimate aims of an interest group. They contrived to be organizations of highly-skilled workpeople without being organizations of 'the working class'.

The traditional political thinking of England had always conceived of society as one in which, although no one 'interest' could be allowed to predominate, the existence of a variety of rival 'interests' was taken for granted; and their harmonization was held to be what political, social and economic life were about. It is therefore unwise to think of the New Model Unions, any more than the friendly societies, as representing a complete 'bourgeoisification' of the labour aristocracy or as in some ways a 'betrayal of the working-class movement'. They were working-class organizations in the only sense that matters: they were run by, and for, working people. The nobility, gentry and the employing class generally, had no part in the trade unions and little in the friendly societies. The fact that they were organizations with little or no ideology of their own means, not that they lacked something, but that they were sensibly and usefully appropriate to the circumstances and needs of their time.[1]

The working-class character of the friendly societies, the trade unions and the cooperative movement is the one feature they shared with Chartism. Whereas there had been an alliance between middle class and working class in the agitation of 1830-1 there had been open hostility between them in the agitation of the 1840s. Bright admitted that the League drew its support entirely from the middle class; O'Connor abused the League as a treacherous attempt to lure the working class into supporting a programme whose fundamental aim was to increase the profits of employers. Hence, even in failure, Chartism added something to the morale of the working class, by virtue of its having been the first political agitation that was exclusively theirs. This, together with the gradual but growing successes of the friendly societies, the trade unions and the cooperative societies, gave dignity, independence and status to men whose rôle otherwise was that of mere 'hands' or industrial 'servants'. They provided workpeople with institutions of their own to which, by the 1870s, society was compelled to offer the protection and recognition of the law. Combined with the persistent, if always slow and obstructed, growth in towns such as Manchester, Leeds and Birmingham of a degree of civic pride without much precedent in English history, the working-class organizations of the mid-Victorian period added a new

---

[1] The point is one it seems almost essential to labour. There is a widespread tendency to assume that an organized body of workpeople is historically noteworthy only if it is class conscious, or revolutionary, or at least contributing in some way to the eventual emergence of a Labour party. This is to display conscious or unconscious bias and, in relation to Victorian society, to be anachronistic.

dimension to society. The foundations were laid of what a century later was at last being discovered and described with some surprise as 'a working-class culture', and one whose character was not revolutionary but conservative, and in many respects a great deal more conservative than the 'culture' of other sections of the community.

One final element in the 1850s and early 1860s contributed to the slow pace of change: the decline in the influence of radicalism through its association with pacifism at the time of the Crimean War. The politically conscious nation, faced as it was with the pacific attitude of Lord Aberdeen to the Czar and the anti-war postures of Cobden and (even more) Bright, swung instead, from 1855 onwards, behind the cheery bellicosity of Palmerston, much as in 1940 it swung from the pacific Neville Chamberlain to the bulldog Churchill. In the 1857 election, Manchester voters unseated Bright and those of Huddersfield rejected Cobden; a development that astonished and distressed even their keenest political opponents. Not only did the pacifism of the Manchester school alienate those Radicals among the middle classes who were at one with their Queen in desiring to give the Czar, the 'bully of Europe', a salutary lesson; as well as dislocating middle-class Radical leadership it may well have deepened the emerging gulf between middle-class Radicals and the working class, the least pacifist and the least internationally minded of the classes.

One of the contributors to the Catalogue of the Great Exhibition of 1851 wrote that among its purposes was that 'of bringing the nations together, of making man better acquainted with his fellow-men and thus destroying those national prejudices which are so many barriers against human progress'. The sentiment was impeccable; but against it was the state of mind illustrated by a working man to whom Gladstone had insisted, during the Reform Bill agitation, that in foreign countries reform had always led to revolution. The reply he got was, 'Damn all foreign countries. What has old England to do with foreign countries?'[1] The Manchester School's attempt to sanctify the pursuit of profit by claiming it as also the pursuit

[1] Philip Magnus, *Gladstone* (London, Murray, 1954), p. 11.

of peace, when combined with condemnation of a war that popular feeling held (at any rate at the start) to be a crusade in defence of the right, had a hollow sound indeed. And so to Cobden's cry, 'Cheapness and not the cannon and the sword is the weapon through which alone we possess, and can hope to defend, our commerce',[1] came Tennysonian demands, representative of the mood of more than the middle class, that no longer should

> Britain's one sole god be the millionaire,
> No more shall commerce be all in all, and Peace
> Pipe on her pastoral hillock a languid note,

that 'God's just wrath shall be wreaked on a giant liar' and that, by attacking Sebastopol,

> We have proved we have hearts in a cause, we
> are noble still.[2]

It was all rapidly seen to have been a mistake; and that Bright's grim anagram, 'Crimea is A Crime', contained something more like the truth of the matter. Yet it argues little feeling of repentance that the enfranchised and the unenfranchised alike should have endured a decade of rule by Palmerston as a replacement for the pacific Aberdeen. An absurd war scare against Napoleon III was whipped up in 1859–60; the Chinese were bullied at the same time; the Czar was abused, even though ineffectively, in 1863, about Poland; and Bismarck was threatened even more unavailingly on behalf of Denmark in 1864. To have persisted in supporting a prime minister whose patriotic gestures in this decade were almost all either unnecessary, dangerous or useless argues that the English must have felt very patriotic indeed in those years; and that they were as patriotic as all that suggests that the English were enjoying a surprising measure both of social stability and social unity.

[1] Asa Briggs, *op. cit.*, p. 222.
[2] See *Maud*, Pt. III, section VI. See also Pt. I, section I, stanzas vi–xiii; section II, stanza viii; section X, stanzas iii and v (Palmerston foreseen). These verses are the most useful guide to the answer to the oft-asked question, 'What were the causes of the Crimean War?'

6 · *Lord Pumicestone*

The Foreign Policy of Palmerston, 1830–41; 1846–51

The system of England ought to be to maintain the liberties and independence of all other nations; out of the conflicting interests of all other countries to secure her own independence; to throw her moral weight into the scale of any people who are spontaneously striving for freedom, by which I mean rational government, and to extend, as far and as fast as possible, civilization all over the world. I am sure this is our interest, I am certain it must redound to our honour, I am convinced we have within ourselves the strength to pursue this course, if only we have the will to do so; and in your humble servant that will is strong and persevering.

PALMERSTON, 21 March 1838
(in Sir Charles Webster,
Foreign Policy of Palmerston, p. 777)

... in international matters ... he was a great practical lawyer. He knew what hardly any one knows, the subject-matter.

WALTER BAGEHOT

Nothing should conduce more caution among analysts of the Victorian period than the dominant part played in its politics by Palmerston. An opportunist beside whom Disraeli appears a model of consistency, his ever-increasing popularity attested both to his own extraordinary astuteness and to the evident fact that the Victorians were a good deal less 'Victorian' than they are supposed to have been. In an age when serious men were guilt-ridden and high-minded he was repeatedly flippant, never high-minded, and if he had a conscience at all, what little he had seems never to have been guilty. He regarded religion as a device for diverting men's minds from socially dangerous thoughts and accordingly subscribed to it as automatically as he subscribed to aristocratic control of Parliament and the army; and, since he ignored theology, and had no personal faith of his own, he was untroubled by doubt. He lived and acted entirely for the moment. For the greater part of his career he displayed an instinct for pursuing at any given moment whatever was the most advantageous course of action, regardless of whether it contradicted what he had said or done previously or would say and do thereafter. He treated all problems, whether of domestic or of foreign policy, in the manner of a shrewd, usually well-briefed but unrelentingly hard-headed lawyer determined to get the best possible terms for his client (and himself) regardless of all other considerations. One would no more expect such a man to be consistent than one would accuse of improper conduct a barrister who accepted a brief from a dishonest share-pusher one day and from a share-pusher's victim the next, or from a peer of the realm in one law term and a radical revolutionary in another. A supporter of constitutional government and of the Habsburg Empire; an opponent of revolution and a verbal partisan of Kossuth (see p. 122); a supporter of slavery and then a persistent abolitionist; a defender of the Six Acts but also of decimal currency and easier divorce; an advocate of the continuance of public executions and an enthusiast for sanitary reform; a supporter of Louis Napoleon's *coup d'état* and a furious if frustrated opponent of the emperor's Italian adventure; the prime minister who 'won' the Crimean War, he devoted more energy to defending the aristocratic control of the army which had nearly lost it than to revitalizing the war effort; adept at barnstorming electioneering speeches, he opposed an extension of the franchise after 1832 without realizing that, at any time after 1848, a widened electorate would almost certainly have voted tumultuously in his favour; brusque, jocular and defiantly English, he was an accomplished linguist who was accounted the best French scholar of his time.

As for his being a typical Victorian, a number of exalted ladies were at various times presumed to be his mistresses, including Melbourne's sister, Emily Lamb, Countess Cowper, who was herself alleged to have had several other lovers and who, two years after Lord Cowper's death in 1837, finally consented to become Viscountess Palmerston, when she was 52 and the bridegroom 55. They had by then been lovers, on and off, for some twenty years. Shortly before their marriage, Palmerston endeavoured, while staying at Windsor Castle, to seduce one of the Queen's ladies-in-waiting. It is characteristic of Palmerston's reputation as an opportunist that it was believed he made his attempt on the lady's person despite having entered her room under the mistaken impression that she was another member of her sex. It is not surprising that Palmerston was known to readers of *The Times* as 'Lord Cupid', or that in 1863, when he was in his 79th year, an Irish Radical M.P. thought it worth while, when taking proceedings for divorce, to cite Palmerston as co-respondent. The case was dismissed; and all that seemed to have emerged from it, despite the deep distress suffered by Gladstone and other of the prime minister's Liberal colleagues, was that Palmerston stayed as popular as ever. Much of the earnestness of Victorianism must have been a response to the evident nostalgia of large sections of the populace for the carefree days of the Regency period.

Palmerston's salvation was his ability to work at a topic and master it. Much of this derived from his exceptionally robust constitution and his lifelong avoidance of the characteristic nobleman's vices of drink and gambling. He displayed this surprising quality of mental industry quite early. Before going to Cambridge he spent three years at Edinburgh diligently acquainting himself with the doctrines of free trade; and on arrival at Cambridge in 1803 insisted on studying for examinations (and doing so successfully) instead of exercising his right as a peer to proceed to his degree without this tiresome necessity. Yet, characteristically, his first political act was to stand unsuccessfully as parliamentary candidate for his university as a Tory opponent of the abolition of the slave trade. He eventually took his seat in the Commons as Tory M.P. for a rotten borough in 1807, being presented with it in consequence of his having been appointed, at the age of twenty-two, one of the junior lords of the Admiralty in the Portland administration of 1807. In 1809 he was appointed secretary at war and held the post continuously until 1828. It was during this eighteen-year tenure of a relatively minor post (he was not elevated to cabinet rank until Canning became prime minister in 1827) that he developed his always surprising and usually unsuspected capacity for bureaucratic attention to detail, becoming in the process authoritarian and legalistic, and already displaying from time to time that arrogant attitude on political affairs that contrasted so sharply with his conspicuous good manners on social occasions. His failure to secure more exalted office over these years laid the foundation of his long-lasting reputation among other politicians as a philandering lightweight. Less attractive, and long remembered in radical quarters, was his vigorous defence of the authorities at Peterloo, his support of the Six Acts, his enthusiastic organization of the army as a weapon against political agitators, his faith in the efficacy of flogging as the foundation of military discipline, and his resolute belief in the social desirability of the repressive Game Laws.

He first began to develop a keen sense of the way the political winds were blowing when, on the death of Castlereagh, he developed sympathy for the emancipation both of the slaves and the Roman Catholics, with the result that he retained his university seat at Cambridge in 1826 with Whig support and entered Canning's Cabinet of 1827. He then veered back into the High Tory fold and served under Wellington in 1828, only to resign before the year was out because of the government's unwillingness to give parliamentary representation to Manchester and Birmingham. He alleged that his support of the proposal arose from his opposition to a general plan of reform; but it may be suspected that once again he was beginning to see the shape of things to come. He quickly produced more evidence of this. Before 1829 he had made no speech on foreign affairs since his maiden speech in 1808; now, he attacked the government for not interfering against a right wing *coup d'état* in Portugal and for its ungenerous policy over Greek independence, and went on to attack the despotic governments of Austria and Spain in terms that delighted the Radicals. He went even further when the July Revolution of 1830 established Louis Philippe as king in France. This he hailed in exuberant style as a victory for constitutionalism and as marking the end of the 'Reign of Metternich'. In these circumstances it is not surprising that when Grey formed, in 1830, the government that was to introduce the First Reform Bill, Palmerston at last cut his ties with the Tories. Yet it was precisely because he was neither a Whig nor a Radical that he was offered the foreign secretaryship. It was felt that the appointment would, for that reason, be less frightening to foreign governments, that of Russia in particular.

As foreign secretary, Palmerston was as hardworking and as finicky over detail as he had been at the War Office, and as inconsiderate in overworking his staff. His insistence on mastering the work of his office was such that it led him to become habitually unpunctual both for his public and private engagements. If he had business he deemed it essential to attend to, he cheerfully, if not imprudently, kept the most exalted persons waiting until he had finished. His predilection for sending important dispatches without first showing them to the Queen as propriety demanded, derived partly from this same offhand arrogance. The dispatch had to be sent off, only he could write it, and to submit it to the Queen would involve a delay which he thought inappropriate. His unpopularity in political circles was further increased by his continuously active social life, which made it seem improbable that he could be a hard worker at all. Yet he wrung approval from two such different people as Talleyrand, who thought he was probably the most able man of business he had ever met, and the exacting Miss Nightingale, who said after his death, 'Though he made a joke when asked to do the right thing he always did it.

He was so much more in earnest than he appeared. He did not do himself justice.'

Palmerston conducted foreign policy in the highly personal fashion of an apparently flippant dandy, armed nevertheless with all the supercilious contempt of a self-appointed professional for uninstructed amateurs. To make matters worse he was, in an age of great parliamentary orators, normally a poor speaker in the House and far from regular in attendance. He regarded himself as the qualified (indeed the only qualified) custodian of British interests. His technique was to handle each problem as it arose, strictly on the facts of the case as he saw them, and to work for whatever solution seemed to him most favourable to Britain. Whether this meant allying with powers or rulers he had previously opposed, or opposing those with whom he had hitherto been on friendly terms, was a matter of complete indifference. He assumed that other states would dislike such behaviour; but his business was to serve his country, not to please foreign governments. To the complaint that his attitude to any particular country changed from one crisis to another his answer would merely have been that different cirumstances required different policies. To the charge that he bullied weak countries his answer was either that he bullied weak countries because he had more sense than to try to bully powerful ones, or that weak countries should realize that their weakness made it the height of folly to oppose a state as powerful as Britain was.

In his first term as foreign secretary, from 1830 to 1841, Palmerston was most deeply involved in the affairs of Belgium and the Middle East. The settlements he achieved were in both cases exceptionally long lasting, are among the major achievements of nineteenth-century diplomacy and are almost wholly ascribable to Palmerston's skill, determination and efficiency. From the start of the Belgian revolt against Dutch rule in 1830, he determined that the outcome should be an independent neutral Belgium. The only factor in his favour was the absorption of the three Northern Courts, Austria, Russia and Prussia, first in the Polish rising and then with the rebellion of Mehemet Ali against the Sultan. As dedicated anti-French supporters of the 1815 settlement that had handed the Belgian provinces to Holland to form a strong United Netherlands as a barrier against France, the eastern powers would otherwise have been energetically opposed to any change in Belgium's status. Their hostile attitude was reinforced by the July Revolution of 1830 in France, as a result of which the Bourbons, whom the Allies had restored in 1814, were replaced by the supposedly Liberal regime of Louis Philippe. But, with Poland and the fate of Constantinople on their minds, they were no match for the tearaway resourcefulness of Palmerston. Their acceptance of his solution was eased by the wholly authoritarian attitude he took throughout an involved diplomatic contest that lasted until 1839.

The object of the exercise was neither Belgian self-determination nor French aggrandisement but the creation of an independent neutral state in the interests of European security. The Dutch must accept that Belgium was lost. The Belgians must accept such boundaries as the Powers allotted to them and the sovereign whom the Powers chose for them; the Belgians themselves had no standing in the matter. Likewise, the French must also keep in line: Louis Philippe's younger son, the Duc de Nemours, must not be king of the Belgians, even though both the French and the Belgians wanted him to be. The solution of persuading the Belgians and the French to accept Leopold of Saxe-Coburg instead, was of almost mathematical beauty. Leopold was the widower of George IV's daughter Princess Charlotte, and the fiancé of Louis Philippe's daughter. Palmerston ran into great trouble over Luxembourg, which the Belgians occupied, and which the Dutch refused to sign away. In the end he let the Dutch keep it, partly because by 1838 he was on bad terms with France, but partly, one suspects, because he refused to be bothered any longer with such trivialities. He twice had to countenance the alarming presence of French troops on Belgian soil acting to restrain Dutch obstinacy, and on each occasion he manœuvred the French out again without any augmentation of French territory, influence or prestige. Indicative of the success of his tireless combination of official and semi-official diplomacy at this time was that, whereas Louis

Philippe was accused in France of knuckling under to Palmerston, Palmerston was more than once accused of knuckling under to France.

The Middle Eastern crisis of 1839 was a legacy of Cabinet caution in 1833. In that year, the Sultan had asked for British assistance against his rebellious subject, Mehemet Ali, whose son, Ibrahim Pasha, had seized Syria and was threatening Constantinople. Since the navy was busily engaged at the time in coercing the Dutch, Palmerston's demand for action to help the Sultan was turned down. Thereupon, Czar Nicholas I of Russia came to the Sultan's rescue instead. Ibrahim withdrew into Syria, and a Russo-Turkish treaty of alliance was signed at Unkiar Skelessi in July 1833. By a secret clause in the treaty, Turkey would allow Russian warships to pass through the Dardanelles whenever Russia so desired, a breach of the traditional rule that excluded all foreign warships from the Dardanelles in time of peace. The fact that the clause was secret resulted in a Turkish official selling the details to the British, and in the long surviving belief that, being secret, the clause was very important. In practice, as Palmerston noted, it added nothing beyond a point of emphasis to the substance of the treaty itself by which, as Palmerston also said, the Russian ambassador became the 'chief cabinet minister of the Sultan'.[1] This was, however, indeed objectionable, and Palmerston was greatly put out to find there was nothing he could do about it. He was all the more irritated because he had hitherto been at pains to adopt a very correct attitude to the Russians, losing much Radical sympathy by his realistic refusal to do more on behalf of the Polish revolutionaries of 1830 than send the

[1] If ever Turkey had allowed Russian warships to use the Dardanelles, other powers would certainly have treated it as an act of war, both by Turkey and Russia, and in 1833 Nicholas I had no intention of going to war with anybody, having been far too chastened by the dismal performance of his troops in the Russo-Turkish War of 1828–9. Moreover, since the Turks had signed just such a secret clause with the British in 1809, indignation about this feature of Unkiar Skelessi was somewhat misplaced. Perhaps the real lesson is that what is officially 'secret' is often neither secret nor important. Students of Bismarck's alliance treaties, for instance, usually forget this.

Czar polite appeals for leniency. The most he could do for the next four years was to persist in a widely unpopular alliance with the France of Louis Philippe in the hope of creating a West European Liberal counterbalance against the 'Holy Alliance' powers of Austria, Russia and Prussia. Indeed, in 1834, England, France, Spain and Portugal signed a Quadruple Alliance with this particular object in view, but the hectic instability of Spanish and Portuguese politics made the alliance productive of little more than bad feeling between England and France.

The Middle East problem burst into life again in 1839 when the Sultan ordered his army to attack Ibrahim in Syria. The Sultan's attack on his vassal was made in defiance of the advice of all the powers, Palmerston's objections being particularly strong. But the Sultan and his ministers knew that, if he did badly against Ibrahim, the British would be bound to come to Turkey's rescue if only to prevent the Russians from doing so. They knew also that the British would not support the French (who were treating Mehemet Ali as a valuable Middle East client) if France tried to protect Syria and Egypt from a Turkish naval attack. The immediate result of the Sultan's (unsuccessful) opening of hostilities was that Palmerston acted at once, not in an anti-Russian sense but out of a firm determination to liquidate the affair before it led to general war. England and France sent fleets to the Dardanelles, to establish their clear interests in the matter, but Palmerston also arranged at once for a conference of all the Great Powers to meet in Vienna to deal with the problem. Once again, as over Belgium, he came forward with his own highly personal solution. The issue should be settled, he said, by making Mehemet Ali give up Syria (which the Sultan showed no sign of being able to reconquer), in return for being made hereditary pasha in Egypt. This would neatly interpose a barrier between Mehemet Ali and the Sultan; limit the influence of the former (and his French sponsors); and preserve Constantinople from Egyptian aggression just as an independent neutral Belgium would protect north-west Europe from aggression by France. To arguments that the Sultan's regime was corrupt and Mehemet's efficient, or that the Turkish Empire was incapable of preservation, Palmerston remained resolutely deaf.

The persistent French opposition to Great Power coercion of Mehemet Ali was a more difficult problem. He did not want to quarrel with France because he knew nothing would please the Northern Courts more; but he was nevertheless prepared to oppose France if, for the moment, there appeared no alternative. Therefore, on hearing that the French were trying to persuade the Sultan to negotiate with Mehemet Ali, he threatened to resign if a policy of coercing Mehemet Ali in defiance of France was not given Cabinet approval. In view of the already palsied condition of his government in 1840, Melbourne had no choice, and Great Britain, Turkey and the three Northern Courts therefore signed an agreement demanding Mehemet Ali's acceptance of Palmerston's original proposals regarding Syria and Egypt within twenty days. When he informed the French two days later, the reactions were explosive. The *Marseillaise* was sung, stones were thrown at the British ambassador's carriage, and the princes of Germany were so convinced that general war would break out at any minute that they asked the Duke of Wellington to take charge of their armies. Reactions in England were hardly less rational. All the best Whig families were pro-French; the Radicals accused Palmerston of joining with the tyrants of Europe to defend the tyrant of Turkey and at Chartist meetings in Birmingham he was denounced as a Russian agent. The Sultan declared Mehemet Ali deposed when the powers' 'twenty days' ultimatum expired; and the French indicated they would fight at least to keep Mehemet in Egypt. Melbourne took fright and caused Leopold of the Belgians to warn Louis Philippe to climb down. Louis Philippe replied that if he climbed down there would be another French revolution. Leopold passed this terrifying message on to Victoria and Albert, who passed it on to Melbourne. Cheerful as ever, Palmerston assured the Queen that it was all hot air but, to show there was no hard feeling, agreed to Napoleon's body being taken from St Helena for ceremonial interment in Paris.

All the same, it was perhaps fortunate for Palmerston that,

not for the last time in their history, the Syrian population suddenly threw off Egyptian rule. Infuriated by Ibrahim's tyrannical regime, the Syrians rose in revolt and were at once given every assistance by coastal activity on the part of the Royal Navy. The expulsion of the Egyptians from Syria being thus achieved, Palmerston insisted on Turkish and Great Power consent to his original plan that Mehemet's control of Egypt be made hereditary. Thus, in a sense, Palmerston, always alleged to be the upholder of the integrity of the Turkish Empire, insisted in 1840 on its partition. The Sultan's objection that the title of Pasha, which was his to confer or remove at will, could not possibly be inherited, was brushed aside, as were the efforts of the French to claim for themselves the credit for Mehemet's improved status in Egypt.

No one was more impressed by Palmerston's conduct in 1839–40 than Nicholas I. Sensibly unwilling to quarrel with England about the Turkish Empire, and himself cured of any desire for military adventure, he welcomed Palmerston's willingness to work with Russia, as with Austria, in the crisis, all the more so because their co-operative endeavours were so conspicuously anti-French. Nicholas was deeply and single-mindedly imbued with anti-revolutionary fervour and viewed Louis Philippe's Liberal monarchy with considerable alarm.[1] He hoped therefore that he could persuade Palmerston into an anti-French alliance. No suggestion could have been more alien to Palmerston's intentions. On the issue of Mehemet Ali he was anti-French; but since the issue had been settled to his satisfaction, he regarded the rivalries and the co-operation it had created as terminated also. He moved into a pro-French and anti-Russian posture on the instant, and arranged the five-power Straits Convention of 1841, by which no foreign warships could enter the Dardanelles in time of peace. This

---

[1] It is (or used to be) well known that Nicholas refused to address Napoleon III as 'Monsier mon Frère' as was customary between monarchs; the fact used to appear in students' notebooks under the heading 'Causes of the Crimean War'. But Nicholas had also refused to call Louis Philippe 'brother', though, since this does not appear to have 'caused' anything, it has tended to be overlooked.

neatly replaced the Russo-Turkish agreement of Unkiar Skelessi by a multilateral treaty in which England, France and Russia were all equally associated – and equally protected. Nicholas accepted the agreement as a concession which was well worth making in return for the prospect of continued Anglo-Russian goodwill.

Although this idea proved a disastrous mistake by Nicholas, the Treaty of London and the Straits Convention (which was reaffirmed by the Treaty of Paris of 1856) effectively settled two major problems of international diplomacy for decades to come (Mehemet's descendants were to rule Egypt till the fall of King Farouk in 1952) and the credit for both of them belongs, as does the Belgian Treaty of London of 1839, almost wholly to Palmerston. It is a pity, therefore, that there is so little else in his record on foreign affairs to match these achievements. For what particularly distinguished Palmerston's diplomacy on these major issues of his first period of office was his ability to secure concerted action by the powers. He did so by a highly individualistic combination of Canning's sense of independence and Castlereagh's sense of Europe's unity; but after 1841 he rarely acted in concert with others. He pursued his own cocksure way, achieving little that was effective and less that was permanent.

Apart from a misguided, discreditable and eventually disastrous interference in the affairs of Afghanistan, Palmerston's other main involvement in the last years of Whig rule was with China. His policy here has proved so easy to condemn, particularly in the hindsight provided by developments in China in the twentieth century, that it is perhaps worth noting that the Chinese authorities behaved throughout with inordinate arrogance, ignorance and incompetence and that it was the Chinese who, in the matter of contemptuously labelling foreigners as barbarians, cast the first stones. To refuse on principle to negotiate with foreigners on terms of equality and to assume, against all the evidence, that they were unable to bring superior physical force into play, no matter how contemptuously they were treated, is indeed to court disaster.

Palmerston approached the problem in his customary

legalistic manner. The Chinese wished to suppress opium smoking. British traders wished to continue to sell Indian-grown opium in China and accordingly smuggled it into Canton from ships anchored just outside Chinese territorial waters. Palmerston took the view that what went on on the Chinese mainland and inside Chinese territorial waters was the affair of the Chinese, but that neither he nor the Chinese had power to interfere with the ships anchored outside China's territorial waters. He further insisted that a British opium trader who threatened reprisals against Chinese ships if his cargoes of opium were seized, would be guilty of piracy. But the Chinese then imprisoned 200 British subjects and released them only after £1·25 million of British-owned opium had been dumped into the sea; and they followed this by trying to attack two British ships as part of their demand for the punishment of an unidentified drunken Englishman who had murdered a Chinese peasant. The British then opened fire on the Chinese and the Opium War had begun.

The war was soon over, since the Chinese resorted to such devices as planning to set light to British vessels by using monkeys with fireworks attached to them, or hoping that an embargo on the export of rhubarb would lead to a swift cessation of hostilities because without their Chinese rhubarb the British would fall victim to their national disease of constipation. Palmerston's demands upon the Chinese were punitive to a degree. He demanded that the Chinese pay the cost of the war, cede an island (Hong Kong) as compensation for their insulting behaviour to the British representative at Canton, pay compensation for the confiscated opium, pay all outstanding commercial debts owed to British merchants, and open the ports of Amoy, Foochow, Ningpo, Shanghai and Canton to British trade. The opposition shown towards his policy by the Tories did not prevent Aberdeen, after the fall of the Whigs, concluding the negotiations for the treaty of Nanking of 1842 without modifying Palmerston's demands. The extreme severity of these demands indicates the lengths Palmerston was prepared to go when unrestrained by well-informed colleagues or by the necessity of adjusting his policies to those of other great powers. His Chinese policy also shows Palmerston's devotion to the doctrines of free trade and his zeal for the furtherance of British Commerce. Yet when his policy was debated in the House, his defence of it was principally in his government-solicitor's manner, devoid of appeals to general principles and marked, as so often with him, by frequent misrepresentations of the facts of the controversy.

Palmerston's return to the Foreign Office in 1846 was marked by ludicrous and unsavoury dealings on the part of the French over the choice of husbands for the sixteen-year-old Queen Isabella of Spain and her fourteen-year-old sister, the Infanta Luisa. Cutting across fairly leisurely Anglo-French negotiations on the point and seizing an opportunity to get their own back on Palmerston for the Mehemet Ali affair, the French got the Spanish to arrange for Isabella to marry a sexually impotent cousin and for her sister to marry Louis Philippe's youngest son, the Duc de Montpensier; the object being to ensure that, eventually, a grandson of Louis Philippe should wear the crown of Spain. This sordid transaction may perhaps in part have been Palmerston's fault for having behaved in a manner calculated to provoke the French into wanting to score off him. But although there was a great anti-French outcry, Palmerston on the whole took it for granted that others would try to do to him as he always tried to do to them, and showed relatively little irritation.[1]

By the time the 1848 Revolutions broke out, Palmerston had contrived to acquire a reputation, both in England and Europe, as a leading defender of freedom, on little evidence, much of that little having been fabricated by himself. He claimed to have supported the Liberal cause in both Spain and Portugal whereas in fact he had usually supported in both countries any group, Liberal or not, which at any given time was opposing some other group favourable to the French. He was believed to have saved the Swiss Liberals from great-power

---

[1] The young are still, however, sometimes taught that the affair of the Spanish Marriages helped to bring about the downfall of Louis Philippe in 1848 by causing him to forfeit Palmerston's friendship.

intervention in 1848 when in fact it was not Palmerston but the outbreak of revolutions in Central Europe that prevented that intervention. During the disturbances in Italy in 1830–1 he had urged moderation on both France and Austria, and urged constitutional reform in Italy. In 1840 he had blockaded Naples on the grounds that its government had violated a trade agreement with England and, when warned by Metternich that this might lead to revolution, he had replied that if the King of Naples were less of a tyrant he would have less reason to fear revolution; and he had undoubtedly seen to it that the British navy was energetic against the slave trade; while in domestic affairs he perhaps purged his enthusiastic support for the Poor Law Amendment Act by voting for Shaftesbury's Ten-Hours Bill – Shaftesbury was the husband of Lady Palmerston's daughter, Minnie Cowper, who was Lady Palmerston's (and possibly Palmerston's) daughter.

During the revolutionary years of 1848–9, Palmerston applauded the revolutions only to the extent that their occurrence proved the truth of his repeatedly uttered warnings that there would be no stability (and certainly no progress) in Europe while rulers refused to adopt a constitutional, representative system of government on the English model. To the extent that they threatened the survival of the Habsburg Empire, seemed likely to provoke French interference, especially in Italy, and to lead to universal suffrage, secret ballot and to attacks on the institution of private property, he condemned them. Being Palmerston, however, his approval became public knowledge both in England and Europe, whereas his condemnation was expressed principally, if not exclusively, in his communications to England's representatives abroad. His exasperating tactic of telling foreign governments how to behave before the revolutions began, and of dressing them down with acid arrogance once the disturbances were afoot, increased his reputation as the one revolutionary sympathizer to be found in high places; and it is a measure of the narrowly repressive character of European governments at this time that it should have seemed so heartening and so important when this 'terrible Milord Palmerston' merely upbraided those governments.[1] What his naïve admirers and his enraged opponents both failed to realize was that he was quite fairly embedded in the pragmatic tradition of English conservatism. He believed revolutions to be bad; while, therefore, he freely condemned the governments which provoked the revolutions, he also condemned all but the most minimal of revolutionaries. Thus, when Louis Philippe was overthrown in France, he entered at once into communication with the Republican government of Lamartine; but when, in the June Days, the workers of Paris burst into revolt against the Second Republic, he applauded their suppression by the right-wing Republican dictator, General Cavaignac. Yet he gave asylum and comfort to the French Socialist leader, Louis Blanc, whom Cavaignac's government sentenced to transportation.

The 1848 revolutions in Germany and the Habsburg Empire were sufficiently dangerous and widespread to stem, at least temporarily, the flow of his unwanted and unheeded advice to the despots on how to save themselves. The survival of the Habsburg Empire was hardly less of an objective of British foreign policy than the survival of the Turkish. Accordingly he showed no approval of either the German or the Hungarian revolutions. Over Italy he pursued a relatively sophisticated but coherent policy: Austria should make concessions to Italian national feeling in Lombardy and Venetia, for fear that war between Sardinia and Austria provoked a French intervention in Italy.[2] But the Habsburgs were able to brush off Palmerston's

---

[1] The same disproportionate significance attaches to Louis Napoleon's verbal condemnations of the principles of 1815: just as Palmerston was the only aristocrat to condemn aristocratic government, Napoleon III was the only head of state to applaud nationalism, condemn the dynastic principle and express sympathy for the working class. The record of both men when it came to translating words into action was meagre; but in the circumstances of their time, the uniqueness of their words was perhaps more important than the paucity of their deeds.

[2] Students of Europe after 1815 rarely appreciate the sharpness of this particular anxiety. Franco-Austrian rivalry in Italy had been for centuries one of the decisive factors in European history. 'Modern' history traditionally begins with a French invasion of Italy in 1494; Napoleon's

reiterated demands for the cession of at least Lombardy to the Kingdom of Sardinia, once Radetzky had defeated Charles Albert of Sardinia at Custozza. When, in 1849, Charles Albert renewed the struggle, Palmerston had caused him to be strongly advised not to do so; and when the Austrians defeated the Sardinians at Novara and Charles Albert abdicated, Palmerston was reduced to showing his annoyance merely by pointedly refraining from congratulating the Austrian ambassador on his country's victory. The most that could be claimed for Palmerston was that he may have had some hand in persuading the Austrians to reduce the war indemnity they imposed on Sardinia; but such was his reputation that the reduction was ascribed solely to his personal influence. He also acquired acclaim for allowing War Office surplus arms to be sold to the rebels in Sicily; this unusual breach of legality by Palmerston led to his having to confess publicly to an error of judgement and to apologize to the King of the Two Sicilies. By contrast, he aligned himself with Russia and against German Liberalism in order to keep Prussia out of Schleswig-Holstein;[1] and he presided over the London Conference of 1850 which regulated the complicated issue of the succession both to the duchies and to Denmark.

Towards the revolution in Hungary he was cool, giving neither aid nor comfort to the rebel government, nor formally protesting when Russian troops entered Hungary to suppress the rebellion in 1849. When it was all over, however, he acted in a manner calculated to give the maximum of offence to the largest number of persons in high places and to produce a heightening of his popularity among the general public. When the leaders of the Hungarian revolution fled to Turkey,

---

invasion in 1796 was the effective beginning of his career as a military giant. British sensitivity in the matter derived also from fear of any extension of French power in the Mediterranean. Fear of what France might do in Italy recurred in 1860 when Napoleon III gained Savoy and Nice from Cavour. See p. 145.

[1] Nominally Prussia had sought to secure these duchies on behalf of the Liberal 'government' set up by the ineffective Frankfurt Parliament.

Palmerston's support of Turkey's refusal to extradite them at the demand of Austria and Russia included approval of the movement of British ships to the Dardanelles at the end of 1849, and of securing the cooperative presence of a French fleet as well. To make the point even more emphatically, he expressed, and encouraged the press to display, strong disapproval of Austrian repression in Hungary.

It was the presence of the British fleet in East Mediterranean waters at this time that prompted Palmerston to use it to blockade the Piraeus in January 1850 and to seize Greek ships in order to compel the Greek government to meet the claims put forward against that government by the notorious Don Pacifico. Pacifico, a Portuguese Jew who was also a British citizen, claimed that the Greek government was refusing him his just rights: over £30,000 was due to him, he said, as compensation for damage done to his house and possessions by a Greek mob in Athens in 1848. Not only was Palmerston's behaviour high-handed: his subsequent behaviour could justifiably be called underhanded. With French mediation, a settlement was agreed with the Greeks in London, but nullified by Palmerston's imposition of a different and stiffer settlement on the Greek government through the British ambassador in Athens. The outcome was that Palmerston had offended Austria, Russia and France and most of his colleagues, and roused the Conservative Opposition to move a vote of censure in the Lords which was carried by 169 votes to 132. Palmerston immediately changed course and softened the terms of the Athens agreement; as a result, Pacifico, in respect of certain legal documents destroyed in his house, received not the £27,000 he had claimed, but £150. This was a victory for France and Louis Napoleon, who claimed after all to have foiled Palmerston's plan to act extortionately against the Greeks.

The Greek kingdom had, no less than Belgium, been established by a treaty of guarantee by all the powers; for England to blockade the Piraeus on behalf of a Portuguese Jew from Gibraltar was analogous to a unilateral blockade of Antwerp by the Russians on behalf of an Armenian from Tiflis.

It is true that King Otto of Greece ruled tyrannically; but greater tyrants than he had over the previous three years been subject to no more than verbal assault from Britain's terrible milord. Given the extremely dubious nature of Don Pacifico's claims against the Greek government, Palmerston's action suggested that Britain would use her preponderant naval power whenever and wherever she pleased without regard for justice or international goodwill.

In the face of the uproar, Palmerston offered to resign; but Russell, unwilling to break up his government, cannily decided to make the issue a matter of confidence in the Commons; and in the last week of June 1850 there took place a four-day debate at the end of which the government had a majority of 310 to 264. The sensation was a speech by Palmerston lasting four and a half hours, which was cheered to the echo. A splendid piece of political oratory by a normally offhand and unconvincing speaker, he concluded with his memorable gloss on the New Testament phrase *Civis Romanus sum*:

> So also a British subject, in whatever land he may be, shall feel confident that the watchful eye and the strong arm of England will protect him against injustice and wrong.

During the final approach to this oratorical summit he took care to compose for his countrymen an unsolicited testimonial that was wholly irrelevant but beautifully calculated:

> We have shown that liberty is compatible with order; that individual freedom is reconcilable with obedience to law. We have shown the example of a nation in which every class of society accepts with cheerfulness the lot which Providence has assigned to it; while at the same time every individual of each class is constantly striving to raise himself in the social scale – not by injustice and wrong, not by violence and illegality – but by persevering good conduct and by the steady and energetic exertion of the moral and intellectual faculties with which his Creator has endowed him.[1]

---

[1] Jasper Ridley, *Lord Palmerston* (London, Constable, 1970), p. 387.

E

It did not detract from the splendid artistry of this encomium that some of it was true.

Nevertheless, Palmerston was by now riding for a fall. His high-handed gestures and his oratorical salutes to freedom's cause created a reputation for troublesomeness and discourtesy which embarrassed Russell and affronted Victoria and Albert, who longed to be rid of him. The Don Pacifico triumph notwithstanding, the Prince Consort quickly renewed his efforts to persuade Russell to remove Palmerston from the Foreign Office, officially because of his habit of failing to show dispatches to the Queen and, less officially, because of his deplorable levity in sexual matters. Palmerston expressed the deepest contrition. Shortly afterwards, London draymen physically assaulted the visiting Austrian general, Haynau, who was notorious for his treatment of defeated Hungarian and Italian rebels; and it was only after vigorous protests from the Queen that Palmerston was persuaded to cancel a dispatch he had sent on the subject, in which a formal apology to Vienna was coupled with the warning that if the draymen were put on trial the defence would inevitably make reference to Haynau's atrocities. Less than a year later, Kossuth, the defeated Hungarian rebel, landed in England and announced his intention of calling on Palmerston to thank him for having encouraged Turkey not to hand Kossuth and his friends over to the Austrians. For a long time, Palmerston stubbornly resisted the demand of both the Queen and Cabinet that he should not receive Kossuth; and, forty-eight hours after giving way, he addressed a Radical deputation in London called together to thank him for his (virtually non-existent) aid to the victims of Austrian and Russian oppression. This conspicuously public act was, if anything, worse than granting Kossuth an audience.

His headstrong behaviour at this time derived from his autocratic temperament, his consciousness of public acclaim and from the fact that none of his colleagues could match either his knowledge of foreign affairs or his dynamic energy. The desperate attempts of Victoria and Albert to hold him in check were undertaken in default of any one in Russell's shaky government who was capable of standing up to him. In the end, like others in Victorian politics, he contrived his own downfall. He incautiously let it be known that he thoroughly approved of the *coup d'état* by which, on 2 December 1851, Louis Napoleon overthrew the constitution of the Second Republic and established himself as dictator. Once again he sent a dispatch before submitting it to the Queen. On this issue, as soon as the full facts became known, Palmerston could expect no public support;[1] and Russell accordingly dismissed him.

Within a year, despite Disraeli's remark, 'There *was* a Palmerston', he was back. Dismissed in December 1851, he took the initiative that led to the overthrow of Russell's government by an adverse Commons vote in February 1852. In December 1852, after a politically flirtatious ten months, during which it sometimes seemed that he might rejoin the Conservatives, he became home secretary in Aberdeen's Whig–Peelite coalition. Nevertheless, with a permanent royal veto on his return to the Foreign Office, it seemed that his greatest days were behind him.

[1] It was as if, acting entirely on his own authority, Sir John Simon had, in 1934, congratulated Hitler on shooting Röhm and other Nazis on The Night of the Long Knives.

7 The People's Darling

Palmerston as Prime Minister

He was a much more complicated character
than tradition would allow.

SIR CHARLES WEBSTER

He prided himself on his exploits in Europe,
but it is by his instincts in England that he will
be remembered.

WALTER BAGEHOT

He was plucky and Palmerston to the last.

LORD CLARENDON

The origins of the Whig–Peelite coalition presided over by
Aberdeen from 1852–5 may perhaps be most precisely located
in an extraordinary outburst of ultra-Protestant hysteria in
1850. Ostensibly, this was occasioned by a papal brief issued in
that year by Pius IX, re-establishing the Roman hierarchy in
England for the first time since the death of Mary Tudor. The
effect would be to divide England into dioceses each with a
bishop with a territorial title, and to create over them a Catholic
archbishop of Westminster. The first archbishop-designate of
Westminster, Cardinal Nicholas Wiseman, at once injudiciously
published from Rome a florid pastoral letter 'from out of the
Flaminian Gate' in which he wrote rhetorically of the 'restoration of Catholic England to its orbit in the ecclesiastical
firmament'. This unleashed a wave of anti-Papism in England
of which, in one more spectacular display of demagogic
Whiggery, Russell decided to be the aristocratic chief trumpeter.

He published an open letter to his friend the bishop of Durham denouncing this 'papal aggression', described the Pope himself as 'an insolent and insidious enemy of Great Britain' and made all the usual rabble-rousing references to Popish 'mummeries' and 'superstition'. To the embarrassment of his colleagues, he had little difficulty in passing through both Houses an Ecclesiastical Titles Act (1851) invalidating the use by Papists of all territorial designations already used by Anglican clergy. The act was always a dead letter if only because the Roman Church did not designate any of its dioceses by territorial names used by the Church of England; and in 1871, Gladstone, who had firmly opposed the act as an interference with religious liberty, repealed it.

Wiseman's tactless handling of what, as an Irishman, he might have remembered was England's obsessive anti-Papism – which equated the act of genuflecting before images with adultery and theft – and, even more, Russell's unworthy attempt to re-enact his ancestors' behaviour when patronizing Titus Oates and the Popish Plot, were a disservice both to the Roman and to the Anglican Churches: the Roman because it launched its new departure in an unnecessarily hostile climate of opinion, and the Anglican because it served to discredit the Oxford Movement, whose members Russell in many ways held responsible for Rome's pretensions. The increasing number of conversions of followers of Newman and Pusey was held to be a species of treason to the nation; and, as a true Whig, Russell was gravely affronted by persons who took religion seriously. It was bad enough that evangelicalism tended to make them troublesomely radical: but when it led true-born Englishmen to desert the national cause (which for Russell was the Glorious Revolution to preserve the Protestant religion from Papists at home and abroad) all his deepest feelings at once ran riot. The furore over 'papal aggression' therefore deepened the xenophobic character of English Protestantism.

It did Russell little good either. It lost him the goodwill of the Peelites, many of whom sympathized with Tractarianism; and it lost the Whigs the support of the Irish. It was these considerations that made it possible in 1852 for Palmerston to stimulate sufficient support for an anti-government vote on the Militia Bill to bring about the downfall of Russell's government. The Whigs could survive only if they acted as the officer-class of the Radicals, the Liberals and the Irish, in an alliance with the Peelites; and it was Russell's failure to lead this mixed body of men effectively from 1846–52 that led to a widespread refusal to serve under his premiership after Derby fell at the end of 1852. He had further aggravated his unpopularity by proposing a parliamentary reform bill. Russell was so discredited that Aberdeen was able in effect to insist that his Cabinet was rather more Peelite than Whig. And though the Aberdeen government was to founder after three years, owing to the Crimean War, Russell was to make himself even more unpopular before it was over, with the result that the sole beneficiaries of the political events of the time were to be Gladstone, who as chancellor of the exchequer showed up the deficiencies of Whig finances from 1846–51 as Peel had their deficiencies from 1835–41, and Palmerston, who was quite undeservedly regarded as the Man Who Could Win The War. But Palmerston was a former Tory (though he had made a Whiggish marriage) whose only steady principles in domestic affairs were a belief in free trade and a disbelief in parliamentary reform; while Gladstone was a Peelite who had once been a very High Tory and who would in due course destroy the Whig power for ever by his obsession with Home Rule. Russell himself went from bad to worse. He was with difficulty persuaded to drop a parliamentary reform bill in 1854 even though a bill might have caused the resignation of Palmerston (and not only Palmerston). Russell's quite justifiable disapproval of the indecisive behaviour of Aberdeen, both before the Crimean War and during it, led him to issue repeated threats of resignation which he failed to carry out; thus giving the impression that his real aim was to replace Aberdeen as prime minister. When he did resign it was because the patriotic Radical backbencher, Roebuck, proposed a parliamentary inquiry into the conduct of the war; Russell declared he must resign now because he would be quite unable to defend the conduct of an administration of which he had from the start been a prominent member. This combination of Russell's folly and Aberdeen's misconduct of the war made Palmerston prime minister in 1855.

When Palmerston had appeared at Windsor to take up the seals of office as home secretary in 1852, Prince Albert had concluded his memorandum on the day's events by recording, 'Lord Palmerston looked excessively ill and had to walk with two sticks from the gout.'[1] Doubtless he was all the more relieved to be able to report this in view of the fear he had expressed in 1850 that, once in opposition, Palmerston 'might so easily force himself back into office as Prime Minister' though even then Lord John had 'thought Palmerston too old to do much in the future (having passed his sixty-fifth year)'.[2] That Palmerston survived in active politics till 1865 was a tribute to his own obstinate vitality, to the outbreak of the Crimean War, and to the errors of Lord John.

That the attempt by Nicholas I of Russia to secure a privileged position of influence over the Turkish government in 1853 should have led to a European war is a retrospective tribute to the diplomatic resourcefulness of Metternich and the early Palmerston. Either together or separately, they had piloted Europe through far more hazardous problems; of all the crises over the Eastern Question in the nineteenth century, that created by the Czar's demands on Turkey in 1853 was by far the least serious. In 1840 there was a strong drive towards war in France; in 1877 an even stronger push towards war in Russia. In 1853 no government wanted war; but no government had the ability to prevent it.

Nicholas seems to have assumed, ever since the Mehemet Ali affair of 1840 and the Straits Convention of 1841, that England understood that his aims in Turkey were limited and pacific; and as a result of conversations he had with Aberdeen in England in 1844 (Aberdeen being at the time Peel's foreign secretary) he assumed that he had made it abundantly clear that he understood and respected England's desire to maintain her

---

[1] Memorandum by Prince Albert, 28 December 1852.
[2] 3 March 1850.

strategic and commercial position in the Eastern Mediterranean. Armed with this simple faith, he demanded Turkish recognition of Russia's right to protect the Turks' Orthodox Christian subjects in the Balkans; backing his demands, first, by the dispatch of a brusque military mission to Constantinople under Menshikov and then, the Turk proving obdurate, by occupying the Danubian provinces of Moldavia and Wallachia.

It is inconceivable that Nicholas could have proceeded thus far had Metternich still been Austrian chancellor, since such a step was inimical to the interest of the Habsburgs as masters of the Danube Valley; and Metternich, who would inevitably have been consulted, would have made this clear to the Czar. But the 1848 revolutions had driven Metternich into retirement and, since acting as saviour of the Habsburgs by crushing the Hungarians in 1849, Nicholas regarded the Habsburg emperor, Francis Joseph, as his political ward rather than his equal. It is equally inconceivable that, had Palmerston not foolishly engineered his own dismissal from the Foreign Office in 1851, he would not have warned Nicholas off before he could invade the Principalities. He had defined his attitude to Russia to Melbourne:

> Russia has advanced specially because nobody watched and understood what she was doing. Expose her plans and you half defeat them. Raise public opinion against her and you double her difficulties. I am all for making a clatter against her. Depend upon it, that is the best way to save you from the necessity of making war against her.[1]

But when Palmerston advised the Cabinet, as soon as Russia first threatened to invade the Principalities, to warn the Czar that England would go to war if the invasion took place, Aberdeen refused to 'make a clatter'. Yet, as the Cabinet bumbled along, it was Lord John Russell who expressed the most openly bellicose opinions, Palmerston causing a certain surprised comment by his readiness to accept with equanimity decisions of which he disapproved. It is hard to assess whether

[1] Sir Charles Webster, *Foreign Policy of Palmerston 1830–41* (London, Bell, 1951), p. 563.

this was a re-assertion of Palmerston's natural courtesy or an unusual caution deriving from his awareness that the Peelites in the government (who had, for instance, voted against him over Don Pacifico) mistrusted him. Perhaps Palmerston's good behaviour was calculated to throw into relief the egregiously disruptive behaviour of Lord John Russell and thus build up his own claim to succeed Aberdeen as prime minister; perhaps it was due to his awareness that he was encouraging the press to counteract his acquiescent behaviour in cabinet by whipping up the storm of anti-Russian feeling among the public that eventually swept Aberdeen reluctantly into a war which was objectionable to him. Palmerston further caused war-fever to mount by temporarily resigning from the Cabinet over the issue of parliamentary reform shortly after the Russians had sunk Turkish ships at Sinope. Outside Westminster, everybody believed he had undertaken this gesture as a protest against the government's continuing refusal to declare war on Russia.

England would not have entered a war against a major European power in the absence of a major European ally, and here again, Palmerston's departure from the Foreign Office was unfortunate. Louis Napoleon had embarked on his own quite separate dispute with the Czar by reviving, for reasons of prestige, a French claim to protect the Roman Catholics in the Turkish Empire; and before leaving the Foreign Office Palmerston had in fact counselled the French against pursuing the claim. But the absence of any British restraining influence meant that France, no less than England, had a quarrel with Russia; and Napoleon III at once seized the opportunity to form an anti-Russian alliance with England in the expectation that if this produced either war or a Russian climb-down, the result would be to give him the diplomatic mastery of Europe.

By the time war came in the spring of 1854, Nicholas did not want it, the Austrians dreaded it, Napoleon III, as usual when it came to it, hoped it could be avoided, and Aberdeen wished he could resign instead. The only enthusiasts for war were the Turks, Palmerston, and British public opinion, now thoroughly determined to 'wreak God's just wrath on a giant liar'.[1]

[1] See p. 102.

Palmerston chose to fan the flames of his now blazing popularity by making offensive attacks on Cobden and Bright in the Commons.

The two great problems of the Crimean War were concerned with where it could be fought and what it was being fought for. It could not be fought for the original purpose of expelling Russia from the Principalities since by the time Anglo-French forces had landed on the Black Sea coast at Varna, Russia had withdrawn from the Principalities, giving place to Austrian troops. The presence of Russian forces athwart the mouth of the Danube offered a much greater potential threat to Austria than to any interest of the Western powers and Russia's withdrawal was a successful bid to secure Austrian neutrality. Accordingly, the Allies decided to adopt the plan put forward by Palmerston of landing in the Crimea and attacking Sebastopol. The question of what would be achieved by the capture of Sebastopol was apparently never discussed. This was largely because Sebastopol took so long to capture. But it was also because the imposition of more than the temporary rebuff to Russia, which was all that the taking of Sebastopol would be, was impossible without the military assistance of Prussia and Austria; and these two powers could not be persuaded to fight Russia in order thereafter to make Napoleon III the master of the continent. It was Austrian and Prussian neutrality that ensured the eventual inconclusiveness of the Crimean War; but, convinced that the seizure of Sebastopol ought to be no more than the first step in a great anti-Russian crusade for freedom, the British public combined great enthusiasm for the war with great rage at the frustrations and delay that marked the Crimean proceedings.

Palmerston, like the commanders on the spot, imagined the town could be taken quickly; in practice the Russians were given time to fortify Sebastopol thoroughly and it had, at enormous cost in casualities, to be invested first, so that it did not surrender till September 1855. During this time, the public was roused and the government shaken by the revelations of *The Times* war correspondent, W. H. Russell; the Charge of the Light Brigade led to demands that the far from energetic secretary for war (Newcastle) be replaced by Palmerston. Russell, as usual, threatened to resign if this was not done and Palmerston showed loyalty (or astuteness, or freedom from ambition) by opposing the idea. Finally Russell deserted the government in time to lend his support to Roebuck's motion for an inquiry. After a debate having something, in its own context, of the debates of May 1940 that brought down Neville Chamberlain, the motion was carried against the government by a majority of 148. The government thereupon resigned.

Palmerston's hour had struck; but there was at once much unwillingness to acknowledge the dread sound. (After all, even in 1940, when it was Churchill's turn, there was a brief hope that Lord Halifax might serve instead.) Not inappropriately, Derby was sent for, since although the Protectionists were in a minority they were the largest single party. But Palmerston (without whom it was felt no government at this juncture could have lasted) found, with some skill, an insuperable difficulty about serving under Derby.[1] Lord Lansdowne, a gouty Whig peer of seventy-five, was then approached. He declined on grounds of his age to serve for more than three months; though not before epigrammatically and inaccurately informing his sovereign that the nation's first-class passengers still thought highly of Lord John Russell despite the contrary view of its 'second-class passengers'.[2] Russell was therefore sent for, only to discover that no first-class passenger would travel with him save Palmerston himself. But, once again, Palmerston made his agreement dependent on Clarendon's joining; and Clarendon informed the Queen,

> The attempt of Lord John ought not to succeed if public morality were to be upheld in this country and because ever since 1852 Russell had had 'only one idea, viz. that of tripping (Aberdeen) up, expel the Peelites and place himself at the head of an exclusive Whig ministry'.[3]

[1] He said he would serve Derby if Lord Clarendon would; everybody knew Derby and Clarendon detested each other.
[2] Memorandum by Prince Albert, 2 February 1855.
[3] Queen Victoria, *Letters*, 3 Febuary 1955.

And so, in Palmerston's own expression, it was recognized that he was '*l'inévitable*'. But not even his good behaviour in cabinet since 1852 could compensate for his lifelong readiness to make political enemies. All the second-class passengers in England were certainly on his side; but the dislike of first-class passengers for Russell was probably equalled by their dislike of Palmerston. Disraeli, furious that Derby, his leader, had made so little effort to form a government, declared of Palmerston (untruthfully) that he was 'an old painted pantaloon, very deaf, very blind and with false teeth which would fall out of his mouth if he did not hesitate and halt so in his talk'. Worse still, the Peelites deeply distrusted him and were shocked by the overthrow of Aberdeen, who evoked from his supporters a degree of emotional loyalty remarkably like that later accorded to that other inappropriate wartime prime minister, Asquith. In his usual impassioned manner, Gladstone spoke of Aberdeen as 'our most noble victim struck down' and as one 'whom I love like a father, while I reverence him almost like a being from another world'; but he said of Palmerston that he 'systematically panders to whatever is questionable or base in the public mind'. Perhaps more magnanimous than Asquith, Aberdeen prevailed on the Peelites to join Palmerston's government; but they resigned from it within a fortnight. This was because Palmerston gave way to a renewed demand by the Commons for an inquiry into the war. Gladstone and his colleagues claimed that to allow the investigation would be unconstitutional; but it seems to be agreed that they could not rid themselves of the suspicion that Palmerston was an uncontrollable warmonger under whom a war that was deeply distasteful to them would be indefinitely and recklessly prolonged.

The result was to establish Palmerston beyond the reach of all other competitors for popular favour. Aberdeen and his Cabinet had mismanaged the war; Russell had been party to that mismanagement, had at the eleventh hour tried to evade his responsibility by a shamelessly self-preservative resignation and then proved not to have a political friend in the world; Derby had ducked the responsibility of office; and the Peelites, as well as being as compromised by the war's failures as their Whig colleagues, had now cravenly deserted the country's man of destiny at the very moment when he put his hand to the helm.

The impression thus created, that Palmerston alone could have turned, and might yet turn, the Crimean War into a brilliantly prosecuted triumph of British arms, was wholly without foundation. Gladstone expressed the opinion, 'the whole world is drunk about a Palmerston government', and John Bright said it was all a 'hoax' perpetrated by an aged and unscrupulous 'charlatan'. It was fortunate indeed that Palmerston had made so few personal enemies, had behaved of late like the gentleman he was at his best and that, despite the various charges of political ambition levelled against him, he was a good deal more honest than he seemed and fundamentally less conceited and self-centred than many another more highly esteemed Victorian politician.

The concluding stages of the Crimean War, once Palmerston was installed as prime minister, indicate (but only to posterity) that the belief that he infused new vigour into the proceedings is almost wholly untrue. The new men he put into responsible positions in the military sphere were worse than those he replaced. He flatly refused to tamper with aristocratic control of the army, to abolish purchase or flogging. He refused to give high command to the lowly-born Sir Colin Campbell, the darling of the press, the public and the Highland regiments, and, when Sebastopol fell at last, it did so as the aftermath of a French victory at the Malakov Redoubt and a British defeat at the Redan, and at the same time as the defeat and capture of a British general and a Turkish army in the Caucasus. The peace negotiations also revealed (though once again it was barely noticed at the time) that Radical hopes and Gladstonian fears that he was an uncontrollably embattled anti-Russian warmonger had little substance either.[1] The truth was that Palmerston's war aims were the only sensible ones, were

[1] Gladstone, it must be admitted, was beyond the reach of argument. To him it was enough that Palmerston would not make peace *before* the fall of Sebastopol; this clearly showed, he said, that Palmerston was encouraging the 'base lust for conquest'.

narrowly limited, and were in fact achieved. He wanted, he said, to hold Russia back for fifteen years in the Near East; and the limits imposed on Russia's power in that area did in fact last for precisely fifteen years, from 1855 to 1871. He tried to browbeat the Russians into accepting harsher terms than were eventually written into the Treaty of Paris (such as the return of the whole Crimea to Turkey); but he resolutely rejected all pleas, whether from exiled foreign patriots themselves, or from Napoleon III, for the inclusion, either in the war's aims or in the peace negotiations, of any measures for the liberation of Poland, Hungary or Italy; and this was in fact the larger (or more praiseworthy) reason for popular support for a war against Russia whose direct and indirect power alone kept these three nations under foreign rule.

The pressures on Palmerston to end the war after Sebastopol's fall, and thereafter to modify his demands upon Russia, came both from his own colleagues and from Napoleon III. The latter now dearly wanted to cement an alliance with Russia against Austria in order to further his hope of liberating Italy and Poland; and, since England had far too few troops to continue the war if France wanted to end it, Palmerston was content to make concessions, as he always was when faced with objections from quarters which commanded respect.

By the Treaty of Paris, Russia was to de-militarize Sebastopol and have no warships on the Black Sea; part of Bessarabia, covering the mouth of the Danube, was ceded to Moldavia which, with its neighbouring principality, Wallachia, would soon form the autonomous state of Romania. Russia's right to interfere in Turkish affairs was formally denied, and the Sultan's full sovereign control over his subjects solemnly confirmed. They were terms which though administering the sharp check to Russian power in the Near East that Palmerston had wanted, fully justified Aberdeen's reluctance to embark on the war.[1] But the responsibility for the inadequacy of the war's results must lie with those who allowed themselves to be bullied into it rather than with Palmerston.

[1] For an analysis of the war's European significance, see the present writer's *From Vienna to Versailles* (London, Methuen, 1955), Ch. IV.

Although when the terms of the treaty were announced in the City of London they were hissed, opinion at large was concerned only with the fact that, once Palmerston became prime minister, the Russians had been beaten; and any decline in popularity there might have been was dramatically increased by another of his displays of patriotic bellicosity at the expense of the Chinese. In 1856, a small vessel, the *Arrow*, which had been registered as a British ship but was owned by a Chinese pirate, was seized by the Chinese authorities when attacking shipping in the Canton river. The British flag was pulled down and the pirate crew arrested. British consular officials at once demanded the release of the crew and an apology for the insult to the British flag, even though they shortly afterwards became aware that the *Arrow*'s British registration had expired. Under pressure, the Chinese released the crew but refused the apology. Canton was bombarded, the Chinese replied with various sorts of violence, and an energetic if quite localized Anglo-Cantonese war then ensued.

Although the actions of British officials in China had been undertaken without prior consultation with London, Palmerston and his Cabinet gave them subsequent full approval. In consequence a vote of censure was moved by Cobden and carried against the government by 263 votes to 247. Support for Cobden's motion and for a similar censure in the Lords came from no less than five of the six prime ministers who held office after Palmerston's death: Lord John Russell, Lord Derby, Gladstone, Disraeli, and the future Lord Salisbury. Palmerston's speech in the debate was to the effect that anybody who took the side of barbarian Chinese against a British colonial governor was no true Englishman; and he followed this by at once holding a general election in which he made the choice appear that of voting in favour of either Palmerston or 'an insolent barbarian' who had 'violated the British flag'. The result was that the Conservatives' representation in the Commons dropped from 290 to 256, the Peelites' from 45 to 26, and Palmerston enjoyed the most spectacular electoral victory since 1832.

Fortified by this unique mark of popular approval, Palmerston promptly embarked on full-scale war with China. And as if this were not enough, the sepoy revolt broke out in India, thus further inflaming the popular conviction that Asia was teeming with threatening barbarian devils who must at all costs be put down. Since in fact the mutiny was suppressed, this seemed further proof of Palmerston's greatness as a patriotic prime minister. In reality his part in the affair was minimal. He adopted his most breezily cheerful manner, delayed the dispatch of reinforcements, with the result that it was the Indian army and not the aristocratically-led British army that defeated the mutiny, and kept rather cannily quiet during the subsequent public argument that raged as to whether Lord Canning's much advertised 'clemency' in forbidding the summary execution of the captured mutineers showed a sufficiently patriotic attitude. In the end he came out publicly in support of Canning, less because he believed in clemency than because, in another of his spasms of bureaucratic legalism, he felt that as head of the administration he ought to support that government's servant in India. All the same, it was good that Palmerston did support Canning; for the mood of the country was such that it would hardly have acquiesced in a defence of justice as against indiscriminate vengeance except from the mouth of Palmerston.

And then, quite suddenly, he stumbled. The Italian patriot, Count Orsini, threw a bomb at Napoleon III in Paris, in January 1858. It was discovered that the bomb had been made (to Orsini's own specification) in Birmingham and that the plot had been hatched in London. The French ambassador in London donned full regimentals and descended upon the Foreign Office, proclaiming 'C'est la guerre!' Palmerston's response was that of a Tory who had served under Liverpool in the days of Cato Street. He at once introduced a bill into the Commons to make it a criminal offence for aliens to conspire in England to commit murder abroad, was hotly criticized and lost both his temper and the division, a hostile amendment being carried by 234 votes to 215. Quick to see the way the wind was blowing, Disraeli had swung the Protectionists into line with the Radicals, with Gladstone and the Peelites (and Russell)

and against the government. Accordingly, Palmerston resigned. Thus the Conspiracy to Murder Bill was a mistake on
Palmerston's part; but it was a mistake that, unlike any of his
triumphs, actually told the truth about him – or at least some of
it: that no matter how bellicose he would be to an insolent
foreigner who was powerless to hit back, he was perfectly
prepared to be civil if the foreigner were powerful or if he
thought it necessary or prudent, no matter how fiercely the
Radicals condemned that ruler as a tyrant, and no matter how
readily Palmerston himself condemned tyranny in general;
and it demonstrated, too, that Palmerston would never tolerate
behaviour that broke the law unless he was absolutely certain
there was some immediate and tangible advantage to England
in so doing.[1] Not unexpectedly, the public deeply resented
Palmerston's failure to conform to the image of the Palmerston
whom they had elected to power so recently. He was hooted in
the streets and in the Commons. His unpopularity in the House
(as well as the dismissal of his ministry) may also have been due
to the revelation of another truth about him, namely how un-
Victorian he was. By the time of the Conspiracy to Murder
debate he had forfeited much respect for having appointed
Lord Clancricarde to his Cabinet. Clancricarde was so
notoriously profligate that his elevation created in political
circles a feeling akin to that aroused sixty years later by Lloyd
George's choice of candidates for the Honours List. Palmerston
lacked altogether the 'true' Victorian's high moral tone.

For the second time, Derby became prime minister at the
head of a minority Tory administration which could survive
only on the unwillingness of the Whig, Peelite and Radical
opposition to coalesce. Disraeli realized this so well that in
1858 he (as well as Lord Derby) tried to lure Gladstone back
to the Tory fold,[2] and in 1859 he tried to woo Palmerston back
also, but without success. In consequence the Tories soon came

---

[1] Even in his dealings with the Chinese he usually took care to respect at
least the letter of international law.
[2] The arctic manner in which Gladstone dealt with Disraeli's effusive
approaches at this time may be studied in Philip Magnus, *Gladstone*
(London, Murray, 1954), p. 133.

to grief. Disraeli decided to gain popular credit for his party by introducing a parliamentary reform bill; but the government was defeated in March 1859 on an amendment put forward by both Palmerston and Russell. Derby decided on a dissolution since the House elected in 1857 had, in barely two years, thrown out two governments. The Tories made gains in 1859 compared with the plebiscitary election of 1857, but were still a minority. The time had clearly come, after well over a decade of the utmost political confusion, to seek for some element of stability.

There was almost general agreement that there was an absence of 'principle' among the politicians of the day, but this was a comment on the total situation rather than on the behaviour of individuals. Given the narrowly restricted franchise established by the 1832 Reform Bill, and the stupefying effects upon the population of a sense of increasing prosperity and of repeated doses of doubt-destroying patriotic pride, there was extraordinarily little to argue about. Protection was dead, the Irish question moribund in the silent aftermath of the Great Famine, and the Church (Cardinal-Archbishop Wiseman and the Tractarians notwithstanding) not in the least in danger; and the aristocracy, thanks in large degree to the popularity of Palmerston, as unchallengeably in the saddle as ever. The only two issues left in politics were the clash between pacifism and patriotism and the matter of parliamentary reform; and of these, the first had produced an unchallenged victory for Palmerston and patriotism, while parliamentary reform was an issue at all only because Russell kept stirring it up owing to his inability to make much capital out of the wickedness of the Pope and the cardinal-archbishop.

In terms of personalities, Palmerston, Gladstone and Disraeli were all in origin Tories. Palmerston had left the Tories because in 1830 he had supported parliamentary reform, a cause to which he was now opposed.[1] Gladstone had ceased to be a Tory because he believed in free trade. Disraeli was still a

---

[1] Though not absolutely. The difficulty was that he would support only a reform bill so minimal that no other advocate of parliamentary reform would have voted for it.

Tory though he no longer opposed free trade. Derby was a Tory because he had resigned from Grey's Whig government in 1834 over Russell's threats to the Church in Ireland. Cobden and Bright could be discounted less on account of their pacifism than of their middle-class origin which was held to unfit them for high office. Russell alone was consistent. But he was also unpredictable; and his political ideology was the most out-of-date of all, his political base in aristocratic Whiggery impossibly narrow. Worse still, all of them in some measure disliked all or most of the others, or were disliked by nearly everybody else. Gladstone was hard put to it to decide whether Palmerston or Disraeli was the greater villain, or whether Derby was all that much less frivolous than Palmerston. Nobody liked Disraeli at all, and nearly everybody was perplexed, if not repelled, by Gladstone's exhausting and tortuous pursuit of political self-righteousness. Palmerston was at one and the same time unmanageable and indispensable; but Russell had turned Palmerston out in 1851 and Palmerston had turned Russell out in 1852. In such circumstances it is perhaps not surprising that Gladstone had said in 1858 he knew no worse minister than Palmerston but in 1859 that nothing would serve but to have a coalition led by Palmerston and Derby in order to eliminate Disraeli; or that in 1859 he was voting with, and Disraeli was inviting Palmerston to join, the Conservatives.

The determining factor after the 1859 election, however, was that Derby and Disraeli were still in and all the rest were out. While the rest remained disunited they might perhaps turn the Tories out; but the fate of the ministries of Aberdeen and Palmerston, and the waywardness of Russell, suggested that they were unlikely to stay in for long unless they undertook to suppress their various disagreements. The political factor that brought Peelites, Whigs and Radicals together was the outbreak in 1859 of the Italian War of Liberation. Russell and Gladstone were emotionally committed to the Italian cause and, like the Radicals, had been affronted by the Derby government's impeccable neutrality, which they interpreted as support for Austria; and Palmerston was as ready as ever to attack Austria, at any rate in words. At Willis's Rooms, in June 1859, the parliamentary opposition met, with Palmerston, Russell and eventually Bright on the platform. The Peelite ex-minister, Sidney Herbert, was also present. Palmerston declared himself happy to serve under Russell; Russell declared himself happy to serve under Palmerston; and Bright said he would support both of them. Satisfied that they would now all stick together, the opposition turned Derby's government out by an adverse vote two days later.

Understandably, perhaps, the Queen, who can hardly have been aware of the jolly goings on at Willis's Rooms and if she knew anything of them probably disapproved of them as some kind of only half-political rout,[1] reacted to the fall of Derby in her own fashion. She invited Lord Granville, who led the opposition in the Lords, to form a government. She did not want to choose between Russell and Palmerston and would have liked to do without either; neither had shown himself particularly good at keeping a government in being. Granville, however, describing himself as a man with 'small pretensions', demurred; the Queen thereupon gave him two identical letters for Russell and Palmerston inviting their assistance and left them all to fight it out between them. Once again Russell took upon himself the onus of being awkward; while Palmerston said he would serve Granville, Russell declined to be number three in a triumvirate in which the other two would be more important than he was. Palmerston therefore yet again became prime minister, and yet again because, in addition to his zest for being arrogant and offensive, when it suited him he had an instinct for recognizing those occasions on which it would pay to be a gentleman.[2] Russell's prickly nervousness and his obsessive notion that as a *Whig* leader everyone must yield

[1] Willis's Rooms had originally been Almack's Club, presided over by a committee of great Whig ladies. It had been exclusive and aristocratic, but not at all distinguished for moral tone. Most of the committee ladies were involved in irregular sexual unions, more than one of them with Palmerston himself. The Queen, even at this much later date, could hardly take cognizance of a meeting held in such dubious surroundings.

[2] Alternatively, one might say Palmerston was a man of great natural courtesy who knew how to be offensive for what he considered to be his own or his country's good.

place to him was forever his undoing. The most he got out of this crisis was the grudging concession of his demand to become foreign secretary; Palmerston wrote to the Queen, 'Viscount Palmerston is sorry to say that Lord John Russell laid claim to the Foreign Office in a manner which rendered it impossible for Viscount Palmerston to decline to submit his name to your Majesty'.[1]

The meetings at Willis's Rooms is regarded by historians, though with some diffidence, as the moment when it first becomes possible accurately to speak of a 'Liberal party'. The diffidence is understandable; the word had been in use for a generation. Hitherto its application had been uncertain; loosely, it could denote a Tory who supported Canning; a non-Tory who was not recognized by the Whigs as being a Whig, or who was accepted by the Radicals as being a Radical; or be applied, at any time, to a temporary coming-together of all or some of them. In the fifties it had become increasingly applied to whoever followed Palmerston. But this held little promise of a permanent Liberal party. For, just as Prussia did not want to be merged into Germany, Whiggery had no fancy to be merged into Liberalism; Radicals disliked Whigs because Whigs were aristocrats, and were divided between those Radicals who wanted to oppose Palmerston because he was a 'warmonger' but to support him because he stood for freedom abroad, and the patriotic Radicals who supported him when he was a 'warmonger' and opposed him when he was not. The Peelites were, by the late 1850s, a decimated tribe of political Red Indians, caught between the devil that was Disraeli and the deep blue sea that was Palmerston, while keeping watch and ward over the grave of their Betrayed Chieftain, Peel, or composing epitaphs for the Beloved Lost Leader, Aberdeen. They said, it is true, that they were 'Liberals'; but in 1855 they had first quarrelled with Russell and then left Palmerston in the lurch. The meeting at Willis's Rooms was, therefore, in essence an *ad hoc* demonstration for Italy and against Disraeli. That it is possible, after it, to observe a Liberal party with a continuous history (though it was forever

[1] Palmerston to Queen Victoria, 12 June 1859.

the history of a party in a gaseous rather than a solid state and one which ought always to be thought of as a coalition) was – and in the circumstances of the time this is unsurprising – due solely to personalities.

One of the personalities was Disraeli, who may thus be said to have a rather better claim to be a founder of the Liberal party than of the Conservative party. It was emphatically the personality of Disraeli that stood in the way of 'Liberal' accommodation with Derby. He had already been shown up by Gladstone as an incompetent chancellor of the exchequer; he had produced no constructive policy on any issue; he was widely believed to be a shady adventurer. More specifically, he was so incompetent that during the debate that, two days after the Willis's Rooms meeting, ended in his government's defeat, he lost his case by default. Documents were available for submission to the House which could have demolished completely the opposition complaint that the government's neutrality in the Italian affair had been unduly favourable to Austria; Disraeli failed to make use of them, and seems not even to have read them.

The other personality was Gladstone. He had served as president of the board of trade (for a time) under Peel and as an outstanding chancellor of the exchequer under Aberdeen. But he had held that post for barely a fortnight under Palmerston; and he was in deep despair about his political career in 1859. The truth was that, temperamentally, Gladstone's passion for moral purity unfitted him for the business of politics; what other politicians did (unless they were Peel or Aberdeen, and both had been politically broken by the burden of their own moral principles) was rarely moral enough for Gladstone, and this made him a most difficult subordinate. Time would prove him an even more difficult chief; his followers could with difficulty breathe the rarefied moral air he favoured. But in 1859 he had no prospects: to compromise his soul by serving Palmerston or by collaborating with Disraeli was horrible to contemplate. It was only the emergence of the Italian problem that gave him the strength to overcome his profound misgivings when, in 1859, Palmerston asked him to be chancellor of the exchequer (or rather to take any office he cared to ask for). For Italy provided him with what alone could justify a political association that otherwise repelled him: a Cause. Aberdeen wrote that a speech by Palmerston in which he said he hoped to see the Germans driven out of Italy 'has secured Gladstone notwithstanding ... the thousand imprecations of late years'. And so, obedient to the call of Duty, and the Will of God that he should serve Italy, Gladstone who, as his uncomprehending niece observed, could not 'swallow Dizzy', nerved himself to 'swallow Pam'. If the meeting at Willis's created the Liberal party, then this was due to this consequent decision of Gladstone. And since that decision was dictated solely by the events in Italy, perhaps the honour of founding the Liberal party really belongs, after all, to Napoleon III and Cavour.

Palmerston's last years of office, from 1859 to 1865, demonstrate to the full the limitations which reliance on sea-power imposed on British foreign policy. British military power was adequate for the (formidable enough) tasks of garrisoning strategic points on the sea routes to India, providing a minimum of colonial defence and, though this was always only just within its capacity, for policing a divided and backward India and its North-western frontier. British soldiers tended to function everywhere as outposts of a power based otherwise on a monopoly of the oceans. Of itself, naval power was adequate to ruling the waves and the commercial littoral of technologically primitive China; it could not impose British power or even influence on inland territories controlled by modern armies or inhabited by westernized societies. Between 1859 and 1865, neither Palmerston nor his public following liked what was achieved by the armies of France, of Prussia, or of the Federal Union on the other side of the Atlantic; but British approval or disapproval of what happened was of little account. Only over defenceless Chinese was Palmerston able to exercise power in his old outrageous fashion; on the main issues of those years, though he still fancied himself the spider, he became much more like the fly. To the Europe and America of the 1860s, milord ceased to be in the least terrible.

Unwilling to believe that Byron, Keats, Shelley, Browning and Gladstone could all have lived in vain, the English have never really accepted the truth of how little they contributed to the unification of Italy.[1] The Italians themselves found it so difficult to believe it that they, too, persuaded themselves otherwise; but the reality is that the first English reaction to the obvious Franco-Sardinian plot to provoke a war with Austria was to disapprove of it and to try, unsuccessfully, to prevent it; and when the war did begin, Malmesbury, Derby's foreign secretary, was rigorously neutral. The reason was simple: the war was a war of unprovoked aggression deliberately engineered by France, in complicity with Sardinia, in order to detach from Austria – a traditional ally of England – two provinces, Lombardy and Venetia, which had been assigned to Austria by the Treaty of Vienna, to which England, like all the great powers, had been a party. Hence, Derby's government had adopted the stance of the mediator seeking to get the disputants to the conference-table; and hence the contemporary view of the Tories as pro-Austrian had something in it, since no European congress was likely to grant Austrian territory to Sardinia. Nor could a proposal for Austrian and Sardinian disarmament be anything but pro-Austrian, given that Sardinia wanted, not disarmament, but war.

Austria, however, by a foolish ultimatum, gave Cavour the suitable excuse for war that British diplomacy had sought to deny him; and shortly after Palmerston became prime minister, the Austrians were defeated at Solferino and Napoleon III signed the agreement of Villafranca, by which Sardinia received Lombardy but not, as Napoleon III had promised,

[1] The proprietorial attitude towards Italy of nineteenth-century English persons of goodwill is well illustrated by Browning's pawky lines,

> Italy, my Italy!
> Queen Mary's saying serves for me –
> (When fortune's malice
> Lost her – Calais) –
> Open my heart and you will see
> Graved inside of it, 'Italy'.
> Such lovers old are I and she
> So it always was, so shall ever be!

Venetia. By the beginning of 1860, Napoleon III and Cavour had conspired together to nullify the other terms of Villafranca and connived at the annexation of the Italian duchies and the Romagna to Sardinia (which henceforth called itself the Kingdom of Italy) in return for the annexation to France of the Sardinian possessions of Savoy and Nice. By May 1860, what looked in every respect a Sardinian-provoked invasion of the Kingdom of the Two Sicilies (Sicily and Naples), led by Garibaldi, appeared likely to carry all before it.

The British were thrown into great confusion by these dramatic and complicated happenings. Wanting Italy to be free, they did not want Italy freed by Napoleon III, and therefore opposed the war against Austria; then (again because they wanted a free Italy) they objected to Napoleon III's ending of the war at Villafranca; and when he annexed Savoy and Nice they exploded with a patriotic fury not unlike that which swept through them when Hitler occupied Prague in March 1939, choosing to see it as the first step in a plan to dominate the whole continent by force. A volunteer association was formed and men practised rifle shooting and drill to be ready against the day of a French invasion. Tennyson sent a poem to *The Times* of 9 May 1859, obviously written under the impression that Napoleon III was worse than 'old Boney' himself, and that, as in the days of Pitt the Younger, reform must give place to the iron necessities of war:

> Be not deaf to the sound that warns!
> Be not gull'd by a despot's plea!
> Are figs of thistles, or grapes of thorns?
> How should a despot set men free?
> Form! form! Riflemen form!
> Ready, be ready to meet the storm!
> Riflemen, riflemen, riflemen form!
>
> Let your reforms for a moment go,
> Look to your butts and take good aims.
> Better a rotten borough or so,
> Than a rotten fleet or a city in flames!

The various passions aroused caused great trouble in the

Cabinet. As foreign secretary, Russell indulged in a ceaseless verbal rampage against the Austrians and the Pope, producing a variety of proposals by which England could make itself the outspoken partisan of every anti-Austrian act that took place, or the architect of ingenious resolutions of Italy's territorial problems, with the object, he said, of combating 'the ruthless tyranny of Austria' and 'the unchained ambition of France'. The Queen was more than usually energetic in her efforts to restrain her impetuous foreign secretary and, aside from her participation in the general anti-Napoleonic frenzy, persistently advocated a policy of absolute non-involvement. Her expostulations, the necessity for which gave her 'deep pain', display a dispassionate understanding of the implications of the processes of the Risorgimento in 1859–60 which makes a refreshing contrast to the prejudice and self-deception which characterized average opinion about it both at the time and afterwards. More than one of her rebukes to Russell shows the Queen as more shrewdly observant of political realities than she is usually credited with being:

> It is true, Lord John says, 'it becomes a great power like Great Britain' to preserve the peace of Europe, by throwing her great weight into the scale that has justice on its side. But where justice lies, admits of every variety of opinion. The Party placed in absolute power by a revolution and foreign invasion is not necessarily the exponent of the real wishes of a people. . . .[1]

Even Palmerston, who kept a great deal cooler than most men about the Risorgimento, could not forbear to insist to the Queen that England ought to intervene in some degree in any 'series of events bearing on the balance of power or on probabilities of peace or war', since not to do so would reduce her 'to the rank of a third-class European state'. Yet all that England really succeeded in doing for the Italian cause before Garibaldi's expedition was to become hysterical about the wickedness of Napoleon III. Palmerston encouraged this because it strengthened his hand in his demand for increased expenditure on defence, and this produced a protracted clash between

[1] Queen Victoria to Lord John Russell, 7 December 1859.

Palmerston and most of the Cabinet on one side and Gladstone, as chancellor of the exchequer, on the other. Gladstone abominated defence expenditure and he abominated war talk; but in insisting that the nationwide hullabaloo about Napoleon III's aggressive designs on England was wholly without justification he was as isolated as was the Queen in her insistence that a cause did not instantly become a just cause merely by proclaiming itself to be a process of national liberation. A compromise was reached with difficulty in time for Gladstone's great budget of 1860; but overwork, bronchitis, the opposition of the House of Lords, his isolation in cabinet and his distaste for Palmerston's flippant jingoism brought him repeatedly to the verge of resignation ('He is terribly excited' the Queen wrote, in the summer of 1860). In sympathy perhaps with Tennyson's expressed preference for rotten boroughs rather than a rotten fleet, Palmerston cheerily told the Queen at one point that, if it came to it, he would sooner lose Mr Gladstone than Portsmouth or Plymouth.

Palmerston's only contribution to the cause of Italian unity was negative. He allowed himself to be prevailed upon to refrain, either unilaterally or in cooperation with Napoleon III, from preventing Garibaldi from crossing the Messina straits that separated Sicily from Naples. Russell was all for action. He endeavoured to persuade the Queen that Victor Emmanuel was to Naples in 1860 what William of Orange was to England in 1688; he assured her, 'The best writers on International Law consider it a merit to overthrow a tyrannical government and there have been few governments as tyrannical as that of Naples.'[1] The Queen replied, devastatingly, that William of Orange had not invaded England in order to make it 'a Province of Holland'. Palmerston, however, disliked Garibaldi on principle as a radical revolutionary, and at first thought he should support the tyrant of Naples against what he assumed to be a joint Franco-Sardinian attack. When he discovered that Napoleon III was equally opposed to Garibaldi (Cavour was opposed to Garibaldi, too, but Cavour kept the fact to himself) he dropped the plan; and Napoleon III there-

[1] Lord John Russell to Queen Victoria, 30 April 1860.

fore abstained also. The result was the series of intricate manœuvres by which, once Garibaldi had conquered Naples, control of the situation was seized once more by Cavour and all Italy, save for Venetia, Rome and the patrimony of St Peter, was 'united'. Palmerston's inability to be better than several moves behind in the game was, however, quite unnoticed; and both he and his countrymen, who had done nothing but cheer lustily from the sidelines, were quite convinced that but for them Italy would still not have been free. It is a tribute to the respect with which England (and Palmerston) were regarded that the Italians felt that the British must have been in some way responsible for the triumphant outcome.

No such illusions were possible over the two other European issues of Palmerston's last ministry. In 1863, the Poles revolted against the Russians, who received the (unwanted) diplomatic support of Prussia, newly come under the influence of Bismarck. This involved Palmerston in months of haggling with Napoleon III. They wanted to make a formal protest; but they could not agree on whether to protest to Russia or to Prussia, or on what legal grounds they would base their protest, or whether to protest separately or jointly. Eventually a sharp protest went from Russell to the Czar and the Czar rejected it. Napoleon III then proposed a European congress and Palmerston rejected that. The Poles by that time had been completely crushed. All Palmerston had done was to antagonize France, Russia and Prussia without helping the Poles.

Over Denmark he pursued this policy of refusing to leave bad alone with even more damaging results. When, in 1863, it became clear that Bismarck was trying to lure Austria into a joint attack on Denmark in order to detach the duchies of Schleswig and Holstein from the Danish crown, Palmerston assured the Commons that those who attempted to interfere with Denmark would find 'that it would not be Denmark alone with which they would have to contend'. Faced by Bismarck's extremely cautious approach to the war, Palmerston thought he had frightened the Prussians. But, early in 1864, the Danes were defeated; and, worse still, were encouraged by Russell to be so uncompromising at a subsequent conference in London about the future of the duchies, that the Austrians and Prussians renewed the war. To universal astonishment, Palmerston then had to admit he was not prepared to help the Danes. His defence of his behaviour was evasive and unconvincing; but the Liberal coalition held firm and Palmerston had won one more parliamentary division against the odds. Yet it is difficult to avoid feeling that he had shrunk by now from being the terror of foreign diplomats to a stature little greater than that of Stanley Baldwin excusing himself for being unable to cope with Mussolini's invasion of Abyssinia and relying for survival, like Baldwin, on the inadequate parliamentary representation of the party in opposition.

Palmerston's attitude to the United States had always been characteristically English, that is, in this context, offensive. One may assume his outlook to have been shaped by his having been a member of the government that had embarked on the war of 1812; he certainly did little to avoid giving the impression that burning the White House only once was a mistake. The prospect of a government of radical ex-colonials being gravely weakened by the armed secession of the Southern States was highly attractive to him; and, to worsen matters, while Lincoln's secretary of state, Seward, was a confirmed Anglophobe, Palmerston convinced himself that the real aim of the North was to attack Canada. When the South appointed two envoys to England, Mason and Slidell, and Northerners removed them from the British ship *Trent* on the high seas, Palmerston and Russell flew into a great diplomatic rage, while, on the other side of the Atlantic, the captain who had seized Mason and Slidell was fêted as a national hero. That the issue was not another Anglo-United States war was due to the beneficent absence of any means of speedy transatlantic communication and to the intervention of the Prince Consort. He persuaded Palmerston to amend his fiery protest to Washington in such a way as to make it possible for Lincoln to disavow the capture of Mason and Slidell and thereupon release them. Lincoln had no wish to provoke the British into war. For his part the Prince Consort, who was virtually on his deathbed, had demonstrated for the last time how necessary it was for

Palmerston to be submitted to the restraining judgement of someone for whom he felt respect and who could to some extent match him in expert knowledge; but with Russell at the Foreign Office, diplomacy was, as the Queen had despairingly remarked, in the hands of 'two terrible old men'.

Hardly less characteristic of the government's anti-Yankee prejudice was its handling of the *Alabama* affair. The Northern representative in London reported that this vessel, launched on the Mersey in May 1862, was in fact being built for the Confederate States as a commerce raider to attack Northern shipping. By a series of delays, some accidental and some avoidable, the opinion that the sailing of the vessel should be banned as a breach of Britain's neutrality was not in Russell's possession until after it had left the Mersey. It had apparently not occurred to Russell at the time to prevent the ship from sailing, pending the results of the investigation; but to all demands for compensation (and to a request for arbitration) from the United States, Palmerston and Russell remained patriotically deaf.

As the war moved to its decisive phase, however, Palmerston's professionalism began at last to get the better of his prejudices. Urged to mediate when it seemed that Lee might invade the North and take Washington and, in effect, to threaten the North with the prospect of active British assistance to the Confederates, he persuaded his colleagues to wait upon the result of Lee's attack; and when Lee was repulsed, Palmerston's public references to the war became markedly less anti-Yankee. Once Lee had lost at Gettysburg and Grant had taken Vicksburg, Palmerston precipitately switched to an attitude of correctness towards the North: it was Palmerston's principle only to bully the weak, and the Federal government had proved after all to be strong. In consequence he now found himself under fire in the Commons for permitting the North to seize British ships believed to be trading with the Confederates, without protest.

Palmerston's only success (in the Palmerstonian sense of the word) in his last years was against the one state, China, which lacked the capacity to resist him. When Palmerston had been turned out over the Conspiracy to Murder Bill, Derby's government (which had opposed Palmerston's China policy) continued his war and imposed a comprehensively humiliating peace on the Chinese by the Treaty of Tientsin of 1858. The Chinese then prevaricated, by declining either to ratify the treaty in Peking or to allow the establishment of a British minister in the capital. In the task of bringing the Chinese to heel in 1859, Palmerston had the cooperation of Napoleon III: an Anglo-French expedition was accordingly dispatched to China. The Chinese displayed their customary ineptitude by imprisoning the expedition's envoys in the dungeons of the Emperor's Summer Palace in Peking. Some died under torture. The result was that the British (commanded by Lord Elgin) burned the Summer Palace to the ground.[1] The justification for this piece of savagery was that it was the most convenient available method for inflicting a purely personal punishment on the Emperor for his duplicity and obstinacy. The proceedings received the unqualified approval of both Palmerston and Russell. The Treaty of Peking, 1860, secured the ratification of all the terms of the Treaty of Tientsin of 1858. Tientsin and other ports were to be opened to foreign trade, diplomatic representatives were to be accepted at Peking and the opium trade was to be 'regulated' – which meant that it was now made legal, with the inevitable consequence of a great increase in opium smoking. Thus was the Chinese Empire opened to the trading activities of all the western barbarian peoples.

Palmerston's electoral victory in 1859 had been in part achieved because he had paid due lip-service to the principle of 'reform' in order to ensure Radical support. Though valuable remedial legislation was passed during his last administration, the free trade Radicals had to rest content with Gladstone's classic budgets and those for whom 'reform' meant an extension of the franchise were forced to content themselves, like Protestants in the reign of Mary Tudor, with the fact that their obdurate opponent could not reign for ever. He remained as popular as ever with the electorate and by now had the status

---

[1] Which was more characteristic of Victorian England, the building of the Crystal Palace in London in 1851 or the burning of the Summer Palace in Peking in 1860?

of a national institution. He had become a political Veteran of Variety; still doing the Halls in his eightieth year, as hearty as ever, always good for a laugh, and a rousing patriotic item to finish with. Improbably, too, the older he grew, the more winning were his ways with those with whom he had to do political business. No longer the offhand, arrogant autocrat, he was courteous and considerate in cabinet and a tactful manager of the Commons; and, once the Italian storm declined, got on well with the Queen. He succeeded (where his predecessors had failed) in securing for Prince Albert the title of Prince Consort; he took a more serious view of the Prince's fatal illness at its outset than the doctors, was moved to tears by his death, and showed deep interest in the plans for the Albert Memorial.

To the end he and Lady Palmerston gave frequent successful parties to which persons of a wide variety of interests were invited. He hobnobbed with newspaper owners, made jovial speeches to Radical deputations, handled hecklers at election meetings with zestful ease, ran up flights of stairs with youthful vigour, believed passionately in fresh air and brisk walks, and ate like a horse. With such assets, he commanded so tribal a loyalty from the electorate that, when he went to the country again in 1865, the Liberals secured a larger majority than they had had in 1859; but, before he could present himself anew to the Commons, he died just before his 81st birthday as the result of optimistically neglecting a chill. No great prime minister in English history before or after him enjoyed a sovereignty as complete as Palmerston's; none contrived so effective or so lengthy a mastery of the commanding heights of political power; and none who earned his countrymen's applause had done so little to deserve it or left behind a smaller legacy of good.

8 · *Leap in the Dark*

Disraeli and the Second Reform Act

'Why is Gladstone like a telescope?'
'Because Disraeli draws him out, looks through him and shuts him up.'

Quoted, MAGNUS, *Gladstone*, p. 189

The Second Reform Act of 1867 was the decisive political event of the Queen's reign. Yet the circumstances surrounding its passing have long been obscured by an excess of both prejudgement and hindsight; and they were indeed so unusually complex as to permit of a wide variety of interpretations.

The oldest tradition is that the act was a natural and inevitable corollary of the act of 1832. This had not only established the principle that the representative system could be changed but, because of its limited character, had made further change merely a matter of time. The 1867 act is thus seen as abnormal only in that its passing was unnaturally deferred because of Palmerston's obstinate longevity and because it was passed, not under a Whig-Liberal, but a Conservative administration. This view depends to a great extent on the frequency with which Lord John Russell,[1] in the years after 1832, either introduced reform bills in the Commons or proposed them to his cabinet colleagues, a practice by which, it was said, Russell transformed himself after 1832 from Finality Jack into Fidgety John.

Another line of approach is to attribute the bill's postponement to the diffusion of prosperity in the 1850s and 1860s, and

---

[1] Russell put forward bills in 1849, 1852, 1854 and finally in 1866. Gladstone came out for reform in 1864; and even Disraeli had launched an unsuccessful bill in 1859.

F

its passing in 1867 to a great outburst of working-class agitation whose deeper social causes are to be found in such economic factors as the financial panic created by the failure of the leading London banking house of Overend & Gurney in 1866, the loss of confidence in railway stocks and shares following revelations of gross mismanagement and corruption in many major companies, the collapse of the Thames-side shipbuilding industry, and a bad harvest in 1866. Among other factors alleged to have contributed to the passage of the bill were the victory of the North in the American Civil War, which was seen as a triumph for 'democracy'; the widely-publicized visit to England of Garibaldi in 1864, which was made the occasion for much radical oratory; the Lancashire cotton famine of 1865–6; the Hornby *v.* Close decision of 1867 which declared that trade unions could not claim the protection of the law;[1] the increasing political activity of the trade unions, which provided the driving force behind the Reform League which had been founded by John Bright in 1864. All this, so it is suggested, culminated in the celebrated tearing down of the Hyde Park railings by a London mob, an event, one is some-times given to understand, as politically effective as the mob violence in Bristol and Nottingham in 1831 and entitled, in its own small way, to rank with the Boston Tea Party or the Fall of the Bastille as a symbol of a people's determination that its urgent will should instantly be done.

Yet, though the Hyde Park railings came down on 23 July 1866, no action was taken by the Tory government of the day to produce its reform bill until almost six months later. Contrari-wise, the original political decision by the Liberals to introduce a bill was taken before the failure of Overend & Gurney and long before the decision in Hornby *v.* Close. The agitation of the Reform League was strongest in areas remote from London; and on the subject of the Reform League and the Hyde Park railings, the diary of a retired army surgeon who lived in London's clubland from 1866 to 1871 contains the following relevant entries for the period, and no other:

[1] See p. 176.

Monday July 23rd, 1866. Walked to Hyde Park: found all gates closed & a mob assembling. About 100 policemen at entrance to my street.

July 24th. Last night the mob broke down the railings near Marble Arch & on south side of Hyde Park: most shameful. Saw some of the prostrate wall and railings. I expect further riots.

July 25th. More riots I hear last night. Walked and witnessed the result of the riots of the 23rd. All the railings in Park Lane & from near Marble Arch to beyond Victoria Gate knocked down &c.

July 26th. Walked to Hyde Park. No mob today.

July 31st. A reform meeting passed off quietly last night which was feared might end in mischief.

December 3rd. A Reform meeting took place. Not so imposing as was expected.

February 11th, 1867. The Reform League had another of their processions. D'Israeli brought in his Reform bill or rather spoke an essay on reform. News came at night that Fenians had taken possession of Chester!!

May 7th, 1867. Another tropical day. Well the expected riots came not off: no enthusiasm in fact is there for reform (except among the Reform league).

Indeed, it is very noticeable that the parliamentary argument in favour of reform was based much more on the fact that the working class had proved itself worthy of the vote by its quiet sobriety and responsibility than on any suggestion that, as in 1832, concessions were imperative to avoid immediate revolution.

The origins of the bill must be sought not in profound socioeconomic factors but in the arena of party political manœuvrings in Westminster, and at a time when settled political principles were a rarer commodity than usual. Indeed, the whole triumph of reform was a defeat for men of principle, since it was an issue about which, after the death of Palmerston, the only coherent principles exhibited were the monopoly of the bill's leading opponents, Robert Lowe on the Liberal side, and Viscount Cranborne (Lord Salisbury from 1868) on the Conservative side. Contemporaries almost all found themselves completely at a loss to explain what had happened and why it had happened.

When Russell proposed a Franchise Bill in 1866, on succeeding Palmerston as prime minister, he was up to his usual Whiggish game of seeking to strengthen Whig support in the constituencies by extending the vote to sections of the community deemed to be favourable to the Whig–Liberal cause. Such an act would give the Whig–Liberal coalition a 'popular' cause for the first time since 1832, or at least since Russell's tactical conversion to Corn Law Repeal in 1846. It would also now receive the approval of Gladstone, a fact which would outweigh the entrenched dislike for any extension of the franchise which was felt by Russell's Whig colleagues. In 1864, Gladstone had delivered one of the most famous of those hieratic utterances of which he was master and which, as was customary, seemed to promise everything while defining nothing. Every man, he had declared, 'was morally entitled to come within the pale of the constitution' unless he was precluded by 'personal unfitness or political danger'. This had led Palmerston to accuse him of advocating universal suffrage and Disraeli to charge him with reviving the doctrines of Tom Paine. Yet, while in theory Gladstone was saying, for the first time, that every man was 'morally' entitled to vote unless cause could be shown for denying him that right, what in practice was proposed by the bill that Gladstone introduced in the Commons in 1866 was that the qualification to vote in borough constituencies should be occupation of property of at least £7 annual rental as against the 1832 qualification of £10.

In an endeavour to stir the pulses of a far from enthusiastic House, Gladstone announced that this would give the vote to men who were 'our fellow Christians and our own flesh and blood', a remark which, as has been pointed out, implied that membership neither of the Christian Church nor the human race was open to those occupying premises of annual rental value of £6 or under. The selection of the figure of £7 was deliberate; to go below it would (according to the available figures) make the working class a majority of the electorate. What, however, doomed Gladstone's bill was not its vulnerable identification of 'moral entitlement' with 'annual rental value' but a revolt against the very idea of democracy. This was expressed

with pugnacious and acid clarity by Robert Lowe, who thus became the leader of those dissentient Liberals, whom Bright nicknamed the Adullamites, and who joined with the Conservatives
to outvote the bill and eventually force Russell's resignation.

Lowe argued that since it would obviously be impossible to
maintain a £7 qualification for any length of time, the bill
tended inevitably towards household suffrage. This would
destroy the traditional mixed constitution, based on a balancing
of interests; it foreshadowed a state in which government would
be wholly subservient to the interest of one class only, the
working-class majority; and Lowe stated firmly that the working
class was unfit for the exercise of political power. In saying this,
Lowe was saying little more than what almost all reputable
politicians believed in principle. Gladstone did not believe in
household suffrage, evidently. Neither did the Conservatives,
in principle; but they sided with Lowe to oust Russell and
Gladstone and for no other reason. In the generally apathetic
state of the country at large on the issue, Lowe's contemptuous
attitude seems to have raised little general ire. Even his most
energetic opponent in the Commons and the country, John
Bright, for all his leadership of the Reform League, did not
believe in household suffrage and would have been content
with a great deal less.

And there, with the fall of the Whigs, the Reform League
notwithstanding, the matter might have rested. The fall of the
Whigs brought Derby in as prime minister of another Conservative minority government. Neither he nor Disraeli had so
far come to the fore on the issue of reform, being content to let
the Adullamites break up the Whig government for them. Nor
did the Hyde Park riots of July 1866 affect the incoming
government; when the session ended soon afterwards, the
government had still not declared its intentions about reform.
And it was Derby who, in September 1866, decided that the
government should take some action about it; just as it was
Derby who suggested in December of the same year that household suffrage, coupled with plural voting, was 'the best of all
possible hares to start'. How far Derby's ideas were influenced
by Bright's campaign (mainly in the North and Midlands) is

uncertain; purely political considerations could provide a sufficient reason in themselves. To introduce a reform bill of almost any sort would keep the Liberals as divided in opposition as they had been in office; and a Conservative act, unlike a Whig one, might be contrived to reduce, and not perpetuate, the Liberal majority in the constituencies.

The difficulty was that a Conservative bill might well split the Conservatives; and accordingly, Derby and Disraeli cogitated in a confused manner from September 1866 until February 1867, changing their minds as to the major details of their proposals ten times in a month. The bill that emerged (and even as passed) was badly drafted and full of anomalies; neither Derby nor Disraeli had much of a head for business. For a long time the government alternated as between straight household suffrage and a £5 qualification before deciding on the former; and to preserve the balance of the constitution, household suffrage was, as Derby had suggested, to be accompanied by so-called fancy franchises. These would enable persons with a certain sum invested in the savings bank or in government funds, those paying £1 or more a year in income tax, or possessed of 'a superior education', to have more than one vote. The fancy franchises were continually being revised; at one time it was proposed they should qualify an elector for two votes and at another for four. None of these shifts averted resignations from the government; Cranborne's was the most notable. Deeply introverted as he was, Cranborne made no personal political capital out of his intense disgust. He contented himself with a 32-page article in *The Quarterly Review* of October 1867 entitled 'The Conservative Surrender', and with the blistering comment on the third reading of the bill that it represented a 'political betrayal which has no parallel in our Parliamentary annals'.

The bill introduced by Disraeli in March 1867 proposed that in the boroughs all householders of two years' residence who paid their rates themselves should be enfranchised; that there should be various fancy franchises; and that in the counties the vote should be given to the £12 householder. By the time it went up to the Lords in August, where Derby secured its passage, little remained of the original bill except the £12 county franchise. As finally passed, the act gave the vote in the boroughs to all householders and all £10 lodgers. The residential qualification was not two years but one, and all the fancy franchises were abandoned. Also withdrawn was the proposal that property owners who also qualified as householders should have two votes. For a number of complicated reasons[1] the differences between enfranchising 'householders personally paying their rates' and 'all householders and £10 lodgers' was such that the latter qualification added a potential half a million voters to the list and effectively destroyed the manifold endeavours of front bench politicians of all shades to extend the franchise without making the working class a majority of the electorate. It was this particular change in the bill that caused most consternation.

Given that it was introduced by a minority government it was not be wondered at that the act should differ from the bill. What excited contemporaries was that an act passed by a Conservative administration should be far more revolutionary and 'democratic' than that which would have emerged under a Liberal administration. Whereas Gladstone's bill had looked like adding only 400,000 voters to the registers, Disraeli's act added something like a million, assuming they all registered. This was (and is) so contrary to accepted ideas that both politicians and historians were soon at work editing the facts to accord with their sense of the fitness of things. The first version was that, whereas the bill represented the anti-democratic aims of the Conservatives, the act represented the more generous philosophy of Liberalism; and that Disraeli unscrupulously allowed the Liberals to change a Conservative bill into an act that appeared Liberal, in the hope that he and his party would get the credit for it. This view seems confirmed by Derby's characteristically cheerful remark that they had 'dished the Whigs' and that the Act was 'a leap in the dark'.[2]

---

[1] These are perhaps most clearly stated in Robert Blake, *Disraeli* (London, Eyre & Spottiswoode, 1966), pp. 461–2.
[2] A less alarmingly original phrase than it seemed. Macaulay had used it of the 1832 Reform Act.

The rival version is a variation of, if not a fantasia on, Disraeli's subsequent assertion that he had 'educated his party' for a future policy of Tory Democracy by cleverly luring them into a ritual baptism in the waters of household suffrage. This would symbolize to them the importance of trying to rule the waves of a democracy which might otherwise sweep them into oblivion.

As is usual in such cases, there are some facts to support each version; but neither is compatible with all the facts. Thus, though the majority of the amendments of the bill were Liberal amendments and, of Gladstone's own proposed amendments, nine out of ten were satisfied by the act, some of the most important changes originated from obscure Radical back-benchers whose names appear in the history books in no other connection. James Clay, J. T. Hibbert, W. M. Torrens, Grosvenor Hodgkinson and Locke King were the prime movers of the most democratic differences between the bill and the act, but they were not the Liberal party but only its radical wing. Of those on the Liberal side who figured most prominently in the Reform Bill debates, the only one subsequently to attain to cabinet rank was Robert Lowe, the most vocal opponent of the whole idea of a reform bill. As for Gladstone, his most important contributions to the debate were two attempts to secure the adoption of a £5 rating qualification in order to limit the newcomers to the electorate to the better-off working class. The first of these efforts was frustrated by a revolt by the Radicals on his own side. The second was thwarted by the combination of a brilliant speech by Disraeli and the abstention or opposition of over forty Liberals. In private, Gladstone described this particular failure as 'a smash without perhaps example'; in public he was white-faced with shock and talked of withdrawing to the back-benches.[1]

---

[1] This was on 13 April 1867. Gladstone had proposed the enfranchisement of all householders whose rates were paid by their landlords, in the hope that this (by enfranchising so many) would be rejected in favour of a move to restore the £5 qualification as a lesser evil. It was wholly characteristic of Disraeli that, after rejecting household suffrage when proposed by Gladstone, he accepted it with casual instantaneity when later put forward by the Radical backbencher, Hodgkinson.

Any claim that the act owed its democratic character to Gladstone must therefore fail; and that its character was 'really' Liberal can be sustained only on the basis that the only M.P.s who were 'really' Liberal were the Radical backbenchers; for the Whig grandees had for the most part wanted no act at all and Gladstone had wanted a much more restricted one. Nor is it true that the new electorate showed their gratitude by electing Gladstone to power in 1868. Those householders who were not themselves ratepayers were not on the registers till after 1869, so that the 1874 election may be regarded as the first to be held under the full terms of the 1867 act, and it produced a Conservative majority for the first time since 1841.[1]

The theory that the passing of the 1867 act was manœuvred by Disraeli in order to educate his party in the philosophy of Tory Democracy is hardly less vulnerable when tested against the facts.[2] The initiative for introducing the bill came from Derby and not from Disraeli; so far from aiming to enfranchise the working class, Disraeli's first intention was to be almost as restrictive as Gladstone. Nor was the scheme of fancy franchises original; it had appeared in an earlier proposal of Russell's. It was only after months of procrastination that Disraeli finally threw himself into getting the bill – any bill – through the Commons, and then only for immediate purposes: to keep in power, to win a parliamentary victory for his party, and to exploit to the full the unresolved divisions in the Liberal party. This amounted, in sum, to a determination to dish, not so much the Whigs, as Gladstone. This was because, in the fluid political situation resulting from the death of Palmerston and the imminent retirement of Russell, Gladstone was clearly destined both to unite Whigs and Radicals under his imperious mantle and to secure popular support by a programme of reform. Disraeli achieved his immediate aims and reaped for

---

[1] Miners, moreover, who did not normally pay rent for their cottages, were not included in the register until 1874.

[2] 'For what he did in 1867 he deserves to go down to history as a politician of genius, a superb improviser, a parliamentarian of unrivalled skill, but not as a far-sighted statesman, a Tory democrat or the educator of his party.' (Blake, *op. cit.*, p. 477.)

himself and his party the hoped-for reward when, at the earliest possible opportunity, the Conservatives were elected in 1874. Thus, though there are facts to forbid large references to Disraeli's statesmanship before the 1867 act was passed, there remains the other fact that, whereas before 1867 the Conservatives were in danger of becoming a permanent minority, they were, after it, in English constituencies at least, almost always in the majority and were only intermittently excluded from office throughout the succeeding century. It is difficult to see how this result could have been brought about had it not been for Disraeli's skilful manœuvres in 1867.

Yet merely to think of Disraeli as a fiend with diabolical cunning or as a Lord High Conjurer is to be Gladstonian rather than historical. For Disraeli's conduct in 1867 raises the not unimportant question as to why it eventually appeared to him (as Gladstone complained) a matter of 'trivial importance' if the bill he was piloting enfranchised a million rather than half a million voters. Carlyle said it was like 'shooting Niagara'; but men do not embark on such hazardous enterprises without at least some balancing of their chances of survival. And the evidence is that Disraeli was less precipitate in the matter than Derby; and that in seeing the working class as manageable electoral material, Disraeli was neither fanciful nor prescient, nor even singular. It was already known that Liberals did best in constituencies with only small working-class electorates and the Conservatives best in the few boroughs where there was a working-class majority. By the time the 1867 bill was being drafted, a majority of Conservatives in both Cabinet and Parliament had already come to favour household suffrage. Thus, Disraeli's claim to have educated his *party* is suspect unless it is realized that he did *not* have to educate his *colleagues*.

It is thus perhaps remarkable, not that Disraeli manœuvred the passage of a broadly democratic Reform Act, but that he hesitated over it for so long in the second half of 1866. But he had to balance two contrary ideas: one that democracy was dangerous, and the other that the working class looked to the Conservatives as their 'natural' leaders. He had expressed the two ideas himself in 1859:

I have no apprehension myself that if you had manhood suffrage tomorrow the honest, brave and good natured people of England would resort to pillage, incendiarism and massacre. Who expects that?. . . . Yet I have no doubt that . . . our countrymen are subject to the same political laws that affect the condition of all other communities and nations. If you establish a democracy you must in due course reap the fruits of democracy.[1]

But in the debates on the Reform Bill itself he expressed what he hoped was the resolution of this contradiction:

The Tory party has resumed its natural function in the government of the country. For what is the Tory party if it does not represent national feeling? If it does not represent national feeling, Toryism is nothing.

When the people are led by their natural leaders, and when, by their united influence the national institutions fulfil their original intention, the Tory party is triumphant.[2]

There is indeed a consistency in the career of one who began as a brilliant opponent of Peel and crowned it as a brilliant opponent of Gladstone. In creating a wide democratic suffrage he did what most Radicals had wanted since 1832 and what had been resisted above all by interests he had consistently attacked both in print and in Parliament: the Whig grandees and the employing middle class. The continuous concessions he made during 1867 to the Radicals suggest that, unlike the foremost men of his day, he was not frightened of the artisan class. He thought that, like the electors newly-enfranchised after 1832, they too could be 'managed', above all if their enfranchisement could be seen as a process from which the Tories (and Disraeli himself) emerged as a triumphant alternative to Gladstone. And it is arguable that Disraeli and his Radical allies showed a great deal more respect for their 'fellow Christians' by enfranchising all householders than did Gladstone, who insisted to the end in wanting to confer this title on them only after attaching a minimum price tag of £5 beforehand.

Of course, Disraeli's sympathy with the working classes was

---

[1] Blake, *op. cit.*, p. 397.
[2] G. Himmelfarb, *Victorian Minds* (London, Weidenfeld, 1968), p. 354.

always mainly rhetorical. Nobody was less likely to go slumming than Disraeli. Thus, he proclaimed in his novel *Sybil* that England was not one nation but two: the rich and the poor. Yet the dénouement of the novel is not in fact a union in marriage between a 'rich' aristocratic Egremont and a 'poor' Sybil. Sybil, it turns out, is of aristocratic origins after all, so that the story line of a social tract for the times proves to resemble that of a romantic novelette or the book of a musical comedy. But what was fully expressed in his career, as well as his writings, was a genuine dislike of the Whiggish–Free Trade coalition out of which the Peelites, and eventually Gladstone, emerged. In attacking them and in the end out-manœuvring them, he expressed, as no other Victorian politician expressed, the deep-seated and widely diffused discontent created in men's minds by the arid philosophy of the ledger and the counting house, for which, when it came down to it, Peel and Gladstone principally stood. The claim of Whigs and Liberals to leadership of the nation seemed to him unnatural, because his distaste for middle-class cant was part of both his private and his political nature. His politics were flexible and opportunist partly because he lacked the disabling rigidity of mind that was the undoing of his high-principled opponents, Peel and Gladstone, and partly because Peelite ideas had such a grip on politics that only by extreme subtlety could he hope to displace them. To think it inappropriate that England should be governed exclusively by the manufacturing middle class and to object when that class sought a prescriptive right to political power over their employees was a reasonable point of view. And to the charge that the landed aristocracy expected to go on monopolizing political power over their tenants, Disraeli's answer would be to contrast, not altogether without justice, the old tradition of Tory paternalism with the cruder Liberal doctrines of *laissez-faire* and self-help.[1]

To translate this nebulous attitude – a combination of nostalgia for a dying past with a largely negative dislike of the present – into political practice was difficult indeed: to solve by

[1] It was the difference between the Speenhamland system and the Poor Law Amendment Act.

administrative action the underlying malaise of a generation deep in the irreversible processes of industrialization and urbanization was beyond the capacity of any government, let alone a Conservative one led, as Disraeli's ministry of 1874–80 was, by a man already old and ill. Yet to appeal, as he did in 1872, for the preservation of Crown and Church and Constitution while at the same time asserting (if only *en passant*) the virtues of sanitary laws and of the Empire and social reform, was astutely to combine an appearance of down-to-earth concern for concrete urban needs with a respect for a traditional past that most men revered but which Whigs and Liberals had been busily denouncing for forty years, and Gladstone seemed ready to cut to its roots.

Disraeli was England's Louis Napoleon; a man who came in from the outside and who, by an ingenious combination of intuition, charlatanism and courage, climbed to the top of a greasy pole. If Disraeli's *coup d'état* of 1867 was wholly bloodless, it was a *coup* all the same, and the work of a consummate political conspirator. Like Louis Napoleon, Disraeli appealed to the people at large over the heads of the conventional politicians. Like Louis Napoleon he operated behind a public mask of secrecy and inscrutability; and like Louis Napoleon, too, he was as unfitted for administrative detail as he was prodigal in contradictory ideas. Both men belonged in spirit to the heyday of the Romantic protest against the new industrial age and against the domination of society by the moneyed bourgeoisie; a portrait of Byron is one of the more obvious embellishments to be noted at Hughenden. Both had mingled, with a certain raffish dandyism, in the far from Victorian London society of the 1840s. And Disraeli, like Napoleon III, impressed his personality upon a large section of the populace because he was the one man in politics to go on record as opposed to the prevailing social and political values of the time. And if it is difficult to prove that Napoleon III did much for the French working class, it is rather less difficult to prove that Disraeli did much for the working class in England; so that though it is perhaps surprising that a trade union official was the only French personage to attend Napoleon III's funeral in

1873, there is substance in the view advanced in 1880 that Disraeli's government had done more for trade unions in five years than the Whigs in fifty. And Disraeli, too, though more successfully and in circumstances appropriate to an essentially civilian society, revived the popular patriotism that Gladstone sought, perhaps rightly, but certainly self-righteously, to suppress; and so, while Napoleon made himself an emperor, Disraeli made an empress out of a little old German widow-woman. There was much to disapprove of in Disraeli's foreign and imperial policy between 1874 and 1880; but on the basis of this disapproval and of the slimness of his administrative achievement, to reduce him to the status of a mere political adventurer is to misjudge the evidence. Disraeli was a symbol, not a cypher.

Disraeli had resembled Louis Napoleon also in seeking to prepare the public mind, in advance of his rise to power, by skilful literary propaganda. *Coningsby* (1844) and *Sybil* (1845) were almost contemporaneous with *Les Idées Napoléoniennes* (1839) and *L'Extinction du Pauperisme* (1844). There is indeed little or no substance in Disraeli's novels on which to construct a positive political programme; and they were not even widely or seriously read when published. Yet they reveal Disraeli's secret: his refusal simply to accept and applaud Victorian economic and political complacency and his awareness of its deeper inadequacies. He struck a blow for the future by damning alike the Toryism of Lord Liverpool, saddling him forever as the 'Arch Mediocrity' in a government of 'mediocrities' (among whom, as is so often forgotten, Palmerston was always numbered) and the arrogant exclusiveness and pretensions of Whiggery. Hence he also attacked the Tamworth Manifesto, as leading to a Conservatism that did not in fact conserve anything, thus putting society at the mercy of 'an age of political materialism that aspires only to wealth' and in which there was none to assert the historic Tory doctrine that 'power has only one duty: to secure the social welfare of the PEOPLE'. In a passage heavy with drama the young Coningsby cries, 'Let me see authority once more honoured; a solemn reverence again the habit of our lives; let me see property acknowledging, as in the old days of faith, that labour is his twin brother, and that the essence of all tenure is the performance of duty.' In *Tancred* (1847) he wrote, 'the European talks of progress because by an ingenious application of some scientific acquirements he has established a society which has mistaken comfort for civilization', just as in *Sybil* he had written, 'If a spirit of rapacious covetousness . . . has been the besetting sin of England for the last century and a half, since the passing of the Reform Act the altar of Mammon has blazed with triple worship.'

It is easy to dismiss this as fustian stuff. Yet Carlyle, who wrote more repulsively to the same effect, was revered as a sage and Mazzini, who wrote no less effusively, was hailed as a prophet. Disraeli alone of these men applied a mind conversant with such thoughts to the actual business of politics. And perhaps this is why he, alone of England's Victorian politicians, was prepared to leap in the dark. In all the great quantity of legislation put on the statute book in the half-century after the repeal of the Corn Laws, only two measures were ahead of their time. One was the Second Reform Act. The other, also passed through a House of Commons led by Disraeli, was the Conspiracy and Protection of Property Act.[1] The first conceded more than responsible advocates of parliamentary reform were asking for; the second gave the trade unions as much as the trade unions were demanding. Almost all the other reforms of the Victorian period were infinitely less than was needed, and the best of them was no more than one last step in a hesitant progress towards meeting demands which had been made by thoughtful and respected men in politics in the 1830s. Disraeli gave working men the vote and trade unions the right to strike. In granting these two reforms, he did not have the weight of informed opinion behind him; and in neither case was he forced into concession by overwhelming public pressure.

[1] See p. 178.

9 · Towards a Modern State
1850–85
(1) Social, Legal and Commercial

> There are no absolute principles in politics. . . .
> In practice everything is done by the arrange-
> ment and execution of the details.
>
> LORD SALISBURY, 1884

The domination of the political scene by Gladstone and
Disraeli in the years after 1867, and the histrionic character of
their political behaviour, deepen the impression that the period
from 1848 to 1868 was a static time when the process of
adjustment to change was almost completely halted. This is
untrue. On coming into office in 1868, Gladstone was obsessed
with Irish and ecclesiastical affairs; on returning to it in 1880 his
mind was so clouded with a messianic desire to purge the land
of the evils of 'Beaconsfieldism' that he had few clear ideas
about anything. As for Disraeli, his arrival for the first time as a
prime minister with a majority was less like his own view of
himself as one who had at last reached the top of a greasy pole
than that of a long distance runner who, having finally breasted
the tape, falls in a heap on the ground because he has nothing
more to give.

The important domestic legislation of the Gladstone–
Disraeli years may therefore be legitimately considered as a
whole and to a great extent without reference to either of them.
Both have had their names attached to reforms which owed
little to their initiative and not much to their encouragement.
Entirely without a sense of proportion, Gladstone absorbed
himself to the exclusion of all else in whatever at any given time

ministered to his passion for conducting a great moral crusade; while Disraeli devoted the best of his now limited energies to the task of presenting himself as an overdressed and vulgar reincarnation of Palmerston at his least likeable. The conventional contrast between the legislative sterility of the twenty years before 1867 and the great burst of reforms that followed it owes more than is realized to the Victorian taste for melodrama. In most respects, the legislative activity of the period from 1868 to 1885 was the culmination of the process of gradual reform that had gone on since 1846. Gladstone and Disraeli produced little that was new; their governments harvested, to the glory of their leaders' reputations, the fruits of the past labours of many professional men, civil servants and others in public life who had secured, given evidence before, or been members of, a considerable number of royal commissions, or had in other ways patiently and persistently sought the ear of any politician they could find who was disposed to listen. In this connection it is relevant to ask whether the institutionalization of the professions in mid-century was not greatly more productive of beneficent change than the parallel institutionalization of the better-paid workers into trade unions and friendly societies. It was not only the civil and mechanical engineers and surveyors who had created professional associations: the Law Society, for example, had been founded in 1833, the Institute of British Architects in 1834 and the British Medical Council in 1854. A growing body of informed professional opinion was thus available to influence politicians otherwise ignorant of day-to-day realities, and to reinforce the deepening expertise of the civil service and its inspectors. It was this growing pressure from the professional middle class that gradually weaned political opinion away from its ingrained English belief that the less a government governed and the fewer laws it made the better it was for everybody.[1]

---

[1] The idea that governments should interfere as little as possible is usually given the label '*laissez-faire*' and sometimes blamed on Adam Smith. Its real origin lies in the circumstances of eighteenth-century politics. The opposite idea, of systematic bureaucratic interference for the sake of efficiency and economy, is usually labelled 'Benthamite'; but most of what

As indicated in Chapter 3, the framework of a public health policy was already in existence by 1866 and the basic problems that remained were enforcement, and the creation of a number of competent local authorities instead of the many hundreds of small ones quite unfitted for the tasks of administering public health adequately. The problem of food adulteration was one of the many health problems which had been recognized and legislated against. An act of 1860 on this subject was the result of a strenuous campaign by the medical profession, most noticeably through the medium of the *Lancet* whose ideas were enthusiastically supported by *Punch* and had already been angrily versified by Tennyson's denunciation of England as a land 'where chalk and alum and plaster are sold to the poor for bread'. The 1860 act empowered local authorities to employ analysts; but few were in fact appointed and quantities of alum could still be found in half the bread offered for sale in London alone.

It was in consequence of shortcomings such as these that a Royal Sanitary Commission, set up in 1868, found that despite the fact that at least twenty-seven major and minor acts concerning public health had been placed on the statute book between 1854 and 1868, the system was still chaotic. Not only was the law confused; so was the machinery by which it was supposed to be carried out. But Gladstone was not greatly anxious to implement either the commission's large plans for public health or a simultaneous plan by the president of the Poor Law Board, Goschen, to reorganize the whole structure of local government. The result was, yet again, piecemeal reform. The Local Government Board Act of 1871 was a fairly paltry measure, coordinating only some of the central departments (notably the Poor Law Board) and officials endowed with the task of overseeing local authorities and consequently their health

---

are called 'Benthamite reforms' would have occurred if Jeremy Bentham had never been born, and were dictated by the lessons of nineteenth-century experience. At no time in the nineteenth century was *'laissez-faire'* generally practised; and to call reforms 'Benthamite' is a lazy device for avoiding the task of trying to discover why they were actually brought into existence.

functions. The Public Health Act of 1872 was a little more adventurous. It divided the country into urban and rural sanitary authorities. The former were the town councils and the existing local boards of health: the sanitary authorities for all other areas were to be the poor law guardians, instead of the previous hugger-mugger of parish vestries, sewage authorities or nuisance authorities. Each sanitary authority was to appoint an inspector of nuisances and a medical officer of health: but no provision was made for government approval of such officers or for the government's right to dismiss them. Beyond setting up more sensible machinery, Gladstone's government made no real effort to see that the machinery actually functioned. In this respect, perhaps its only virtue was that it made it easier for the sanitary authorities to borrow from the government. Nor did the government either consolidate or extend the existing law on public health itself. Thus, the struggle for a proper system of health administration was to go on as before, being conducted by administrators and officials without a positive lead from the politicians, who remained mainly concerned with more dramatic matters of high policy.

The new Local Government Board immediately became the battleground between Simon and the new political nominees who came to dominate it. Like Florence Nightingale and Edwin Chadwick, they had no real use for medical experts in the sphere of public health; Simon lost his right to make annual reports or to make direct approaches to the political chief of the board. One result was that authorities were lax in appointing medical officers; many worked only part-time or for absurdly low salaries. The law was given merely lip-service in this respect in far too many places. The board cut down its medical inspectorate and failed to intervene when local sanitary authorities neglected their statutory duties. The medical profession began energetically to campaign against the board's apathy; and the hostility of medical men to the board has been considered one of the factors contributing to Gladstone's electoral defeat in 1874.

Thus, though it was contrary to his own and to Tory precedent, Disraeli's ministry could hardly avoid being more energetic in sanitary matters than Gladstone's. The Adulteration Acts of 1875 and 1879 made it no longer possible for a vendor to escape prosecution on the grounds that he was unaware that the goods he was selling were adulterated; and local authorities were at last compelled to appoint public analysts.

On larger matters of policy, although Disraeli began badly by downgrading the Local Government Board by excluding its president from the Cabinet, a Public Health Act of 1874 did increase the board's powers of enforcement, particularly over water supply, and brought infected milk within the category of a 'nuisance'. Simon was also given back some of his old influence and was allowed to resume his annual reports. In 1875 he declared that the 1,558 English sanitary authorities were between them responsible for an estimated 120,000 deaths every year through their failure to carry out their duties under the Public Health Acts. His last major contribution to legislation came with the passage of the Public Health Act of that same year, 1875.

Its character owed little to Disraeli, and almost everything to the labours of the Royal Sanitary Commission of 1868 and to the work of Simon and the lawyers who collaborated in its drafting. The act was in almost all respects an end-product of nearly thirty years of effort, most of it conducted without benefit of active political support at Westminster, and was the result of the pressures, patience and propaganda of professional men. Most of its provisions had been on the statute book at least since the act of 1866. It added little to the actual content of the sanitary laws. Nevertheless, its clear drafting and its comprehensiveness were sufficient to make the 1875 act the basis of the public health service for the next forty years; and although there had perhaps been more sanitary activity by local authorities since 1848 than is sometimes claimed, there can be no doubt that, after 1875, progress was rapid. Among its most important consequences was a sharp fall in smallpox deaths, since it at last set up an efficient system of compulsory vaccination. In the last quarter of the century, deaths from cholera were few; deaths from that other dirt-borne disease, typhus, declined and so did deaths from tuberculosis.

Since the urban population continued to increase, this was an achievement made inadequate as much by the magnitude of the problem as by the shortcomings of politicians, both central and local. At least in the first part of the reign, the immature state of the science of civil engineering, the unreliability of inexperienced public works contractors, the conflicting financial claims of rival forms of local amenity development, the absence for so long of satisfactory units of local government, and the medical profession's limited understanding before the 1870s of the origins and spread of diseases, were formidable obstacles to improvement. Even the Chadwickian emphasis on sanitary engineering was the outcome of a desire to make haste in the one direction in which speedy progress seemed feasible; and even in this respect it is remarkable that the Victorians were able to plan, produce and organize the supply of so many reservoirs, taps, wash basins and water closets and so many thousands of miles of sewers. In the long run, the development of preventive medicine was to be the more important factor; but this was not only a slow process, but something to which the early- and mid-Victorian mind was not attuned. Drains, they could be made to understand; germs were a harder matter for them. Experts laying down the law to them was something they utterly mistrusted. Nevertheless, while the national death rate stood at 22·4 per thousand in the 1840s, it was down to 18·4 by 1900; that this was considered still to be too high was a measure of the growth of men's expectations by the end of the century. That much more still needed to be done was clear enough from the fact that infant mortality rates stood as high in 1900 as in the 1840s.

In the sphere of housing a modest beginning was made by acts of 1851, 1853 and 1855, which provided for the inspection of lodging houses and permitted local authorities to build lodging houses themselves, though few of them did so. Following the passage of private acts by a number of municipal authorities in the 1860s empowering them to clear and replace insanitary dwellings, the Torrens Act of 1868 extended similar powers to all municipal corporations. Under Disraeli came Cross's Artisans' Dwellings Act of 1875, which widened these powers to include the right to rebuild entire slum areas and to erect what would now be called council dwellings. Not only were these powers merely permissive, however; the urban sanitary districts set up in 1872 did not receive such powers until 1885. Apart from the well-known example of Birmingham under Joseph Chamberlain, the acts had a limited effect, if only because of the high compensation costs likely to result from any compulsory purchase.

As noted earlier[1] the mid century had seen much legislation about working conditions. The abolition in 1853 of the shift or relay systems and the effective establishment thereby of the ten-hour day was largely the result of pressure from the now professionalized factory inspectorate. In 1860, women and children employed in the bleaching and dyeing industries, and in 1861 those in the lace factories, were brought within the scope of the acts already applicable to the textile factories. Apart from coalmining, however, all other occupations were still untouched by factory legislation. In 1862, therefore, Shaftesbury secured the appointment of a Children's Employment Commission with wide terms of reference. The commission's five-year-long labours resulted in extending the Factory Acts to the potteries in 1864; and in 1867 a Factory Act brought under regulation almost all industrial premises employing fifty workers or over, while a Workshops' Act covered virtually 'any room or place' where women and children were employed 'in handicraft'. These acts were put through with an ease that testified to the way in which knowledge of human and economic realities had triumphed over the emotional ignorance which had obstructed factory legislation earlier in the reign. Even some of those who employed needlewomen in the dressmaking trades admitted that they grossly overworked their girls, but that they did so for fear of being undercut by their competitors and thus looked to general legislative limitation as the only practicable solution. Legislation to limit hours was also the only way to cope with the situation created by those fashionable women who were reported to have the habit of ordering ball dresses at teatime and expecting them to be

[1] See pp. 55–9.

delivered complete some time before midnight.[1] Finally, in 1878, the Factory Act of that year consolidated over a hundred previous acts.

Despite pertinacious efforts by the Early Closing Association, however, legislation to establish a compulsory half-holiday apart from Sunday met with no success despite ample evidence that shop assistants often worked a ninety-hour week. Indeed, as late as 1888, it was to be affirmed by a junior member of Lord Salisbury's second administration that it was a proposal that would 'degenerate the people's moral fibres'.

In the coal industry, acts of 1850 and 1855 provided for regular inspection of safety and ventilation in mines. A further Coal Mines Act of 1872, after a series of colliery disasters, required colliery managers to have government certificates attesting their competence, stipulated that there should be a daily inspection of pit safety conditions, and gave the miners themselves the right to appoint inspectors from their own ranks to check the management's fulfilment of the safety regulations. An act of 1860 prohibited the employment of boys under twelve in mines, while the acts of 1834 and 1840 to protect child chimneysweeps, which were widely evaded, were strengthened in 1864. They were still ineffective until chimneysweeps were, by an act of 1875, required to be licensed. Women and children in rural areas were protected by the Gangs Act of 1867 and the Agricultural Children's Act of 1873, which forbade the employment of children under eight and provided for them to receive education. In 1876, the first of the Merchant Shipping Acts, dramatically sponsored by Samuel Plimsoll in the face of the indifference of Disraeli's front bench, prohibited overloading and took one step forward for the benefit of men whose work, though vital to the country's economic dominance, was often carried out in the worst possible conditions.

Legislation to benefit organized labour began promisingly. In 1853, the Truck Act, introduced by Palmerston, forbade employers to pay their workmen in goods or to compel them to buy goods from company shops, thus ending 'tommy rot'

---

[1] This far from uncommon practice is a reminder that in the Victorian period women were not 'exploited' only by men.

as a phenomenon if not as an idiom. From 1855 onwards, trade unions were able to register as friendly societies under the Friendly Societies Act of that year, which set up the Registrar of Friendly Societies. This appeared to give the unions legal protection, at any rate for their social benefit funds. In 1859, peaceful picketing was legalized by the Combinations of Workmen Act, when undertaken in trade disputes over wages and hours of work. In the 1860s, the Scottish unions in particular began a campaign to mitigate the harshness of the Master and Servant Acts. These made breach of contract, if committed by an employer, a civil offence, but a criminal offence if committed by an employee. Thus, as a 'servant', a workman could be arrested for 'leaving work unfinished'. Accordingly the law was made less severe in 1867, though a workman could still be imprisoned rather than merely fined if the magistrates decided he had been guilty of 'aggravated' breach of contract.

This problem was overshadowed at the time by the 'Sheffield outrages' and by the Hornby *v.* Close decision, both in 1867. Various violent acts committed by unionists in Sheffield against non-union workers culminated when the explosion of a tin of gunpowder blew up a workman's house. The result was the appointment of a royal commission to inquire into trade unions and to trace the origins of the Sheffield outrages. Meanwhile, in the Hornby *v.* Close case, the Court of Queen's Bench had decided that the Boilermakers' Society could not sue for the recovery of £24 of its funds, which had been appropriated by its treasurer, on the grounds that, though trade unions were not criminal bodies, they tended to operate 'in restraint of trade' and were therefore illegal. The doctrine that nothing should be allowed to 'restrain trade', though long established within the common law, was a significant dogma within the creed of the moralist economics of the Victorian period. It provided the justification for the freeing of trade; it lay behind Gladstone's fight to abolish income tax; and it was a principle with which not only to hamper the trade unions but also to belabour the Chinese, since their obstinate refusal to open their ports to Europeans was likewise an act in restraint of trade.

The unions now pressed the commission to deal with the implications of the Hornby *v.* Close decision as well as the other matters. They were much embarrassed by the evidence that came to light, not only about the violence of trade unionists in Sheffield and Manchester, but also about restrictive practices in general. Fortunately, the unions exercised great skill in the presentation of their evidence. As the result of well-organized efforts on the part of five leading union officials (later nicknamed 'the Junta'), of whom the most famous was the secretary of the Amalgamated Carpenters, Robert Applegarth, they secured the appointment to the commission of two powerful sympathizers. One of these was Thomas Hughes, who was an M.P., a Christian Socialist and the author of *Tom Brown's Schooldays*. The commission decided that violence was on the decline and that there was little evidence of it outside Sheffield and Manchester; it praised the unions' financial prudence and stability. It recommended that steps be taken to legalize the unions and, perhaps even more important, presented a view of them that greatly increased public respect for them. Accordingly, in 1868 an act was passed allowing unions to prosecute fraudulent officials and another in 1869 allowing them to take legal action to recover their funds.

The situation was regularized by two acts passed in 1871 under Gladstone, a Trade Union Act and a Criminal Law Amendment Act. The Trade Union Act removed the possibility of unions being regarded as criminal and gave full legal protection to their funds. The Criminal Law Amendment Act, however, repealed the Peaceful Picketing Act of 1859 and made molestation, obstruction, intimidation, persistently following individuals and 'watching and besetting' premises all criminal acts. The scope of the statute was so wide that for a union member to give a non-striker nothing more unpleasant than a nasty look could be characterized as criminal; a year later, the mere planning of a strike by London gasworkers led to their union leaders being sentenced to a year's imprisonment on the grounds that they had conspired to molest their employers. In effect, Gladstone's legislation abandoned, by the first act, the principle that unions were illegal, but reaffirmed in the second that any industrial action they took was criminal. The intention was the classically Gladstonian Liberal one: a majority of workers should not be given legal authority to use methods of mass-coercion against free citizens.

As a result of Gladstone's refusal to budge from this position, the unions decided to put pressure on parliamentary candidates in the 1874 election by urging their members to vote only for candidates prepared to support the amendment of the offending legislation. This technique was made possible by the 1872 act establishing secret ballot. The result was confusing. It contributed to the Conservative victory of 1874, and secured the election to the Commons of two trade unionists. But the two M.P.s concerned had had Liberal support, and sat in the Commons as Liberal, not Conservative, supporters.

Among those who had been regarded by the unions as acceptable candidates was Richard Cross, whom Disraeli made home secretary; and in 1875 Cross produced the Conspiracy and Protection of Property Act and the Employers and Workmen Act. The former made peaceful picketing legal and removed from the trade dispute the character of 'conspiracy', though interruption of supplies of gas or water, or any breach of contract likely to cause loss of life or serious damage to property, remained criminal offences. The Employers and Workmen Act made breach of contract on either side a purely civil offence. Taken together, the two acts completed the process of absorbing workmen's combinations within the institutionalized life of society.

There was much legal reform, partly as the result of two royal commissions set up in the 1840s. Both common law courts and Chancery procedure were reformed by various statutes between 1852 and 1860. The profusion of courts, some administering the common law and others the law of equity, was not however satisfactorily reduced until Selborne's Judicature Act of 1873 united them all into one Supreme Court and established that both common law and equity should be administered in every court by every judge. Selborne's act replaced judicial appeal to the House of Lords by an Appeal Court; but in 1876 the Lords was re-established as a final court of appeal, its functions being carried out by Lords of Appeal in Ordinary. Like most of the more valuable legislation of the period it owed little to political considerations and much to the accumulated weight and wisdom of expert professional judgement.

The criminal law was much reformed in the 1860s, particularly by the Offences against the Person Act, 1861, and such antique survivals as the penalties of beheading and quartering, as well as the law that the children of those found guilty of treason could not inherit their parents' possessions, were at last removed from the statute book. In the same decade, in 1868, imprisonment for debt was ended, as were public executions. It was during the same period that in lieu of transportation or the incarceration of offenders in the rotting hulks of former naval vessels at Woolwich or Gosport, in Bermuda or off Gibraltar, national prisons to supplement the town and county jails came into existence. Prisons were subject to government inspection only after 1835, but it was not until the Prisons Act of 1865 that the Prison Commission was established to create a national system, chiefly by closing down many locally-controlled prisons whose management was frequently scandalous. The changes may be said to have achieved an equitably uniform standard of treatment; it remained harsh but became relatively hygienic; it became less barbarous though remaining wholly soulless.

The new system went along with the more systematic treatment of long-term imprisonment under the Penal Servitude Act of 1853. The transported convict was often set free on ticket of leave and it was considered that a term of imprisonment in one of the newly-built penitentiaries was a severer punishment than an equivalent term of transportation. The 1853 act substituted penal servitude for transportation, but reduced maximum sentences and introduced the ticket of leave system for convicts in home prisons. Palmerston had difficulty in getting the ticket of leave system accepted in Parliament and ten years later its operation was much restricted. The new prisons also introduced the principle of solitary confinement for short-term prisoners for the first time. This was considered a progressive reform; it protected short-term offenders from contact with the depraved influence of long-term prisoners.

The County and Borough Police Act of 1856 compelled all counties to organize police forces under the systematic control of the Home Office and subjected them to government inspection. The inspectors of constabulary judged as 'inefficient' half of the police forces inspected in the course of the following year.

A major reform was the Matrimonial Causes Act of 1857. The laws concerning divorce until then resounded with echoes of the pre-Reformation Church and had certainly ceased to be consonant with the social needs of any period subsequent to the trial and imprisonment of Archbishop Laud. Basically, divorce was still a matter for the ecclesiastical courts and therefore technically not divorce at all, since the church courts took their stand on the indissolubility of marriage. They could nullify a marriage on the grounds of non-consummation; but where matrimonial offences were alleged they would offer nothing beyond a judicial separation. To secure the freedom to remarry, the 'innocent' party had to involve himself in the further labour and expense of a private act of Parliament pronouncing the marriage at an end. Apart from the enormous cost, the system was rendered further objectionable by the legalization in 1836 of civil marriages before a registrar. Accordingly, the 1857 act established a secular Divorce Court which would grant a divorce to a male petitioner whose spouse had committed adultery but to a female petitioner only if her spouse had, in addition to adultery, also been guilty of cruelty or desertion. There was as much objection to the permission that divorce gave to 'guilty' parties to marry each other as there was to the act's discrimination against wronged wives. But the government stood as firmly by the principle that adultery by a woman was a more grievous offence than when committed by a man as it did by its resolve to let a divorced person marry a co-respondent. Gladstone was in the forefront of the opposition to the act and he and his supporters used against it tactics of obstruction and filibustering not unlike those later used by the Irish Nationalists under Parnell. Palmerston remained obdurate but cheerful through it all and the most that Gladstone got was the concession that beneficed clergymen would not be compelled to conduct the marriage service for divorced persons. The main effect of the act was to extend divorce facilities from the very rich to the more prosperous of the middle classes. In the decade ending in 1885 there were 460 petitions a year; and the reporting of divorce cases did much for newspaper circulations.

Before 1870, a husband became by matrimony instantly and perpetually endowed with all his wife's worldly goods and indeed could disinherit her of all of them, a fate otherwise reserved, until the 1860s, for proved traitors. The only way out, akin to that by which the ecclesiastical ban on divorce was evaded before 1857, was to indulge in the expensive and complicated business of setting up a trust on behalf of one's daughter before she married. This elaborate legal precaution was not available to women in humbler circumstances; a working-class woman could not even protect her post office savings book from her husband or prevent him selling off the entire home over her head. A Married Women's Property Act was passed in 1870; but it was so emasculated by the Lords that it did no more than give wives possession of any money they happened to earn. This was fifteen years after a petition in favour of a bill had been presented to Parliament with 26,000 signatures; the proposal had then been stigmatized as contrary both to the common law of England and to the law of God. A second act, in 1882, gave a married woman the right to separate ownership of property of all kinds; and a further act in 1893 finally assimilated her position to that of an unmarried woman.

Another legal battle on the matrimonial front met with no success during the Queen's reign: the right of a man to marry his deceased wife's sister. It was a subject which provoked jests in the press and on the music halls for half a century. The proposal was resisted on the grounds that it would imperil the virtue of all spinsters with married sisters and inflame all married women with jealousy towards their unmarried sisters. It would open the way to bigamy, polygamy and, according to Gladstone, 'to more horrible forms of incest' (though he later changed his view). The rejection of the proposal was almost an annual parliamentary event until its eventual success in 1906. The persistence of the opposition to it reflects not only the unthinking bibliolatry of the Victorian mind (the text which, it was alleged, forbade such marriages contained in fact no such prohibition) but also its terrified awareness of the sexual licence that existed only just below the surface of the time. This feeling was more obviously manifested in an unavailing attack on pornography by way of an Obscene Publications Act in 1857.

The most universally applauded development of the mid-century was the steady process by which state regulation of external trade was finally dismantled by Gladstone as chancellor of the exchequer, from 1852–5 under Aberdeen, and from 1859–66 under Palmerston and Russell. As Ireland was to be from 1868, as the plight of political prisoners in Naples had been in 1850, and the sufferings of Bulgarians were to be in 1877, the final achievement of free trade, combined with the reduction of public expenditure and direct taxation, was for Gladstone an obsession, a creed and a passionate moral obligation. Once his mind had become captivated by the details of the fiscal system during his term as president of the Board of Trade under Peel, he concentrated upon them with the burning zeal of an Elijah confronted by the priests of Baal. To him, the freeing of trade and the removal of taxes were part of a great scheme to confer upon the middle classes the prime moral good of individual freedom and personal responsibility. Only in the unfettered exercise of free moral choice did man become truly himself, in Gladstone's view of things; and it was because he combined a frightening mastery of his subject with the fervour of a prophet that his immensely long budget speeches were listened to in the Commons with fascinated awe.

In 1853 he abolished most duties on foodstuffs and partly-manufactured goods, while halving almost all those on manufactured imports. In particular, he abolished the duty on soap and reduced those on tea, on life assurance and advertisements. In 1860, he reduced the number of articles still significantly taxed to only sixteen, and sponsored the free trade Cobden Treaty with France which operated (to the great misfortune of Coventry's lacemakers) until 1872. In 1863 and 1865, he again reduced the duty on tea. As part of his budget of 1861 he abolished newspaper duty, though only after an exhausting struggle, first with Palmerston and then with the Lords. It was a measure which, when combined with the abolition of the tax on advertisements in 1853, and of the stamp duty in 1855, greatly accelerated the growth of the press as well as lowering the price of books.

Concurrently, Gladstone fought, with all the embattled zeal of a man of God determined to give no quarter to the forces of the Evil One, a fierce and ultimately unsuccessful battle against income tax. In 1853 he proposed to abolish it altogether by 1859. He believed that money should be left to 'fructify in men's pockets' and that it was a breach of the principles of a free society that a man should be required to disclose to the state the size and nature of his income. Once again, Gladstone was expressing a doctrine of individual moral responsibility. For government to take part of a man's income from him was to deprive him of that much of his personal responsibility for learning how rightly to dispose of that which was his own. Only through freedom could man reach his true moral stature; if the state limited his freedom it diminished him. Gladstone thought, too, that what he described as 'an engine of great national power' was not lightly to be placed at the disposal of governments save 'for great national purposes'. And in his view, that meant, ideally, only for the cost of waging a war of which he approved. Since Gladstone came as near as a practising politician has ever come to disapproving not only of all wars but of all preparation for wars, he was in constant trouble throughout the last forty years of his long political career. One year after his promise to abolish income tax, he had, in 1854, to increase it owing to the outbreak of the Crimean War. Even so, he defended his action by informing the Commons that the expense of war was a design by the Almighty to place a check upon 'ambition and lust of conquest', a view hardly calculated to appeal to the patriotic spirit; and to his wife he wrote, 'War! ... it will swallow up everything good and useful.' This was doubtless why, in a manner that was also characteristic of him, he tried to pretend not to notice the war by involving himself in university and civil service reform; and why he confessed to a bad conscience about the Crimean War forever after. It explains, too, the revulsion he felt at the prospect of serving Palmerston as chancellor in 1855, and why he resigned within a fortnight.[1]

Back again in Palmerston's last ministry in 1859, he was as distressed as ever by the prime minister's encouragement of the war fever of 1860 and was once again compelled to raise income tax. But in 1861 he got it down to ninepence, in 1863 to sevenpence, in 1864 to fivepence and in 1865 to fourpence. He thus contrived for three years in a row to reduce both direct and indirect taxes. But he had done more. While the national income had been steadily increasing, government expenditure had been steadily decreasing. Gladstone achieved this by a fanatical insistence on economy in public spending; he concerned himself, as he said, with saving 'candle ends and cheeseparings in the cause of the country'; as long as income tax survived he was sure that Whitehall would be extravagant, so that to his mind it was important to urge a department to use less expensive notepaper.

In the short run, much was gained by Gladstone's long crusade against extravagance, corruption and waste in government, since no crusade is, in most countries at most times, more likely to be necessary. Not only is ostentatious display the oldest of government public-relations techniques; in a pre-industrial society, the perquisite and the tactic of feathering one's own nest represented a necessary device to compensate for the lack of such sophisticated refinements as reliable life insurance, adequate regular salaries and guaranteed pensions. While the age of patronage lasted, government employment would always tend, at the lower levels if not usually at the highest, to be a boon to be enjoyed rather than a duty to be performed; as a means to the acquisition, in however small a way, of a power over one's fellows which one would tend as a matter of course to exercise in favour of those who might have favours to offer in return. A rigorous scrutiny of public expenditure and the abolition of patronage were essential to the efficient, just and

[1] See p. 132.

reliable administration of a modern industrial society. In the context of Victorian change, too, it appeared essential to liberate an expanding economy from a clutter of archaic regulations. Under the stimulus of free trade, exports boomed until 1875; and the boom was unquestionably assisted by a government policy which took as little as possible from the profits that were made, and demanded as small a proportion as possible of the national wealth for the cost of administration, while at the same time improving that administration's efficiency.

In the longer run – and this is why, though Gladstonian finance lived on well into the 1930s, Gladstonian Liberalism died before Gladstone – its effects were to be less beneficent. It tended, because of the moral passion of its creator, to become a dogma in the bad sense, a moral absolute rather than a financial policy appropriate to a particular phase of social and economic history. It established in too many minds the belief that government expenditure was not only a financial but a moral evil, so that what a community spent as a community came to be regarded as 'waste'. It produced the ultimately fallacious idea that if 'waste' were obviated the result would be the universal cultivation of the virtue of 'thrift'. If the state practised thrift, this would encourage that virtue in the individual. To Gladstone, a virtuous artisan was one who took care to put money into the post office savings bank which he established in 1861; and it was as a further step to encourage thrift that he launched the halfpenny postcard in 1871. Characteristically, the populace soon ceased to see the point; by the end of the century the sending of picture postcards to one another became a middle-class cult, and not at all a means of practising 'thrift'.

Gladstonian finance, however, was based on the assumption that all individual spending would be thrifty spending by highly moral and economic beings, for highly moral and thrifty ends. No doubt it was a glimmering realization that this was not happening that caused Gladstone in his later years to speak so darkly of 'the west end of London' and to appeal 'from the classes to the masses'. The principles of Gladstonian finance, like most systems claiming a basis in high moral principle, were kinder to the strong than to the weak. The profits and the opportunities for personal development that Gladstonian finance so greatly encouraged mostly went to the rich; the poor, who needed communal expenditure if they were to be raised up, got little from governments devoted to the avoidance of waste, and not much, despite the volume of Victorian good works, from the charity of the wealthy whom Gladstone had done so much to enrich. A total concern with personal morality left Gladstone blind to basic social problems.

In the institutionalizing of industrial and commercial life, a major step was the Limited Liability Acts of 1856 and 1862. These made possible the creation, for the first time, of industrial and commercial joint-stock corporations, controlled by a committee of directors and answerable to members of the public who became shareholders. The liability of directors of a joint-stock company was now limited to the value of their subscribed shares. Previously, the norm had been the family business or the partnership, with each partner liable for the debts of the concern to the full extent of his wealth and property. Such businesses were largely unprotected against the normal human processes of mortality preceded by a decline in energy and capacity. Partnerships were dissolved whenever any partner died; the head of a family might be over-committed to outdated methods and the son who succeeded him might take to drink, or women, or a 'Bohemian' life devoted to the arts. Revivification might be dependent on such unpredictable contingencies as the circumstance of one's only daughter having the good sense (or the naïvety) to take in matrimony an upstanding young employee capable of putting his father-in-law's business on its feet again.

The creation of incorporated companies, managed by directors and appealing to the public for shares, had been virtually prohibited by the Bubble Act of 1720, as a result of the losses suffered by those who had invested in the South Sea Bubble. The absence of limited liability companies before the 1860s, however, had not been due solely to fears of encouraging speculation. In the earlier phases of industrial development,

the high degree of risk involved, the difficulty of rapid communication, the absence of any system of company law, or an
accountancy profession, all meant that private enterprise
could be effective only if it were personal enterprise, personally
controlled. For both managerial support and for finance, the
early entrepreneur relied almost exclusively on his friends and
his relations; merely, that is to say, carrying over into the fields
of industry and commerce the traditional practices current in
all other fields of social life. Whatever one achieved in the
eighteenth century and through most of the nineteenth was
achieved by making use of the influence of one's family and
one's friends and (with luck) a powerful or wealthy patron who
might, if one kept in his favour – and he kept in the favour of
whichever even more powerful personage patronized him –
obtain for one a commission in the army, a living in the Church,
a post in government service, or the East India Company, or a
place in an endowed grammar school. The strong Dissenting
character of early entrepreneurial activity in the industrial
revolution is perhaps ascribable less to the Protestant ethic than
to the fact that socially-disadvantaged religious minorities
tended to act as extended but very close-knit families.

The theoretical advantages of limited liability were that it
facilitated the raising of finance by the offer of shares to the
investing public at large; that corporations, though the
directors who controlled them remained mortal, fallible men,
were not themselves subject to the processes of inevitable
decline and death; and that the limitation of liability encouraged
enterprise. By and large, these advantages were eventually
operative; but there seems little evidence that the Limited
Liability Acts themselves were overdue or revolutionary.
Firms initially founded to take advantage of the opportunities
provided by the acts had a high failure rate. In the absence of a
sophisticated system of commercial law, and until there was an
adequate labour force of trained clerks to keep proper records,
the transition from the old personalized system to the large
depersonalized corporation did not really begin to make
headway till the last two decades of the century. It might be
difficult to assert that corporate institutions displayed in practice

much greater reliability or longevity than the older family businesses; and, for most of the century, appointments to directorships were determined principally by family connection and the patronage that went with it. The age of the managerial class had hardly begun.

10 · *Towards a Modern State*

1850–85

(2) Education and the Public Service

> There is no cloud so dark and dangerous in our
> political horizon ... as the existence of ...
> perhaps half a million children ... who are
> growing to man's estate ... to be a cause of
> poverty, instead of a cause of wealth, to the
> nation that has given them birth.
>
> GEORGE MELLY, M.P., 1869

> ... those whose abilities do not warrant an
> expectation that they will succeed in the open
> professions ... and those whom indolence of
> temperament or physical infirmities unfit for
> active exertions, are placed in the Civil Service,
> where they may obtain an honourable
> livelihood with little labour, and with no
> risk.
>
> THE NORTHCOTE-TREVELYAN REPORT, 1853

The establishment by the Education Act of 1870 of elementary
schools maintained wholly out of public funds was long
overdue. Its tardy achievement was due, in detail, to Palmerston's unwillingness during his last ministry to sponsor a
reform with which he came to agree in principle; but more
general reasons for the delay were the sustained resistance of the
Established Church and the survival of fears among the
propertied and employing classes that almost any form of
education would cause the labouring poor to become

insubordinate. The issue, like almost all the issues tackled by Gladstone's administration of 1868–74, had first become a major topic of political controversy well before the 1830s, and that it was still a matter of controversy forty years later is further evidence of the essentially conservative character of the decades that followed the Great Reform Act.

The Whig Education Grant of 1833 made available £20,000 a year for the construction of new schools by the two existing voluntary bodies then maintaining schools for the children of the poor. The purpose of the grant was to evade the proposal put forward by Roebuck, the Radical, that the government should establish a national system of education. The Church of England was resolutely opposed to the idea, being convinced, and not without reason, that an education system which the Church itself did not control would be either radical and secularist or radical and nonconformist. Believing itself threatened, in the 1830s, along with the landed aristocracy, by the radical revolution that had produced the Reform Act, it could easily see a state education system as the prelude to disestablishment, if it were not, indeed, a form of disestablishment in itself. And Grey was not prepared to attack the Church to please his Radical rank and file.

Moreover the Church was already engaged in a counter-attack against Dissent and the terms of the Whig grant assisted their campaign. The creation in 1807 of the non-denominational organization known, from 1814, as the British and Foreign Schools Society, had been largely responsible for the developing agitation for a national system of education; and it was this which had stimulated the Church to support Andrew Bell's National Society for the Education of the Children of the Poor in the Principles of the Church of England, founded in 1811. Under the system of aid begun in 1833, the government provided up to half the cost of new school building by the societies, subject to the overall £20,000 maximum; and this was at once seen to operate to the advantage of the National Society. By 1838 it had built 700 schools with government aid compared with the British Society's figure of 200. Thus, whereas a state education act would have weakened Anglican control of education, the grant system stimulated it to extend its control and subsidized it for so doing.

It was soon clear that the grant was inadequate and a parliamentary committee urged in 1838 that it should be increased. Melbourne appointed a Committee of the Privy Council in 1839, and its recommendation that the annual grant be increased to £30,000 was accepted: so also was the appointment of two inspectors, one for the schools of each of the societies; they were, however, to report, not to the appropriate society, but to the Privy Council Committee. This insistence on the insinuation of state control at the expense of the powers of the parochial clergy, the school managers and the societies was put through only with difficulty; and the Church was successful in ensuring that diocesan bishops were to be consulted about appointments to the inspectorate. The government also proposed to establish a completely non-denominational teacher-training, or 'Normal', college to train the school-teachers who were so badly needed. Both this clause, and a plan by the government to secure a fairer allocation of the grant between the two societies by making it dependent on local educational needs and not only the volume of local voluntary contributions, were successfully opposed. Under the leadership of Peel and with the support of the young Gladstone, clergy and laity had mounted a campaign to forestall the bill by making plans for diocesan teacher-training colleges; and by the time the bill reached Commons and Lords it faced such resistance that even the clauses that survived were passed by the narrowest of margins.

But the bill, the Normal College proposal in particular, was not merely opposed by the Church. The nonconformists were as ready to kill the Normal College by objecting to the provision that it should have an Anglican chaplain, as the Church was by objecting to the provision for separate doctrinal instruction for non-Anglicans. There were also other forces at work: secularists who wanted no religious instruction at all and 'voluntaryists' who objected to the whole principle of state education, though chiefly on the grounds that it would inevitably be Anglican. Had the working class been consulted (or had they been enfranchised rather than disfranchised in 1832) they would almost certainly have been, if not secularists, at any rate utilitarian about it; they would have insisted that, if schools there must be, the sole criterion of their suitability should be their success in teaching reading, writing and arithmetic.

Obstruction of educational progress by denominational partisanship continued throughout the 1840s. Graham's Factory Bill of 1843 proposed that textile factory children receive three hours schooling a day. Mill owners would be given government help to build the schools and the cost of their maintenance would be a charge on the local poor rate. Since the Church had all but wrecked the innovations of 1839, the Tories sought to secure the passage of this bill by proposing that the factory schoolmaster should be an Anglican nominated by a bishop and that the parish priest and the churchwardens should be *ex officio* among the school's managers. The result was that Methodists, Roman Catholics and Quakers joined the older Dissenting denominations in such an explosion of wrath that the bill had to be abandoned. In the long run, this non-conformist victory had the effect of making it clear beyond doubt that the Established Church would never make good its claim to control national education; in the short run, it damaged the educational prospects of the children then actually working in the factories. The 1844 Factory Act prescribed that factory children should attend school; but for this to have effect it was necessary to wait upon the success of the two societies in building more schools.

The intensity of nonconformist fear of the Established Church in the sphere of education is easy to understand, however. The Newcastle Commission[1] found that, in 1858, the National Society claimed 1,187,000 out of the total of 1,566,000 pupils for whom state aid was granted; the British Society had only 150,000; the Roman Catholics had 86,000, the Wesleyans 60,000, the Congregationalists 33,000. The figures testify to the energy that the Established Church had been provoked to display in the field of education, and to the organizational

[1] See also p. 193.

advantages resulting from its nationwide diocesan and parochial system.[1]

In 1846, Russell's government was able, despite the customary obstructionism, to make a forward move. From 1846 onwards grants were available for the maintenance of society schools as well as for the building of them. For the first time, the grant system was extended to the Roman Catholic Poor School Committee, even though all its school managers were to be nominated by the priests. To improve teacher-training the government paid salaries to apprentice pupil-teachers and fees to schoolteachers who taught such pupil-teachers. Survival of five years' apprenticeship could be rewarded by a scholarship to a three-year training-college course. The government undertook to contribute to the cost of the salary of any teacher who had been trained in this fashion. The initial cost of launching the scheme was as much as £100,000 and the size of this sum, together with the absence in the scheme of any discrimination in favour of Anglicans, naturally called forth protests; but already, by the 1850s, controversy was beginning to assume the more modern form of a conflict between the statistics of social need and the statistics of treasury finance: on the one hand too few children were getting too little schooling, and on the other the government was, as is the way of governments, convinced that it was spending too much of the public's money and getting too little value for it.

In 1858, therefore, Derby's government set up the Newcastle Commission whose terms of reference were to report on the 'present state of Popular Education' and on the measures needed to extend 'sound and cheap elementary education'. The report was issued in 1861. It decided that just under 2·25 million children of the poorer classes were 'receiving elementary instruction' and that this was as high a proportion of the total population as could reasonably be expected; but that, even in the schools subject to government inspection, only a quarter of the children received a good education. It found, on the one hand, that government expenditure had risen from

[1] See also G. Kitson Clark, *The Making of Victorian England* (London, Methuen, 1962), pp. 175–6.

£125,000 to £800,000 since 1850; on the other, that only one child in five stayed at school beyond the age of ten, and that about one child in three attended for less than a hundred days in the year. Though only a minority took the view that the way ahead lay in the direction of gradually withdrawing state aid altogether, the commission was unanimous that compulsory school attendance was 'neither attainable nor desirable'.

Combining severe practicality with a high moral tone, and the poor law mentality with characteristically Anglo-Saxon suspicion of education as such, it declared,

> Independence is of more importance than education; and if the wages of the child's labour are necessary, either to keep the parents from the poor rates, or to relieve the pressure of severe and bitter poverty, it is far better that it should go to work at the earliest age at which it can bear the physical exertion than that it should remain at school

and then, with a sudden gush of compassionate feeling, opined that a child who was a burden to his parents because he was not earning was likely to be less 'kindly treated at home'.

The Commission proposed to simplify and bureaucratize the grant system, with a view to enabling the state to ensure that it got value for its money and, further to that end, to prescribe firmly that the instruction given should be strictly elementary – on the grounds that the demands of the labour market required a sufficient supply of persons thus minimally equipped. They commented unfavourably on the tendency of the better-trained teachers to want to escape from the drudgery of elementary instruction in the three Rs by trying to teach more ambitious subjects, and were even more severe on teachers who, having been educated at the public expense, wanted an improved and progressive salary scale. The Commission's proposals for financing the schools were, with modification, incorporated in a Revised Code of Regulations drawn up in 1861 by Robert Lowe who, as vice-president of the Council, headed the Department of Education in Palmerston's second government. Lowe financed the aided schools by means of a grant per pupil, graduated according to each child's record of attendance, and his success in passing, at the first attempt, an examination in the three Rs at each of the six annual 'standards' between the ages of six and eleven.[1] This was the notorious Payment by Results system and Lowe presented it to the Commons with the chilling words, 'If this system is not cheap, I can promise it shall be efficient; if it is not efficient, it shall be cheap.' To contribute to this aim, the payment for teaching pupil-teachers was stopped and the training-college grant reduced. The results were splendidly in keeping with the principles of Gladstonian finance: after four years the system had taken in 161,500 more children but cut the cost by £177,450.

The system of payment by results was condemned by the inspectorate at the time and by all subsequent writers on the subject of education. Like the monitorial system used in the earlier history of the society schools, it was an attempt to spread scarce resources thinly but nevertheless widely. The monitorial system by which, in effect, teachers taught able children and they in turn taught the others (usually there was a monitor per twenty children), though treated with pettish disapproval by most historians of education was perhaps the only practical solution to a pioneer attempt at mass education conducted by barely literate teachers supported by exiguous financial resources. Payment by results was the recognition that it was socially and economically desirable that as many children as possible should be taught, as quickly as possible, to read, write and calculate. The system was depressing to imaginative teachers; but not all teachers were (or are) imaginative and the system may have kept the mediocre ones up to the mark. It may be suspected that at least some of the dislike of payment by results derived from its severe restriction of teachers who desired to develop the potential of their brightest pupils. The payment by results system, like the monitorial system, certainly encouraged mechanical methods of instruction and the rote-learning of 'facts'; but the Victorian fascination with facts was not merely silly; it was also an intellectual revolution. To

---

[1] The examinations would be conducted by the department's inspectors; there seems little doubt that this is the original cause of the nervous panic created in state schools by visits from inspectors throughout the succeeding hundred years.

disseminate even trivial facts among the masses was an advance; and to mount a campaign against illiteracy among a rapidly expanding population was an unprecedented undertaking. The achievements of English popular education before 1870 may well prove to have been underestimated through being judged in relation to what remained to be done rather than, as is more proper, by comparing the situation in 1870 with that of 1830.[1]

It may well be that the worst feature of the voluntary system was that it was, like so much of the progress made all through the reign, stopping short of those most in need. Just as the Church and the friendly societies and trade unions were reaching the upper section of the artisan class and no lower down that that, so was the voluntary education system. The payments by results system itself encouraged the respectable, well-dressed, regular-attending child rather than the neglected children of the very poor; they could not be reached without more schools than the voluntary system could build and without some element of compulsion. It was with this problem in mind that Forster introduced the 1870 bill, not to create a scheme of compulsory national education but 'to fill up gaps' in the voluntary system, so that in due course compulsory attendance should become practicable. (Advocates of a truly national system tended to speak in terms of 'sweeping the streets of the thousands of children' still to be found in them.) Forster pointed out that the 1·5 million children on the registers of aided schools included only two-fifths of the children of the working classes under ten and only one-third of those between the ages of ten and twelve. Accordingly, the act divided the

---

[1] This consideration ought to be borne in mind when considering the cliché that the 1870 Education Act was an inevitable consequence of the 1867 Reform Act, on the lines of Robert Lowe's usually misquoted remark that now the working class had the vote it was necessary to 'compel our future masters to learn their letters'. One would like to know how many illiterates were in fact enfranchised in 1867; and there is so much evidence of continuous Radical pressure for a national system of education over the previous forty years that it is possible to question whether the 1867 Reform Act, or the idea of 'educating our masters', had all that much to do with the 1870 Education Act.

whole of England and Wales into districts, each with an elected school board, empowered to levy an education rate to supplement the government grant, the voluntary subscriptions and the parental fees. The voluntary societies were given six months in which to claim grants for new school building; but, from the start, the school boards could, if they thought fit, build and maintain 'board schools' themselves. The government would continue to contribute to the cost of maintenance of existing voluntary schools. The boards were also empowered to pass by-laws compelling the attendance of all children between the ages of five and twelve, a right which the school board for London exercised almost from the first.

The religious issue naturally caused trouble. Since the Church was established by law, it thought that publicly-financed schools should teach its doctrine; and the provision that the board schools should give 'simple Bible teaching' failed to prevent their being labelled 'Godless'. From the point of view of the Established Church it was indeed anomalous that its ordained priests were excluded from the board schools, whereas a Methodist lay preacher was not. The conferment of what Disraeli not unjustifiably called 'sacerdotal' status upon the board school teacher propounding 'simple Bible teaching' did not of course make the schools 'non-sectarian'. It made them, at least potentially, sectarian. Nonconformists, however, objected to public funds continuing to be used to subsidize the building, and thereafter the maintenance, of church schools; others demanded the exclusion of all religious teaching. In the end, by the so-called Cowper-Temple clause, parents were given the right to withdraw their children altogether from prayers and scripture lessons.

Although Forster intended neither a free nor even a predominantly state-administered system of elementary education, the energy of the school boards and the officials of the Department of Education tended to outpace the politicians; and, particularly in the urban areas, the board schools were soon much larger and, by the necessities of the case, more modern than the voluntary schools. Thus, Forster's original estimates of costs were soon proved inadequate. Progress was such that

Sandon's act of 1876, passed under Disraeli, put a legal compulsion on parents to ensure that their children received 'efficient elementary instruction' and forbade the employment of children under ten; and to stop evasions of the act, Gladstone's second ministry put through the Mundella Act of 1880. This compelled school attendance for all children between five and ten, and restricted the terms on which a child between ten and fourteen could leave school for employment.

In view of the ever-widening extent of state education since 1870 it is sometimes too easy to forget that the school board system was intended to ensure that no more than a strictly elementary education should be available to all the children of the poor; and Forster set his face against the principle of free education even while providing for exceptions from it in practice. He pointed out that in 1869 parents paid a total in fees of £420,000; that, as more schools were built, this figure would be trebled; and that for the government to assume responsibility for such a sum would be unfair both to the middle classes and 'the best portion of the working classes' who would then also demand free education.[1] Thus there was no question in 1870 of a national system of education and no question of using board school education as a means to the widening of individual opportunity. Its sole purpose was to fit poor children for their station in life, not to raise them above it. Almost none of the developments towards a state education system after 1870 was intended by the act of 1870; its development, even in its first decade, was largely unforeseen and unwished for by its creators.

Palmerston had appointed two royal commissions to report on what would now be called secondary education. In 1861, the Clarendon Commission inquired into the affairs of the nine major public schools and, in 1864, the Taunton Commission began inquiring into the newer public schools and the endowed grammar schools. The Clarendon Commission had been set up

---

[1] School boards could charge fees up to a maximum of ninepence a week; but, by the 1880s, in London at any rate, it was apparently considered that a maximum of sixpence would be high enough to make a board school relatively 'select'.

because of fears that the upper classes might suffer in comparison with the middle and lower classes if the schools they attended were inefficient. It concerned itself mainly with the administration of the schools with which it dealt and, by the Public Schools Act of 1869, put some of its recommendations into effect.

The Commission found the schools too conducive to the development of idleness in the aristocratic young, recommended that subjects such as modern languages, geography and history be taught and noted that, for all their excessive concentration on classical studies, the schools often failed to produce proficient classicists. In keeping with the spirit of the age, they urged the institutionalization of school life – the love of learning should receive institutional reward in the shape of daily marks and prizes and be tested by frequent examinations. Leisure should be institutionalized also: and the development of manly sports was encouraged. The commission also recommended the exclusion of poor boys or local scholars. These, it was felt, could now find an education elsewhere.

The Taunton Commission led to the Endowed Schools Act of 1869. The Commission concerned itself with that wide range of schools that lay between the nine great public schools and those concerned with the children of the labouring poor. The Commission thought the schools should be graded. The first-grade schools would keep pupils aged up to nineteen, take in the sons of the wealthy and, like the old public schools, make classics the core of their curriculum, but include languages, science and mathematics, and prepare the best of the pupils for the university. Second-grade schools should keep pupils to the age of sixteen and prepare them for the army and the middle ranks of the medical and legal professions as well as civil engineering. The subjects taught should be of practical use in business. Third-grade schools should educate the children of small farmers and shopkeepers and 'superior artisans' for clerical posts in commerce, and only to the age of fourteen. Like the Clarendon Commission, the Taunton Commission was concerned to institutionalize differences of social class and produced similar recommendations for the exclusion of local boys or poor boys. Instead they advocated scholarships for boys of 'real ability' – i.e. to the already better-educated. The commission thought any admixture of lower-class children with those more gently born embarrassed the former and was 'mischievous' for the latter.

Gladstone's Endowed Schools Act incorporated few of the Taunton Commission's organizational recommendations. It did not, as recommended, appoint provincial boards to categorize the schools, or to seek financial support from local rates for second- and third-grade schools. Nor did it establish the recommended national system of secondary school examinations. The act merely appointed three commissioners to do what they could without supporting administrative machinery. It is to Gladstone's failure to implement the Taunton Report that the country owed the extraordinarily miscellaneous character of all secondary education outside the state system for almost another century. It was as a reaction to the plans of the Taunton Commission that the Public School Headmasters' Conference was set up in 1869. Gladstone's failure to establish a national examination system for secondary schools led to the establishment of the Oxford and Cambridge Schools Examination Board in 1874 and thereafter to the other university examination departments administering public examinations for secondary schools.

The Newcastle, Clarendon and Taunton Commissions, taken together with the acts of 1869 and 1870, were thus intended to set up a system of education based on the careful segregation of the classes. Gladstone's failure to implement the Taunton Report, and the extreme exclusiveness of the public schools, defeated the aim in the long run because only the state elementary system was endowed with the sinews of finance, the effectiveness of an organization under central control, and the impetus deriving from the sense of public service eagerly displayed by many of those elected to the new school boards. By the end of the century it was clear that the state system was ready to invade the secondary sphere also.

A common feature of the reforms resulting from the work of the Newcastle, Clarendon and Taunton Commissions was the emphasis upon examinations: even the great public schools were to submit their pupils to them, following the example of Thomas Arnold at Rugby; the endowed schools were soon to be served by the setting up of the first of the university examining boards; and the annual examination system imposed on the elementary schools by Robert Lowe's Revised Code of 1861 continued with only minor changes until 1890. This new emphasis on examinations was not confined to the schools. The older universities had already begun, at last, to pay more serious attention to written degree examinations. The creation of so many professional institutes and associations led naturally to the increasing use of the examination as a means of attesting qualification; and from the 1830s onwards there was a slow but steady drive to test by examination the suitability of candidates for the civil service.

The growing complexity of public administration in the nineteenth century and the increasing employment of men of the calibre of Chadwick, Kay, Simon and Southwood Smith, led to a desire to establish higher standards of both efficiency and economy. These could not be secured under the traditional system of patronage, which frequently resulted in the appointment of the idle and the incompetent. Posts in the public service were for the most part in the gift of government politicians or obtainable through the good offices of influential peers, and were thus a principal element in the complicated system of patronage which constituted the only normal machinery through which a man's advancement in life was organized. Furthermore, it remained well past mid-century the principal social institution by means of which governments rewarded political supporters and kept a majority in the Commons.[1] In consequence, the idea of selection of candidates by examination appeared the only way to ensure the elimination

[1] E. S. Turner's *Shocking History of Advertising* (Harmondsworth, Penguin, 1965), quotes the following advertisement from *The Times* of 16 April 1807: '500 Guineas will be given to any lady or gentleman who can procure the Advertiser a Permanent Situation of proportionate value in the Exchequer or any other office under the Government where not more than three hours' daily attendance is required. Strict secrecy may be relied on if requisite.'

of persons of idle habits and inadequate intellectual powers. From the outside, such a reform would also seem a natural extension of the Radical campaign to break down the monopoly of public life by aristocratic privilege and to end corruption and waste.

Government was in fact much harassed during the Crimean War by the foundation in 1855 of the Administrative Reform Association, one of whose leaders was Roebuck.[1] Government acted, however, before the association was formed, though naturally with less radical results. The government departments had been investigating the possibilities of economies since 1848; and in 1853 Gladstone appointed the Northcote–Trevelyan Committee to examine the whole question of civil service reform. The witnesses from inside the departments were already strongly in favour of an examination system. The Committee accordingly recommended that the service be divided into a higher and a lower grade; that both grades should be recruited by open competitive examination; and that promotion should be by merit and not seniority. In 1853, the Government of India Act (Macaulay being the driving force) established the examination system in the Indian service. An Order in Council of 1855, passed under Palmerston's first administration, established the Civil Service Commission to conduct 'the examination of the young men proposed to be appointed to any of the junior situations in the civil establishments'. Competition was not yet, however, 'open'. Departments were not compelled to appoint persons who had passed the commission's examination and continued to nominate candidates for the examination. From 1859 onwards, only persons certificated by the commission could receive pensions, however, and finally, in 1870, Gladstone established the open competitive system for all departments under Treasury control. The Foreign Office was excluded from the new system.

Like the educational reforms of the time, the establishment of the examination system was in no sense designed to let down ladders by which persons from the middle and lower classes might raise themselves in the social scale. The object was, in

[1] See p. 190.

the interests of efficiency and economy, to professionalize the public service, not to democratize it. For one thing the examinations devised by the Civil Service commissioners for higher-grade entrants were based on the traditional literary subjects, so that success in them remained the privilege of the expensively educated products of the great public schools and the universities. The open examination system opened new avenues of employment for intelligent public schoolboys and thus closed those avenues off from the rest of society, reinforcing the changes in the 1860s that had closed public schools and secondary schools to the children of the poor.

The older universities naturally escaped any serious interference from outside pressures, although, as noted above, they had begun to make use of written examinations. Degree examinations in science, law and history were begun in the 1850s. In 1850, two commissions of inquiry into the affairs of Oxford and Cambridge were set up in the face of intense opposition, and all that emerged was a first breach in the privileges of the Established Church.[1] Acts of 1854 and 1856 enabled non-Anglicans to matriculate at Oxford (they could already do so at Cambridge) and to take degrees at both universities. It was not until Gladstone's Universities Test Act of 1871 that religious tests were abolished in respect of fellowships and posts in the universities and their colleges. The social effects of these changes appear to have been slight. The stratification of the school system and the increasing emphasis on examinations meant that the likelihood of a poor boy reaching Oxford or Cambridge in the second half of the century was probably more remote than ever.

The need to apply the doctrines of economy and efficiency upon the army was clearly manifested during the Crimean War but this was the one major field in which change was wholly resisted until Gladstone's first premiership, and in which Palmerston may be properly accused of being immovably opposed to reform. The reason was almost certainly that he had been in civilian charge of army organization for the first twenty years of his political career and had involved himself intensely

[1] See Philip Magnus, *Gladstone* (London, Murray, 1954), p. 117.

in the question of military expenditure for the whole of it. Against his formidable combination of expert knowledge and entrenched conservatism, no headway could be made. To Palmerston's opposition was added that of the commander-in-chief, who was the Queen's cousin, the Duke of Cambridge.

It was due to the skill of Gladstone's secretary for war, Edward Cardwell, that a series of reforms was devised which achieved the remarkable result of increasing the size and efficiency of the army but reducing its cost. In abolishing flogging in peacetime in 1868, and in withdrawing colonial garrisons, he also conformed both to humanitarian ideals and the Liberal dislike of overseas military commitments. Cardwell's labours must therefore be accounted unusually successful in satisfying almost the whole of the ideal specification for a typical nineteenth-century reform. In the face of stiff opposition he also achieved the abolition of the system of purchase, by which officers bought commissions and promotion.[1] Virtually all senior serving officers opposed abolition; there was obstruction in the Commons, and so much hostility in the Lords that Gladstone decided to get round it by persuading the Queen to abolish purchase by the issue of a royal warrant. It was a

---

[1] The Army List for 1855 sets out the prices of commissions as follows:

Rank	Full Price of Commission	Difference in value between the several Commissions in Succession
	£	£
Life Guards		
Lieutenant-Colonel	7250	1900
Major	5350	1850
Captain	3500	1715
Lieutenant	1785	525
Cornet	1260	
Regiments of the Line		
Lieutenant-Colonel	4500	1300
Major	3200	1400
Captain	1800	1100
Lieutenant	700	250
Ensign	450	

shrewd move, and though not, as his opponents claimed, unconstitutional, it was the kind of artful dodge which, if it had been employed by Disraeli, Gladstone would have attacked as craftily unscrupulous. The Lords' opposition, unlike that directed against much later Liberal legislation, was that more obviously of a class than of a party. To the major objection that abolition was yet another attack on the aristocracy were added the objections of the Whig peers. Russell, still at the approach of the last quarter of the nineteenth reliving the last quarter of the seventeenth century, reaffirmed the view that to transfer control of the army from the aristocracy to a professional class would create a military caste with a will of its own; and that this would be a threat to civil liberty. Cardwell, however, went on to weaken aristocratic control still further by taking away from the lord lieutenants the right to appoint officers to the militia, vesting it instead in the War Office. Further to professionalize the army he abolished the long service system which had recently served the French so badly and substituted the short service system favoured by the Prussians. Men were no longer enlisted for twelve years,[1] much of that time being spent overseas with disastrous effects upon their physical condition. Instead they were to serve for six years with the colours and then for six in the reserves; and by the linked battalion system he ensured that there would always be at least one battalion in each regiment serving at home. Unable to reorganize the cavalry he did better with the artillery; and though he was unable to woo the latter from their faith in muzzle-loading guns he did succeed in equipping the infantry with a breech-loader. He also stimulated recruitment by substituting county regiments for the old numbered regiments of the line.[2]

---

[1] Until 1847 they had enlisted for 21 years.
[2] All the numbered regiments had in fact also had names before 1870, some of them territorial. The 87th Regiment of Foot was the Royal Irish Fusiliers, the 12th Regiment of Foot was the East Suffolk Regiment and the 53rd, as readers of A. E. Housman are aware, was the Shropshire Regiment.

11 · Beaconsfieldism and Midlothianism

Foreign and Colonial Policy 1868–85

> If *we are* to maintain our position as a *first-rate* Power we must, with our Indian Empire and large Colonies be *Prepared* for *attacks* and *wars*, *somewhere* or *other*, CONTINUALLY.
>
> QUEEN VICTORIA to Lord Beaconsfield,
> 28 July 1879

It was between 1868 and 1886 that certain characteristic political attitudes of the 'Right' and 'Left', as they were to exist well into the middle of the twentieth century, were first shaped; and the shaping was done by Gladstone and Disraeli. The particular differences for which they were responsible have little to do with social problems at home, however. Even if it be accepted that there is at least something in the view that Disraeli's government from 1874 to 1880 paid more attention to working-class living and working conditions than Gladstone's first two ministries, the Conservative party after his death, even when associated, as it was after 1886, with the Liberal Unionists, did little in its domestic policies to commend itself to the working classes. 'Tory Democracy' was little more than a colourful theory about Disraeli's Conservatism invented by Lord Randolph Churchill in the 1880s for the purpose (in which he was ultimately unsuccessful) of embarrassing Lord Salisbury. Nor, owing to Gladstone's obsession with Ireland, the consequent loss to the party of Joseph Chamberlain, and the political disarray into which the party fell after Gladstone's resignation in 1893, did the Liberals after 1880, whether in office or in opposition, appear to possess a relevant social policy until after 1905. The differences which Gladstone and Disraeli symbolized were almost wholly within the spheres of foreign and imperial policy. In this respect, Gladstonian Liberalism established the normal (though never universal) attitude of the Liberals, and their heirs in the twentieth-century Labour party; while Disraeli established the normal (though not quite universal) Conservative attitude to foreign and colonial affairs until 1956.

It was Disraeli who was the greater innovator of the two, though Gladstonian Liberal foreign and imperial policy was almost as different from Palmerstonian Liberal policy in such matters as Disraeli's was from that of most of his Tory predecessors.

In his first ministry Gladstone insisted on making Liberal policy conform to the tradition he had inherited from his old Tory chieftains, Peel and Aberdeen, thus in effect bequeathing to the Liberal party a mainly Tory foreign policy, and one as wholly unlike that of Palmerston's as possible, and almost as unlike that of John Russell. Thus, whereas Palmerston and John Russell had refused to submit the *Alabama* case to arbitration, Gladstone insisted on doing so; and accepted an award that was held to be more than generous to the United States. He and his colleagues persuaded the combatants in the Franco-Prussian war to undertake to respect the neutrality of Belgium; both Gladstone and his foreign secretary, Lord Granville, secured the informal agreement of all the powers not to intervene in the conflict, and refused to depart from the strictest neutrality, even when Prussian victories caused opinion in England to veer for the first (and last) time in the reign in favour of France; and Gladstone himself made unofficial attempts to persuade Bismarck not to annex Alsace and Lorraine. When the Russians took the opportunity of the outbreak of the war to announce their unilateral abrogation of the clauses of the Treaty of Paris neutralizing the Black Sea, Gladstone insisted on a conference of powers in 1871. The Russian action was legalized after the event, and this was accompanied by a solemn declaration that treaties ought not to be abrogated save with the consent of all the signatories. These were unheroic acts, not at all in accordance with Palmerston's view that any matter affecting the European balance was one in which England 'ought to intervene'.[1] That they were in the best sense realistic, because there was nothing more that could have been done without courting the kind of humiliation Palmerston had suffered in 1864, was not however accounted to the government's favour; and it remains a convention that Gladstone's foreign policy in this ministry was 'weak', when all that is really meant is that it was neither blustering like Palmerston's nor 'realistic' in the ruthless Bismarckian sense of the word. Public opinion was, however, partly mollified by Cardwell's subsequent army reforms.[2]

The contrast when Disraeli became prime minister was so great as to dazzle his contemporaries for part of the time and posterity almost all the time. The first event to catch the public imagination was the purchase of the shares in the Suez Canal Company owned (or rather mortgaged for the next twenty years) by the bankrupt Khedive of Egypt. Disraeli was able to do this quickly, partly because the French foreign minister accepted the warning that the British would object strongly to the Khedive's shares passing into French hands, and also because, Parliament not being in session, Disraeli borrowed the necessary sum of £4 million from the Rothschilds (who charged a stiff rate of interest). It was a personal *coup* on Disraeli's part, conducted with skill and resolution. But all that the government had done was to secure a large minority holding of the shares of the Canal Company. The British had not secured control of the company, and not even any voting rights until twenty years later, since the purchased shares were mortgaged till 1895. Neither had Disraeli prevented the French government from 'controlling' the canal itself as he pretended, since navigation of merchant ships through it was already legally free to all, solely on payment of dues to the company. Nevertheless it was still an advantage to prevent the French having the great influence on the Khedive they would have

[1] See p. 146.
[2] See p. 204.

had, had French interests acquired almost all the company's shares. Gladstone showed his usual capacity to see ahead of Disraeli's actions in foreign affairs when he prophesied that the acquisition of a financial interest in Egypt would lead in the end to political interest.

Disraeli was less personally committed over two other matters which came to be associated with his mythical 'imperialism'. The visit of the Prince of Wales to India in the winter of 1875–6 originated from the Prince himself and not from either Disraeli or his colleagues. It caused Disraeli some difficulty both because the Commons was unwilling to subsidize the visit adequately, and because Princess Alexandra had to be dissuaded from accompanying her husband to India and the Queen had to be dissuaded from forbidding the Princess the consolation prize of a visit to her native Denmark. Nor was the proposal to confer on the Queen the title of Empress of India the brainchild of Disraeli; it had been mooted ever since the Indian Mutiny and had come to seem even more necessary now that Russian power was feeling its way towards Persia and Afghanistan. The Indians, it was felt, might be less open to subversion by the agents of a Russian emperor if they had an empress of their own. That the Royal Titles Bill came when it did, in 1876, was due largely to pressure from the Queen herself. There was Liberal opposition in both Houses and Gladstone later described it as 'theatrical bombast'.[1] Nevertheless, since these minor acts of theatrical showmanship were almost simultaneous with Disraeli's apparently triumphant progress towards the attainment of peace with honour at the Congress of Berlin, it is hardly surprising that they appeared part of a conscious Conservative policy of 'maintaining the greatness' of the Empire, to which Disraeli had referred in the course of a speech at the Crystal Palace in 1872 when alleging also that the Liberals were seeking to disrupt the Empire.[2]

[1] Philip Magnus, *Gladstone* (London, Murray, 1954), p. 264.
[2] Disraeli used the expression again when resisting Gladstone's strictures after the Bulgarian atrocities (see p. 212): 'What our duty is at this critical moment is to maintain the Empire of England' (Robert Blake, *Disraeli*, London, Eyre & Spottiswoode, 1966, p. 594).

The Eastern question erupted in 1875 with a revolt against the Turks by Serbian peasants in Bosnia and Herzegovina. This raised once again the spectre of Russian action against Turkey on behalf of persecuted fellow-Slavs and fellow-Orthodox Christians. The prospect, as the revolt was joined by the Serbs and Montenegrins, both still under Turkish suzerainty, deepened the alarm of the Austro-Hungarian government, who were unwilling to see the emergence of independent, but almost certainly Russian-dominated, Slav states immediately to the south of the Habsburg Empire, which already ruled many South Slavs (chiefly Croats and Slovenes) and which already wanted Bosnia and Herzegovina for itself. Alexander II, an indecisive and by this time greatly detested Czar, was hardly less alarmed: he did not want another Crimean War, did not want to forfeit Habsburg friendship and had no personal sympathy with Balkan Slavs. Since Bismarck did not want an Austro-Russian quarrel of any sort and regarded the Balkans as not worth the 'bones of a single Pomeranian grenadier', it was clear that the prospects for some kind of concerted great-power action to localize the conflict and to put pressure on the Turks to fulfil the promises of Balkan reform they had made in 1856 were quite good. Since the French were in no position to make trouble by themselves, everything therefore depended on the British government.

In December 1875, the British did in fact join with the other powers in demanding reforms from the Turk, in the Andrassy Note. Since this produced no result, Andrassy (the Austro-Hungarian foreign minister) produced another diplomatic request for reforms, the Berlin Memorandum of May 1876. On the grounds that it threatened Britain's ally, Turkey, with 'effective measures' if the reforms were not forthcoming, Disraeli refused to agree to it, pretending that it was nothing but a plot by the Three Emperors' League of Austria-Hungary, Germany and Russia to destroy the Turkish Empire. To indicate to the world that the British were not to be trifled with, and that it was he, and not the 'weak' Gladstone, with whom foreigners now had to deal, he ordered British ships to Besika Bay, just outside the Straits. Shortly afterwards, the revolt spread not only to Serbia and Montenegro but also to Bulgaria. The Serbs and Montenegrins were defeated and the Turks attacked the Bulgarians (who were much more accessible from Constantinople) with murderous ferocity. This development, combined with the failure to secure great-power collaboration and the signature of an agreement with Austria–Hungary to share the spoils of war if any, pushed Alexander II further along the path to war against Turkey. Even so, he hesitated to run the risks of European intervention; and Disraeli's foreign secretary, Lord Derby, and eventually Disraeli himself, were persuaded to let England be represented at a Great Power Conference at Constantinople in December 1876 by Lord Salisbury, the secretary for India.

Disraeli lacked Palmerston's authority, his capacity for work and his robust good health (he withdrew from the Commons in July 1876 and thereafter led his government and party from the Lords as the Earl of Beaconsfield).[1] He was unable to drive his Cabinet towards the vigorous anti-Russian policy he was trying to achieve; his foreign secretary, Lord Derby, appeared desperately anxious to avoid any action whatever; and at the Constantinople Conference, Salisbury, who found his prime minister politically and personally distasteful, cooperated with the Russians in proposing large plans for the Balkans, including the establishment of an autonomous state of Bulgaria. It was fortunate, from Disraeli's point of view at any rate, that the Sultan sabotaged the conferences in the confident expectation that England would always defend Constantinople from the Russians; on the other hand, it was less fortunate that Gladstone had dramatically intervened with a resounding condemnation both of the Turks and of the Conservative prime minister who supported these murderous infidels and opposed Christian Russia.

Disgusted by the chilliness of his Whig supporters and disillusioned by his party's substantial defeat in the 1874 election, Gladstone had announced his retirement from the Liberal

---

[1] Disraeli, on resigning the premiership in 1868, had persuaded the Queen to grant a peerage to his wife; her official title was Viscountess Beaconsfield. She died in December 1872.

leadership. But Disraeli's cavalier attitude, throughout the summer of 1876, to well-substantiated reports that in May the Turks had massacred 12,000 Bulgarian men, women and children, finally provoked Gladstone into writing, in September 1876, in what he himself described as 'a righteous passion', a pamphlet full of frenetic fury against the Turks entitled 'The Bulgarian Horrors and the Question of the East'. It sold 200,000 copies in three weeks and Gladstone followed it with an impassioned speech to an open-air meeting at Blackheath, claiming that his pamphlet had created a truly national movement of protest and declaring that his personal message to a Russia that sought to drive Turkey from Bulgaria was 'Go on and prosper!' Gladstone continued to attack Disraeli's policy of propping up Turkey as immoral well on into 1877 and even after Russia had at last declared war on Turkey in April of that year. As well as raising a good deal of opinion against Disraeli's policy of supporting Turkey, Gladstone's frenzies alienated the Whigs, one of whom, the Marquis of Hartington, had become Liberal leader in succession to Gladstone. Hartington had no wish to oppose the government's Eastern policy; and the outcome was that Gladstone came to be regarded as the chief and most dangerous spokesman of extreme Liberal and Radical idealism. He himself heightened the impression by announcing in the Commons, 'what I may call the West End of London . . . does not express the true sentiments of England. Looking over all the great achievements that have made the last half century illustrious, not one of them would have been effected if the opinions of the West End of London had prevailed.'[1] This caused Hartington, with some justification, to say of Gladstone, 'He does not cease to be leader of the Party by merely saying that he will not be the leader. If, as he has done since the autumn [of 1876] he takes the lead, he *is* the leader.'[2]

Unable to secure the active assistance of Austria–Hungary, the support of an energetic Cabinet or, thanks to Gladstone, a united public opinion, Disraeli was compelled to look on as, during the early summer of 1877, the Russians advanced into

[1] Magnus, op. cit., p. 24.
[2] Ibid., p. 248.

the Balkans. It was the stubborn fighting quality of the Turks which eventually gave Disraeli back some freedom to man-œuvre. At the fortress of Plevna, the Turks, under Osman Pasha, held the Russians up for six months, and thus succeeded in transforming themselves in the eyes of the British public from bloody butchers of Bulgarian Christians into heroic fighters resisting the onslaughts of the gruesome Russian bear. Gladstone had laboured in vain; now, as crowds hooted him in the streets and other patriotic persons broke his windows, the music halls resounded to cries of –

> We don't want to fight,
> But by Jingo if we do,
> We've got the men, we've got the ships,
> We've got the money too.

culminating in the defiant Palmerstonian cry:

> The Russians shall not have Constantinople!

What Russia's aims had been when the war started is impossible to assert with any exactitude. But in the event they stopped short of Constantinople; when the Turks asked for an armistice after the fall of Adrianople, the Russians agreed to preliminary peace talks on 31 January 1878. Of course, the Russians would have liked to take Constantinople. But the arguments against doing so, even now they were within sight of its walls, were weighty: their army was almost as exhausted as that of the Turks; even if they had succeeded in entering Constantinople the result was certain to be a degree of opposition from England, Austria–Hungary and France which the Russians could not hope to resist; and whether they then realized it or not, Bismarck had no intention of assisting Russia against such a combination. The Czar was as indecisive as ever and so was his brother, who was in command of the army. The Russians might well have taken Constantinople had they screwed up sufficient courage to risk the possible consequences. Rumours reached London that they had in fact done so. But still Disraeli's Cabinet dithered. A week before the Russo-Turkish armistice Disraeli proposed that the fleet move from Besika Bay into the

Dardanelles off Constantinople. Derby resigned as foreign secretary and only returned when the proposal was dropped. It was put into effect however, in February 1878, to the accompaniment of an intensification of Russophobia, principally in London. The Queen wished she 'were a man' so that she could 'go and give those horrid Russians a beating'. Russia was warned that diplomatic relations would be broken off if Constantinople were entered; and when the Russians said they would not allow their peace treaty with Turkey (the Treaty of San Stefano) to be reviewed at a European congress, Disraeli called up the reserves and secretly ordered Indian troops to Malta with the object if necessary of seizing Cyprus. At last Lord Derby resigned, to the accompaniment of suggestions from some quarters that he be hanged on the nearest available tree in Hyde Park,[1] and was replaced by Lord Salisbury, whose dislike of Disraeli was now lessened by Disraeli's readiness to oppose the Russians at Constantinople.

Encouraged by this show of resolution on England's part, Austria–Hungary began to make threatening diplomatic gestures also. The Czar's advisers accordingly counselled him to make no further move towards either Constantinople or the Straits, and to accept the proposal for a European congress. To keep things on the boil, Disraeli now announced publicly that Indian troops had been ordered to Malta.

The Treaty of San Stefano was regarded as objectionable by the British on the grounds that it provided for the creation of an autonomous 'Big' Bulgaria which would include, not only the Bulgarian state as it has existed since 1945, but also the greater part of those areas of Macedonia which are today part of Jugoslavia and Greece. It was also to have an outlet to the Aegean Sea at Dedegeach (also now in Greek hands). Broadly speaking, 'Big' Bulgaria would have extended from the Danube to the Aegean and from Albania to the Black Sea, cutting Turkey in Europe into two quite disconnected portions. Austria–Hungary also objected. Not only would 'Big' Bulgaria be administered by Russian army officers; the treaty contained no provision for Austria's acquisition of Bosnia which had been understood as

[1] Blake, op. cit., p. 639.

one of the rewards that Austria should have for her neutrality. The British also objected to the proposed Russian gains in Asiatic Turkey, Batum and Kars, on the grounds that this would enable Russia to penetrate further into Asia Minor towards the Persian Gulf. By the time the congress met in June 1878, Disraeli and Salisbury had signed in secret three preliminary agreements. By an agreement with Russia at the end of May, the plan for a 'Big' Bulgaria was abandoned; by an agreement with Austria–Hungary, the latter would support the partition of Bulgaria and England would support Austria's claim to Bosnia; by an agreement with Turkey, England would be allowed to occupy Cyprus and would defend Turkey against any Russian attack in Asia. This last agreement was designed to counter Russian control of Batum and Kars.

Despite these preceding negotiations, the Congress of Berlin was not a mere formality even though doubts have been cast on the story that, when the Russians showed signs of being obstructive, Disraeli theatrically ordered a special train to be ready to take him away from Berlin. Despite the fact that it made him seriously ill before it was over, Disraeli was the most picturesque and forceful personality at the congress, though Salisbury did most of the donkey work. And though Disraeli failed rather pathetically to get limits placed on the Russian control of Batum[1] he more than got his way over Bulgaria. Liberated Bulgaria was allowed to stretch no farther south than the line of the Balkan mountains. An area to the south, known as Eastern Roumelia, was kept within the Turkish Empire, but given a Christian governor. The rest of 'Big' Bulgaria – almost all Macedonia – remained an integral part of the Turkish Empire. Since Austria was permitted to occupy Bosnia and Herzegovina, both Russian ambitions and Slav nationalist aspirations were alike regarded as decisively checked. It was because of these decisions, together with the occupation of Cyprus, that Disraeli claimed he had brought back from Berlin 'peace with honour', meaning, in plainer language, that he had

[1] ibid., p. 649, and A. J. Grant and H. Temperley, *Europe in the 19th and 20th Centuries, 1789–1950*, 6th edn (Harlow, Longmans, 1952), p. 305 footnote.

secured a resounding defeat of Russia's nefarious aims without putting his countrymen to the trouble and expense of actually fighting a war in order to achieve this felicitous result.[1] Nothing could have been more acceptable to the bulk of public opinion than to be presented with a victory without having to have a war first, and Disraeli was received back home with enthusiasm. The Queen wanted to make him a knight of the garter and a duke. He contented himself with the K.G. and with bland generosity (and indeed some justice) requested that the same honour be bestowed upon Salisbury. Gladstone, however, was splenetic with indignation, much of it righteous, but some of it jealous. He described the Cyprus Convention as 'insane' (a word which both the Queen and Bismarck several times considered more appropriately descriptive of Gladstone himself) and 'an act of duplicity not surpassed and rarely equalled in the history of nations'. This nonsensical outburst provoked Disraeli's celebrated public retort that his rival was 'a sophisticated rhetorician inebriated with the exuberance of his own verbosity' and determined on all occasions 'to malign an opponent and to glorify himself'.

On balance, the crisis in the Near East from 1875 to 1878 may be said to have been to a great extent created by Disraeli's initial abandonment of concerted action when refusing to associate England with the Berlin Memorandum. The basic assumption that Russia aimed in 1875, or even later, to set up puppet Slav states in the Balkans and seize Constantinople regardless of the interests and fears of the rest of Europe was a compulsive reflex reaction, not a logical deduction from the situation as it really was, though it can be ascribed in part to the combination of divided counsels and evasive inscrutability normally characteristic of the Russian government, particularly under Alexander II. But in arguing at the outset that the Eastern Question should be settled by the Concert of Europe and not by taking Turkey's side against Russia, Gladstone was

---

[1] 'Great Britain won a bloodless victory with a music-hall song, a navy of museum pieces, and no land forces at all, except the 7,000 Indian troops sent demonstratively to Malta.' (A. J. P. Taylor, *The Struggle for Mastery in Europe 1848–1918*, London, O.U.P., 1954, p. 250.)

in the right, if only because any breach between England and the other great powers inevitably encouraged Turkish obstinacy.

Gladstone was also in the right in claiming that Balkan nationalism ('the breasts of free men' as he dramatically put it) would prove a more effective barrier against Russia than the maintenance of the incompetent Ottoman Empire. The contempt with which Disraeli treated Slav nationalist aspirations derived partly from the normal West European prejudice against the Slavs[1] and partly from a romantic notion (derived from his meetings with *Arabs* in his earlier travels) that the Turks were splendid fellows. To refuse to acknowledge that Turkish rule in south-east Europe was objectionable, purely on the grounds that any alternative to it would increase Russian influence and endanger the route to India, had been a sterile and negative policy at least since the outbreak of the Greek revolt in 1820, and Gladstone's view that it was cynically immoral to persevere in keeping Balkan Christians in subjection because this was held to be a British strategic interest is one from which (despite the intemperate way in which it was expressed) it is difficult to dissent.

In its handling of the Balkan situation, the Treaty of Berlin was bad both in the short term and in the long. From the start, Congress Bulgaria proved as anti-Russian as it had previously been anti-Turk; the Turks made no attempt to maintain their authority in Eastern Roumelia and its inhabitants proclaimed their independence as South Bulgaria in 1885, offering themselves instantly as subjects of Prince Alexander of Bulgaria. There followed a three-year diplomatic conflict in which after nearly going to war with Russia in 1878 to keep Bulgaria small, England and Austria all but made war on her in order to let it become large. From 1885–7 Russia tried desperately to prevent the union of the two Bulgarias on the grounds that the Bulgarians were so strongly anti-Russian; while Salisbury used all his diplomatic skills, precisely because the Bulgarians had proved anti-Russian, to ensure that the union was preserved.

[1] A prejudice that was to dominate British foreign policy again in the 1930s and reached its lowest depths in 1938.

H

Thus did Salisbury publicly demonstrate that he and his master (who had died in 1881) had, in Salisbury's own words, 'backed the wrong horse' in 1878 and that Gladstone had been right about the Bulgarians after all. Bulgaria remained consistently anti-Russian until its second 'liberation' in 1944.

The return of Macedonia to Turkey and the assignment of Bosnia and Herzegovina to Austrian occupation were both the source of much evil. The Macedonian area was at this time almost wholly Bulgarian in population.[1] But, once returned to Turkey, it became an inevitable attraction to the Serbs. Their ambitions had hitherto been concentrated largely on Bosnia and Herzegovina whose population was almost wholly Serb; but now, the Austrian occupation barred Serb progress northwards. Hence, the Treaty of Berlin created two wholly new problems in both Bosnia and Macedonia, setting up Austro-Serbian and Serbo-Bulgarian tensions that led, eventually, to the Balkan Wars of 1912–13 and the outbreak of European war a year later. Added to this was the fact of continuing Turkish misrule in Macedonia. There is a good case for the argument that the Treaty of San Stefano would have gone a long way to settling at least the Balkan aspect of the Eastern Question, and that the Congress of Berlin went a long way to unsettling it. The fact that there were no major wars in Europe between 1878 and 1912 has very little to do with the Congress of Berlin.

Little of Disraeli's conduct in all this had anything to do with the Imperialism of the last two decades of the century. As with most elderly politicians (Gladstone was no exception) his con-duct of affairs was based less on contemporary fact than on recollections of things past: his policy over the Eastern Question was almost slavishly imitative of Palmerston in his heyday, as well as based on a conscious desire to be as unlike the irresolute pacifist Aberdeen in his handling of Russia's Balkan policies, or as 'weak' as Gladstone had been over the abrogation of the Black Sea clauses. Like Canning in the 1820s and Palmerston in the 1830s he was also concerned to break up the alliance of St Petersburg, Berlin and Vienna which Metter-

[1] On this point A. J. P. Taylor, op cit. and Grant and Temperley, op. cit. are insistent. Blake, op. cit., p. 651, asserts the opposite.

nich had engineered in his day and Bismarck had revived after the Franco-Prussian war. The objection of all three, of Canning, Palmerston and Disraeli, to the so-called Holy Alliance of the 1820–40 period and its ghostly successor, the Three Emperors' League, was based on the patriotic illusion that the collaboration of the three powers somehow minimized England's position as a great power, and on the unverifiable thesis that they wanted to handle the questions of Constantinople and the Straits in complete disregard of England's clear interests there. Disraeli's attitude was thus not merely 'immoral'; it was both unnecessary and, in the larger issue of what was to be done about the Balkans, reactionary.

It is significant that Salisbury had agreed with the Russians at Constantinople at the end of 1876 that an autonomous Bulgaria be set up, that he supported Disraeli fully only at the point where it seemed likely that Russia might take Constantinople at any minute; that it was Salisbury's Circular of April 1878 that revived the principle of concerted action, that Salisbury pursued an anti-Russian policy after 1885 by supporting Bulgaria's nationalism and by a virtually secret diplomacy; that it was during Salisbury's premiership that the British government quietly came to the conclusion that Constantinople could fall to the Russians without danger to the Empire; and that there was no future in the old policy of 'maintaining the integrity' of the Turkish Empire. Salisbury may or may not be accurately described as an Imperialist; Disraeli, however, was a one hundred per cent Palmerstonian. And, while Salisbury conducted foreign affairs in an almost Byzantine seclusion from public opinion, Disraeli had learned from Palmerston, and with advantages, the technique of playing the anti-Russian game in full view of a patriotic public opinion.

Disraeli ought also to have learned from Palmerston that the penalty for playing the patriotic role in public was instant obloquy if he failed to keep it up. From 1878 onwards his government was associated with two serious colonial muddles, which did much to rob him of the laurels he had won at Berlin. By the end of 1878, Disraeli found himself faced, while the Eastern Question was still unsettled, with a war in South Africa against the Zulus, and another on the North-West Frontier against the Afghans.

In South Africa, the weakness of the Boer republic of the Transvaal was considered so grave a temptation to the Zulus to attack it – and thereafter Cape Colony – that Disraeli's colonial secretary, Carnarvon, appointed Sir Bartle Frere as governor of Cape Colony and high commissioner for South Africa, with instructions to form a South African Federation. By the time he reached South Africa in April 1877, Sir Theophilus Shepstone, minister for native affairs in Natal, had, on instructions from Carnarvon, annexed the Transvaal to the British Crown as the only way to ensure the defence both of the Boers and the British in South Africa against the Zulus. Frere was all for extending British power in South Africa and decided that the Zulus must be crushed. Ignoring a Cabinet veto, Frere started his war; and promptly a Zulu force of 20,000 men overwhelmed 1,200 British troops at Isandhlwana, in January 1879. Reserves had to be sent from England, but little progress was made against the Zulus after the shock of this initial defeat. A further public humiliation was that Napoleon III's son, the Prince Imperial, who had gone out as an eager volunteer after undergoing military training at Woolwich, was speared to death by a Zulu ambush and in circumstances that suggested that the officers accompanying him had been so anxious to escape from the Zulus that they did not notice he had failed to remount his horse and was not in fact riding with them. It was not until June 1879 that the British commander, Lord Chelmsford, was able to defeat the Zulus at Ulundi. And before that had happened the government had made itself unpopular by rebuking, but not dismissing, Frere and by sending out Sir Garnet Wolseley to oversee both Frere and Chelmsford.

So far from approving what happened in South Africa, Disraeli was enraged by the behaviour of both Frere and Chelmsford and contemptuous of Carnarvon (who had resigned along with Derby over the calling up of the reserves during the Eastern crisis). But, as prime minister, Disraeli could not evade some responsibility for failing to exercise sufficient supervision

over both Carnarvon and Frere. Carnarvon's appointment of the
headstrong Frere as high commissioner in 1877 was in its way
almost as foolish as Gladstone's later decision to send Gordon
to evacuate the Sudan.

Disraeli was rather more positively behind the almost contemporaneous trouble in Afghanistan. In 1876, Disraeli and
Salisbury (the latter still at that time secretary for India)
appointed Lord Lytton as viceroy of India with the intention
that he should adopt a stiff line with the Afghans, who had
committed the dangerous offence of entering into friendly
relations with the Russians. The Afghan amir, Sher Ali, was to
be persuaded to receive a permanent British mission. But in
July 1878, Sher Ali, much against his will, found himself
receiving a Russian military mission in his capital, Kabul.
Lytton asked for London's authority to send a British mission
to Kabul. Once again, poor communications and inattention
led to precipitate action on the spot against the wishes of the
home government. The latter's intention was that Lytton
should take no action pending the result of a formal diplomatic
approach by London to the Russian government. But London
was slow to tell Lytton; and even when, very late in the day, he
did get a clear warning from London not to proceed for the
time being, he nevertheless went ahead. The British mission
departed for Afghanistan by way of the Khyber Pass and was
promptly turned back at the Afghan frontier. This left Disraeli
and Salisbury with no alternative but to support Lytton against
this display of oriental insolence. Thanks largely to the military
skills of General Roberts, the campaign succeeded in driving
Sher Ali from his throne. He was replaced by his son Yakub
Khan who, in May 1879, gave the British the control both of
the passes into Afghanistan and of Afghan foreign policy; and
a British minister, Sir Louis Cavagnari, took up residence in
Kabul. In September 1879, however, Sir Louis and the whole
of his staff were murdered by mutinous Afghan soldiers and
thus the second Afghan war had to be followed by a third.
Thanks once more to Roberts, resistance in Afghanistan was
broken by the middle of October 1879.

The Zulu and Afghan wars both cost a great deal of money

and though both had ended in victory each had been attended by confusion and humiliation. Combined with the bad harvests consequent upon four wet summers in succession, a sudden halt in economic expansion, a number of bank failures and a dramatic rise in unemployment, these colonial bunglings induced a mood of disenchantment in the public mind. This mood Gladstone set out to exploit to the Liberal advantage. Neither Gladstone nor any of his fellow Liberals could promise good harvests or economic recovery, since they could understand or control the economic changes of the time hardly better than they could understand or control the weather. But what could be done was to campaign against the evils of what Gladstone decided to call 'Beaconsfieldism'. (It is perhaps significant that he used this label and not the word 'Imperialism'.) Both in the winter of 1879 and the spring of 1880 Gladstone addressed a series of meetings at railway stations and in large public halls en route to Midlothian for which, at the instigation of Lord Rosebery, Gladstone had agreed to be a candidate at the general election due in 1880. With the added attraction now and again of bonfires, firework displays and much torch-carrying, Gladstone denounced Beaconsfieldism as the work of the devil. He spoke of the government's 'mischievous and ruinous misdeeds' and its pursuit of 'false phantoms of glory' and declared that it had endangered 'all the most fundamental interests of Christian society'. The invasion of Afghanistan had been 'wanton' and he called upon his hearers to remember 'that the sanctity of life in the hill villages of Afghanistan among the winter snows is as inviolable in the eye of Almighty God as can be your own'. Zulus had been struck down by the forces of Beaconsfieldism for no other offence than that of seeking 'with their naked bodies' to defend 'their hearths and homes, their wives and families' against the attacks of British artillery. In March 1880 he broadened his attack to include not merely 'Beaconsfieldism' but the wicked in high places who (apparently) connived at it. The aristocracy, the landed interest, the clergy of the Church of England, the 'wealth' and the 'rank' of the country could none of them be relied on. Over against these dreadful personages Gladstone invoked 'the nation itself'.

Nobody on the government side offered a reply to Gladstone's stump-oratory of November 1879. This was partly because it was considered vulgarly American to campaign in this manner and partly because most of Disraeli's Cabinet, the prime minister included, appear to have fallen ill in the first month of 1880. Gladstone of course continued to abound in vitality, some of it purely physical, much of it the product of intense emotional excitement. By contrast, Disraeli had bronchial asthma and so had the lord chancellor: Salisbury was confined to his bed at Hatfield, the chancellor of the exchequer had influenza and the postmaster-general had a hunting injury.[1] Even when they all recovered they thought they had little reason for political alarm, since the Conservatives proceeded to win two by-elections. Accordingly a snap decision was made to dissolve Parliament in March, and very little was done to answer the denunciatory oratory of Gladstone's second Midlothian Campaign. The elections resulted in the Liberals raising the number of their seats to 353 from 250, the Irish Nationalists raising theirs from 51 to 61, while Conservative representation fell from 351 to 238.

The extent to which the Conservative defeat was the decisive rejection of 'Beaconsfieldism' that Gladstone (and most historians afterwards) took it to be, is a speculative matter. The relevant point is that it was so regarded. Gladstone, in the interval of felling trees, saw the cumulative Liberal victories as a sign that 'the arm of the Lord' was at work and congratulated the Almighty for His intervention: 'to God be the praise', he wrote. The impression that 'Beaconsfieldism' had indeed been overthrown was reinforced when Hartington, who officially still led the Liberals, declined the Queen's request to form a government on the grounds that no Liberal government could function without Gladstone and that Gladstone would accept no subordinate office. When consulted, Gladstone confirmed that he would accept no office save that of prime minister and complained that he had intended Lord Granville and not Hartington to succeed to the leadership in 1875. In spite of this further example of Gladstone's outrageous behaviour to his

[1] Blake, op. cit., p. 702.

senior colleagues, both Hartington and Granville agreed to serve under his premiership. The Queen, who had responded to the news of Disraeli's defeat by saying she would rather abdicate than have Gladstone as prime minister on the grounds that he was a 'half mad firebrand' who would be 'a Dictator', gave way to the inevitable only with the greatest reluctance. Gladstone at once did much to confirm the suspicion that he would be 'a Dictator' by acting as his own chancellor of the exchequer until the end of 1882.

This, together with his obsession with Ireland,[1] helps in part to explain the blunders committed during his second term as premier. He was further hampered by the fact that he filled his Cabinet with Whigs, save for three Radicals: Bright, now fairly conservative-minded, Dilke and the energetic, ambitious Chamberlain. The government thus disappointed many of its own supporters. It ran into almost endless trouble over the question of whether Charles Bradlaugh, the Radical M.P. for Northampton, could take his seat without taking the normal oath of allegiance which he declined to do on the grounds that he was a professed atheist. Gladstone also faced continuous obstruction by the Irish Nationalist M.P.s, led by Parnell, and many deliberately provocative attacks on him by Lord Randolph Churchill and a group of younger Tory M.P.s who became known as the Fourth Party. To add to Gladstone's misery, the Queen had as little to do with him as possible and continued to correspond with Disraeli almost until his death in April 1881.[2]

In clearing up certain matters outstanding from the Berlin Congress, Gladstone sought to demonstrate his faith in the Concert of Europe by trying, not at all successfully, to get joint action to force Turkey to cede territory to Montenegro and to Greece. It was fortunate for Gladstone that the Turks gave way,

---

[1] See Chapter 12.

[2] The Queen failed to invite the prime minister and Mrs Gladstone to the wedding of her third son, the Duke of Connaught; Gladstone declined to attend Disraeli's funeral on 19 April 1881, did not himself move the proposal that a memorial to Disraeli be erected in Westminster Abbey, and only after a stiff battle with his conscience did he at last bring himself to make a suitable Commons speech about his dead opponent.

since Gladstone in fact failed altogether to get France, Germany and Austria–Hungary to act with him; had the Sultan not given way Gladstone would have found himself left alone to carry out a plan to seize Smyrna in order to bring the Turks to heel. His ill-considered action persuaded both Austria–Hungary and Russia that he was bent on destroying Turkey and this helped Bismarck's design of re-creating the Three Emperors' League in 1881. He then proceeded to alienate France by making public the promise made by Salisbury that England would support a French occupation of Tunis, an action which also alienated Italy who also had designs on Tunis. In addition, he let it be known that he still disliked the assumption of Anglo-French dual control of the Egyptian government's finances in 1879.

But, before Egypt could claim his attention, the Afghans and the Boers claimed it almost immediately. Gladstone's Mid-lothian speeches had led the Boers to expect the immediate restoration of the independence they had signed away in 1877. Instead, the Cabinet reverted to the Carnarvon scheme of federation and, impatient of the delay, the Transvaal Boers began to fight for what Gladstone appeared to have promised but had failed to give. British forces were defeated first at Laing's Nek and then, decisively, on Majuba Hill where the British commander, Sir George Colley, was killed. Gladstone refused to consider the issue of prestige: after the Convention of Pretoria in August 1881 the Transvaal became the independent South African Republic, and by 1883 it had as its president the leader of their successful revolt, Paul Kruger. British 'suzerainty' was reaffirmed in 1881; but a supplementary London Convention of 1884 omitted the word.

On a variety of counts, Gladstone was open to criticism here. He had committed himself to the Boer side when speaking as a stump-orator without the responsibilities either of government or party leadership; he had failed to act promptly in accordance with his demagogically offered pledges; his granting of independence (on insufficiently precise legal terms) immediately after a British defeat encouraged the Boers in general, and Kruger in particular, to feel that they had indeed been wronged, but that they were well able to challenge the British by the use of force. Even if it be conceded that Gladstone was right to restore the Boers' independence when it came to the point after Majuba, his conduct up to that point had been either foolish or erratic, so that if he did what was right he did it in the worst possible way. He also made it all too easy for patriotic minds to assert that whereas Disraeli had stood for the greatness of Empire, Gladstone stood for its humiliation.

In July 1880, a British force had been heavily defeated by Afghan rebels outside Kandahar and the remainder of the British were besieged in the city until relieved by yet another heroic march and consequent victory by General Roberts. But just as the defeat at Majuba was followed by a diplomatic and territorial retreat, so also was victory over the Afghans at Maiwand. The British made no further attempt to install a resident in Kabul and merely contented themselves with a military defence treaty with Afghanistan and control of its foreign policy, both being sweetened by a subsidy.

Over Egypt, however, for reasons which made complete sense only to himself, he pursued a totally different policy. A nationalist revolt under Arabi Pasha led, in June 1882, to riots in Alexandria and the death of fifty Europeans followed by the mounting of guns by Arabi on the forts protecting Alexandria as a threat to the British Navy; and Gladstone at once intervened.

The factor which Gladstone decided to use to justify intervention against Arabi was Arabi's expressed intention to repudiate Egypt's huge debt to European bondholders (mainly British and French). He also adopted the line that Arabi was aiming to establish a dictatorship in Egypt. He tried to secure concerted action by Europe, perhaps by putting pressure on the Sultan of Turkey, which still had rights of suzerainty over Egypt. Nobody was prepared to act, not even the French whose government at the last minute withdrew their fleet from Alexandria because of an unwillingness, for fear of what Bismarck might do behind their back in Europe, to allow their forces to be simultaneously engaged in Egypt as well as in Algeria and Tunis. Accordingly, the British acted unilaterally, though Gladstone kept pretending to himself and to everybody else that action was being taken on behalf of the European concert and in the interests of the sanctity of legal contracts and freedom from arbitrary government. Arabi Pasha's force was annihilated by Sir Garnet Wolseley at Tel-el-Kebir in September 1882 and the British were masters of Egypt. Not unreasonably, John Bright declared that all this was worse than Disraeli, and resigned from the Cabinet.

Despite an initial burst of almost jingoistic excitement, Gladstone did his best to put as unpatriotic an appearance as possible on this achievement. A circular was sent to the powers promising that the British would withdraw from Egypt as soon as law and order had been established. Moreover, like the squabble with the Turks over Greece and Montenegro a year earlier, British intervention in Egypt further alienated the Continental powers. The French were particularly incensed since, although they knew they could not acquire Egypt, they did not want the British to occupy it. In order to reform Egyptian finances and protect the interests of foreign bondholders, a task which Lord Cromer, head of the financial house of Baring, undertook with great skill, England had to secure European cooperation through the formation of an international commission (though not until 1885). On this commission, both France and Russia were usually uncooperative and this forced the British to rely on the uncertain support of Germany; and Bismarck went out of his way during most of Gladstone's second term as prime minister to be exceptionally amiable to the French. The events in Egypt in 1882 therefore bedevilled Anglo-French, and to a certain extent Anglo-German, relations for the next twenty years. The first consequence of this situation was that the British acted as helpless onlookers while Bismarck seized control of south-west Africa, Togoland and the Cameroons and also New Guinea.[1] These developments helped to show up the contrast between England's dominating position among the great powers when Disraeli attended the Congress of Berlin and its humiliating isolation now Gladstone was at the helm.

[1] See p. 360.

Far worse for Gladstone was that the occupation of Egypt led to involvement in the Sudan, which had long been misgoverned by the Egyptians. Under their leader, the Mahdi, the Sudanese revolted and, in November 1883, almost completely destroyed an Egyptian army of 10,000 men commanded by an English officer, Colonel Hicks, sent out by Cairo to reconquer the Sudan. With that remarkable capacity he had for producing resounding phrases to provide the loftiest moral justification for whatever policy he wished to pursue at any given moment, Gladstone, who had described the Egyptian nationalist Arabi Pasha as 'one of the greatest villains alive', decided that the Sudanese ought properly to be considered as 'struggling rightly to be free'. If this was how he saw it, he and his foreign secretary, Granville, should have vetoed the sending of Hicks into the Sudan in the first place. Now, Gladstone refused to take any action to punish the Mahdi, and decided that the most that should be done was to send such help as was necessary to enable the Egyptian garrisons to evacuate the Sudan. For reasons which baffled both contemporaries and posterity the government decided in January 1884, and Gladstone agreed, that General Charles Gordon be sent to report on the best method of extricating the Egyptian forces garrisoning the Sudan.

Gordon's previous career had included taking part in the capture of Peking in 1860, in winning over thirty battles on behalf of the Chinese government against the Taiping rebellion from 1863 to 1865, and two periods of service in the Sudan in the 1870s, restoring order and suppressing the slave trade there. The most melodramatic kind of evangelical military crusader, he was as invincibly convinced of his mission to civilize the Sudan as Gladstone was that the Almighty required a withdrawal from it. Accordingly, Gordon went first to Cairo, where he got Lord Cromer, with the foolish concurrence of Granville, to appoint him governor-general of the Sudan. Proceeding thence to Khartoum, where he arrived in February 1884, he then began at once to demand reinforcements to enable him to crush the Mahdi. Gordon remained convinced, as the Mahdi's forces began to move towards Khartoum, that Gladstone would be forced to reverse his declared policy. At home, public opinion regarded Gordon as a national hero; and Gladstone's refusal, throughout the summer, either to send reinforcements to Khartoum or to order Gordon's recall caused him to become almost universally unpopular. Not until August did Gladstone reluctantly authorize the dispatch of an expedition to relieve Gordon. It did not make contact with Khartoum until 28 January 1885, two days after Gordon had been killed and the town taken by the Mahdists. The Queen put the blame firmly and almost publicly on Gladstone and the music halls pronounced that the G.O.M. (Grand Old Man) had become the M.O.G. (Murderer of Gordon). Miserably, Gladstone decided to tell the Commons that it was necessary after all that the Mahdi be crushed; but, even so, the government survived a censure vote by a mere 14 votes and would probably have resigned, had not Gladstone, almost in isolation, held out against doing so.

Salvation came from the East. Russian forces probed their way into the Afghan border village of Penjdeh at the end of March 1885, and this was at once regarded by the public as the first step in a Russian advance towards India; and, by Gladstone, as a heaven-sent excuse for reviving his policy of leaving the Mahdi in possession of the Sudan. He secured a vote of £11 million from the Commons to deal with the 'wanton aggression' of the Russians and announced that the forces in the Sudan must be made available to meet the greater danger in Asia. The Russians agreed to negotiate and eventually, though they in fact kept Penjdeh, agreed to limit their advances towards both Persia and Afghanistan. This agreement, however, took place after the fall of Gladstone's second ministry, so that what was still uppermost in the public mind was not only that Gladstone had 'murdered' Gordon but that he had refused to avenge that murder by crushing the Mahdi.

There is little to be said in favour of Gladstone's handling of foreign and colonial affairs from 1880 to 1885. However laudable his basic intentions and fundamental principles – and they were on the whole a good deal more laudable than

Disraeli's – his attempts to apply them in the diplomatically and psychologically unpleasant world of the 1880s were marked by almost continuous incompetence, administrative inefficiency and at times almost wilful self-deception. It was impossible to take seriously a prime minister who thought Arabi a villain but the Mahdi a patriot; who abandoned the Transvaal but occupied Egypt; who proclaimed the virtues of a Concert of Europe that Bismarck had wrecked in the 1860s and whose restoration it was a major object of his policy to prevent; who had proclaimed in 1878 that Russia had been doing God's work but in 1885 that it was doing the Devil's. And when, to all this, was added Gladstone's apparent condonation of Home Rule violence in Ireland it is easy to see how, given the contrast with Disraeli, the Conservative party seemed the only safe refuge for the true patriot. Henceforth, too, Gladstonian Liberalism and Liberal Radicalism would be permanently associated with pacifism, internationalism and high moral attitudes; and would be forever faced with the insoluble conflicts between such attitudes and the facts of the increasingly competitive world of international rivalries, and between those (such as Rosebery, and later Grey) who sought to adjust to that world and those (such as John Morley, Campbell-Bannerman and the young Lloyd George) who regarded it as 'immoral' to do so. And, given the elusive characters of Disraeli's successors, Salisbury and Balfour, the outcome was that the popular heroes of the last two decades of the Queen's reign were soldiers, like Garnet Wolseley, Gordon and Roberts, whose deeds had 'won the Empire', or equivocal apostles of Anglo-Saxon supremacy like Joseph Chamberlain and Cecil Rhodes. That this Imperialist attitude claimed to descend from Disraeli was only in part the result of Disraeli's record; it was equally a natural reaction against the reckless and offensive vehemence of Gladstone's oratorical attacks on 'Beaconsfieldism' and the result of his unmanageable combination of high but unattainable moral principle with bungling incompetence and an inconsistency which, though it was not hypocritical, bore all the outward signs of being so.

Though Gladstone indeed believed 'the sentiment of

Empire was innate in every Briton', and though, whereas Disraeli merely acquired Cyprus, Gladstone acquired Egypt, the simple view prevailed: under Disraeli and the Conservatives England had been great; under Gladstone England had been humiliated.

12 · *Cloud in the West*

Ireland! Ireland! That cloud in the West! That
coming storm! That minister of God's retribu-
tion upon cruel, inveterate and but half-atoned
injustice! Ireland forces upon us those great
social and great religious questions. God grant
that we may have courage to look them in the
face!

GLADSTONE, 1845

What is this horrid government going to do
with Ireland? I don't exactly wish they'd blow
up Mr Gladstone but if a mad bull would chivy
him there and he would never come back any
more, I should not be sorry.

THEOBALD PONTIFEX
(Samuel Butler, *Way of All Flesh*, Ch. 86)

In unforgettable words Gladstone declared, when it became
clear in 1868 that he was to become prime minister, 'My mission
is to pacify Ireland.' He had already acknowledged to John
Bright that an attempt to fulfil this 'mission' might 'lead the
Liberal party to martyrdom';[1] but he had informed his sister
that he would proceed with his task as an agent of 'the God of
truth and justice'. This 'mission' of Gladstone's was to rend and
distort the politics of England for most of the next thirty years
and his failure to carry it out – a failure perhaps made inevitable
by the intemperate, holier-than-thou methods he adopted –
was a disaster. Had he employed the rapier of political subtlety
he might possibly have succeeded, but given that his favourite

[1] See Philip Magnus, *Gladstone* (London, Murray, 1954), p. 191, but
curiously, see also ibid., p. 196 on this question of 'martyrdom'.

political device was to try to bludgeon friend and foe alike into an admission that he alone was righteous, he was indeed justified in speaking of 'martyrdom' even before his 'mission' had begun. The spectacle of a political leader who claimed, in his public utterances, to have a monopoly of moral conviction, was bound to generate an intense and eventually insurmountable hostility.

He was right to sense that only through the maximum exercise of crusading zeal could anyone persuade an English legislature to do anything to Ireland's advantage; and he was correct also in believing that nobody but he was prepared to attempt this impossible task. It would be difficult to imagine any people with whom the average Englishman in any decade of the Victorian period was more likely to be totally unsympathetic than the Irish. They were poor; they married young; they had large families; they lived on potatoes; many of them were undesirable immigrants in the slum districts of Liverpool and London; and, save in the predominantly Presbyterian north, they were Roman Catholics[1] and therefore 'priest-ridden'. Every one of these characteristics was a violation of the principal tenets of Victorian morality. If they were poor it was because they were shiftless; to marry young and produce large families contravened the English Victorian practice of late marriages preceded, where necessary, by secret recourse to prostitutes or the seduction of servant girls and accompanied (in theory at any rate) by abstention from breeding above one's income whenever a high infant mortality rate failed to compensate, in its own gruesome fashion, for the absence of birth-control technique. To live on potatoes was equally sinful, because potatoes were too easy to cultivate and therefore an encouragement to idleness, and sufficient explanation of why potato blight had led to the horrors of the Great Famine in the 1840s. To be a source from which immigrants crowded into the poorest quarters of the largest English cities, bringing with them their lax and alien habits and their false religion, was a further occasion for disapproval among all classes, while their

---

[1] 'Their religion,' says a children's primer of the mid century, 'is the Roman Catholic, which teaches them many wrong things.'

ingrained Catholicism singled them out among all the non-English nationalities in the United Kingdom as quite exceptionally contumacious. Worst of all, perhaps, was the circumstance that most of the Irish tenants were so poor and had holdings so unproductive that they were often unable to pay their rents, and thus cheated their absentee English landlords of their rights. There were so many tenants too, that intelligent landlords saw salvation only in reducing their number by evicting them and destroying their miserable shacks; but this led to agrarian outrages and the formation of 'terrorist' organizations, of which the latest representatives were the Fenians of the years 1865–7, who caused disturbances in Chester and Manchester, and at Clerkenwell in London. It was, in fact, Fenian violence, for all that it lacked universal support in Ireland, which triggered off Gladstone's decision to begin his mission forthwith.

At once there were difficulties. He had already, before the 1868 election, carried a resolution in the Commons, supported by the whole Palmerstonian Whig–Liberal–Radical coalition, in favour of the disestablishment of the Anglican Church in Ireland and the Conservatives had hopes that Gladstone's commitment in this direction would rally Anglican voters to the Conservative cause. But it effectively rallied the Radicals and Nonconformists to the Liberal cause, since disestablishment of the Church had been in the Radical programme in the 1830s.[1] Indeed, Matthew Arnold firmly asserted in 1869, 'The actual power by virtue of which the Liberal party . . . is now trying to disestablish the Irish Church, is not the power of reason and justice, it is the power of the Nonconformists' antipathy to Church establishments.' It was, he said, an aim pursued 'in view of a certain stock-notion or fetish, of the Nonconformists'.[2] He was provoked to this view because there was no provision to use the confiscated endowments of the Anglican Church in Ireland (about £16 million) for the assistance of the Roman Catholic Church, the national church for most of the Irish;

[1] See p. 66.
[2] *Culture and Anarchy*, ed. J. Dover Wilson (Cambridge, C.U.P., 1961 reprint), pp. 167–8.

indeed the Maynooth Grant[1] and the state grant to the Presbyterians were simultaneously abolished. That portion of the wealth of the churches in Ireland which was not used to compensate incumbents and curates went to Irish education, to the relief of distress and to sundry other secular purposes. This was to implement the pure Nonconformist–Radical doctrine of no state support for any religious organization and to raise, once again, the possibility of the disestablishment of England's own National Church at the behest of the Irish Nationalists, Welshmen, Scotsmen and fringe-Radicals who were increasingly providing the votes that sent Liberals to Westminster. The Lords, on this issue, as later, took the Conservative (and, as things were, the 'respectable' English) view, and contested the bill strongly; it was not only a Conservative, but a respectable and autocratic Whig view too. Whig peers and Whigs in general (who felt themselves under-represented in Gladstone's government) opposed disestablishment hardly less in 1868 than in 1834 and 1838. The Lords eventually gave way largely as a result of energetic efforts by the Queen to avert a head-on constitutional clash. She did not like what this 'dreadful old man' was doing and her sympathy for Irish extremists had been reduced still further by the fact that a Fenian had shot her second son, Prince Alfred, in the ribs when visiting Australia in the spring of 1868; but she was anxious to avoid serious damage to the English political system. The bill became law in 1869.

Matthew Arnold was thus correct that on this, as on almost all other Irish issues in the following half-century, political factors in England, Scotland and Wales, and not the condition of Ireland, were the ones that counted. Not least among them at this stage was the apparent hypocrisy and demagogy of Gladstone's own position. Time and again in his career, ever since the 1830s, he had opposed disestablishment and disendowment; and now he was (as he admitted to himself) pursuing an entirely contrary policy. To the devoted few, he was a noble character doing what was right for Ireland; to the uncharitable many he was indulging in vote-catching, and

[1] See p. 73.

bowing down to the 'fetishes' of the least respectable elements in the now enlarged electorate. Disraeli summed it up precisely, even if the precision was purely rhetorical: 'We have legalized confiscation, we have consecrated sacrilege, we have condoned treason, we have destroyed Churches.'

Gladstone next turned to piloting through the Irish Land Act of 1870. This extended the system already existing in Ulster by which a tenant was to be compensated for 'unjust' eviction and for any improvements he had made to his holding. It did not exclude eviction for non-payment of rent and thus gave no protection either against rack-renting or against the fact that, when agricultural depression set in in 1875, many tenants found it impossible to pay their rents. Provisions of the act protecting tenants against 'exorbitant' rents, by appeal to the courts, proved of little use, as did the provision of facilities for advancing loans to tenants wishing to purchase their holdings.

The bill produced more dissent in the government than either the Commons or the Lords, both of which passed it without difficulty. While Gladstone's colleagues tended to oppose the bill on principle, Commons and Lords by and large supported it because it was realized that it would make very little difference in practice and penalize only the worst of the landlords. Those who understood the Irish peasants' problem best warned Gladstone of the act's inadequacy, but for the moment he believed he had got as much out of Parliament as was practicable and that Irish agrarian violence was now certain to decrease.

The trouble Gladstone had with his Cabinet was vocalized with his usual acerbity by Robert Lowe. Compensation for disturbance when a tenant was evicted was 'a precedent under which any amount of spoliation might as far as principle goes be justified, the fining of one class for the benefit of another and the forcing of new terms into existing contracts'. Lowe's attitude in this reflected the same purity of *laissez-faire* Liberal doctrine that had made him oppose Reform in 1866.[1] The Duke of Argyll took a lot of persuading before he could be made to

[1] See p. 157.

dissent from Lowe's opinion; and other Whigs in the Commons also made difficulties on the similar ground that interference with the unfettered rights of landlords in Ireland would lead eventually to a like interference with landlords' rights elsewhere in the United Kingdom. Palmerston, himself an Irish landlord, had earlier on summed it up pithily: 'Tenant's right is landlord's wrong.'

In the end, nearly everybody was right except Gladstone. The act did establish as a principle that the rights of landlords were not absolute. The act did prove completely inadequate; it did not prevent eviction and the perhaps economically desirable, though in the short run socially brutal, process of consolidation of their estates by the landlords, and it contributed nothing whatever to the pacification of Ireland. Agrarian crime and violence continued to increase and by acts of 1870 and 1871 habeas corpus was virtually suspended in Ireland. The outcome was that Gladstone had failed on all counts. He had in the first place appeared to condone Irish violence by responding to Fenian extremism in passing discriminatory acts against the Church and the landlords; yet his actions had not eliminated that violence but seemed rather to have encouraged it, and in the end he had to resort to repression in Ireland. Final evidence that Gladstone had done nothing to pacify Ireland was the succession of victories at by-elections in Ireland by candidates advocating Home Rule for Ireland.

Undeterred, as always, by failure, or indeed by consideration of the relevance of his proposals to the realities of the situation he was handling, Gladstone turned in 1873 to the problem of higher education for Irish Catholics. Since they refused to attend the existing Irish universities, the Queen's Colleges at Cork and Belfast and Trinity College, Dublin, Gladstone proposed the establishment of a University of Dublin which Roman Catholics and Protestants could attend on equal terms, though at the sacrifice of some of the revenue of Trinity College, Dublin, a specifically 'Protestant' foundation. More objectionable still, the new university would teach no theology, moral philosophy or modern history, on the grounds that these subjects would upset religious susceptibilities; and any teacher in any other subject who offended students' religious feelings would be liable to dismissal.

The prospects that such an institution could work were remote. The Roman hierarchy in Ireland wanted a purely Roman Catholic university; Cardinal-Archbishop Manning of Westminster tried to persuade them to approve Gladstone's plan, but the Irish bishops knew their flock (and their problems) better than Manning and, given that it would offend Protestants without in the least placating Catholics, the bill was rejected on second reading by three votes. Gladstone promptly announced that his government would resign but not ask for a dissolution. Disraeli refused to take office and thus forced Gladstone back to continue through eleven more confused and muddled months of office, from which he was swept away by the election of February 1874, despite holding out to the voters the promise of a total abolition of income tax. His Irish policy, so objectionable in principle and so ineffective in practice, combined with his domestic reforms (including the introduction of the ballot in 1872) and his 'weakness' in foreign affairs had upset the aristocracy, the gentry and the clergy; and Gladstone had even upset the masses whom he claimed to represent as against the classes, by supporting a proposal of Robert Lowe that a tax should be placed on matches. Yet the most numerous victims of the Disraelian triumph were the more aristocratic and Whiggish of the Liberal candidates. And this perhaps helps to explain why, though Gladstone announced his retirement from the leadership, he was, as early as 1876, already once more seeking to rouse the masses against the classes. The latter, including the Whigs, had already very little liking for him by 1874.

An ominous result of the 1874 elections, underlining Gladstone's Irish failure, was that the new Parliament contained, under the leadership of Isaac Butt, 58 Irish M.P.s elected to support the cause of 'Home Rule', a euphemism introduced by Butt as likely to be less offensive to English ears than the reality it expressed: a demand for the Repeal of the Act of Union of 1800. Butt annually introduced a Home Rule Bill during Disraeli's premiership, but it was invariably tossed aside, with never more than a handful of English M.P.s giving it their votes. A pattern later to become familiar in all parts of the world was duly established: the search for political liberation through ordinary constitutional means being rebuffed, moderate men were replaced by more uncompromising leaders. Butt resigned the leadership of the Home Rulers in 1878 under pressure from those who felt that the attempt to act properly through English parliamentary channels was leading nowhere. He was replaced by Charles Stewart Parnell who, already by 1877, had begun to show his passionate skill at disciplining the Irish groups into the concerted tactic of deliberately obstructing the whole business of the Commons and thus periodically paralysing it.

The obstructionism of the Irish M.P.s is one of the several reasons for the absence of much notable legislation in the last years of Disraeli's 1874–80 government. Worse still, what little relief had been provided by the 1870 Land Act ceased to be effective after 1875. With tenants unable to pay rents because of the great fall in agricultural prices, landlord–tenant relations were further embittered. In 1879, Parnell became president of the Irish Land League with four prominent Fenians, among them Michael Davitt, who had already launched an Irish agrarian revolt and who was to be an M.P. from 1880 to 1899. Parnell took over the presidency of the Land League partly to control its excesses (in this, again foreshadowing the pattern of later events in other lands, he largely failed), partly to keep the leadership of the Irish movement in his own hands, and partly in order to use it as a weapon against government at Westminster. Though careful not himself to advocate violence, Parnell advised all members of the Land League to pay no rent at all if landlords refused to accept what tenants chose to regard as a 'fair rent'. Evictions, and all their subsequent misery, were added to the already heavy burden of impoverishment under which the Irish peasantry were suffering.[1]

Parnell demanded that any tenant who bid for a farm from which his neighbour had been evicted was to be shunned as a

[1] See R. C. K. Ensor, *England 1870–1914* (London, O.U.P., 1936), p. 72 footnote.

leper (the fact that the first victim of this tactic was a certain Captain Boycott gave the English language a more dramatic substitute for the phrase 'to send to Coventry'). Violence increased rapidly. Assaults by night on landlords' cattle, ricks and homes became commonplace, all of them, it was gruesomely alleged, the work of 'Captain Moonlight'. Parnell and other members of the Land League were charged with conspiracy at the end of 1880 and saved only by the failure of the jury to agree. W. E. Forster, now Irish secretary in Gladstone's second ministry, insisted on introducing a new Coercion Bill for Ireland, against the wishes both of the prime minister and of John Bright. Parnell replied with a renewed campaign of parliamentary obstruction so effective that the bill did not get through the Commons for a month. When made law in March 1881 it gave the authorities in Ireland complete powers of arbitrary arrest, all rights of habeas corpus being suspended. The final session of the Commons on the bill lasted for 41 hours and was 'final' only because the Speaker took the initiative of putting the question from the chair on his own personal responsibility. After this, Gladstone duly introduced measures by which a closure motion could be put to terminate a Commons debate. This amounted to a breach in the hitherto unrestricted freedom of speech of M.P.s and it has remained ever since as one of the enduring consequences of the Irish Question.

Gladstone had reluctantly accepted the principle of coercion because he was determinedly working on a new Land Act, which he introduced, without consultation with Parnell, in April 1881. He had already failed at a first attempt to secure immediate relief for the Irish tenant by a bill to compel landlords to compensate evicted tenants. It had passed the Commons only with difficulty and had been overwhelmingly rejected in the Lords in August 1880. It was a measure of how deeply the Whigs were outraged that almost all the Whigs in the Lords voted with the Conservatives. The Second Land Act of 1881 provided Irish tenants with fair rents, fixity of tenure and the freedom to sell their holdings. Judicial tribunals would be set up to review rents; no tenant could be evicted so long as he paid the rent fixed by the tribunal. Despite ingenious and complicated efforts by Gladstone to disguise the new proposals as mere amendments to the act of 1870, these drastic incursions upon the rights of landlords were too much for the great Whig grandee, the Duke of Argyll, who resigned from the Cabinet in protest in May 1881; an event which together with the Whig rebellion over the Compensation Bill of 1880 presaged the mass Whig defections of 1886. Over the Land Act itself, however, the Whig peers contented themselves with abstaining in the division in the Lords, feeling compelled to agree that the state of Ireland was such that, without the act, the prospects of restoring law and order were almost nil. But, a leading Whig peer gloomily observed, 'the tendency of the extreme section of the Liberal party is to buy the support of the masses by distributing among them the property of their political opponents and it is towards a social rather than a political revolution that we are tending', adding that the precedent established in Ireland 'is almost sure to be applied elsewhere'.[1]

At the Irish end of the political spectrum, Land League violence continued, if only on the grounds that the 1881 act did nothing for the 100,000 Irish tenants, who, since they were heavily in arrears with their rents, were still liable to eviction. Parnell played a skilful role: he attacked the bill's limitations, persuaded the majority of Irish Nationalist M.P.s to oppose it, but helped to ensure it was not emasculated in committee. He then got himself suspended from the Commons as soon as the bill was through and continued to urge tenants to boycott the Land Courts (which in due course were to reduce rents by something like a fifth). The Land League still argued that no rent whatever should be paid by Irishmen to foreign, English, landlords and that as violence had produced some concessions from Westminster, more violence would result in more concessions. Gladstone's wrath was roused: 'If,' he declared at a public meeting in Leeds in October 1881, 'there is still to be fought a final conflict in Ireland between law on one side and sheer lawlessness on the other . . . then . . . the resources of

[1] Quoted in Donald Southgate, *Passing of the Whigs* (London, Macmillan, 1962), p. 376.

civilization are not yet exhausted.' Parnell's retort was to describe Gladstone as a 'masquerading knight errant' who had at last 'thrown off the mask' and shown himself ready 'to carry fire and sword' into the homes of the Irish people. A day later, Parnell was arrested under the Coercion Act and imprisoned in Kilmainham jail. The Land League was declared an illegal organization, and its other leaders imprisoned also. The result was a dramatic increase in violence in Ireland and every likelihood that leadership of the peasantry would pass into the hands of the most extreme of the secret societies.

The whole situation was the prototype of the dilemmas which were to face the English in so many of their overseas possessions in the half century after 1919. To begin with, a failure to listen to reasonable men before the situation got out of hand (as the Commons had failed to listen to Isaac Butt in the 1870s); then, as social and economic order broke down, a harassed, hurried attempt to appease the unappeasable by inadequate concessions combined with an equally hopeless attempt to maintain law and order by a suspension of civil liberty which merely added to lawlessness, and at the same time deprived the rebellious movement of the restraining control of its acknowledged political leaders through whom alone a settlement could be reached. The most obvious lesson to be drawn from the Irish problem of the 1880s is that the English learned nothing from it.

Ultimately, however, this result was to some extent Parnell's fault, since he who seemed likely in a few years to be the obvious first prime minister of a self-governing Ireland was to end by destroying both himself and the party he led – a procedure which those such as Nehru, Makarios and Nkrumah, for instance, to whom he was otherwise an archetype, were destined not to imitate for the benefit of English predominance. Of all rebels against established authority, Parnell was potentially the most dangerous and the least politically corruptible. A Protestant landlord from Wicklow and a Cambridge man, he had little in common with the Irish Catholic peasantry he led, but too much in common with the aristocratic English parliamentarians he opposed to be susceptible to that process of slow assimilation into their *mores* which regularly tames the lowly or alien-born rebel.[1] Deep psychological factors arising from his devotion to his American mother and his dislike of his father gave him a scalding contempt for the English upper class, and an aloof and coldly intelligent arrogance which he set aside only in his ardent private life as the lover of Kitty, wife of the Irish M.P. Captain O'Shea. It was his concern for Kitty O'Shea, whose child by Parnell had recently died, as well as for the maintenance of his political leadership of the Irish, that made him the readier to come to terms with the government in order to secure his release from Kilmainham.

Through the instrumentality of Joseph Chamberlain, who saw clearly enough that coercion was not the answer to the Irish problem, and the Irish M.P.s, Justin McCarthy and Captain O'Shea, Kitty's husband, Gladstone's government agreed to Parnell's release from prison on condition that he supported the Land Act and used his influence to calm down Irish violence; in return, the government would introduce an Arrears Bill extending the benefits of the 1881 act to peasants whose rents were in arrears. This 'Kilmainham Treaty' of April 1882 seemed yet again to imply that Irish violence had got results, and the Irish secretary, W. E. Forster, who had been personally responsible for the Coercion Act, resigned in protest. It was yet again the classic dilemma; how could a government inspire confidence if, after proscribing political opponents as criminals and rebels, it nevertheless negotiated with them?

Forster was replaced as Irish secretary by Gladstone's young nephew by marriage, Lord Frederick Cavendish. Lord Frederick was stabbed to death within twenty-four hours of reaching Ireland, when endeavouring in vain in Phoenix Park, Dublin, to defend a government official, T. H. Burke, from death at the hands of members of an Irish organization known as 'The Invincibles'. The effect of this calamity was to lower still further the government's shaky reputation, and in particu-

---

[1] One could here mention such trade union M.P.s of the early twentieth century as John Burns and J. H. Thomas and later personalities such as Herbert Morrison. More recent examples still will readily spring to the reader's mind.

lar to cause some revulsion, which Arthur Balfour strenuously encouraged in the Commons, against the virtual alliance between the Irish Nationalists and the Liberal party created by the Kilmainham Treaty. It was all too easy to represent it as an unscrupulous bid by Gladstone for the Irish vote, and in the light of Lord Frederick's murder, to treat Parnell's undertaking to curb Irish violence as worthless. It also ensured the stormiest possible passage for the Arrears Bill, when it was introduced in May 1882, providing for the cancellation of all arrears where tenants occupying land worth less than £30 a year were unable to pay.

With the Arrears Act on the statute book by August 1882, and opinion in England still strongly anti-Irish, Parnell chose for the time being to play a waiting game. The increasing impatience of the Whigs, who detested Gladstone's Irish policy, and of the Radicals, particularly Joseph Chamberlain, who resented Gladstone's inattention to social reforms, meant that the Liberal party was rapidly losing such cohesion as it had ever had, and, by its shambling imperial and foreign policy, rapidly losing public favour. Out of this Liberal weakness, Parnell hoped to make suitable capital at the next general election.

This indeed came to pass. The government was, by 1885, demoralized by its failures, torn by internal tensions, and held together by little more than the personality of the leader whose policies and actions had divided it; and who had so divided it while dominating it that he had no obvious heir-apparent despite the fact that in 1885 he was already seventy-six.

The small group of Radicals on the government side (Joseph Chamberlain and Sir Charles Dilke were the only cabinet ministers who could be considered Radical) were increasingly becoming so infuriated by Gladstone's bungling involvement in foreign affairs and in Ireland and the paucity of social reforms, that they had already begun to make speeches so oratorically Radical in content as still further to antagonize the Whigs, to whom Gladstone had given most of the places in his Cabinet but whose principles he had persistently forced them to abandon not only in Ireland but elsewhere in the United Kingdom. The only reason that Whigs continued to serve

Gladstone was that without him Liberalism would become more radical; the only reason the Radicals stayed with him was that he was still, despite his declining powers and the diminishing number of facts to support the notion, regarded by and large as 'The People's William.' The Married Women's Property Act of 1882, the Corrupt Practices Act of 1883, the Third Reform Bill of 1884 and the consequent Redistribution Act of 1885 largely made up the sum of the government's domestic legislation and they weighed little enough in the balance against the unsolved Irish question and the muddle in South Africa, Egypt and above all the Sudan.

In the spring of 1885, the Cabinet began to quarrel once more over whether or not to renew the Coercion Act of 1882. Chamberlain and Dilke wanted coercion dropped and a system of elected county councils in Ireland. Almost all the Whigs in the Cabinet opposed the plan; and when Gladstone proposed instead to renew most of the clauses of the Coercion Act but to introduce a scheme of state land purchase in Ireland, Chamberlain and Dilke were prevented from resigning only by the government's unexpected defeat by 12 votes over the budget in June – largely as a result of heavy Liberal abstentions.

The new electoral registers not yet being ready, there could be no general election for several months to come and accordingly, when Gladstone resigned, Lord Salisbury, at the head of yet another minority Conservative government, became prime minister for the first time. For Gladstone the problem now was that he had made up his mind that the Irish, like the Italians, the Bulgarians, the Afghans, the Zulus and the Sudanese (though not, of course, the Egyptians), were a people rightly struggling to be free and that Parnell's demand for Home Rule ought to be conceded. For one thing, it would end that Irish obstructionism at Westminster which explained, in part, the lack of major social reform since 1877. By the end of the summer Gladstone therefore became obsessed by the last and most disruptive of these various 'missions' in his political career: the achievement of Irish Home Rule. He had failed to 'pacify' the Irish; instead, he would give them that status of free men through which alone they could achieve the dignity, self-respect and moral responsibility they appeared so incapable of displaying so long as their destinies were wholly decided for them at Westminster.

In the light of subsequent history, Gladstone's decision was no more than a belated display of blinding common sense. The union of 1800, which had destroyed the separate Irish Parliament, had been forced through against the wishes both of the Irish Catholics and of the 'Protestant ascendancy' in Ireland. The English record in Ireland both before 1800 and after might be said to render mythological in advance the spate of arguments that were already beginning to be poured forth from high political and academic circles about the special fitness of 'the Anglo-Saxon race' to govern other peoples for their own good. By 1885, Gladstone had reached the conclusion that Mazzini had reached much earlier: that no good ever ensued either to rulers or ruled when one nation dominated another. But the problem was how Gladstone's new 'mission' could be fulfilled. It must not, he decided, become a 'party' issue. He declined, as the election approached, to give any public indication of his new intention, because it would lay him open to the charge of deliberately angling for the Irish vote, and would almost certainly split the Liberal party. The hostility he had aroused by Majuba, Kilmainham, Phoenix Park and Khartoum was such that he realized, correctly, that, if he did appeal to the country as a Home Ruler, so much bitterness would be aroused against both himself and against Home Rule that both would almost certainly be defeated. 'The production at this time of a plan by me,' he told Lord Rosebery in November 1885, 'would . . . destroy all reasonable hope of its adoption.'[1] The Whig old guard and the Radical rebels would desert him and reduce the Liberal party to a Gladstonian 'rump'. He was further impelled towards silence by the knowledge that the Conservatives were angling for Parnell's support also. Parnell, aware that the Conservatives were the weaker party, was also prepared to accord them Irish support, since he aimed to be the real victor of the election by securing that the Irish

[1] Magnus, op. cit., pp. 333–4.

Nationalists held the balance between the two major parties. Highmindedly, Gladstone played Parnell's hand for him by refusing to commit himself publicly to Home Rule or even to give the slightest hint of his intentions to his colleagues. In consequence, Parnell advised Irishmen in England to vote Tory; and similar advice was given to them by their Catholic bishops because of Joseph Chamberlain's advocacy of universal free state education.

Thanks almost entirely to the popularity, among the newly enfranchised county voters, of Chamberlain's widely publicized Unauthorized Programme of radical reform, which Gladstone had at no time fully endorsed, the Liberals won 335 seats and the Conservatives only 249. But Parnell was the real winner. His Irish Nationalist party won 86 seats, which exactly equalled the Liberal majority over the Conservatives. Since in the absence of any statement from Gladstone the Parnellites were still in nominal alliance with the Conservatives, Lord Salisbury remained in office.

Gladstone, meanwhile, continued in contemplative isolation. From the meditational depths he dredged up the conclusion that it was Lord Salisbury's duty to pass a Home Rule Bill which he could get on the statute book without difficulty since it would be supported in the Commons by the Gladstonian Liberals and the Irish Nationalists and, as a Conservative measure, would also secure a safe passage through the predominantly Conservative Lords. The result, it was true, would perhaps be to split the Conservative party as well as the Liberal party, but Gladstone was now so far removed from considerations of party that this seemed a matter of little concern compared with the necessity of doing justice to the Irish. Gladstone, therefore, like MacDonald in 1931, devoted more of his energies to consultations (albeit very discreet consultations) with his political opponents rather than his political allies. Lord Salisbury, however, was not prepared to be the second Conservative prime minister of the century to receive a poisoned chalice from the hands of his political opponents. Although there were depths in his character even more obscure than the dimmer areas of Gladstone's, he was aware of

the damage Disraeli had done to Peel in 1846 and the trouble he
had himself caused Disraeli over the 1867 Reform Bill; and he
was aware even more that, just as Chamberlain was waiting his
opportunity to replace Gladstone, the belligerently demagogic
Lord Randolph Churchill would seize without hesitation the
first chance that came his way to replace Salisbury, as yet
merely on trial as prime minister.

Salisbury's political realism was Gladstone's undoing. The
Liberals were in confusion. It was harder now than ever for
their leader to plump for Home Rule; given the abuse Parnell
had heaped on Gladstone and the Liberals in the election
campaign, it would look more than ever like an obstinate, self-
centred old man's determination to get back into power if
(given the state of the parties in December 1885) he did so now.
He even took refuge in obscurities when his son, Herbert, also
a Liberal M.P., endeavoured to rally the party to his father's
side by a series of interviews to the Liberal press indicating that
Gladstone was indeed personally committed to the Home Rule
cause. He did nothing in fact until, after announcing its
intention to preserve the union with Ireland, the government
also indicated that it would proceed to a new Coercion Act.
Gladstone immediately secured the agreement of all his former
cabinet colleagues, except Lord Hartington, that the government be brought down, though on an irrelevant domestic, and
not an Irish, issue. Nevertheless, though the government was
defeated, Hartington and seventeen other Liberals voted with
the Conservatives and over seventy other Liberals abstained.
Though the full Liberal and Irish Nationalist majority over the
government stood at 172, the majority by which it was overthrown was only 79.

Gladstone's state of mind was perfectly illustrated by his
reply to an astonished Sir William Harcourt (Gladstone's
home secretary from 1880–5 and his chancellor of the exchequer in 1886), who asked him, 'Are you prepared to go
forward without either Hartington or Chamberlain?' Gladstone's reply was that he was 'prepared to go forward without
anybody'. It was in Gladstone's view 'one of the great imperial
occasions which call for such resolution'. In this exalted frame

of mind it did not matter that he now had to form a Liberal government to implement a policy for which it had no mandate and for which officially his followers had almost no previous notice; or that he had, by his impulsive behaviour, created exactly the impression he had set out with such earnestness to avoid, namely that he had sold out to the Parnellites merely to be prime minister yet again. Also, in the early months of 1886 English opinion was more hardened than usual against the Irish both because of Parnell's contemptuous speeches and a recurrence of Irish outrages in London.

It is often said that it is difficult not to admire the vigour and indeed exhilaration with which the aged Gladstone flung himself into the battle for Home Rule that now ensued. It could be said with equal justice that it is impossible not to regret the way in which Gladstone's conduct guaranteed that the issue should be dealt with in so inflammatory a manner. Randolph Churchill's gibe that he was 'an old man in a hurry' has much truth in it. Gladstone underestimated the extent to which the normally hostile feeling of the English towards the Irish had been aggravated by the bitterness of Parnell's speeches and the violence of his Irish followers. He may well, in proposing the large degree of autonomy for Ireland contained in the first Home Rule Bill, have unduly antagonized the English by over-estimating the amount of self-government that would satisfy the Irish. He seems to have ignored the certainty that, with the wholesale flight of the Whig peerage from the Liberal side, any bill that survived the struggle in the Commons would be thrown out by the Lords. He convinced himself also that he need make no change in his schemes with a view to keeping Chamberlain in the party. He failed to see that by his deviously passionate tactics he was rousing Irish hopes and English fears to fever pitch on a matter which, more than any other in the century, called for a softening of passions and not their intensification. It was all too easy for Randolph Churchill to lend his oratorical talents to the arousal of Protestant prejudice – Home Rule is Rome Rule; Ulster will fight and Ulster will be right. The simple truth was that, swept along by the undisciplined self-righteousness of a personality which had caused his whole

I

political career to be marred by emotional and intellectual incontinence, Gladstone was trying to prove that politics was the art of the impossible

Yet foolish though he was, and on the grandest possible scale, the other actors on the political stage at this time were, in their less grandiloquent fashion, hardly less foolish. At some stage, and somehow, the liberation of Ireland from rule by Westminster would surely have to come; and in realizing this, Gladstone, for all his mistakes, put himself on a higher moral level than his opponents. Salisbury was open to the charge that, having extended the Conservative hand of friendship to Parnell during the election campaign, he had dropped him as soon as the election was over. The Tories thus opposed Home Rule partly because it might have been politically inconvenient but principally because it was Gladstone who was proposing it. The Whigs, who had swallowed so many of their principles since 1832, refused to stomach Home Rule to a large extent (though again understandably perhaps) because they had been driven far too hard by Gladstone; and Chamberlain likewise opposed Home Rule with something of the arrogance with which Gladstone proposed it, and to a great extent because a Home Rule struggle would defer the adoption by the Liberals of policies advocated by him at the time but soon thereafter replaced in his mind by quite different ones. In these circumstances, Parnell was the only protagonist who had yet to behave with maximum stupidity; and his turn would come in a few years' time. By 1886, however, his greatest blunder had been, not so much that he had advised Irishmen in England to vote Tory in 1885, but that, although what he wanted could be brought about only by an English legislature representing English electors, he had nevertheless treated both Parliament and Englishmen with arrogant and destructive contempt.

In the circumstances it is a tribute to Gladstone's ascendancy that during the sixteen-day debate on the second reading it was evident that most of the Liberal constituency organizations remained loyal to his proposals. But on 8 June 1886 the second reading was defeated by 343 to 313. Over 90 Liberals voted with the Conservatives; and the decisive factor had been the resignation of Joseph Chamberlain from the Cabinet. So far from attempting to conciliate Chamberlain in recognition of his national standing as a Radical leader Gladstone had offered him no more than the minor post of president of the Local Government Board and affected to be delighted when, the details of the proposed Home Rule Bill being presented in cabinet for the first time, Chamberlain, together with Sir George Trevelyan, had at once resigned.

Defeat of the bill merely induced in Gladstone a renewed attack of Midlothianism. He would not resign, but would appeal once more to the 'masses' against the 'classes'. He poured out torrents of words in speeches, letters and telegrams; and his opponents poured out like torrents of invective, the most powerful coming from Randolph Churchill and *The Times*. The result was what Gladstone called 'a drubbing'. In the new House of Commons there were 316 Conservatives and 78 Liberal Unionists (led by Hartington and Chamberlain) as against only 191 Gladstonian Liberals and 81 Irish Nationalists. Lord Salisbury once again became prime minister, this time with an effective majority of 118 since the Liberal Unionists regularly voted on the government side. For the moment, there was no question of a Conservative-Unionist coalition: Chamberlain's attacks on the aristocracy were too bitter and too recent for Salisbury to contemplate having Chamberlain with him in the Cabinet.

The Conservatives had put through Ashbourne's Land Purchase Act for Ireland in 1885, by which tenants could be advanced 80 per cent of the purchase price if they wished to purchase their holdings; and in 1890, Balfour's Land Purchase Act established a central office to deal with all land questions in Ireland, including the settlement of the purchase price of land, and the government took the power to advance the whole price to a would-be peasant proprietor, repayments being spread over 49 years. A Congested Districts Board was also set up to take steps to ease the situation in those areas where the holdings were too small to sustain a multitude of individual holdings. The object of these measures was, it was hoped, to 'Kill Home Rule by Kindness'; but since the policy was accompanied by strict measures of coercion (defined by Salisbury as the start of 'twenty years of resolute government') it was the coercion that attracted most attention. The new Coercion Act of 1887 was the government's response to the 'Plan of Campaign' organized in Ireland (and without Parnell's approval), by which tenants on an estate were to offer what they considered an adequate rent and if the landlord disagreed they were to pay it instead into a campaign fund. The Plan of Campaign was sufficiently successful to provoke more evictions, and the Coercion Act of 1887 authorized the Irish secretary (Salisbury's clever nephew A. J. Balfour) not only to suspend trial by jury but to treat as crimes, in any 'proclaimed' area, a number of actions which were not normally considered criminal. The act was so offensive to Liberals and Irish Nationalists alike that in order to get it passed as quickly as they desired, the government had to alter the rules of the parliamentary game. First it was established that the closure could be applied to a debate on a majority vote, provided the Speaker agreed and 200 members voted for it. In the committee stage, the government introduced the guillotine by which a limit was fixed to the time to be spent in debate on particular clauses. Armed with his new powers, the willowy Balfour proceeded, to the general surprise, to use them rigorously, earning for himself the improbable title of Bloody Balfour. For the next three years there was violence on both sides, with Balfour insisting that, if anything, political offenders in Ireland be treated worse than common criminals. An eviction at Mitchelstown in County Tipperary in the autumn of 1887 led to two men being shot dead by the police, against whom a coroner's jury returned a verdict of wilful murder. Though the verdict was quashed by a higher court, Gladstone's subsequent call, 'remember Mitchelstown', was indeed long remembered.

Simultaneously with the parliamentary struggle over the passage of the Coercion Act, *The Times*, which was vigorously opposed to Home Rule, printed, as the culmination of a series of strong articles under the general heading of 'Parnellism and Crime', the facsimile of a letter, alleged to have been written by Parnell, in which it appeared that he had condoned at least the

murder of Burke in Phoenix Park in 1881. Other facsimile
letters, also alleged to be in Parnell's handwriting, and all
tending to sustain the argument of *The Times* that Parnell and
the Land League had deliberately encouraged and approved
acts of violence by Irish extremists, were also published. Not
only had *The Times* believed the letters genuine: the leading
handwriting expert in the country supported this view.

The obvious course was for Parnell not only to deny the
letters' authenticity in the Commons (which he did) but to sue
The Times for libel; this, to the consternation of many, he was
in no haste to do, for reasons which did not become apparent
until later. Fortunately for Parnell, though most unfortunately
for *The Times*, instead of appointing a select committee of the
Commons to inquire into the matter Salisbury's government
chose to appoint a special judicial commission to investigate,
not merely the authenticity of the letter *The Times* had published, but the whole range of its lengthy accusation that
Parnell and Davitt were associated closely with murder and
arson for the express purpose of achieving the complete separation of Ireland from the United Kingdom.

The commission began to sit in September 1888. Though the
handwriting expert was never allowed to give evidence, the
man from whom an intermediary had bought the letters printed
in facsimile in *The Times* was produced. A shifty character called
Richard Pigott, it became apparent that he had not only forged
at least one of the letters himself but had been paid for doing so;
he had then tried to extract money from the Irish bishops by
warning them that the letters were to be published and indicating that he knew how their authenticity could be disputed.
Crumpling under particularly severe examination by counsel
acting for Parnell, Pigott fled the country and shot himself.

The whole case which *The Times* had made against the Irish
leaders was thus assumed to be totally discredited. This did
more than restore Parnell's reputation; it also revived Liberal
sympathy for him by appearing to reveal the dastardly lengths
to which the opponents of Gladstone and the Home Rule
movement were prepared to go. Combined as this was with
revulsion against the coercive policies of Bloody Balfour, and

with the feeling that, at bottom, all that the opponents of Home Rule were really interested in was to preserve the privileges of selfish landlords, the prospects for Parnell and for Ireland began to look brighter. By the autumn of 1890, lost by-elections and the return of some Liberal Unionists to the Gladstonian fold had reduced the Conservatives' majority from nearly 120 to a mere 70; yet the final report of the judges on *The Times* affair, which had not appeared until nearly twelve months after Pigott's suicide in March 1899, though it had completely exonerated Parnell had by no means exonerated all of his Land League associates from all the charges *The Times* had made against them. Nor had Parnell reacted to his rehabilitation in a way that increased his stature in the eyes of the Commons. At the time of Pigott's exposure he had been greeted in the Commons with a standing ovation from all parties except for the majority of the Conservatives; but Parnell's response had been an icy speech marked by a complete absence of warmth. All the same, Gladstone now declared that unless he or Parnell were removed from the scene, Home Rule was a certainty.

But all this new hope was already imperilled. At the end of 1889, Captain O'Shea at last decided to take notice of the long-lasting infidelities of his wife, Kitty, and filed a suit for divorce against her, naming Parnell as co-respondent. When the case was finally heard in November 1890, O'Shea was granted a decree *nisi* within two days, there being no defence. The vindicated hero who had been too proud to sue *The Times* in 1887 was now suddenly revealed as an adulterer, long engaged in a furtive liaison with the wife of one of his own followers, forever slipping in and out of hotel rooms, or desperately avoiding the discovery of his shameful behaviour by use of the fire escape.[1]

[1] O'Shea's decision to proceed against his wife was so surprising to the large number of M.P.s who had long been aware of the situation that it was subsequently asserted that Chamberlain put O'Shea up to it as part of a deliberate scheme to ruin Parnell. There is apparently no evidence for this charge. O'Shea's reasons are believed to have been more sordid: he held his hand for so long because Kitty was expecting to inherit a large fortune from an aunt. O'Shea took proceedings when he did because, on the death of Kitty's aunt, the inheritance failed to materialize.

Parnell was now to be undone by his extraordinary arrogance. The English code was that if there had to be adultery, it must not lead to scandal by flaunting itself before the public gaze – and that meant, first, that adulterers must not be found out; and second, that if proved adulterous by the courts they were to retire at once from public life. Melbourne and Palmerston had both survived divorce proceedings unscathed, but in 1885 Sir Charles Dilke had not. Melbourne and Palmerston continued their public careers because their private lives were kept out of the public notice. In 1889 Hartington himself was engaged in a liaison with the Duchess of Manchester which was as well known to society as Parnell's with Mrs O'Shea; but Hartington, unlike Parnell or Dilke,[1] continued his political career because the public had no opportunity to probe his private life. Over the O'Shea divorce, however, Parnell seems to have believed that he could defy English social convictions as serenely as he had defied English politicians. At first, he pretended the case was a trumped-up one and then, just as it was due, airily announced that there would be no defence and it would merely be a 'nine day wonder'. In his view, he was answerable to nobody in England, was the acknowledged leader of the Irish National Movement and therefore absolutely nothing was changed except that in due season he was free to marry Kitty O'Shea.[2] *The Times*, naturally, had a field day and (killing two birds with one stone) described the incidents revealed in the divorce court as 'comparable only to the dreary monotony of French middle class vice, over which the scalpel of M. Zola lingers so lovingly'.

Gladstone was taken wholly by surprise. He had always re-fused to listen to 'gossip' about Parnell's private life[3] and at first,

[1] 'The fall of Parnell left Ireland with a dead god instead of a leader and the fall of Dilke left Liberalism without a brain'. G. M. Young, *Portrait of an Age* (London, O.U.P. Paperback, 1960), p. 174.

[2] A less arrogant man would not have left himself wholly undefended so that only the case against him and the animadversions of a hostile judge were made public. A very astute man could probably have proved collusion; but Parnell positively wanted Kitty to be divorced.

[3] Sir George Young's *Portrait of an Age* carries on its title page the Victorian precept, 'Servants talk about People; Gentlefolk discuss

when pressed to condemn Parnell publicly, he very properly declined to do so on the grounds that leadership of a political party gave him no right to act as 'a judge of faith and morals'. But nonconformist Liberals were so manifestly hostile to a continuance of the alliance with Parnell after the divorce that Gladstone was finally prevailed upon to write a letter to his faithful friend, colleague and eventual biographer, John Morley, for Morley to show to Parnell. This intimated that the situation was such that Parnell's continued leadership of the Irish party 'at this present moment' would be disastrous for Ireland and would render Gladstone's own leadership of the Liberals 'almost a nullity', based as it was 'mainly upon the prosecution of the Irish cause'.[1]

The Irish Nationalist M.P.s, however, re-elected Parnell as their leader for the new parliamentary session in November 1890 before Morley was able to place Gladstone's letter before Parnell. To his party, Parnell, as usual, refused either to explain or to apologize; one of his followers said his attitude was as imperious as if it were they and not he who had committed adultery. When thereafter Parnell did read Gladstone's letter, he admitted that Gladstone would have to attack him, but said it was all a 'storm in a teacup' and that he had no intention of retiring even temporarily. Gladstone was so indignant at this reply that he had his letter to Morley sent to the newspapers.

Thus, one more blunder had been committed. Publication of the letter turned a private warning into what looked like the political excommunication of Parnell and a demand either that Parnell retire or that the Irish Nationalists throw him over. Parnell's response was a tempestuous manifesto to the people of Ireland, accusing Gladstone of having all along intended to

---

Things'. Given what there was to say about what some of the best people were often up to, it was a necessary precept in Victorian times.

[1] Parnell also received advice from another quarter (or other quarters?). Thus, 'The advice cabled by Cecil Rhodes from South Africa to Parnell was "Resign – marry – return!"' (Magnus, op. cit., p. 389) and/or '"Retire – marry – return" – so cabled Andrew Carnegie from America to Parnell'. (J. A. Spender, *Empire and Commonwealth, 1886–1935*, London, Cassell, 1936, p. 35.)

betray the Irish. In addition, he spent twelve hectic days of passionate, disorderly debate with the Irish Nationalist M.P.s, insisting that he was their leader and that he could not be displaced, even by them, at the bidding of Gladstone. The issue was made the more heated because to nonconformist disapproval was now added public condemnation of Parnell by the Irish Catholic bishops. The outcome was that a majority of the Irish Nationalists (44 out of 70) deserted Parnell and formed a separate group under Justin McCarthy. Within the next few months, at three Irish by-elections, Parnellite candidates were soundly defeated. Parnell pursued his way relentlessly, with self-destructive energy. He married Kitty O'Shea, a further affront to Catholic opinion, in June 1891, but was dead by early October of the same year. The Irish Nationalist factions continued to execrate each other and this rendered the acceptance of Home Rule by English opinion less likely than ever. At least while Parnell lived a self-governing Ireland had an obvious first prime minister and a united group of experienced parliamentarians, to whom some measure of power could be transferred. Now Ireland had neither. And, as ever, the English were held responsible: Gladstone's letter to Parnell via Morley was held by the Irish to have been a deliberate attempt to wreck Parnell and the Irish Nationalists so that he could go back on all his Home Rule promises.

So, although, just before his 83rd birthday, Gladstone was prime minister again, it was with the smallest majority he had ever had. At the 1892 election Gladstonian Liberals won 273 seats, the Irish Nationalists 81 and one independent Labour M.P., Keir Hardie, was elected for West Ham. But ranged against them in the Commons were 269 Conservatives and 46 Liberal Unionists, now led by Chamberlain, since Hartington had by now become the 8th Duke of Devonshire and gone to the Lords; and in the Lords itself, ready to strike Home Rule down at the first opportunity, were now, as there had been since 1886, not only the large ranks of the Conservative peerage but their newly recruited allies, the bulk of the great Whig aristocracy. When, for the fourth time in her life, the Queen suffered the pain of the first audience of a Gladstonian premiership, she said to him (they were both leaning on sticks and although she always now referred to him as 'old' she was herself by 1892 in her 73rd year): 'You and I, Mr Gladstone, are lamer than we used to be!' The remark was a great deal truer of Gladstone than of the Queen. His own version of his difficult situation was that there was ranged against the admittedly small majority he led 'the sense of nearly the entire peerage and landed gentry and of the vast majority of the upper and leisured classes'. This armed him with a new argument: that unless Home Rule was settled at once there would be class warfare.

Gladstone did in fact have more success with the second Home Rule Bill than the first in that it passed through all stages of the House of Commons and the issue was thus thoroughly debated in detail as well as in principle for the first time. In addition to the parliament of their own to deal exclusively with Irish affairs but not with defence, trade and foreign affairs (this had been the main feature of the first Home Rule Bill), the Irish were to send 80 M.P.s to Westminster, but with the power to vote only on matters concerning Ireland or the Empire in general. Introduced in February 1893, it passed its third reading by a majority of only 34 on 2 September, after months of heated and sometimes virulent debate and astounding oratorical feats by Gladstone; and as soon as it reached the Lords no fewer than 419 peers arrived to vote against it, while only 41 could be found to vote in its favour.

On 3 March 1894, Gladstone at last gave up. His colleagues had refused to agree on a dissolution and an election fought on the issue of the powers of the Lords; and they had added to their sins a determination, in spite of his complete condemnation of such un-Gladstonian 'madness', to increase naval expenditure. He was so enraged that he left the country, giving strict orders that no Cabinets were to be held in his absence; and he again demanded an appeal to the country on the issue of curbing the powers of the Lords. Faced with unanimous opposition, Gladstone returned to London; but it was only after a great deal of shilly-shallying on both sides that the final moment came. Gladstone referred to it afterwards as his 'blubbering cabinet'. The Queen found it impossible to express to Gladstone the slightest personal regret at his final resignation.

He was succeeded as prime minister by Lord Rosebery, who was very rich, very clever, owned racehorses that won the Derby for him (twice) but suffered from continuous insomnia. His premiership lasted eighteen dismal months, and in 1895 Salisbury was back in office with a substantial majority: 340 Conservatives and 71 Liberal Unionists faced the inevitable 82 Irish Nationalists but only 177 Liberals. Home Rule ceased to be an issue for another fifteen years, and the Liberals ceased to be a credible alternative government for another ten. The Whigs had ceased to have a separate existence; and Radicalism had, in Chamberlain, a leader almost wholly suborned by the glamour of Imperialism.[1] The alliance between Liberal Unionists and Conservatives became so close that 'Unionism' was to acquire the character of a formula as politically sacred as had been such concepts as Transubstantiation or Predestination in earlier centuries. Imperialism could be secretly distasteful to some members of that alliance and in the early years of the twentieth century the slogan of Tariff Reform was to create public dissension within it; but Unionism – an insistence on using the Protestantism of Ulster as sufficient grounds for governing all Irishmen, Catholic majority and Protestant minority alike, from Westminster was so tribal a word that for the first quarter of the twentieth century it was the normal official label used by all those who were Conservatives or ex-Liberal Unionists.[2]

Resistance to Home Rule thus intensified the process which Disraeli had begun. Conservatism in its post-Gladstonian, Unionist phase, seemed the only natural party for the true English patriot. By contrast, Liberalism tended to derive too much of its support from the non-English races of the British Isles – the Irish, the Welsh and the Highland Scots – together

---

[1] Tory Radicalism had also died the death: Lord Randolph Churchill had been forced by his own arrogance out of Salisbury's second Cabinet and died in 1895.

[2] See Oscar Wilde's *The Importance of Being Earnest* (London, 1899). '*Lady Bracknell:* What are your politics? *Jack:* Well, I am afraid I really have none. I am a Liberal Unionist. *Lady B:* Oh, they count as Tories. They dine with us. Or come in the evening, at any rate.'

with men of the west country, who lived remote from the main centres of English life.

The Home Rule issue was one of the factors making the Unionist/Conservative alliance appear as the party of the rich. This was due largely to the desertion of Liberalism by the Whig aristocracy[1] and by the Liberal right wing, with its strong opposition to state intervention and to radical social reform. The Home Rule issue also helped to make Conservatism much more the party of the men of property who were not wealthy; for the whole of Gladstone's Home Rule policy seemed directed towards abandoning the inherited authority of England under the pressure of violent extremists whose principal weapons were attacks on English-owned property. The Unionist emphasis on Ulster's Protestantism also further perpetuated the notion that Conservatism was the natural party of the Church of England; even if the Church of England was not 'the Tory party at prayer', the Tory party certainly entered the next century at least as much the political arm of Anglicanism as it had been when Gladstone had been called the rising hope of the stern unbending Tories in the 1830s.

The further result of the long Home Rule struggle was the alienation of both major parties from the economic and social aspirations of the urban workers. To the extent that their politics (like that of men of all classes) was instinctive rather than rational they were as likely to vote Unionist as Liberal. That the Unionists were rich men disqualified them only in the eyes of a politically conscious radical or socialist minority; there were in the last quarter of the century large numbers of urban working-class voters who disliked the Irish and rejoiced in the party's Imperialism. Nevertheless it was to become increasingly felt that, for the working classes' more material needs, the Unionists were doing little or nothing. Yet the Liberals after Gladstone had little to offer the radical–socialist working classes either. It is difficult to see how a Labour party could ever have been nursed into the noticeable existence it possessed a few years after the Queen's death had not

[1] Most of both groups were, by the century's end, more and more reliant for their wealth on industry and commerce.

Gladstone's Irish policies destroyed both the effectiveness and the radicalism of the Liberals; and it is significant that when radicalism returned to Liberalism in 1906 its established spokesman should have been, not a prophet out of early-Victorian Manchester like John Bright, or of late-Victorian Birmingham, like the early Joseph Chamberlain, but that 'Bible-thumping pagan' from a remote corner of rural Wales, David Lloyd George, a man to whom the urban working classes of England were never to give more than a temporary allegiance.

13 · The Great Depression: Fact and Fiction

> We may think of English history in the
> years . . . between the Jubilees as the epilogue
> to one age or the prehistory of another. But . . .
> the proud and sober confidence that irradiates
> the mid-Victorian landscape, that will not be
> seen again.
>
> G. M. YOUNG,
> *Portrait of An Age*, p. 148

Though the word 'Victorian' lives on in the vocabulary of the late twentieth century, to outface historians with a permanence not unlike that which by 1887 the Queen had begun to acquire for herself, historians rightly persist in their academically reputable dislike of dividing English history in accordance with the accession and death of its monarchs. And almost all are agreed that, at some point which they hesitate to specify, and in a variety of ways they are uncertain how to elucidate, the late-Victorian age had characteristics profoundly unlike those of early- and mid-Victorian times. That most felicitous of writers on the Victorian age, Sir George Young, clearly found the Victorians distasteful long before he had fully reached the terminal date of his study, asserting that, whereas he found the early- and mid-Victorian public 'so alert, so masculine and so responsible', their late-Victorian (and Edwardian) successors 'were ceasing to be a ruling or a reasonable stock'. They were become 'easily excited, easily satisfied', and guilty of remissness 'of intelligence, character and purpose'. More cautious in declaring the scope of his own later study, *The Making of Victorian England*, George Kitson Clark goes so far as to describe the year 1886 as 'a turning point in political history', but after looking forward a few pages later to the survival of great wealth among the nobility in 1901, shelters himself from the late Victorians two pages thereafter behind an analysis of Jane Austen's *Pride and Prejudice*. Two recent economic and social historians stop short in the 1880s.[1] Another well-known historian writes on *The Age of Improvement* and appears, no doubt unintentionally, to accept Sir George Young's despondent view of the late Victorians by ending his volume in 1867.[2] With a fine disregard for the earliest economic historians (and perhaps for the meaning of words) two joint authors of another work entitle it *The Agricultural Revolution 1750–1880*.[3] Basil Willey's *Nineteenth Century Studies* studiously avoids reference to any writer after Matthew Arnold. Raymond Williams, in *Culture and Society 1780–1950*, writes with somewhat more assurance, 'The temper which the adjective Victorian is useful to describe is virtually finished in the 1880s', but then retreats into the uncertainty of most other writers by lamely describing the years from 1880 to 1914 as an 'Interregnum'.

But the late-Victorian age was not the mere start of a hectic and rather inexplicable 'interregnum'. Nor was it merely a period when by some mysterious process of degeneration, Victorians began to fail; it was a time when major social, economic and psychological changes began to take place in English society and when, though much that was admirable in mid-Victorian society began (slowly) to disappear, much that was a good deal less than admirable came under attack and likewise began (slowly) to disappear.

The first indication of the changing forces at work in late-Victorian times was the decreasing significance of the ownership

[1] S. G. Checkland, *The Rise of Industrial Society in England 1815–1885* (London, Longmans, 1964) and Harold Perkin, *The Origins of Modern English Society, 1780–1880* (London, Routledge, 1969).
[2] Asa Briggs, *The Age of Improvement, 1783–1867* (London, Longmans, 1959). The terminal date is a reasonable one for a history book; but the title has, on reflection, the gloomiest of implications.
[3] J. D. Chambers and G. E. Mingay, *The Agricultural Revolution, 1750–1880* (London, Batsford, 1966).

of great tracts of land as the primary source of combined
wealth and social status. This did not mean that the landed
aristocracy which the Victorians had inherited from the pre-
industrial age, and whose dominance had been so little diminished by radical agitation or political reform before 1880, began
in general to fall upon hard times or to lose its political and
social pre-eminence. But, for the future, its members were
increasingly compelled to share their pre-eminence with
financiers and industrialists, and increasingly compelled to
divert more of their wealth from investment in land to investment in commerce and industry, at home and overseas, than
they had done in the first four decades of the Queen's reign.
The second victim was, not so much commerce and industry or
even businessmen and manufacturers themselves, but the confidence of businessmen and manufacturers in their prospects of
future prosperity.

The manifestation of these developments of the late-Victorian period was sufficiently evident to contemporaries for them
to call the period from 1873 to 1896 the years of The Great
Depression, and for them to appoint royal commissions which
reported on the agricultural Depression in 1882 and 1897 and
on the commercial and industrial Depression in 1886. Modern
economic historians insist that the Great Depression of those
years is 'a myth', as if to tell the late Victorians that they ought
to have pulled themselves together and should have stopped
making a fuss about nothing. But what most people believe and
what many people suffer, at any given period of history, is
usually more important historically than the long-term views
of historians who suffer much from the occupational disease of
believing themselves to be so much cleverer than the dead.[1]

---

[1] A brief outline of exactly how widely economic historians have disagreed about the Great Depression may be read in *The Myth of the Great
Depression 1873-1896*, by Professor S. B. Saul (London, Macmillan, 1969),
whose conclusion reads: 'We are far from a full understanding of all the
problems. . . . But this at least is clear: the sooner the "Great Depression"
is banished from the literature the better.' In similar style, economic
historians are busily proving that the other Great Depression (in the
England of the 1930s) was really a very minor matter when set alongside
the steady increase in living standards between the wars. It should be

And the facts are that there was a serious depression in arable farming, and in industry and commerce a wide tendency for prices to fall and for the rate of growth to be much slower than expected.

The truth would appear to be that, by the last quarter of the century, agriculture though still a major industry was a declining one and that the sharpest decline afflicted the wheat growing areas, to which prosperity did not return until the outbreak of war in 1914. In 1872, 3,599,000 acres of land were devoted to the cultivation of wheat; by 1895 the figure had fallen to 1,417,000.[1] In 1870, wheat accounted for half the output of arable land, by 1895 for only one-sixth. The reasons for the decline were a succession of bad harvests beginning in the mid seventies, and the challenge of imported wheat. 'The corn counties,' wrote G. M. Young, 'were stricken, it seemed, beyond recovery. Great wars have been less destructive of wealth than the calamity which stretches from 1879 the wettest, to 1894 the driest, year in memory. . . . Never again was the landed proprietor to dominate the social fabric.'[2] To this woeful tale of falling prices and uncollectable rents was added the general spectacle of a flight from the land. In the last thirty years of the reign the numbers employed in agriculture fell from 962,000 to 621,000. By 1899 (estate duty of 1 per cent on estates over £10,000 having been introduced by Goschen in 1889 and death duties on a graduated scale by Harcourt in 1894) Lady Bracknell could be assured of a sympathetic response to her other famous remark in Wilde's *The Importance*

---

mandatory for all economic historians to undergo a minimum period of three years' enforced dependence exclusively on social security benefits before writing on English economic history since 1919, or a similar period in complete destitution before writing about earlier times. This would do much to broaden their perspective.

[1] For the purposes of the *late-Victorian* period alone, the more consoling figures of 3,368,000 acres under wheat in 1867 and 2,636,000 by 1918 are irrelevant. The statistics are from Peter Mathias, *The First Industrial Nation* (London, Methuen, 1969).
[2] G. M. Young, *Victorian England: Portrait of an Age* (London, O.U.P., 1953), p. 145.

of Being Earnest: 'What between the duties expected of one during one's lifetime and the duties enacted from one after one's death, land has ceased to be either a profit or a pleasure.'

The royal commission of 1897 on the Agricultural Depression named the principal sources of the foreign competition which British agriculture had met in the previous twenty years: the United States and Argentina sent most wheat and meat, the United States and Romania most maize, and Russia also sent wheat. Australasia was exporting wool, mutton and butter, though nearly 50 per cent of imported butter came from Denmark; there were great imports of cheese from the United States and Canada and of margarine from Holland; the report concluded, somewhat desperately, that it could see no near prospect of any slackening of such competition.

But the traditional answer – the re-imposition of duties on foreign corn – was politically out of the question. It may be, therefore, that the decline of the landed aristocracy was as much a cause as a consequence of 'The Great Depression'. The landlords had lost the fight to maintain the price of bread in 1846; by the 1880s, no matter in what other respects it was losing ground politically, Liberalism's gospel of Free Trade still remained the central dogma of the day. During the 1850s and 1860s agriculture had prospered in spite of the Corn Laws,[1] and wheat prices had fallen hardly at all. From the 1870s onwards, with the railway and the steamship drastically reducing costs, the newly exploited soil of the United States could send wheat to England at a price that undercut the home producer. Russia's grain exports increased as the need to export Russian wheat increased in order to secure foreign currency for the beginnings of industrial development in that country. But by now, the majority of Englishmen were town-dwellers (only 15 per cent of the working population was engaged in agriculture in England and Wales by 1871) and the depressed state of the wheat areas itself increased the pull away from the land to the towns. Hence, with a much widened franchise after 1885,

---

[1] Wheat was 57·87 shillings a quarter before Peel's act of 1846, 49·03 just before the Crimean War, 57·61 during it and 55·00 in 1870–4. See figures quoted in Mathias, op. cit., p. 474.

it was a national (or at any rate a political) necessity to avoid any policy that increased food prices. The fact is sufficiently illustrated by the care with which Chamberlain's programme for Tariff Reform, launched in 1903, excluded a tax on wheat imports, and by the fact that Protection in general, though not then officially adopted by the party, was seen as an attack on cheap food and therefore brought the Unionists to electoral catastrophe in 1906. Moreover, to put up the price of bread would add still further to the burdens borne by the perpetually overworked and underpaid agricultural workers themselves.

The fate that overtook the wheatlands was, however, only one part of the agricultural jigsaw in late-Victorian times, though it attracted most of the attention of contemporaries and subsequent historians. Livestock producers, who bought cereal for feeding purposes, benefited from the lowered prices. With the rise in real wages that accompanied the Depression, the market absorbed the import of cheap, low-quality foreign meat – the price of which fell heavily during the Depression – and home meat prices fell less than prices in general. Despite the growth of imports in butter and cheese, the dairy farmer was sustained by the lively domestic market for milk (effective because of the development of the railways) while, contrary to the normal trend, the price of eggs went up. The population increase of about ten million which occurred during the years of Depression enlarged the market for agricultural products, but the increase of real wages produced a further difficulty for the wheat farmer in that the commonest sign of a rise in standards of living among the labour force is a decline in the proportion of income that is spent on bread. Agriculture was thus compelled to adjust itself to its own success in expanding sufficiently in the first three-quarters of the century to sustain the great industrial growth of that period. That same industrial growth made it inevitable that England should export manufactured goods and import foreign food surpluses in exchange.

Nor did the rapid decline of those employed in agriculture in the last decades of the century necessarily reflect a deep economic malaise. Though the numbers employed fell drastically, output was up by around 10 per cent and productivity per man by about 15 per cent. Various factors accounted for this. Among them were the introduction of machinery, often steam-driven, and the fact that dairy farming required a smaller labour force than arable farming. But there was undoubted social strain, and much migration to the towns and emigration over-seas were the unavoidable alternatives to destitution in, for example, the western counties of England, where much land was converted to dairy farming, or in Cambridgeshire and Essex, where traditionalists hung on to corn-growing longest in the hope that the tide of change would turn back, and then had to sell up for whatever price they could get.

As every townsman knows, for it is part of universal folk-history, farming is 'a way of life', which is, perhaps, only to say that members of the agricultural community, even more than townsmen, tend to want to go on doing what they have always been doing; nevertheless it was during the late-Victorian period that that particular way of life finally ceased to be the typical way of life of Englishmen in general. Nor is it surprising (except to economists) that the disappearance from the scene of two million acres of arable land should have seemed the most significant as well as the most melancholy feature of the history of late-Victorian agriculture. The fields of waving corn and the golden sheaves of harvest-time were powerful symbols, bespeaking history and fertility and the virility of a 'bold peasantry, their country's pride'. Eggs and milk, and butter and cheese may well have been more flourishing now; but some-thing precious had been lost, for such commodities had some-how enfeebling, unmasculine qualities about them: suggesting perhaps a nation of milksops and dairymaids. What sort of a people was this, the journalists asked, that was content to rely on foreigners for its staple food? What would happen in war-time? Not only would we starve, but the rank and file of our armies would be, not sturdy men from the plough but white-faced clerks from the cities. That these propositions were not all of them very rational is irrelevant. History is made by the irrational beliefs of the dead.

But there was nothing irrational about the beliefs of many agricultural labourers that for them this old 'way of life' was for them a lifetime of long or irregular hours of work (or both), of low wages and excessive deference. They were repeatedly told that they were doing better in relation both to the farmers and the landowners during the years of the Depression and that they were better off than their predecessors; but though everybody else believed this (and the economic historians agree) they refused to believe it. It is significant that Joseph Arch's attempt to form a National Agricultural Labourers' Union began in 1871 before, and not after, the start of the Depression. The Depression doomed it to failure; but its foundation and such limited successes as it had suggest that the rosier view of the 'way of life' that the Depression ended in so many parts of the countryside should be held as strictly within limits as should be more melodramatic views of the Agricultural Depression itself.

The real nature of the 'Depression of Trade and Industry' on which a royal commission was reporting in 1886 is even more in dispute than that of the Depression in agriculture. The seminal Cambridge economist, Alfred Marshall, informed the commission itself in 1886 that the previous ten years, marked as they had been by 'a gradual fall in price', had 'conduced more to solid progress and true happiness' than the wide fluctuations of activity and recessions of 'every preceding decade of this century'. There had, he conceded, been 'a depression of prices, a depression of interest, a depression of profits' but no 'considerable depression in any other respect'. By contrast, Lord Randolph Churchill, who, even more than his illustrious son, was wont to let his words run away with him, told the public that the iron industry was 'dead as mutton', the silk industry had been 'assassinated' by foreigners, the cotton industry was 'sick', the shipbuilding industry had 'come to a standstill' (it had done nothing of the sort) and that in every branch of British industry they would 'find signs of mortal disease'. On the whole, Marshall's judgement is closer to the ideas of subsequent study: the Depression of trade and industry with generally falling prices, interest and profits, was a phenomenon from which the articulate middle classes suffered much more than their workers, whose real incomes went up fairly steadily until 1895. Indeed it has been calculated[1] that nearly all the 50 per cent rise in the standard of living of the working population in general that took place between 1880 and 1913 occurred in fact between 1880 and 1896, the years of 'Depression'. Another calculation[2] is that real income per head in the United Kingdom (and most 'heads' were working-class heads) grew at about 25 per cent in each of the last three decades of the century.

That the Depression was a middle-class phenomenon, just as, to a lesser extent, the collapse of the wheat market was a bitter blow to the more prestigious of the landlords, ensured that it received the maximum publicity and generated the most widely-advertised gloom. Businessmen blamed it on the competition of foreigners, particularly the Germans and the 'Yankees', on foreign tariff barriers, on increased taxation, the trade unions, on the limitations placed by Parliament on the hours of work. It came to be an accepted theory that the English were altogether incapable of meeting the threat of American and German competition; and one of the drives that contributed to the Imperialism of the late Victorians was perhaps a desire to assert in colonial spheres a virility that it seemed impossible to display in the industrial and commercial spheres. It may be that the one reason why the progress of British industry slowed down after 1873, or at any rate why it failed to adapt to changing circumstances as well as it might have done, was psychological: businessmen thought themselves into a pessimistic frame of mind that inhibited growth and the ability to change. Certainly, no single economic factor appears to offer an explanation either of the causes of the sense of malaise in the late-Victorian economy or of its real nature or even of its precise duration. Looking beyond the period, there is certainly an apparent similarity of psychological attitude to that displayed in the years from 1922 to 1939: a general feeling that there was not a great deal to be done about the declining

---

[1] A. L. Bowley, *Wages and Income in the United Kingdom since 1860* (Cambridge, Cambridge U.P., 1937).
[2] W. Ashworth, *Economic History of England, 1870–1939* (London, Methuen, 1960).

growth rate of areas of the economy and a marked tendency to let things go on as before in the hope that eventually some promising corner might be turned. And of both periods it is true that progress was occurring and adjustments were being made that contemporaries either ignored or deplored.

Certain factors of long-term consequence began to be apparent in the last quarter of the century which ought to have produced a more positive response. The simple facts of economic geography were that both the United States and Germany were, once historic events had given both states a guarantee of the political unity needed to facilitate their exploitation, far richer in human and natural resources than the United Kingdom. The simple facts of economic history were that the railway and the steamship now made it physically possible for both countries to export their goods in competition with Great Britain to all parts of the world. That they protected their industries with tariffs and bounties was, in the first instance, itself a tribute to the highly competitive character of British manufactures. It was no reflection on anybody that percentage rates of growth in the United States and Germany after 1871 were far higher than the growth rate in Great Britain; to produce even a mere thousand tons of coal where less had been produced earlier represents a percentage growth rate which would be pitiful in absolute terms; and even in percentage terms the United Kingdom's industrial production rose by an average of over 2·1 per cent per annum over the whole period from 1870 to 1914. The fact that the corresponding figure for the United States was 4·7 per cent per annum and for Germany 4·1 says as much about the industrial backwardness of these two latter countries in 1870 as about their energy and inventiveness.

But what attracted more attention than these figures was that whereas the volume of British exports had for thirty years before 1870 been expanding by 5 per cent per annum, it increased at the rate of only 2 per cent a year from 1870 to 1890 and only 1 per cent a year in the last decade of the century. The actual value of Britain's annual exports did not reach the figures attained in the early 1870s until after 1895. Over the same period, production rates per man fell; so did the rate of capital investment and, with it, the pace of introduction of new equipment and new technologies. And, although against this gloomy picture has to be set the continued world-domination of British shipbuilding and heavy engineering, the fact remains that industrial growth was less for the whole period between 1870 and 1914 than between 1919 and 1939 (despite the World Depression) and much less than after 1945. It seems, therefore, that even if one is forced to abandon the notion of a Great Depression between 1873 and 1895, it is still valid to regard this as the beginning of a long period during which Britain, having lost (for largely inevitable and in no sense unworthy reasons) her hold on the largest share of world trade in the traditional industries created between 1780 and 1870, found it difficult (for reasons that are understandable if perhaps less worthy) to adjust to, and innovate for, a dramatically changing situation; and despite the soothing noises economic historians now make about the years between 1919 and 1939, the duration of this period of inadequate adjustment and innovation could well be regarded as extending until 1945.

One practical reason for a failure to innovate in the late-Victorian era was the large amount of capital investment already sunk into existing equipment. Other countries, starting afresh, were freer to use the most developed, or the newest, technological processes. Existing equipment in Britain might still work well enough, but with less efficiency and therefore less productivity than the products of the newer technology. This offers an explanation of why Britain was slow to develop its electrical industry; for decades, the country had been committed to gas-lighting, and its dense and over-capitalized railway system was even more committed by its enormous investment in the steam locomotive. Thus, in some respects, Britain suffered inevitably from the effects of being the pioneer industrial state; though, against this, it was an advantage to have so much accumulated capital and such a large reservoir of skilled labour.

Yet even where there was expansion during the Depression, as in the coal and steel industries, there was a sluggish attitude to innovation. Britain needed to introduce mechanical methods of coal mining at this time more than did either the U.S.A. or Germany, since in Britain the working seams were already farther from the surface than in the new mines abroad. But, since even coal prices were falling, and profits and business confidence with them, little or no mechanization took place. And in steel, the heavy investment in the decade before 1873 in the Bessemer steel process and to a less extent in the Siemens-Marten open-hearth furnace after 1866 seems to have inhibited the adoption of the Gilchrist-Thomas process invented in 1879, which, unlike the other processes, enabled steel to be made out of readily available low-grade iron ores. The less efficient Bessemer converter, largely abandoned in Germany, continued to dominate the British steel industry.

While coal and steel exports nevertheless doubled in the last twenty years of the Victorian age, this was due to an expanding world market rather than to any conspicuous managerial drive (this is reflected in the declining prices of both after 1875); and textile exports sagged badly at a time when textiles were the largest industry in the country and the largest export manufacture. This again was due to a failure to use new techniques even though these were being developed in England and were readily available.

There is also alleged to have been a failure of inventive genius in Great Britain in late-Victorian times, ascribable to the fact that the supply of gifted amateurs had dried up and had not been compensated for, as in Germany and the United States, by an adequate system of technical education or a due attention to science in the the public schools and universities. The list of innovations from abroad at this time is certainly large: most new agricultural machinery, the equipment and processing required for the expanding dairy industry, the sewing machine and the typewriter all came from the United States or Western Europe. Advanced technology in glass making, mining and electrical engineering and above all in the chemical industry came (like most professors of chemistry in British universities) from Germany. Yet even this may amount to little more than complaining that, when only the British played football, all the best players were British, but that when all the world took to playing football many of the best players were foreigners for the sufficient reason that there were more of them.[1]

It does seem impossible to deny that the social climate in both the United States and Germany was more conducive (because the pre-existence of British predominance necessitated it) to an aggressive and innovating economic and technological attitude. Since no nation can predict that brilliant individual inventors or commercially worthwhile intuitions will emerge merely by a process of waiting for them, it was inevitable that Germany and the United States should nurse their infant industrial economies by systematic technical and scientific education whereas the British industrialist, with his capital heavily invested in the inventions and technologies of previous decades, should continue prudently along traditional lines in order to get out of that investment as much as he could. Scientific education and, above all, what later came to be called research and development are extremely costly processes, not lightly to be embarked upon at a time of falling prices and profits such as faced the British entrepreneur in the late-Victorian period. But there is a distinction between the development of new processes and the adoption of them. The first may depend either on unpredictable originality or on a massive expenditure on scientific education and investigation; but the adoption of such processes after somebody else has borne the usual losses involved in research and development is sometimes a purely managerial decision. This rather than anything else would seem to explain the laggardliness of the British chemical industry and the dynamic progress of the German.

Such broad new developments as there were in late-Victorian times were in directions that contributed little to exports but ministered to the domestic needs of an ever-expanding internal market. Sir George Young comments on this development with fastidious disapproval: 'After the age of the great producers . . . comes the age of great shops and great advertisers . . . the

[1] This defence will not however serve to explain such facts as that as early as 1893 France had an output of 500 motor cars a year, a figure not reached by the United Kingdom till three years later.

springs of invention are failing, and, for the successors of the Arkwrights and Stephensons we must look to America or France or even to Italy.'[1] The names of Beecham, Lever, Cadbury, Fry, Guinness and Bass, which first made a national impact in the years of the Great Depression, like the names of retail or multiple traders such as Lipton, Maypole Dairies, Boot and Whiteley, hardly suggest a drying-up of entrepreneurial activity or an unawareness of market possibilities. And though these new developments did not at this period add much either to the gross national product or to the export trade, and were dependent for their success upon strident advertising, they represented a real forward step in the quality of the goods available to the ordinary housewife.[2] It is illogical to complain that too little of the gross national product was devoted to the welfare of common people in the early stages of the industrial era and then to complain when at the close of the Victorian age a larger, though still small proportion of it, was being devoted to that end. The period of the Depression was also remarkable for a boom in house building, particularly in the suburbs of the great towns.

That problems should arise in an age of transition caused by the entry into the world market of the powerful tariff-supported industries of two larger and more populated countries may well seem more obvious to posterity than it did to the late Victorians. Well before they began to boast of an Empire on which the sun never set, Victorians tended to assume that they had an ever-prospering and expanding commerce on which no sun would ever set. The discovery that this was not, after all, likely to be so, seems to have caught them unprepared, and contemporary

---

[1] *Portrait of an Age*, pp. 159–60. One can feel the shudder with which the writer contemplates shopkeepers and advertisers and the possibility of even the Italians actually inventing anything.

[2] Beecham's Pills were not 'worth a guinea a box' but self-medication was an ineradicable habit and a standard advertised product was less inimical to health than some of its predecessors. The extraordinary health-giving properties attributed to cocoa by its manufacturers at this time were indeed excessive; but though Whiteley's department store in Westbourne Grove, London was not 'the Universal Provider' it claimed to be, it did provide, under one roof, a very great deal.

attitudes seem to have wavered between complacency and despondency. They called for retaliatory tariffs which they knew no government would impose; they wanted increased working hours just at the time when the franchise was being widened, and asked for the maintenance of low wages just when the trade unions were becoming stronger. And to the unwillingness of late-Victorian governments to interfere in the economy on behalf of entrepreneurs for fear of the electoral consequences was to be added the circumstance that in late-Victorian times governments were less rather than more sympathetic to the entrepreneur than they had been earlier. There was certainly at least as wide a gap between the ultimate decision-makers in London after 1875 and the entrepreneurs as there had been at the start of the reign.

Although all such generalizations must be treated with caution, making a lot of money out of trade and commerce was never considered quite respectable in Victorian society. The doctrine of self-help was useful as a means of persuading the poor that they could be comfortably off if they were thrifty and hardworking and refrained from appealing to or opposing government; but it was never a doctrine for gentlemen. Businessmen got to the back benches in the Commons; they might even get peerages. But a businessman who made a fortune and became, by purchase, a landowner and, by contribution to party coffers, a peer, was never as good as a man who was a peer because he inherited land, even though he (or his father) had saved the family fortunes by marrying the daughter of an American millionaire or by investing in industry and commerce or by obtaining lucrative company directorships. Trade and industry were not so socially acceptable, at least until their practitioners had done sufficiently well to be able to devote the bulk of their energies into turning themselves into gentlemen. And if they despaired of doing this for themselves they did their best to do it for their sons.

The public schools were designed to produce gentlemen, not entrepreneurs. They aimed to produce leaders of the state; their interest was not to educate tomorrow's 'captains of industry' but to assimilate the sons of today's uncouth businessmen into gentlemanly society. Politics and the public service, the armed services and the liberal professions were the 'vocational' termini of both public schools and universities, though a number of public school men would 'go into the city'. The heroes of late-Victorian society were soldiers and empire-builders; their hidden élite was the handful of utterly unknown first division civil servants chosen by the competitive examination system from the most academically-gifted products of the best public schools and of Oxford and Cambridge; and politicians were public heroes almost for the very reason that they were so unlike businessmen.[1] Politicians counted for less in the United States because they were assumed to be venal; they counted for less in Germany because neither before nor after 1871 did Bismarck provide scope for any politician other than himself. But in England, Palmerston's outstanding feats of quick-change artistry which enabled him to present himself, according to the taste of his audience, as The Scourge of The Tyrants, The Saviour of his Country, The Darling of the People or The Defender of Property were succeeded by Disraeli's magnetic act 'fresh from the inscrutable East' and by Gladstone's tremendous and enduring performance as a God-intoxicated Superman; hardly less compelling in the public mind were Charles Stewart Parnell and Randolph Churchill, each doing his own individual Dive to Death; and then, with only a brief interlude from 1892–5, the reassuring assumption by Lord Salisbury of the role of a perpetual Prospero forever re-enacting the last scene of the last act of *The Tempest* – only such bronzed soldiers as Wolseley, Gordon, Roberts and Kitchener, an empire-builder such as Cecil Rhodes or a missionary hero like Livingstone could begin to compete for public acclaim with performers such as these. If in such a society businessmen could be with any justice accused of lacking aggression and a drive to innovate in comparison with their German and American competitors, it could well be because German and American businessmen were not automatically regarded like English businessmen as ungentlemanly. The

[1] Walter Bagehot clearly believed they should not look like businessmen. (See p. 78.)

best-educated men in England went into politics and into the public service at home and abroad; they were educated for the art and science of government, not for the arts and sciences of industry and commerce. In 1872, when there were only twelve candidates for the natural sciences tripos in Cambridge, Germany already had eleven technical universities; in England, Oxford and Cambridge as well as the public schools 'had their backs turned towards the industrial economy'.[1]

This remarkable policy of creaming the top layers of academic ability within the middle and upper classes and diverting them towards a 'liberal' education, liberal indeed though it often was, constituted a deliberate conditioning of the mind so that it turned away in distaste from workshop, factory, manager's office and laboratory. After the Queen's death, it was applied to the lower middle classes as well, as a result of the creation, by Balfour's Education Act of 1902, of the state-aided and maintained grammar schools. And, although science gradually became first respectable and then prestigious, applied science had still not acquired anything like equal status almost a century after the Great Depression is supposed to have begun. The best that England could supply (Scotland did better) was a wholly inadequate system of technical education which was in no sense designed to lead on to any form of higher education. The voluntary 'mechanics' institutes, of which there were 622 in 1850 with 600,000 members, made no appreciable contribution to the problem in the second half of the century. In 1889 county and county borough councils[2] were empowered to provide technical schools; from 1859 the state helped to set up the Department of Art and Science at South Kensington and in 1879 the City and Guilds of London Institute was established to take over a system of examination in 'technological subjects'. Here, too, the state subsidized only in relation to examination successes, but in any case the best that was provided in this field – the technical schools set up by some counties after 1889 – went no further than at best a secondary school level of education.

[1] See Mathias, op. cit., pp. 421–4.
[2] See p. 312.

It would be altogether too facile to contend that a defective education system and a fairly rigid class structure 'caused' the Great Depression; but they may well have affected England's ability to adapt to changing economic circumstances. The chief objection to such an explanation is that it cannot be quantified; but there are also still too few accurate statistics to substantiate purely 'economic' explanations either. Thus it has been argued on the one hand that wages were too high and on the other that they were too low. Yet probably a more relevant contention is that the gap between owners and managers and their workers was perhaps wider in England than in either the United States which, unlike England, believed itself to be classless, or in Germany where, again in contrast to England, the whole concept of individual freedom was alien, and where, since too many thinking minds had been poisoned by the Hegelian concept of the State as an Absolute and unthinking minds had long been schooled to obedience, an aggressive patriotic fervour united both workers and employers in a manner quite out of the question in England, with its long-standing traditions of what would now be called bloody-mindedness among employers and employed. The basic problem would seem to be the problem of a lack of investment in new staple industries, principally electricity and chemicals, and the persistence in relying on the old basic industries; and it is difficult to see, on present evidence, how this lack of investment could have been overcome. It looks indeed as though agriculture adjusted better than industry to the challenge of the 1880s and 1890s. Agriculture as a whole settled down by 1900 on a more diversified if slightly less prosperous over-all level; industry seems to have been confirmed in its old ways by the recovery of the old basic industries after 1896, resulting in the main from the artificial stimulus of the worldwide increase in armaments that enabled it for the most part to resume its traditional course until the slump of 1921. This may – or may not – mean that there was no Depression from 1873 to 1896. But it does seem to mean that for avoidable – or unavoidable – reasons, British industry failed adequately after 1873 to adapt itself to the changing patterns of trade.

14 · Death of Liberal England

> If you once desert the solid ground of indi-
> vidual freedom, you can find no resting place
> till you reach the chasm of Socialism.
>
> A. W. DICEY,
> *Fortnightly Review*, October 1885

> ... that vast portion ... of the working class
> which, raw and half-developed, has long been
> half-hidden amidst its poverty and squalor, and
> is now issuing from its hiding place to assert an
> Englishman's heaven-born privilege of doing
> as he likes, and is beginning to perplex us by
> marching where it likes, meeting where it likes,
> bawling what it likes, breaking what it likes. ...
>
> MATTHEW ARNOLD,
> *Culture and Anarchy*, p. 105

Socially and politically, the late Victorians never escaped from
the shadow of the Second Reform Act. The affair of the Hyde
Park Railings and Disraeli's subsequent 'leap in the dark' shook
the morale of all who were not radicals almost as much as did
the uncertain fortunes of wheat and coal and textiles. For the
rest of the century they drifted rather despondently along in the
direction to which the act had pointed them, allowing themselves to be dragged towards Democracy, and what they were
pleased to call 'Socialism', in the hope that if they did not
struggle too much they might somehow manage to keep afloat.
In a sense it was fortunate for them that Gladstone, though he
talked so often about the virtues of 'the masses', diverted
everybody's political attention in the 1880s to the Irish question
and in doing so left Liberalism without a head and Radicalism

without a home, while at the same time bequeathing the Conservative Unionist alliance the valuable electoral assets of patriotism and Imperialism. It was also fortunate for the men of property that Salisbury, though opposed on principle to the Reform Acts of 1867 and 1884, was by nature non-belligerent and, whether in foreign or domestic politics, usually in favour of doing whatever was least spectacular. He accepted that the stirring dogs of democracy were unlikely ever to lie down again; he was sure that, in the end, no good would come of this; but he was always as careful as possible not to excite them. When it became evident that under his premiership the Empire was becoming larger and larger, he waved no flags himself because he so greatly detested vulgarity and because his deep private Christian convictions were of a sort that made him the only Victorian minister after the irreligious Melbourne who believed that nothing whatever that one did in the political sphere would ever transform a sinful world into a virtuous one. He regularly dodged the limelight because he knew it would reveal a countenance as firmly fixed on the past as Prince Metternich's. Thus, Salisbury quietly accumulated a fund of popular goodwill which was all the greater because he seemed so majestically aloof from all the stridencies of the era over which he presided.

By the time Salisbury became prime minister, however, Gladstone had gone far to complete the work that Disraeli had begun in 1867. In 1872 Gladstone at last achieved what the Radicals had demanded in the 1830s, the introduction of the secret ballot. Its object was primarily to prevent corruption: open voting was still so productive of scandal that there had been as many as 111 petitions against successful candidates in the 1868 elections. Palmerston had taken the view that voting in secret was 'unmanly'; and to most peers it was objectionable on the grounds that it deprived property owners and employers of their traditional rights, at election times, to 'influence', though sometimes at a price, their social inferiors. It is unlikely that the use of the ballot for the first time in 1874 changed traditional ways altogether though it is usually believed that it was one reason for the increased number of Irish Nationalists who were elected in that year. More effective in purifying electoral procedures was the Corrupt Practices Act of 1883, which fixed election expenses in proportion to the number of voters.

In 1884, Gladstone, once again belatedly, found time to fulfil the Liberal pledge (made by Hartington in 1877) to extend the franchise to householders in the county constituencies on the same terms as had been enjoyed by those in the boroughs since 1867. The Third Reform Bill was, however, rejected in the Lords. Salisbury disliked the bill as heartily as he had disliked that of 1867; but although much was made by Conservatives of the unfitness of agricultural labourers (and Irish peasant farmers) for the vote, they chose rather to reject the bill on the grounds that it was not accompanied by a Redistribution Act. Whereas the 1832 act had increased the electorate by 500,000, and the 1867 act increased it by about a million, the 1884 act would increase it by two million; and unless seats were redistributed there would be a great imbalance between the many large county, and the many small borough, constituencies. The counties were the last stronghold of the Tory landholders and the conviction was that – particularly after the acts of 1872 and 1883 – the rural workers would all vote Liberal.

The rejection of the bill by the Lords on 9 July 1884 at last gave the Radicals something to expostulate about. It was a case of 'the Peers versus the People' according to Joseph Chamberlain; and from John Morley came the call to 'End Them or Mend Them'. Gladstone himself made dark speeches against the Lords in the autumn, despite a fierce message from Her Majesty:

> The Queen will yield to no one in TRUE LIBERAL FEELING but not to destructive, and she calls upon Mr Gladstone to *restrain as he can*, some of his wild colleagues and followers.

Since Hartington largely sympathized with the Conservatives' objections and the Queen was determined that it was better for agricultural labourers to have the vote than for Radicals to be encouraged to attack the House of Lords, a compromise was achieved. Gladstone and Salisbury were persuaded to meet for tea at 10 Downing Street accompanied by Hartington and Sir Michael Hicks-Beach and it was agreed that the Reform Bill should go through the Lords and be followed at once by a Redistribution Act.[1] This in itself saved the Tories from what they considered the certainty of defeat if an election were sprung on them before a Redistribution Act. The act of 1885 disfranchised all boroughs with fewer than 15,000 inhabitants; and boroughs with fewer than 50,000 inhabitants were in future to return one member and not two or three members. From now on, the single member constituency became the rule; and since this was held to be a very Radical notion, Gladstone was surprised at the eagerness with which the Conservatives favoured it. Indeed, the 1885 act dished the Whigs hardly less than the act of 1867. The acts of 1872 and 1883, the increase in the electorate in 1884 and the redistribution of 1885, virtually ended Whig control of many nomination boroughs and many of the county constituencies they had previously controlled. The number of aristocratic Whig M.P.s was drastically and permanently reduced as a result. In the larger two- or three-member cities, Tory voters had hitherto been swamped by Liberals; but in the 1885 election the Tories had a bare majority in the English boroughs for the first time in the Queen's reign and thereafter were never again in a minority in these constituencies till 1906. Similarly, the old Liberal practice of Radicals and Whigs running in harness in English constituencies and Home Rulers and Liberals in Ireland was also ended. Thus, in 1884–5, as in 1867, the Conservatives abandoned their principles for the sake of gaining Conservative votes.

From a purely constitutional point of view all that now remained to achieve full political democracy was to give the vote to women, to abolish plural voting and to secure a greater approximation to equal electoral districts, though the 1885 act came much nearer to this than before. The Redistribution Act also virtually ended the old tradition that the Commons represented *communities*; now, with the preponderance of single-

---

[1] And, Gladstone may have thought, if they could reform the electoral system by private conferences in 1884 why could they not, in 1885 or 1886, give Home Rule to Ireland by the same technique?

member constituencies (643 out of 670), it represented *majorities*. This in itself caused alarm, for it was basic to respectable mid-Victorian social ideas that majorities were bound to be wrong, since majorities were under-educated and envious of those who were more prosperous and more propertied than they were.

By the time that reform came again in 1884–5, it served to reinforce the development of new methods of vote-collecting appropriate to a period when there were so many more potential voters to attract and when 'influence' of the old sort could no longer be exercised. In 1873 Joseph Chamberlain helped to organize the Birmingham Liberal Association to see that every ward of the city was canvassed. By 1877, a National Liberal Federation was at work helping to form Liberal associations throughout the country. The Conservatives had indeed founded a National Union for the same purpose in 1867 but this was less important than the establishment in 1870 of what by the end of 1871 was generally known as the Conservative Party Central Office. This Central Office imposed itself upon local Conservative associations in a manner which henceforth usually made the Conservatives a more efficiently organized party than the Liberals. The National Liberal Federation, which developed out of the Birmingham Union, aimed at imposing a radical policy on the leadership, and lost its principal figures with the withdrawal of Chamberlain from Liberalism and the social and therefore political downfall of Dilke in the divorce court; but Conservatism was, from 1884 onwards, led firmly from the top. From the time of Gladstone's conversion to Home Rule onwards, however, his party had no effective leadership and a headless organization in the constituencies. Toryism, however, fared better. Salisbury completely defeated Lord Randolph Churchill's efforts to use the constituency associations against the leadership in the 1880s. He manœuvred Churchill out of the chairmanship of the National Union in 1884 and then manœuvred him out of the Cabinet in 1887: when Churchill flamboyantly sent Salisbury a letter resigning from the office of chancellor of the exchequer in the expectation that Salisbury's reply would be to change his policies at Churchill's bidding,

Salisbury called his bluff by accepting Churchill's resignation and appointing George Goschen[1] chancellor in his place.

Thus early, therefore, the political system had begun to defend itself against its democratic appearance by the tighter organization of M.P.s. The widening of the franchise had already begun to erode the M.P.'s independence. He was on the way to his twentieth-century position as a delegate rather than a representative, and a delegate ultimately responsible more to the party machine than to his constituents, though the opposite impression would always be sedulously cultivated.[2] The days of loose affiliations, when the Commons was an impressionable body of men capable of being swayed by oratorical prima donnas to preserve or overthrow governments, were numbered. After 1886, no government with a majority in the House of Commons would suddenly find itself without one.[3] After 1886, also, it became normal, though not invariable, practice for a prime minister to resign immediately after an electoral defeat in the country. Before 1867, few governments in office were overthrown by general elections; after 1867, and even more after 1886, it was automatic for an adverse vote in a general election to be followed by the government's immediate resignation:[4] the House of Commons itself no longer either made or

[1] Goschen had held government or cabinet office in Liberal administrations from 1885 to 1874.

[2] Realistically considered, a modern M.P. is a delegated representative of party headquarters, selected by his constituency association (an unrepresentative minority) from a number of other political delegates approved by party H.Q., for the purpose of securing votes in his constituency for the party which first put him forward or gave him its *nihil obstat*. Hence the theory sometimes advanced that M.P.s since 1886 have ceased to be representatives of their constituencies but are only their delegates is inadequate.

[3] The Lloyd George coalition, like the Asquith ministry and coalition before it, fell to intrigue behind the scenes; and when Chamberlain resigned in 1940 it was not because he lacked a majority in the Commons, which is why he was on the whole so reluctant to give up.

[4] Baldwin did not resign immediately after losing the 1923 election because it was not clear until Parliament met in January 1924 just who would succeed him, since though the Opposition had a majority it was divided between two parties, Liberal and Labour.

unmade governments. Characteristically, Gladstone tried to resist this change in 1874, asserting that it was still the Commons' function to dismiss a ministry, not that of the constituencies.

The power of the Commons was further diminished (without necessarily in any way increasing the real power of the electorate) by the increased control which these developments gave to the Cabinet. Given that, until 1911, no M.P.s were paid a salary, the tendency not to risk the high cost of another general election by wrecking the government proved a further source of strength to the Cabinet. By the end of the reign it could be said with truth that the traditional theory that the Commons controlled the executive had already been reversed. And although this looked very democratic in that the electoral body had become the real political sovereign and the final arbiter of the fate of the Cabinet, it was, until after 1911, a sovereignty that could be effectively exercised only once every seven years and even then only in favour of whichever party happened at that time to be more effectively organized; a vote for a party that lacked unity or enthusiastic and nationwide constituency associations was so much a vote wasted that it would tend to be withheld. Thus, nothing but the profound demoralization of the Conservative-Unionist alliance in 1905 by the split over the issue of Tariff Reform could have let the Liberals win in 1906, because they had previously been so disunited.

Thus the age of the virtuoso parliamentary orator was over; those who sought to secure power within the Commons by combination of demagogy outside and debating skill within it – like Joseph Chamberlain and Randolph Churchill – were broken by the party system because, in future, demagogy outside Westminster would have to be combined with conformism inside it. The party boat must not be rocked. Accordingly, the many Jeremiahs, such as Matthew Arnold, who supposed that democracy would sweep all before it, were mistaken. Their fears were little more than an over-reaction to the declining power of M.P.s over the executive; much as the view that English agriculture was ruined was an over-reaction to the difficulties of one area of it. Had English politics really become democratic in the late-Victorian era it would hardly have seemed necessary to attempt to form a parliamentary Labour party at the end of it.

Another major step towards political democracy, at any rate in theory, was the County Councils Act of 1888, passed by Salisbury's second administration. Outside the incorporated boroughs covered by, or incorporated under, the Municipal Corporations Act of 1835, local government was administered at Quarter Sessions by those members of the local gentry who had succeeded in getting themselves nominated as justices of the peace. By the act of 1888, all the powers of the justices, other than their purely judicial and licensing duties, were transferred to sixty-two elected county councils. The powers given to county councils were also given to certain boroughs, usually those with populations in excess of 50,000. These henceforth became county boroughs, administratively detached from the counties in which they were located. The franchise in the counties was granted to householders; and though they could not stand as candidates, unmarried women were allowed to vote in county council elections.[1] Responsibilities of the new councils extended in the first place to highways, bridges and drains. In 1889 the county councils were made the authorities responsible for carrying out the provisions of the Technical Instruction Act. The 1888 act was a further inroad into the traditional view that the landed gentry and aristocracy should rule over the rural areas as of right but, although there was an initial period of useful innovation, county councils almost always appeared rather too large, too recent and also too humdrum to arouse any long-term popular enthusiasm.

The displacement of rule by hereditary landowners by the rule of persons with sufficient leisure (and money) to devote their time to unpaid council work did not make county councils 'democratic' in the eyes of any section of the community except the section they displaced; and, for long, the average county alderman and councillor was the old justice of the peace in an only moderately democratic fancy dress. Otherwise,

[1] Women, subject to the same limitation, had had the right to vote in borough council elections since 1872.

he was a successful local shopkeeper or builder; and this meant if anything a lessening of local government prestige. The greatest practical change was probably that in London, whose sole large-scale administrative body was still the Metropolitan Board of Works set up in 1858. Henceforth the whole area covered by that body became an administrative county governed by the London County Council, replacing the absurd system by which the local affairs of a world metropolis had been in the incapable hands of thirty vestries and twelve district boards. The only area within its bounds where its writ did not fully operate was the historic City of London, which retained much of its former autonomy and an elaborately-preserved medievalism.

Despite the fact that the area assigned to it was far too small, the L.C.C. soon developed such enterprise and energy, under councillors whose political designation of 'Progressive' covered an amalgam of Liberal, Radical and Fabian Socialist personalities, that in 1899 the Conservatives limited its powers by the creation within its area of the 28 metropolitan boroughs that, like the L.C.C. itself, survived unchanged until the London Government Act of 1963. One Conservative aim in setting up metropolitan boroughs was to limit the powers the L.C.C. might have to use the rates levied on wealthy boroughs to subsidize social improvement in the poorer ones.

The other administrative counties were also subdivided into districts (urban and rural) and into local government parishes by the Local Government Act of 1894, one of the few legislative achievements of Gladstone's government. The new elected urban and rural districts had wider sanitary powers than the old local health boards (or in rural areas, the boards of guardians) and were elected on a wider, that is to say, household, franchise. The act also allowed married, as well as single, women to vote and to stand as candidates if they qualified as electors. The villages did not gain much from their parish councils; the powers it was intended to give them were seriously reduced by the Lords who decided (since the measure had been introduced by a Liberal government) to be as awkward as possible about any proposal to democratize village life more than was un-avoidable.[1] In particular, they objected to the prospect of local affairs in the countryside passing out of the hands of church-wardens and vestries in the parishes and into those of elected councils, many of whose members might well turn out to be nonconformists. It is easy to forget that what may not appear particularly 'democratic' to the observer a century later would, in the context of the time, seem very 'democratic' indeed. Throughout the nineteenth century, any measure that caused even a small transfer of religious, social or political influence from the Established Church to Nonconformity could properly be called 'democratic' and be applauded or condemned accordingly. A similar abstention from applying late twentieth-century interpretations is needed when considering measures which involved even the slightest diminution of the social, political and economic influence of the aristocratic and employ-ing classes. Any such diminution could, pejoratively or approv-ingly, properly be called 'democratic' in the Victorian social context.

Similar considerations apply to the word 'socialism'. In-creasingly fashionable as a term of abuse from at least the mid forties, it almost became a necessary addition to the political vocabulary in late-Victorian times as a label for men and pro-grammes that were, so to speak, post-Radical, in that they looked beyond the reforms which Radicals had been demanding since the first years of the Queen's reign and a large number of which had been almost achieved by the 1880s. By that time, a start (it was felt) had been made on disestablishment, with the Irish Church Act of 1869; the social and political power of the landowner was clearly being eroded in a variety of ways, if

[1] The creation of elected parish councils (where the population of a local government parish was below 300 there was merely an annual parish meeting) led to much confusion of nomenclature when in 1920 the Church of England established its quite unrelated system of parochial church councils. Parish councils after 1888 were units of local govern-ment; parochial church councils were bodies elected by persons on the 'electoral roll' kept by the parish church, and their sole function was to assist (or embarrass) their parish priest in the discharge of his duties as incumbent.

only by acts such as Gladstone's Land Acts and the County and Parish Council Acts; there was secret ballot, universal male household suffrage and even women's suffrage in local government elections; and there was a state elementary education system. Almost everybody realized, whether they liked it or not, that the newly-enfranchised electorate wanted something beyond the relatively minor changes needed to complete this outdated programme, most of which was at least half a century old by the 1880s. In addition, the difficulties of both agriculture and industry after 1873 (and there were serious periods of unemployment in both the 1870s and the 1880s) had begun for the first time since the 1840s to direct the attention of thinking minds, either towards the threat to society posed by so much continuing poverty, or towards the need to relieve it. The triumph of free trade principles and Gladstonian finance had not after all proved enough to guarantee the supremacy of the British economy, since it was manifestly suffering from competition from abroad; nor had they guaranteed adequate prosperity for everyone. The general increase in wages and living standards which economic historians detect in late-Victorian times was almost certainly unsuspected by the unskilled members of the working class, and liable to be rendered non-existent for most working-class people, whether urban or rural, if they fell on hard times through sickness or unemployment or the death of a family's principal wage earner. In practice, it was not only Gladstone's Irish obsession that failed to satisfy the electorate; Conservative Imperialism did not satisfy them either. In spite of his 'forward policy' Disraeli lost the 1880 election; in spite of all Gladstone's calamitous weaknesses in this respect, he can hardly be said to have been given the 'drubbing' in 1885 that he got over Home Rule in 1886; the 1892 election produced a Liberal rally despite the defection of both Whigs and Radicals; the 1895 election was lost, even though Rosebery was a Liberal Imperialist; and in the last election of the Queen's reign, the Khaki election of 1900, the Conservative Unionist alliance scraped home by the narrowest margin, despite the most energetic appeals to the patriotic feelings of a nation at war.

The significance of both Joseph Chamberlain and Lord Randolph Churchill is that each realized the inadequacy of his party's leadership to the needs and opportunities of the time. To dismiss either of them as actuated solely by intense personal ambition is to be superficial. Both indulged in what to their contemporaries seemed demagogy, and in this respect Churchill was perhaps the wilder; it was essential to shout very loud indeed if either was to be heard above the thunderous oratory of Gladstone. Chamberlain's extremer radical notions, which he himself was prepared on occasion to describe as 'socialist', had broader origins than Churchill's ideas, being those of a successful nonconformist and screw manufacturer and an outstandingly successful Lord Mayor of Birmingham, who had used the Artisans Dwellings Act of 1875[1] to effect a large rebuilding programme in that city. For a man with such origins (he was a shopkeeper's son) and such a record to sit on any government front bench[2] was something of a novelty. The violence of his public pronouncements derived from his belief that there was no future for Liberalism until it had rid itself of its Whiggish elements and unless it freed itself from Gladstone's messianic obsession with Ireland. As early as 1883, Salisbury was rebuking both Chamberlain and Sir Charles Dilke for their claim that the radical Liberals were alone the true spokesmen for the 'poorer classes' and was declaring that a party that set out to live upon the discovery of discontents was likely to manufacture those discontents. Chamberlain's bitter retort was that Salisbury had constituted himself the spokesman of 'the class to which he himself belongs, who toil not neither do they spin', who had sprung from a line of courtiers enriched by kings and whose fortunes had grown 'while they have slept, by levying an increased share on all that other men have done by toil and labour to add to the general wealth and prosperity of the nation'. After his further denunciation of the aristocracy when the Lords tried to obstruct the 1884 Reform Bill, he continued to make ominous threats in the election campaign of

---

[1] As well as a special private act.
[2] His first cabinet post was as president of the Board of Trade under Gladstone from 1881 to 1885.

1885. Those, he declared, who imagined that the two million newly-enfranchised voters intended to make no use of their new opportunities were in for 'a rude awakening'. Though denying that he was intent on 'wild and revolutionary projects' he also thought it necessary to assert that he was 'not a Communist, although some people will have it that I am'. But in between these two disclaimers he also said:

> I want you not to accept as final, or as perfect, arrangements under which hundreds of thousands, nay millions, of your fellow countrymen are subject to untold misery with the evidence all round them of accumulated wealth and unbounded luxury. . . . I believe that the great evil with which we have to deal is the excessive inequality in the distribution of riches.[1]

In fact the so-called 'Unauthorized Programme' of radical reforms for which Chamberlain campaigned so energetically with a view to its official adoption by Gladstone and the whole Liberal party at the time of the 1885 election was not revolutionary, not socialistic, not communist; it contained proposals for elected county councils, the provision of smallholdings or allotments for agricultural labourers, free education, and the preservation of poor people's rights in common land, most of which were in fact put into practice, shortly afterwards by Salisbury's Conservative governments. Indeed it was both an old-fashioned and a short-term programme, in that it was designed to attract the newly-enfranchised farmworker and offered nothing to the urban working class whom the general development of the economy was already making much more important. But contemporaries were quick to see that, even if the Unauthorized Programme was itself relatively innocuous, the language of social revolution and class warfare in which it was couched had serious possibilities for the future. In one respect, the unauthorized programme was, however, as alarming in detail as in theory. Chamberlain proposed that taxation should be graduated and that by differential rates of tax the 'landlords' (though if it were applied to landlords today it

[1] H. W. Lucy, *Speeches of the Rt. Hon. Joseph Chamberlain, M.P.* (London, 1885), p. 161.

could be applied to all men of wealth tomorrow) could be made to compensate the masses from whom, it appeared, the landlords had stolen their land. Suddenly, property became stigmatized as theft; suddenly, the tax system was being attacked, not on the Gladstonian grounds that it stultified initiative and should therefore be reduced, but for the contrary reasons that there should be more of it, and that more of it should be taken from the rich in order that it could be used to benefit the community at large. If this was not socialism it was certainly state socialism; and great was the outcry at the time and severe the rebukes of many historians, who saw (accurately enough) 'the shadow of the People's Budget'[1] in Chamberlain's programme.

If Chamberlain's bite was less dangerous than his bark – and after 1886 he virtually ceased even to bark – Lord Randolph Churchill's Tory Democracy had no real bite at all. He was brilliant at the not altogether difficult task of making Gladstone appear ridiculous during the Parliament of 1881–5, in later describing Home Rule as the work of 'an old man in a hurry', and in attacking it for its complete disregard for the feelings of Ulster. But beyond that, his parliamentary and platform performances are best thought of as those of a young man in a hurry – a hurry both to displace his party leaders by himself and to recapture for the Tories that broad appeal to the popular imagination which it had lost with the death of Beaconsfield and was in fact never to acquire again. Nevertheless he, like Chamberlain, talked of 'social revolution'. But in practice all he seems to have asked for is that the Tories should recognize that such a revolution had been contained in Disraeli's joke of 1871 to the effect that the phrase 'vanitas vanitatum, omnia vanitas' in Ecclesiastes ought to have been written as 'sanitas sanitatum, omnia sanitas'.[2] Disraeli's utterance encapsulated,

[1] It would be more accurate to describe the People's Budget as the ghost of at least this part of the Unauthorized Programme.

[2] It is perhaps a tribute to this witticism of Disraeli's that even forty years after his death one of the most widely-used preparations for disinfecting lavatory pans was still that bearing the trade name 'Sanitas'. The witticism disguises the fact that Disraeli's usual attitude to sanitary legislation was one of hostility, mellowing only into indifference.

said Churchill, a 'social revolution' which involved, beyond improved public health, the possibility of improved dwelling places for the poor, compulsory national insurance, the preservation of commons, the establishment of parks, museums, libraries and art galleries, and public baths and washhouses. No less than Chamberlain, Churchill confidently envisaged increased taxation for these purposes: 'Public and private thrift must animate the whole, for it is from public thrift that the funds for these largesses can be drawn and it is by private thrift alone that their results can be utilized and appreciated.' All this was 'Tory Democracy'; all its elements already existed and their translation into a coherent possibility 'may some day possibly be effected by the man, whoever he may be, upon whom the mantle of Elijah has descended'.

Churchill was quite clear that he was the man upon whom Elijah's mantle had fallen. When he recklessly resigned from the Exchequer, it was on the grounds that social reform should take precedence over naval expenditure and in the expectation that he was politically irreplaceable. But when Salisbury let him go, the Cabinet sighed with relief and the repercussions outside Westminster were negligible. Churchill made only one convert to the idea of Tory Democracy and that posthumously; his son, Winston, who derived from it that paternal concern for social welfare which characterized him until 1945 whenever he was not preoccupied with matters of foreign policy and defence.[1]

The substance of the more innocuous of the proposals of both Chamberlain and Churchill was put on the statute book quietly and unobservedly for the most part before the opening of the twentieth century. In 1894, after Gladstone's retirement, Harcourt, chancellor of the exchequer under Rosebery,

[1] There were few major developments in the history of social insurance in the first half of the twentieth century with which Winston Churchill was not associated; and it is historically appropriate that the major forward step between the wars, the Widows', Orphans' and Old Age Pensions Act of 1925, should be jointly the work of Lord Randolph's son, Winston, and Joseph Chamberlain's son, Neville. Yet, if the fathers had been less precipitate, they might well have seen through in their own day what had to wait until the middle age of their sons.

imposed both graduated income tax and death duties, measures which have been described as 'a funeral wreath for the old Liberalism'.[1] Salisbury, continuing to believe that politics was a matter of attending to details rather than to principles, was not a stony-hearted reactionary. He showed a considerable interest in the problems of working-class housing. He moved successfully for a royal commission on the subject when still in Opposition in 1884 and became a member of it, demanding action by the state. It was in reply to the accusation that this must mean he was becoming a Socialist that he made his retort that there were 'no absolute truths or principles in politics'. Disliking ostentatiously wealthy people, he was moved to announce in 1895, 'we have got, as far as we can, to make this country more pleasant to live in for the vast majority of those who live in it'. In 1886, in his first short term as prime minister, an act was passed penalizing the owners of insanitary premises and empowering the Local Government Board to pull them down. In 1887, the first, though largely abortive, Allotments Act was passed. In 1891, he gave his approval to the establishment of free education in those elementary schools where the fees were not more than threepence a week; and did so, not because he believed in state education, but because the state, having imposed the system, ought therefore to bear the cost. In the same year, the onus of paying tithe was transferred from the occupier of land to the landlord. There was an act for the inspection of weighing machines, a further act to protect merchant seamen and a large set of new regulations was drawn up for observance by railway companies. In 1897, in his third ministry, a Workmen's Compensation Act was passed and yet another Merchant Shipping Act; and in the same ministry, the prime minister took a personal interest in a bill which, among other regulations designed to protect people at their place of work, made it a breach of the law for housemaids to sit on window sills when cleaning the outside panes of (the then almost universal) sash windows. In 1899 there was a Seats for Shop Assistants Act and an act to encourage occupiers of small

[1] Carlton Hayes, *A Generation of Materialism, 1871–1900* (New York, Harper & Row, 1941), p. 215.

houses to become owners; in that year, too, the Board of Education was set up to coordinate the work of the higher grade elementary schools, the county technical schools and the endowed grammar schools, while, for the first time, a government grant was made to the university colleges in Wales, the Midlands and north-west England.

If one adds to these miscellaneous pieces of legislation others passed from the 1880s onwards, either by Liberals or Conservatives, it is possible to see the force of the arguments (or at any rate to see the fears) of those who believed they were watching a steady march towards a collectivist, interventionist state. Other acts of the last twenty years of the reign were designed to protect occupiers of land against damage to their crops by game animals; to prohibit the practice of paying workers their wages in public house premises; to allow local authorities to establish electricity supply undertakings; to regulate quarries; to prevent cruelty to children; to isolate persons suffering from cholera and other infectious diseases; to raise the age of consent for girls from 13 to 16; and to close (in 1886) the brothels for registered prostitutes set up in various dockyard and garrison towns by acts of the 1860s. This increase in the coercive powers of the state and the continuous expenditure of money collected by the state in taxes, and by local authorities through the rates, caused both parties to be accused of intervention, collectivism, paternalism and socialism.

Both Herbert Spencer, the founding father of sociology, and Professor Dicey, whose Whiggish interpretation of the operations of the British Constitution[1] was for so long venerated in academic circles, inveighed against the tendency of the times and were supported by a host of minor publicists and pamphleteers. Herbert Spencer went so far as to assert, as early as 1884, that Liberals had really become Tories, since in his interpretation of constitutional history, the Tories had always been the advocates of coercive state power, while Liberalism stood for individual liberty and self-help. In 1885, Dicey defined 'true' Liberalism as the defence of the liberty of the subject, freedom of trade and labour as well as of expression, and argued that

[1] *The Law of the Constitution* (London, 1886).

there should be no interference with liberty where it did not interfere with the liberty of others. Whatever went beyond this was therefore not Liberalism at all. The reality behind these somewhat large assertions as to what Liberalism was,[1] and what it was not, was that whereas, by and large, the prevailing climate of political opinion from about 1846 to 1874 had been Liberal, Sir William Harcourt's opinion (expressed in the 1880s), 'We are all Socialists now', was an equally valid description of the late-Victorian period, subject always to the important consideration that most Socialists would even then have dismissed the thought as absurd.[2] The abstract aridities of John Stuart Mill, Dicey and Spencer had always been as psychologically inadequate as the gospel of self-help was socially and economically inadequate.

For better or worse, by the late nineteenth century, society was seen as requiring to be governed in a manner suitable to the social and economic needs of a more closely-knit, a more thickly-populated and a more economically and technologically interdependent kind of civilization. The doctrines of pure individualism and the unreal myths of *laissez-faire* which, even at the height of their theoretical predominance, had neither of them been capable of complete practical application, were, by the 1880s, increasingly being regarded as unreal and unattainable. They stood revealed as involving not, as they once had done so significantly, freedom from religious intolerance and the restraints of antiquated institutions and regulations, but, rather, as standing for little more – in practice – than the right of businessmen to get rich, and powerful landlords to stay rich and powerful. And since (as they themselves believed) businessmen were not getting rich as fast as they expected and landlords were less powerful than they were and ceasing to be rich merely because they owned land, Liberalism was being abandoned because too many inescapable facts made it impossible to go on

---

[1] At best it was no more than a set of abstract propositions, some of which a few persons calling themselves Liberals may from time to time have claimed to believe in.

[2] But then, how many of the ideas of classic Liberalism had Palmerston accepted before 1865?

believing in it. T. S. Eliot's lines could well apply to Liberal thought by the mid 1880s:

> For last year's words belong to last year's language
> and next year's words await another voice.[1]

Henceforward Liberalism survived as a complex of ideas on which to justify the preservation of the private life and the questing mind against intolerance, censorship and oppression. It ended by becoming what it had begun by being in England: not a philosophy of government but part of the philosophy of dissent. Satisfactory intellectual armour for those who would (rightly) set limits to the power of the government, it was no longer appropriate armament for those who recognized that modern society required a multifariousness of regulation if it was to survive, and if it was to satisfy the imperative need for some measure of social justice.

[1] T. S. Eliot, *The Four Quartets*, 'Little Gidding', pt. II.

15 · Birth of the Twentieth Century

I should be curious to find out the system of reason which would reconcile the various phenomena of English society at this time. . . . the force of habit is continually exposed to fresh assaults; and that combination of worldliness and Bible worship which was renowned for two centuries under the name of Puritanism has at length begun to stagger, to lose confidence in itself, and to reel beneath the blows of science, critical as well as economical. Its young men dream dreams and its old men see visions. The keystone of the English constitution . . . is getting shaken out of its place, and the edifice shows rents and fissures in every direction.

WILLIAM BARRY,
The Nineteenth Century, May 1894

The Present is a dungeon dark
Of social problems. Break the gaol!
Get out into the splendid Past
Or bid the splendid Future hail.

JOHN DAVIDSON,
A Fleet Street Eclogue, 1895

The trend towards state Socialism and the decline of business confidence in the late-Victorian years both stimulated and sprang from the many-sided attacks on the whole philosophy and structure of the society which had emerged as a result of a century's devotion to industrialization and material progress.

Although there had been much criticism of the evolving industrial society right from its beginnings, its effects had been overborne by the confident general belief in the almost inexorable progress of 'improvement' in the middle of the century. Dickens had criticized through ridicule and verbal caricature; in *Heroes and Hero-Worship* Carlyle declaimed,

> I, for my share, declare the world to be no machine! I say that it does *not* go by the wheel-and-pinion 'motives', self-interests, checks, balances; that there is something far other than the clank of spinning jennies and parliamentary majorities. . . .

But once he had extended his dislike of industrial society to include the newly-enfranchised masses after 1867 and had taken refuge in glorifying the Hero he no longer had much to contribute: in the end Carlyle offered not so much Old Testament prophecy as a synthesis of Samuel Smiles with *Mein Kampf*.

Ruskin likewise belonged to the mid-Victorian period, despite his survival till 1900, and his various contributions to the early development of English Socialism properly so-called. In a footnote to the printed version of a series of lectures given in 1864–5 under the title *The Crown of Wild Olive*, he comments scathingly on a sentence contained in an article contributed by Baron Liebig to the *Daily Telegraph* of 11 January 1866, in which the baron declared 'Civilisation is the economy of power and English power is coal'. Ruskin retorts,

> Not altogether so, my chemical friend. Civilization is the making of civil persons . . . and does not at all imply the turning of a small company of gentlemen into a small company of ironmongers.

Earlier still, in a chapter on 'The Nature of the Gothic' in *The Stones of Venice*, published in the 1880s, he had written:

> The great cry that rises from all our manufacturing cities, louder than their furnace blast is . . . that we manufacture everything there except men; we blanch cotton and strengthen steel and refine sugar and shape pottery; but to brighten, to strengthen, to refine or form a single living spirit, never enters into our system of advantages.

Unfortunately, despite his obvious links with early English Socialism, Ruskin like Carlyle was essentially backward-looking.[1] His insistence that Gothic was the only proper architecture for religious building gave further encouragement to the construction of those glowering edifices, secular as well as religious, which were such a feature of the Victorian urban landscape. Worse still, he belonged to the ranks of the mid Victorians in his revulsion from democracy. It was not true that all men are equal. The upper classes must continue to exist, to carry out the function of keeping order among their inferiors and to 'raise them always to the nearest level with themselves of which those inferiors are capable'.

Matthew Arnold was no less critical but rather more naïve when he looked quizzically down his nose at the state of the nation in *Culture and Anarchy*, in 1869. The aristocracy were healthy 'Barbarians'; the middle classes were canting 'Philistines'; and the rest of the nation constituted 'The Populace'. The two former groups were called upon to abandon their obsession with Old Testament Hebraism and to think of the Greeks instead. They were to aim at 'sweetness and light', rather than at physical fitness in the one case, or devotion to nonconformist fetishes if they were Philistines. All this badly needed saying. In a society in which intellectuals who found religion incredible turned for salvation to George Eliot's view that though God was inconceivable and immortality unbelievable, Duty was 'peremptory and absolute', it was all to the good to hear a cultivated mind object that '*strictness of conscience*, the staunch adherence to some fixed law of doing we have got already' must be compensated for by 'spontaneity of consciousness, which tends to enlarge our whole law of doing'. He was on sure ground in calling attention to the private as well as the public evils of the intense concentration on purely personal material and spiritual salvation which marred even the better

---

[1] At almost no time in the century did radical and socialist thought escape from its unhistorical nostalgia for the world that preceded not only the factories but also the Age of Enlightenment. The whole silly fiction of 'Merrie England' distorted, and indeed tended to inhibit, rational thought about either the present or the future.

men among the Victorian Philistines. Referring to reports that the secretary of an insurance company had committed suicide while 'under the apprehension that he would come to poverty and that he was eternally lost' he wrote:

> The whole middle class have a conception of things . . . just like that of this poor man . . . how generally, with how many of us, are the main concerns these two: the concern for making money, and the concern for saving our souls! and how entirely does this narrow and mechanical conception of our secular business proceed from a narrow and mechanical conception of our religious business![1]

In a sardonically elegant attack on the sillier intellectual excesses of free trade thinking he was moved to an almost radical frame of mind, induced in part no doubt by his lifelong experience as an inspector of schools: 'the increase of houses and manufactories, or the increase of population' were not 'absolute goods in themselves, to be mechanically pursued and to be worshipped like fetishes'. Instead, he asserts, we can

> conceive of no perfection as being real which is not a *general* perfection, embracing all our fellow men with whom we have to do. . . . So all our fellow men, in the East End of London and elsewhere we must take along with us in the progress towards perfection.[2]

Arnold's prescription for society's cultural deficiencies was to end the contemporary philosophy of 'do as you like' and to charge the state with the duty of educating the Populace in the principles of sweetness and light, and in the knowledge of all 'the best that has been known and thought in the world'. But this highly optimistic view of the state as the communal custodian of culture and of the schools as disseminators of sweetness and light[3] was all but nullified by the backward-

---

[1] M. Arnold, *Culture and Anarchy*, ed. J. Dover Wilson (Cambridge, C.U.P., 1961 reprint), p. 192.
[2] ibid.
[3] Can H.M. inspectors of schools be said ever to have become much more realistic than their great Archetype?

looking element in Arnold's thought. He put himself out of court as a guide for all but the most donnish of late Victorians by a dogged adherence to the principle of an Established Church and by his insistence that the populace was bent on a course of anarchy (Arnold was yet another victim of the Hyde Park Railing syndrome). All in all, Arnold was an intellectually fastidious mid-Victorian with a passion for universal education, a detached distaste for the vulgarity of prevailing mid-Victorian attitudes and a characteristically academic disapproval of industry and commerce. That he therefore figures prominently in all the books about the Victorians is understandable; but in practice he failed to cut much ice.

Carlyle, Ruskin and Arnold (and, of course, in his early writings, Disraeli)[1] all had this in common, however, that they saw that the individualism which classic Liberalism had so sedulously preached implied a selfish, and therefore fundamentally heartless, society. Beneath its bland exterior, Liberalism, in so far as it implied *laissez-faire*, was the philosophy of the 'I'm-all-right-Jacks', whose characteristic attitude to the problem of those who were poor was quite simply, 'That's your bad luck, mate'. They looked backward to Edmund Burke and forward to both the Communist and anti-Communist totalitarians of the twentieth century in their demand for a society which was a harmonious and organic community instead of one based, as mid-Victorian society was, on self-help and individual competitiveness. But none of them (except the 'opportunist' and 'superficial' politician Disraeli) could face the consequences of their own social criticism: that the Populace, the Democracy, the 'residuum', could never be assimilated into society for so long as their social and economic needs were constantly neglected, and while it was assumed, as it was by all these writers, that they ought not to have been born in such numbers and were merely objects of contempt, pity, irrational fear, or unthinking repression. Thus, Matthew Arnold, the apostle of 'sweetness and light', quoted as an opinion he could 'never forsake' the view of his headmaster-father, Thomas Arnold: 'As for rioting, the old Roman way of dealing with *that* is

[1] See p. 166.

always the right one; flog the rank and file, and fling the ring-leaders from the Tarpeian Rock!'[1]

Late Victorians, however, showed a greater awareness of the problems of the poor and a greater anxiety to do something about those problems than, generally speaking, their predecessors had. It was at last beginning to be acknowledged that the poor were real people, even though a good proportion of those who did concern themselves with the poor were still neurotically anxious to distinguish between the 'deserving' poor and the 'undeserving' poor. The reasons for this new concern are still a matter for speculation, though one of them may well be that there were more manifestations of discontent in London in late-Victorian times than there had been since 1848 and that there was an increase in the number of the very poor owing to migration into the city from the areas of agricultural decline. There may have been an increase in poverty as a result of a temporary decline in the expenditure of the rich in the capital, owing to the falling rents of the great aristocrats and the declining confidence of businessmen. There was an increase in the number of immigrants, particularly Jewish ones, from Eastern Europe, who would have swelled the ranks of the poor. In the bad years of 1879, 1886 and 1894 unemployment reached an alarmingly high figure. Yet another reason may have been simply that the cumulative pressure of all the literature of condemnation which had been written earlier in the reign at last began to take effect, making the more serious middle class more aware of the contrast between wealth and poverty that existed on so great a scale in London, and more receptive to the new wave of published works, fictional, polemical or quasi-sociological, which uncovered more and more of the evidences of London poverty. It may be that the fashion for interventionist legislation also furthered the idea, not simply that something ought to be done, but that it could be done. Christianity, too, began to renew that more lively sense of its social mission which Christian Socialism had sought to create. Contributory also may have been the insatiable Victorian desire for facts and particularly sensational ones. It is perhaps not accidental that at

[1] Arnold, op. cit., p. 203.

a time when explorers, missionaries and empire-builders were opening up Darkest Africa, stay-at-homes should console themselves by exploring Darkest London. One lady contributor to *The Nineteenth Century* wrote in January 1879,

> Rich people with tender hearts have been having a hard time of it lately in many ways. Never, surely, before, were so many and such harrowing appeals made every day to their feelings on behalf of sufferers of every description. The sufferings of the poor in sickness and old age, our neglected children, pining needlewomen, hard time, strikes, workhouses, crowded alleys, fever-nests, polluted water-supply, smallpox, pauperism, monotony, dreariness and drink haunt our thoughts by day if not our dreams by night,

and Octavia Hill, in the same journal in 1884, wrote,

> I notice . . . a depraved hunger for rags, sharp need and slums, which pollutes some who profess charity. 'I should like to go where there is condensed misery' a lady said lately in the cheeriest tone. But, short of this utter callousness, there is a certain excited temper abroad which almost amounts to a longing to see want. There is, in a court I know well, a great blank, high bare wall, which rises within a few feet of the back windows of a number of rooms inhabited by the poor. I have shown it to many . . . and have said how cheerless it makes the rooms. Some feel it and seem to realise what sitting opposite it day after day would be. Some say it isn't so *very* dark and almost seem to add, 'Can you show us nothing worse?'

Apart from the multitude of voluntary social organizations run by the middle classes in an endeavour to explore, to expose and charitably relieve at least some of the misery of the poor, there was an abundant literature on the subject. Much attention was devoted to the loaded subject of prostitution. The view that poor girls were so shockingly exploited in the sweated trades that prostitution was an altogether less degrading way of life was elaborated in so lively a manner in Bernard Shaw's play, *Mrs Warren's Profession*, that, though published in 1894, it was kept off the stage by the lord chamberlain until 1904: Mrs Warren explained her adoption of prostitution as due to her desire to avoid her sister's death from poisoning after working in a white-lead factory for nine shillings a week. In 1885, the journalist W. T. Stead, editor of *The Pall Mall Gazette*, provoked the introduction of the Criminal Law Amendment Bill[1] by luridly exposing the white slave trade in very young girls in a series of articles entitled 'Maiden Tribute of Modern Babylon'. To prove his point he arranged to procure a fourteen-year-old 'maiden' by giving her mother money through an intermediary and arranging for the child's dispatch across the Channel, an action that landed him in court.

The attention given by middle-class reformers to prostitution among the poor was only to be expected; it enabled them to press for social reform, to castigate the heartlessness and hypocrisy of traditional Victorian 'respectability', and it ensured maximum publicity among a class accustomed to condemn sexual irregularity because of their not always successful attempts to avoid being guilty of it themselves. On closer examination, some of what was loosely labelled 'prostitution' derived from the not unreasonable tendency of destitute young women to attach themselves to lonely and hardly less destitute young men who were financially incapable of transforming a not always exclusively sexual union into a legal marriage. The girl might thereafter drift from man to man in a similar fashion. A proportion of them, though indeed driven into this irregular sexual life by their economic situation, could be termed 'prostitutes' in an emotive sense rather than in the technical sense more properly applicable to the young women who sought wealthy male clients in the 'promenade' of the Empire Theatre, Leicester Square. Henry Mayhew's inquiry into the allegation that needlewomen were forced into prostitution by their low wages suggests that, in 1849–50, those who gave evidence that this was indeed true in their particular cases were rarely professional 'prostitutes', not only because they avoided this condition whenever they could, but also because they were very ashamed of it.[2] Charles Booth's inquiries in the 1880s con-

[1] See p. 196.
[2] E. P. Thompson and E. Yeo, *The Unknown Mayhew* (London, Merlin Press, 1971), pp. 167–78.

firmed this; he distinguished clearly between the professional and those

> who take to the life occasionally when circumstances compel: tailoresses or dressmakers, for example, who return to their trade in busy times; girls from low neighbourhoods who eke out a living in this way; or poor women, neglected wives or widows, under pressure of poverty. . . . Some jealousy is felt by those who are more strictly professional, of incursions into the field occupied.[1]

Charles Booth's seventeen volumes on *The Life and Labour of the People in London* was published between 1889 and 1903, and written in collaboration with Beatrice Potter (who married Sidney Webb in 1892).[2] It provides a survey of the poor of London which, though less lurid and more detached than that provided by Henry Mayhew in *London Labour and the London Poor* which had related to the years 1849–50, appears to have had more influence on contemporaries and on subsequent historical writings about the Victorian period.[3] Yet, save perhaps for the most dedicated of sociologists, there seems very little in Booth that was not in Mayhew. There is still the sorry tale of minimal wages, maximum hours of work and

[1] *Charles Booth's London*, ed. A. Fried and R. Elman (Harmondsworth, Pelican, 1971), pp. 193–4.
[2] See p. 314.
[3] One reason for this is that through Beatrice Webb, the Fabian and Socialist movements had something of a vested interest in Booth's findings. Another is the allegation that Booth was a more scientific and less anecdotal writer than Mayhew; this view is now in dispute (see Thompson and Yeo, op. cit.). Other factors are that Mayhew was disapproved of at the time for his obvious feeling that something serious should be done for the poor whose plight he uncovered; that, for various reasons, his serious inquiries were not, like Booth's, sustained over a long period of time; and that, in general, Mayhew wrote against the mainstream ideas of his day whereas Booth began a habit of systematic investigation into the phenomena of poverty that has continued almost uninterruptedly ever since. Mayhew, however, entered far more imaginatively into the lives of those he described than Booth and was in that sense more 'real'. There is something coldly blue-bookish about Booth; perhaps this was encouraged by Miss Beatrice Potter. It may have been due also to the fact that, as a Conservative, he avoided the stock-in-trade reactions of the liberal-minded.

uncertainty of employment in the many casual or sweated trades for which London had long been notorious; there are still the dismal living conditions, the same stories of drunken male treatment of common-law wives; there is the same evidence of recourse to the streets by destitute women, a not dissimilar assortment of weird and pathetically odd ways of scraping together any sort of living, the same combination of improvident spending in good times with its consequent recourse to pawnshop or bread ticket in bad. To choose at random, Booth gave this account of the occupants of one house in Parker Street, Covent Garden:

At No. 19 on the ground floor there was a woman with two grown-up daughters, all looking hardened in sin. They would beg for a bread ticket as though they had not broken fast for days. But if refused the face would alter to a fiendish grin and the most fearful language would follow, the strength of voice and expression leaving no doubt as to the absence of food or ill-health. In the first floor front lived the Neals. The man had been a soldier and now earns his living as a market porter; his wife was fast breaking up and the son, a tall young fellow of twenty-two appeared to be in rapid consumption; the daughter, also grown up, sold flowers in the street. All four lived and slept in this room. In the back room lived a family consisting of mother, a son of twenty, a daughter of twelve, and an old grandmother who looked eighty – a spare tough woman – who gets her living as a crossing sweeper and gets a lot of food and coal tickets given. The mother sells in the streets but suffers from asthma, and the son a few months ago was at the point of death from the same complaint. The girl also looked very ill. Their room was in wretched condition – patches of plaster protruding where the walls had been roughly mended, windows stuffed with rags or mended with paper – vermin everywhere.[1]

A state of affairs not greatly unlike that to be found in Parker Street in 1890 is related in an interview secured by Mayhew with a near destitute shoemaker in 1850:

I have lived at the East-end nearly two years. Some months back, I took a shop in Great Saffron-Hill, Holborn; being a low

[1] Fried and Elman, op. cit., pp. 133-4.

neighbourhood, and having a good stock to start with, I thought in such a place we might do. I bought and sold old clothes, mended old boots, &c, for sale; but all my efforts were useless. I lived there four months; and as fast as I sold my property the money was spent to support my family. Not being able to obtain employment we began here to feel the pinching of poverty, and got in arrear for rent.

The man then took to women's tailoring, being allowed by some kindly Jews to occupy their kitchen for 1s 3d a week rent, which he was rarely able to pay:

The kitchen we lived in was dark, damp and dirty. The ceiling was six feet only from the floor. The health of myself, wife and children suffered much here, with the bad quality of food we were obliged to eat, bad ventilation and many hours of toil.

He got work making women's cloth button boots at 1s 5d a pair:

I was obliged to work from five to six in the morning till twelve at night. At this work, bad as the pay was, we could, by long hours, get bread and coffee, and school-money for two children – meat we could not get. I could not get Sunday's dinner. . . . We would reserve 2d on Saturday night to buy pudding for (the children) on Sunday.

Things then got worse as he took even lower-paid tailoring work and his wife took in sewing. Now, they could not often buy bread. 'We lived upon boiled rice and hard biscuits, sold at 2d per pound in the East-end.'[1]

Other less patiently persevering accounts of London life in the period include *The Bitter Cry of Outcast London* (1883) by G. R. Sims, *In Darkest England, and the Way Out* (1890) by General William Booth of the Salvation Army, and *The White Slaves of England* (1897) by Robert Sherard, which exposed yet again the horrors of life endured by working-class girls. All were widely read and it is significant that General Booth's book should have been one of them. William Booth had founded the Salvation Army in 1878, and made of it the first large-scale effort to take

[1] Thompson and Yeo, op. cit., pp. 261–3.

Christianity into the urban back streets in a manner capable of being understood by at least some of the people who lived in them. Its success (after the inevitable initial disapproval of reputable religious bodies and the physical resistance of the ruffianly element) was ascribable to the quite exceptional contemporaneity of its methods. The not particularly original concept of an army of the saved at war with the Devil was made pictorially visible by the army's distinctive martial uniform, and although it relied greatly on the verbalism so traditional in evangelical religion it brought to its aid a colourful ritual and a music-hall type of music more immediately comprehensible and less initially intimidating to the unconverted than the liturgical splendours either of Rome or the Anglo-Catholics, comparatively active though both now were in their attempts to reach the poor. Salvationism systematically and unashamedly combined the saving of souls with the service of the physical needs of the destitute. It was, in the best sense of the word, a brilliant form of religious vulgarization; and Booth himself was at pains to deride the kind of Christianity that believed that 'once a man is down the supreme duty of a self-regarding Society is to jump upon him' and to insist that until Christians did something about poverty it would, to the poor, be merely a 'mockery'.

None of this was new, but in the late-Victorian era it at last began to strike home: so much so that the older Churches quickly responded by imitation, with the establishment by the Anglican Church, of the Church Army in 1882 and of the Boys' Brigade in 1883. At the far extreme of the religious spectrum from William Booth, Cardinal Manning, Roman Catholic archbishop of Westminster, was quick, in the spirit of Leo XIII's encyclical *Rerum Novarum*, to associate himself with the cause of the poor. It was not enough to regard the manufacture of goods at a price that would undercut the foreigner as an adequate social end if the consequence was to destroy family life by turning the working man into a 'beast of burden', he declared. And, shrewdly though he penetrates the man's pseudo-virility, Shaw vividly portrays in *Candida* (1895) a typical socially-conscious Anglican priest of the period in the

Reverend James Mavor Morell, 'a Christian Socialist clergyman of the Church of England, and an active member of the Gild of St. Matthew and the Christian Social Union'. His bookshelves include, in addition to theological works (and the poems of Robert Browning), such works as 'Fabian Essays,[1] A Dream of John Ball, Marx's Capital, and half a dozen other literary landmarks in Socialism'. The outward appearance Shaw ascribes to Morell is also illustrative of the 'muscular' Christianity which was much favoured in the period (and afterwards) and which often resulted from a conscious attempt to combine godliness with manliness.

> ... A vigorous, genial, popular man of forty, robust and good-looking, full of energy, with pleasant, hearty, considerate manners, and a sound, unaffected voice, which he uses with the clean athletic articulation of a practised orator, and with a wide range and perfect command of expression. He is a first-rate clergyman, able to say what he likes to whom he likes, to lecture people without setting himself up against them, to impose authority on them without humiliating them, and, on occasion, to interfere in their business without impertinence. His well-spring of enthusiasm has never run dry for a moment; he still eats and sleeps heartily enough to win the daily battle between exhaustion and recuperation triumphantly. Withal, a great baby, pardonably vain of his powers and unconsciously pleased with himself. He has a healthy complexion: good forehead, with the brows somewhat blunt, and the eyes bright and eager, mouth resolute but not particularly well cut, and a substantial nose, with the mobile spreading nostrils of the dramatic orator, void, like all his features, of subtlety.[2]

It is thus important to recognize that Christianity contributed much more to the stirring of the social conscience in late-Victorian England than simply to provide in Methodist meetings the early training of a number of future Labour party leaders. The grown men and women of the 1880s and 1890s had spent their formative years in the 1850s and 1860s, well before either biblical criticism or the furore caused by Darwin's works

[1] See p. 314.
[2] G. B. Shaw, *Candida*, stage direction at beginning of Act One.

had penetrated very far into the public consciousness; and the decline in Christian belief, though heavily publicized at the time and excessively emphasized in most histories, clearly provoked much fresh thinking among intelligent Christians and a great deal of revivalism. The first Quintin Hogg based the whole polytechnic movement in London on a religious revivalism which he had absorbed and fostered at Eton in the 1860s.[1] When the Moody part of the Sankey and Moody partnership[1] first came to London in 1871, Hogg was the first to befriend him, and in 1884 he organized the Chicago evangelist's campaign for him. This experience reinforced the altogether Anglo-Saxon circumstance that the development of technical education within the L.C.C. area (most early polytechnics[2] in London were inspired by the results of Hogg's lavish expenditure of time and his own money[3] on transforming a ragged school, first into a Youths' Christian Institute and then into the Polytechnic Institute in Regent Street) owed at least as much to revivalist, evangelical, muscular Christianity as it did to the County Councils Act of 1888, the Technical Instruction Act of 1889 or the influence upon the L.C.C. of Mr Sidney Webb. Brightly cheerful, fervently evangelical, ready at the drop of a hat to produce a sermon packed with biblical texts, so resolutely muscular that he still played football at fifty-seven, a manly supporter of Imperialist ideas, Quintin Hogg's determination to bring the poor young lads of the metropolis to Jesus was matched only by his determination to get them into night classes (and eventually day classes as well) in every conceivable subject. The polytechnic he created was, like William Whiteley's store, a universal provider of instruction on everything from hairdressing to engineering surveying, from shorthand and typing to carriage building, from plumbing to Dante readings; of every kind of social club from mock parliaments to brass bands; of holidays by the sea and on the Continent; and of regular Sunday services which made what was, on weekdays, a night school-cum-temperance and social institute into a

---

[1] See p. 9.
[2] The Woolwich Polytechnic was a notable example.
[3] About £100,000.

self-contained place of worship, as distinctive in its way as Whitfield's Tabernacle; and there were, of course, Bible classes without end.

The gap between humanitarian and Christian concern on one side and the working class itself on the other continued, however, to be hardly less wide than in the past. This was not only because little of this earnest middle-class concern led to any noteworthy legislation but also (and this was not often recognized) because almost all the social reformers (even the most earnest of them) either pitied or disliked the working classes because their behaviour was so unlike that of the middle classes or out of a suspicion that they either did not want to behave like the middle classes or were incapable of so doing. It was not an accident that university and public schools set up 'missions' in the poorer parts of London; the poor were often treated, even by those most anxious to improve their lot, as if they were 'poor black men' who needed to be converted from nakedness and dependence on witch doctors.[1] Moreover, there was a geographical factor. The London-based writers and investigators had relatively little knowledge of the stable artisan classes of the great industrial areas in 'the provinces', and were a good deal too ready to see the lower orders as largely composed of, either what they patronizingly looked down on as 'little' or 'shabby' clerks, or else of the 'great unwashed'. A deep-seated bourgeois dislike of the working class is one of the distinguishing features of the plays of Bernard Shaw, for instance; and it is significant that Doolittle in *Pygmalion* (1912) is simultaneously a boozy scrounger and a derider of 'middle-class morality'. Conversely there was, as Shaw frequently pointed out, a certain amount of emotional self-indulgence in the late Victorians' interest in the poor: some of the desire to 'do good' derived from the pleasurable feeling of 'being good' that resulted.[2]

[1] Lord Salisbury, in that slightly absent-minded manner that often characterized his utterances, came very near, in a public speech in May 1886, to saying that the Irish were not really much more fitted for free representative institutions than 'the Hottentots'.

[2] A widespread phenomenon among the socially conscious middle class Leftists of the 1930s also.

L

Perhaps the most notable lack of sympathetic understanding of the working class as people was to be found in those architects of the Fabian Society, Sidney and Beatrice Webb, from whom Shaw derived, or so he claimed, most of his Socialist ideas.[1] History has recorded to the Webbs a disproportionate role in the development of political Socialism at the end of the nineteenth century, whereas their major contribution belongs to the twentieth century. The Fabian Society of which they were the principal luminaries was founded in 1884, originally as an offshoot of the Fellowship of the New Life founded in the previous year, which was primarily ethical in character. The Fabian Society proposed to concern itself with the social movements and needs of the day, and above all with the patient examination and dissemination of facts about society through discussions, public meetings and pamphleteering. Its first pamphlet was entitled *Why Are the Many Poor?* Later pamphlets in the 1880s, mostly written by Sidney Webb, included *Facts for Socialists, Facts for Londoners* and *Figures for Londoners*. In 1887, it issued a basic constitution, announcing that the society (which then had 150 members) 'consists of Socialists'. Its aims were to emancipate 'Land and Industrial Capital from individual and class ownership' and to vest them 'in the community for the general benefit'. It would work for 'the extinction of private property in Land' and 'for the transfer to the community of such industrial Capital as can conveniently be managed socially'. These Socialist ends were to be achieved 'by the general dissemination of knowledge as to the relation between the individual and Society in its economic, ethical and political aspects'. *Fabian Essays in Socialism* appeared in 1889. These sought to base Socialism 'not on the speculations of a German philosopher but on the obvious evolution of society as we see

[1] He also claimed to owe much to Samuel Butler, author of *Erewhon* and *The Way of All Flesh*. Beyond the fact that Butler attacked the stupider forms of Victorian pseudo-Christianity and exposed so much of the cant of the day there is little else in Shaw's claim. All the same, the tendency to disparage Butler as a case of arrested development is regrettable. *The Way of All Flesh* is a recognizable representation of the worst aspects of Victorianism and the *Notebooks* contain more good sense than weightier volumes of Victorian writing.

it around us' and 'proved' that Socialism was 'the next step in the development of society, rendered inevitable by the changes which followed from the industrial revolution of the eighteenth century'. Other characteristics of the society are revealed by its title 'Fabian', which it assumed on the (incorrect) grounds that the Roman general Fabius only struck hard against Hannibal after a long period of patient waiting; and by Sidney Webb's celebrated if rather laboured joke about 'The Individualist Town Councillor', who declared self-help was the only true gospel and that Socialism was 'a fantastic absurdity', all the while walking along 'a municipal pavement lit by municipal gas and cleansed by municipal brooms with municipal water' en route to meet 'his children coming from a municipal school hard by the county lunatic asylum and municipal hospital', or using 'the municipal tramway' to get to 'the municipal art gallery, museum or library'.

The strong emphasis in Fabian writings on 'gradualism' and on the claim that since 'socialism' already existed at the municipal level its application to national administration was merely a further step forward in the direction in which society was already going, has usually been seen as a piece of brilliantly successful propaganda designed to convert those to whom Socialism was otherwise still as fearful a word as Jacobinism had been a century earlier. It would perhaps be more realistic to see it rather as a manifestation of middle-class intellectual complacency. At its widest, Fabianism was mostly a matter of a tiny middle-class minority demonstrating its intellectual and statistical superiority before a (largely indifferent) middle-class audience; the humanitarianism it displayed was usually perfunctory; the contacts it made with the working class at this stage were few. It worked, if at all, in influencing administrators, civil servants and the occasional politician and, via Sidney Webb, the L.C.C. H. G. Wells was one of its early members; but, nearer than they were to the realities, if not of the working class, at any rate of the lowest strata of the non-industrial classes, a Cockney by nature if not precisely by birth, he soon found the Fabian Society intolerable and left it, only to deride its principal figures in his fiction.

Bernard Shaw was the most iridescent of all the Fabians but, though he shared their narrowly middle-class outlook, his real life-work was to popularize, not Fabianism, but himself; and this, whether as controversialist or dramatist, he did not succeed in doing to any great extent until the 1920s. For longer than was remembered by the time longevity had turned him into a national institution, Shaw's policy of being deliberately outrageous had the result that most people who read him, or, as was more usual, read about him, were outraged by him.

None of this detracts from the long-term influence of Fabianism, and of the Webbs in particular. Already before 1900 (in 1894 and 1895 respectively) the Webbs had published a monumental and elaborately researched *History of Trade Unionism* and had been actively responsible for the foundation of the London School of Economics and Political Science, though it is interesting to recall that having prejudged the issue in accordance with their theories, they took it for granted that scholarly research and teaching in economics was bound to further the cause of Socialism. And, although they had little to do with the formation of the parliamentary Labour party and regarded both it and trade union leaders in general with a fastidious snobbery that was not solely intellectual (Beatrice in particular regarding them with middle-class feminist asperity as muddleheads who smoked too much and drank too much), their long-term contribution to the social thinking of the mid-twentieth century is probably difficult to overestimate. The Fabians in general, and the Webbs in particular, provide an outstanding example of how many of the ideas of the post-Victorian world were conceived by the late-Victorians. Yet, in their devotion to fact and statistical inquiry and in the almost total absence of feeling for any section of the community except a small left-wing element of middle-class intellectuals, they ought perhaps to be regarded as looking back to Chadwick and Bentham and forward to what James Burnham was later to christen 'the Managerial Revolution'. True, they also disliked the aristocracy, what was called 'society', the surviving power of privilege and rank and the growing power of finance and capital; but the central weakness of the Webbs' Fabianism was that they believed that the problems of poverty and of the subordinate position that labour held in society was essentially a matter of large-scale social engineering to be undertaken exclusively by a fully-informed intellectual élite like themselves. This is not to underestimate, but merely to describe, their true place in history.

Another contemporary influence which touched Socialism and the nascent working-class movement in a less clinical manner was William Morris, a many-sided man who, again however, influenced the middle-class rather than the working-class mind. His first influence was on interior decoration, with his demand that rooms should contain only what was known 'to be useful' and believed 'to be beautiful'. This began the long slow process of uncluttering middle-class drawing rooms. He then turned to wallpaper and textile design and to the revival of fine printing typefaces. This aesthetic revolt against machine-made artifacts led him to a proper attack on capitalism, a backward-looking contempt for machinery and to a revival of the cult of the craftsman. This was to put the social as well as the aesthetic clock back, leading in time to the quite arbitrarily silly equations, 'craft-made equals good' but 'machine-made equals bad'. But it also forced Morris into the Socialist camp since it was indeed a fact that manufactured domestic articles were at that time usually very ugly. Fortunately Morris was also a poet and this led him to write not only some 'Chants for Socialists' but a long-remembered (though never widely-read) account of a Socialist Utopia in *News from Nowhere* (1824). Though the only work in Socialist literature that is graced by a genuine love of life and human nature, it is, alas, a Utopia populated almost entirely by arty-crafty people chatting and basket-weaving their way along the banks of the higher part of the Thames valley in a climate from which the onset of the Socialist Commonwealth has miraculously excluded all possibility of wet weather. Much of the same combination of Socialism and the simple life is to be found in Edward

Carpenter, who was much influenced by Morris and produced *Towards Democracy* in 1883.[1]

Inevitably, some of these essentially middle-class ideas filtered down to the leaders of the working classes themselves; and there was a good deal of personal collaboration between leading trade unionists and the Webbs and William Morris and others in publicity campaigns, in public meetings and in the organization of the evidence placed before royal commissions. Yet it was in the long term rather than the short term that what one must perhaps call 'intellectual' Socialists of the eighties and nineties had most influence; and even then mainly upon a dissentient, though vocal, section of the middle class, disposing them to favour the working-class movement because it seemed both to be suffering the most from the social injustices of industrial society and because the workers, too, like the 'leftist' middle class, were in apparent revolt against that society. Yet, if indeed the writers and investigators and charitable workers did strengthen the working-class movement by providing it with allies, many of whom had the ear of influential people in central and local government and administration, it could also be said to have helped to stiffen the resistance of the employing class by appearing to threaten it not only with recalcitrant workers but also an insidiously dangerous set of hostile ideas. The strong element of Socialism and quasi-Socialism to be found in areas of secular and religious middle-class thinking ensured that any political movement that arose out of working-class aspirations would never in the conventional sense be wholly 'working class'. For more than a century after the 1880s many of the voices that championed the workers' cause

[1] In addition to his Socialist writings, Edward Carpenter, the other main influences on whose work were the American poet, Walt Whitman, and the English sexologist, Havelock Ellis, later wrote two curious apologias for homosexuality, *The Intermediate Sex* and *Ioläus, an Anthology of Friendship*. Socialism was hindered rathei than helped by its tendency to attract 'cranks' (Shaw was a teetotaller and a vegetarian) and was felt to be so continually hindered by this characteristic that much of George Orwell's *Road to Wigan Pier* (1937) is taken up with a rather over-written attack on such people.

in 'the class struggle' would do so in obviously educated, middle-class accents. What the late-Victorian period perpetuated in English life was a different division altogether: one between those of all 'classes' who assented to the existing social, economic and political order and those, also of all 'classes', who dissented from it. Such a division may be supposed to exist in all societies, even the most totalitarian, and it certainly existed before 1880 in England. But before 1880 the characteristic public form that dissent took was a Liberalism that also comprehended all classes: from Whigs, remembering their forbears' great political act of dissent in 1689, through the new mercantile class thrown up by the industrial revolution, the religiously dissenting nonconformists of the new towns, and the poor labourers of Flora Thompson's '*Lark Rise*', singing of Gladstone in all their rustic innocence,

> God bless the people's William,
> Long may he head the van
> Of Liberty and Freedom,
> God bless the Grand Old Man.[1]

As soon as Liberalism was seen to be developing as the prevailing creed, however, Toryism might have been expected to be the creed of dissent from it; and it is in this sense that Disraeli can with justice be credited with insight in accusing Peel of betraying Toryism by his adhesion to Liberal economic principles and it is in this sense, too, that beneath the personal irresponsibility and runaway tirades of Lord Randolph there was a vein of genuine political understanding. But from the 1880s onwards, the division that needed organized political expression was no longer that between landlord and farmer, or farmer and agricultural labourer, but between urban employer and urban worker and, more than ever, between those who, on much wider grounds, differed fundamentally about the nature and purpose of industrial society, the one a group who regarded the right of the individual to make a profit as its principal determining factor and the other a group who sought to subordinate

[1] Flora Thompson, *Lark Rise to Candleford* (London, O.U.P., 1954), p. 59.

both the profit motive and the progress of technology to the needs of the community as a whole. With the exception of the more bloodless Fabians all the critics of industrial progress saw it as involving the sacrifice of human dignity, as stultifying to the emotions and as inimical to spontaneity and therefore to man's creative instincts. It is wholly appropriate that the late-Victorian period should have simultaneously been a period of mounting social criticism, and one of aesthetic revolt, and that many leaders of the latter called themselves Socialists. William Morris was by no means alone in this. Shaw was Socialist, playwright and dramatic and music critic. Max Beerbohm proclaimed the rebirth of 'the Dandy' in the 1890s and it can no longer be considered merely frivolous to see signs of social transformation in any startling change of male fashion. It was in a typically frivolous context that Max Beerbohm wrote 'For behold! the Victorian era comes to an end and the day of *sancta simplicitas* is quite ended', but this is as characteristic of the end of the century as the fact that Oscar Wilde, the most wittily brilliant of playwrights to use the English language, was not merely also the author of a great deal of aesthetically mannered prose which, though now nauseating to the mind, may perhaps be regarded as having, at the time, been therapeutically emetic; he also professed to be a Socialist and attempted to answer a question too profound for most Socialists even to ask by writing on *The Soul of Man Under Socialism*. When, by due process of law, Oscar Wilde was publicly disgraced in 1895, the established order was doing a great deal more than imprisoning a great writer for being a homosexual. It was defending itself against a whole complex of ideas and attitudes which called in question the received ideas of Victorian England as destructively as the writers of the Enlightenment attacked those of the *ancien régime* in eighteenth-century France. As one of the lesser figures of the aesthetic movement of the 1890s wrote, 'The one certainty is that society is the enemy of man' and

> A man who goes through a day without some fine emotion has wasted his day, whatever he had gained by it. . . . And the making of one's life into art is after all the first duty and privilege of every

man. It is to escape from material reality into whatever is our own form of spiritual existence.[1]

To provide effective political expression to this miscellany of discontents was of course virtually impossible, if only because so many of them were manifestations of a revolt against the entire political system and because there was (and is) no political machinery capable of reversing developments so socially and technologically fundamental as those which had shaped Victorian society out of the industrial revolution. The critics of the age, whether social or artistic, looked back to a utopian past and forward to a utopian future. This is why, in the long run, it was the Webbs who were to have most influence on post-Victorian social policy; they were only interested in facts and in transforming society by slow patient plans for social improvement on lines they considered were already being laid down by the collectivist legislation of their own day. Apart from periodic visitations during which Beatrice was vaguely aware of some higher spiritual force at work in the universe, the Webbs were impatient of feelings. The aesthetic movement ran away into disaster: the disgrace of Wilde and the 'decadence' of Aubrey Beardsley left the way open to sneering voices describing all its practitioners as 'greenery-yallery'; they were laughed at by Gilbert and Sullivan, mocked unpleasantly by Owen Seaman in *Punch* and overwhelmed by the loud imperial themes proclaimed most noisily by Kipling.[2]

Inevitably, middle-class Socialist feeling had its effect upon some of the more energetic leaders of organized labour. The Fabians had their long-term influence, but initially more important, though more ephemeral, were the activities of H. M. Hyndman (described with somewhat startling confidence in the 14th edition of the *Encyclopaedia Britannica* (1929) as 'founder

---

[1] See Holbrook Jackson, *The Eighteen Nineties* (Harmondsworth, Pelican edition, 1939), p. 13.
[2] Max Beerbohm produced a drawing of Kipling blowing a tin trumpet and clutching the arm of a bowler-hatted, rather blowsy Britannia, and feelingly captioned it, 'Mr. Rudyard Kipling takes a bloomin' day aht, on the blasted 'eath along with Britannia, 'is gurl'. It appeared in *The Poets' Corner*, 1904.

of British Socialism'). A Cambridge man, a City stockbroker and a smart dresser, his claim to distinction rests primarily on his having been the first Englishman to study the work of Karl Marx.[1] A characteristic Victorian egocentric, he published works expounding Marxist theories without acknowledging their provenance, to the great indignation of both Marx and his collaborator Engels. By 1884, he had founded a Social Democratic Federation; William Morris was one of his disciples, as were such leaders of organized labour as John Burns, who became a Liberal minister from 1905 to 1914, Tom Mann, who became a founder member of the Communist party of Great Britain in 1920, and George Lansbury, who in the interregnum between the expulsion of Ramsay MacDonald in 1931 and the election of Attlee in 1935 was leader of the Labour Opposition in the Commons. The S.D.F. was certainly the first Socialist political organization in Britain; the only approximate precedent to it is to be found in the activities of Robert Owen. Meetings and marches of the unemployed were organized, particularly in the bad winter of 1885–6, and one of these, diverted from Trafalgar Square, led to much smashing of windows in Pall Mall and an unsuccessful prosecution of both Hyndman and John Burns at the Old Bailey. More spectacular still were the events in London on 13 November 1887 of what came to be called 'Bloody Sunday'. This was the culmination of an indecisive attitude by the commissioner of police for the metropolis during the preceding months, when he had forbidden some S.D.F. gatherings and permitted others. The meeting of 13 November 1887 was banned in part because its professed aim was to protest at the imprisonment of William O'Brien, one of the Irish M.P.s chiefly responsible for the 'Plan of Campaign'.[2] The police sought by baton charges to keep the demonstrators from approaching Trafalgar Square from Holborn, the Strand and Parliament Street. Many reached

---

[1] He did so in a French translation, no English translation of *Das Kapital* being available until 1887.

[2] See p. 252. Ireland's wrongs then, as always, provided useful ammunition to Radicals and Socialists, being represented as typical of the oppressive wickedness of the British government.

the square nevertheless and mounted guards were called out to disperse them. The police and demonstrators suffered considerable casualties and two civilians subsequently died from their injuries. Various leaders of the demonstration, John Burns among them, were given prison sentences.

Although these events, highly uncharacteristic of Victorian London, made the S.D.F. something of a bogey, neither it nor Hyndman contributed much after this. Hyndman did not merely ensure the non-cooperation of continental Social Democrats by his quarrel with Marx and Engels; he cut himself off from British realities by his contemptuous attitude to the trade unions and to those who worked to create a separate political party to represent organized Labour.

The two factors that had instilled new life into the organized working-class movement by the end of the Queen's reign were a new surge of activity in the trade union movement and the attempt to form a working-man's, that is to say, Labour, party. Neither development was specifically Socialist but both were strongly influenced by the Socialist or quasi-Socialist propaganda of the time; and both received a larger measure of middle-class support in consequence of the enlarged social conscience which the multiplicity of writings about the plight of the poor had created. More specifically, both Tom Mann and John Burns, both of the Amalgamated Engineers, who did much to render trade unions more militant, were both members of the S.D.F. Mann criticized the unions for their over-cautious policy, and in particular for confining their activities solely to the protection of members' wages and being indifferent to the problem of unemployment. Most progress was made, however, in spreading unionism from skilled to unskilled workers, and in adding to the traditional unions, whose membership was usually confined to those exercising a particular skill or craft, general or industrial unions embracing all those employed in a particular industry. There was also, with increased urbanization and better communications, a tendency for local unions to amalgamate either into national unions or unions embracing a large industrial region. Thus the

1880s saw a tendency to general unionism on Tyneside among railway employees[1] and merchant seamen.

In 1888, seven hundred girls employed making matches for Bryant and May went on strike for better conditions, and won. They had apparently read an article by the Fabian lady, Mrs Annie Besant, condemning the way they were being treated. In August 1889, Tom Mann, John Burns and a gasworker called Will Thorne demanded an eight-hour day for gasworkers employed by the South Metropolitan Gas Company. They also got their way and other gas companies fell into line. Before the month was out, Mann and Burns together with a dock labourer called Ben Tillett, organized a complete shutdown of the London docks and announced, with the support of the Stevedores' and Lightermen's unions, who constituted the aristocracy of dockland, the creation of a Dockers' Union. Their chief demand was for a minimum wage of sixpence an hour.[2] Burns, Mann and Tillett conducted great mass meetings on Tower Hill, and for something like a fortnight they led the dockers in orderly marches through the City of London, all the more impressive because Burns cooperated with the Metropolitan Police about the routes to be taken. These were more than mere demonstrations: they were necessary fundraising devices also, since, without financial help from sympathizers, the strikers had no resources. Their employers therefore held out, making use of blackleg labour; the situation was only saved at the last moment by a sudden rush of subscriptions for the dockers from Australia, which stimulated the flow of money from sympathizers in Britain. Apart from the £30,000 sent from Australia, every trade union in the country, and many football clubs, sent money to the dockers, while the Salvation Army contributed money from the proceeds of its official journal *War Cry*. The lord mayor of London set up a conciliation committee. Cardinal Manning was indefatigable in the dockers' cause, and he was the member of the committee who

---

[1] They called themselves the Amalgamated Society of Railway *Servants*.
[2] The young find this so hard to believe that they tend to convince themselves that the dockers wanted 'an extra' sixpence an hour. The normal dockers' pay before the strike was fourpence or fivepence an hour.

duly presented the dockers' strike committee with what amounted almost to an unconditional surrender by the employers.

The result was a rapid increase in the number of general or industrial unions and a marked increase in the membership of the older unions. The successful strike in 1889 for 'the dockers' tanner' was the central event in the history of trade union growth in late-Victorian times; membership rose from about 400,000 in 1872 to nearly two million by the end of the reign and most of the growth took place after 1889.

On the whole, however, it remained true that while Socialists sympathized with, and at particular times and on specific issues actively assisted, trade unionism, the trade unions, both before and after 1889, sympathized very little with Socialists. Thus, whereas Socialists were from all the classes, trade unionists came from, and served the interest of, only one particular section of one particular class, the organized 'industrial' employee. It is for this reason that Socialist propaganda, with its hostility to 'capitalist' society as such, with its often intellectual and theoretical approach, made relatively little progress among trade unionists in general. The 'New Unionism' was perhaps more militant than the unions based on the tradition of the 'New Model'; but such Socialism as it exhibited was part of its militant trade unionism, not part of a grand design to replace an old society by a new one. Trade union aims remained industrial rather than political. They agreed with the Socialist view that they were being robbed by their employers of the full reward for their labour, but this merely led them to demand shorter hours and higher wages. Political or revolutionary aims were perhaps for the long term, a matter of jam for tomorrow or even pie in the sky. What the trade unionists wanted was jam for today, a bigger wage packet as soon as possible, along with more time in which to spend its contents.

Nevertheless the developments of the eighties had brought younger men to the fore in the trade union movement; most of them had Socialist ideas of some sort and many began to see the potential value of specifically political agitation. They wanted an eight-hour day established by law; and they were instrumental in influencing municipal politics by increasing the number of trades councils, which contained representatives of all the unions in a town and were thus capable of influencing urban and borough councils and elections. In the main, however, the movement was quite sharply divided, between those who sought to secure trade union aims by Socialist propaganda and political activity, and those who did not. The parliamentary committee of the T.U.C. was content to sponsor a number of 'Lib-Lab' M.P.s who in fact accepted the Liberal Whip in the Commons, despite a T.U.C. resolution in 1893 that candidates should receive union support only if they believed in collective ownership of 'the means of production, distribution and exchange'. The two principal factors which produced this resolution were the writings of Robert Blatchford, editor of the Socialist weekly, *The Clarion*, and the rise to prominence of Keir Hardie.

Blatchford's most celebrated work was a book called *Merrie England* (1894) consisting of articles reprinted from *The Clarion*. It was a clever amalgam of moral indignation, patriotism, appeals to Christian ideals, vigorous condemnations of capitalism and direct, simply-written expositions of Socialist ideas; and it sold in tens of thousands of copies. He also insisted that trade unions were not sufficient by themselves to secure the workers' victory. His readers were urged to forget the Liberals and Tories alike and vote only for representatives of Labour; he described it as foolish for trade unionists to vote, as they mainly did, for members of the employing class.

The first steps in the direction to which Blatchford pointed had already been taken. Keir Hardie, a Scottish miner, abandoning his faith in the Liberal party, attacked the parliamentary committee on this account in 1888, and in 1892 got himself elected as an independent Labour candidate for south West Ham. Two other M.P.s also elected in 1892 as independent Labour men, John Burns and J. Havelock Wilson, soon came to accept the Liberal whip, but in 1893 a meeting of 120 persons at Bradford, under Hardie's chairmanship, announced the formation of an Independent Labour party. Among those attending were representatives from the S.D.F. and the Fabian

Society, as well as the Scottish Labour party, and various trade union branches. Significantly, the S.D.F. found the I.L.P. programme insufficiently revolutionary and the Fabian Society also withheld its support, preferring its own technique of spreading the gospel among persons of influence. John Burns refused to join and even Blatchford, who was also at the meeting, left the party quite soon.

In consequence, Hardie became the only spokesman of the I.L.P. in the 1892–5 Parliament, outraging M.P.s by wearing a cloth cap[1] and having some of his constituency supporters brought to the Palace of Westminster in a coach that supported also a small brass band. But in 1895, although the I.L.P. put up 28 candidates none, not even Keir Hardie himself, was returned. Working-class Socialism was thus a spasmodic thing, reacting sharply to immediate crises and shifting its allegiance to different leaders in turn, and tending always to subside beneath the dead weight of apathy. Successively, Hyndman, Tom Mann and Burns, and then Blatchford and Keir Hardie had had their spells of influence, and by 1895 all appeared to have fizzled out.

What caused a revival, if not of Socialism at any rate of militancy, by the end of the reign, was the failure of Salisbury's government from 1895 to produce major social reforms, and a mounting attack on the unions by the employers. The Conservatives, seeing the formation of the I.L.P. as potentially inimical to the prospects of the Liberal party, gave the impression in the election campaign of 1895 that they would provide an alternative to Socialism by themselves introducing major social reforms. But Chamberlain's sole achievement in the 1895–1900 period was a far from satisfactory Workmen's Compensation Act in 1897; on the matter of old age pensions, despite what appeared to have been explicit election pledges, Chamberlain did nothing, chiefly because of the cost of the Boer War. The truth was, also, that as the landed interest increasingly turned from the Liberals to the Conservatives, so also did financiers and merchants for fear of Socialism; Cham-

[1] The expression 'cloth-cap image' contains a folk-memory of this dramatic event, as well as of the survival of this typically working-class headgear during at least the first half of the twentieth century.

berlain could not lead a party so supported in the direction of social reform.

Employers began during the 1890s to recruit blackleg or non-union labour. The Shipping Federation made willingness to work alongside non-union men a condition of employment. In 1893 a union strike at Hull led to strong police action to protect blackleg labour. A National Free Labour Association was formed to provide blackleg labour during strikes. This raised the vexed question of picketing and a series of court decisions in the 1890s went against the unions. Most notable was the case of Lyons *v.* Wilkins. A leather goods manufacturer successfully secured an injunction to prevent picketing of his premises during a strike in 1896 and Lyons' case was upheld in the Court of Appeal. In the same year, an Employers Federation was established in the engineering industry; and in the following year it countered a strike in London by ordering a nationwide lock-out, an unprecedented act which brought about a complete capitulation by the Amalgamated Engineering Union after a struggle lasting from July 1897 to January 1898.

The result was to force a closer collaboration between the T.U.C. and the I.L.P. This was partly because their superior drive and ability were enabling Socialists to rise to the top in several important unions and partly due to an increased feeling that since the government was producing little or no positive social legislation and the courts were apparently whittling away union rights, the idea of political activity had become more relevant. The T.U.C. congress of 1899, though by a narrow majority, agreed that its parliamentary committee join with the Cooperative movement and the various Socialist bodies in a conference to discuss the representation of the Labour movement in Parliament. The conference met in Farringdon Street, London, in 1900. Fifty per cent of the unions were not represented and the Cooperative movement was not represented at all. The trade union delegates who did present themselves were supported by the I.L.P., the S.D.F. and the Fabians. It was resolved to establish a Labour Representation Committee, with the object of securing the election of Labour candidates who would pursue an independent policy in Parliament under their own Whips. James Ramsay MacDonald who, twenty-four years later, found himself prime minister at the head of the jubilant, but very surprised, first Labour government, was appointed secretary. But the S.D.F., true to its quasi-Marxist cantankerousness, soon withdrew its support; John Burns announced his disapproval; and MacDonald, effective organizer though he was in his earlier days, was never more than a socialistically-inclined Liberal. Nevertheless, the L.R.C. did represent, even at the time, one step forward: it declined to be content with sponsoring trade union members prepared to act as hangers-on of the Liberals. Beyond that, however, it had little support, save from a proportion of trade unionists and the I.L.P. itself. The Fabians attended the L.R.C.'s meetings as detached and rather disapproving advisers; and the L.R.C. had to soft-pedal its Socialist ideas for fear of affronting the non-cooperating trade unionists and all those who, in the midst of the Boer War, were filled with a patriotic desire to support the Queen's government and therefore little likely to vote for those who were (however moderately they might express themselves) believed to be bent on its overthrow. In the so-called Khaki Election held in October 1900, of 15 L.R.C. candidates, only two were elected, Keir Hardie being returned for Merthyr.

A new offensive by the employers, however, suddenly gave the L.R.C. (or Labour party as it was already being called) a new significance. In 1900 the employees of the Taff Vale Railway Company in South Wales went on unofficial strike. The company replied by importing blacklegs; the Amalgamated Society of Railway Servants thereupon recognized the strike, gave the men strike pay, and sent its general secretary to aid and organize them. The railway companies were well known for their dislike of the unions and the manager of the Taff Vale Company therefore sued the A.S.R.S. for the losses which the company had suffered as a consequence of the strike. The High Court decided in favour of the company; the Appeal Court decided in favour of the unions; but, in July 1901, the Law Lords supported the decision of the High Court. The A.S.R.S. was to pay £23,000 damages to the company, plus legal costs amounting to almost £9,000. The point of law insisted on by the Lords to justify their decision was that since Parliament had made a trade union a body which 'can own property, which can employ servants or which can inflict injury, it must be taken ... to have impliedly given the power to make it suable in a court of law for injuries purposely done by its authority and procurement'. It was this discovery that the courts of law could in effect nullify what Parliament had appeared to have given the unions in 1871 and 1875 – the right to strike – which caused the trade unions to give much more support to the Labour party, particularly as the Conservatives were to show no willingness to introduce new legislation to make another Taff Vale decision impossible.[1]

Hence, Queen Victoria's death in 1901, the year of the Taff Vale judgment, may be said almost to have coincided with the real birth of the twentieth-century Labour party. It was to bear all through its childhood before 1918, its adolescence until 1939, and its adulthood thereafter, all the marks of its accidental birth and its mixed and largely unintentional parentage. It would assuredly never have come into existence at all but for the total failure of both of the older parties in the nineties to respond to the needs of the times as the Tories had responded in the 1820s, 1840s and 1870s and as the Whigs and their Liberal allies had done in the 1830s and, though less resolutely, from 1859 to 1874.

---

[1] The decision in the Taff Vale Case, having been promulgated by the Lords sitting as a final Court of Appeal, could not be, and therefore never was, 'reversed'. The only remedy was a new statute to alter the law in the unions' favour for the future. This new statute was the Trade Disputes Act of 1906.

16 · Imperial Pre-Eminence

1837–80

> The sentiment of empire may be called innate in
> every Briton.
>
> GLADSTONE, 1878

> To say that our Empire is 'bone of our bone,
> flesh of our flesh', is not to express an opinion
> but to assert a fact. So long as Englishmen
> retain at once their migratory instinct, their
> passion for independence, and their impatience
> of foreign rule, they are bound by a manifest
> destiny to found empires abroad, or, in other
> words, to make themselves the dominant race in
> the foreign countries to which they wander.
>
> EDWARD DICEY, 1877

> I awoke once more and on my way I went,
> And my heart was overflowing with a deep content:
> In the dear homeland, far across the sea,
> They had missed me and they loved me,
> And they prayed for me.
>
> *The Emigrant's Dream* (popular ballad)

Just as there have been strenuous attempts to show that there
was no Great Depression in the late-Victorian period, so has
there also developed a body of opinion that the 'New Imperialism' so often regarded as distinctive of the last quarter of the
nineteenth century was not really 'new' and that, so far from
being the outcome of any new philosophy of Empire, it was a
rather harassed, if not desperate, reaction to the force of un-

looked-for circumstance. However, attempts to play down the Imperialism of the 1880s and 1890s must be seen against the undoubted fact that Imperialism was a burning public issue at the time; that between 1871 and 1900 there were added to the British Colonial Empire around 66 million people and 4¼ million square miles; and that this great accession of peoples and territories, though obtained at a time when France, Germany, Italy and Belgium were all for the first time simultaneously involved in the race for colonies, was greatly in excess of the gains made by any of these powers. Just as nothing quite like the economic phenomenon rightly or wrongly called The Great Depression had happened before, so was the Imperialism of the 1880s and 1890s without precedent.

The starting point of most historical thinking on late-Victorian Imperialism was the celebrated remark of Sir John Seeley, then professor of modern history at Cambridge, in the first of a series of lectures published in 1883 with the title *The Expansion of England*. 'We [the English] seem, as it were, to have conquered and peopled half the world in a fit of absence of mind.' The book quickly became a classic, and stayed one for half a century. The implication that before Seeley's day the English cared little about their Empire but thereafter woke up to develop a new, more thrusting and virile approach to it rapidly became an accepted doctrine. It received wide support in academic circles, and its popular manifestations were widespread. The Queen's Jubilee in 1887 was made the occasion of the first Imperial conference, and her Diamond Jubilee in 1897 was a great Imperial spectacular in its own right and accompanied by another conference of the Empire's chief ministers. The music halls resounded to 'Soldiers of the Queen' and 'Sons of the Sea'. In 1899, Rudyard Kipling issued perhaps the most famous of his calls to Englishmen to fulfil their manifest destiny:

> Take up the White Man's burden –
> Send forth the best ye breed –
> Go bind your sons to exile
> To serve your captives' need;

To wait in heavy harness
On fluttered folk and wild –
Your new-caught, sullen peoples,
Half-devil and half-child.

and A. C. Benson had put words to the first of Elgar's Pomp
and Circumstance marches that turned it into a second national
anthem:

Wider still and wider shall thy bounds be set;
God who made thee mighty make thee mightier yet.

Among popular books of the time were Rider Haggard's *King
Solomon's Mines*, which made Africa more mysterious even than
it was, Fitchett's *Deeds That Won The Empire* (frequently
presented as a school prize) and *With Roberts to Kandahar*.

Evidently, something about the Empire stirred the British
people at this time in a way they had not been stirred since
the brave days of the mid-eighteenth century, whose successful
wars with France gave rise to the traditional patriotic songs
that indeed outlasted those of late Victorians – such as 'Hearts
of Oak', 'Rule Britannia' and 'God Save the King'.

There were, in fact, several quite new characteristics about
the Imperialism of the late Victorians. It was heavily (though
not exclusively) concentrated upon Africa. It was more concerned than at any time since before the Napoleonic wars with
the annexation of large tracts of territory. As the conventional
label 'Scramble for Africa' suggests, it was consequential upon,
and productive of, rivalry with many other European powers.
It was accompanied, and encouraged, by far more defiantly
positive publicity than previous imperial activity and justified
by vigorous appeals to a philosophy that was at bottom one of
racial superiority, based on pseudo-scientific nonsense about
'the survival of the fittest'. It was possible at all only because of
the steamship and the railway; and it was one manifestation of
that peculiar outburst of vulgar and unthinking megalomania
which, called into existence perhaps by Germany's victory over
France in 1871, reached its climax when the states of Europe
plunged into war in 1914. Finally, in that it concentrated on
Africa, it was almost entirely lacking in economic value and was

productive of expense rather than of profit. It is true that the British had possessed the largest, if not the only large, overseas empire long before the 1870s, and had been proud of it; but the prevailing mood had been patriotic rather than Imperialist; there had been more thought of self-government in the Empire than of a search for additions to it; and it had been a source of profit at an annual cost before the 1880s of only 2 or 3 per cent of the national income.

Broadly speaking 'the Empire' was hardly less miscellaneous before 1870 than it was afterwards. In the Americas, there survived from the old 'first British Empire' the oldest of the so-called 'colonies of settlement', Canada, together with the Carribean Islands. The latter had been of prime importance in the eighteenth century, as what might be termed colonies of exploitation, on account of their slave-produced sugar. In the nineteenth, they were in constant economic difficulty, partly because of the social dislocation caused by the abolition of slavery and partly by the competition of slave-produced cane sugar and beet sugar from outside the Empire, which resulted from Britain's free trade policy. Upon these disturbed territories the British had been compelled by the 1870s to impose crown colony government, thus removing from them the never very representative institutions, dominated by white minorities, which they had had in the seventeenth and eighteenth centuries.

If the West Indies were already neglected problem-children rather than the area (outside India) that the British had been most anxious to defend, acquire and exploit in the days of the Elder and Younger Pitt, Canada, or North America as it was then usually called, was a source of constant anxiety until after the end of the 1860s. Those historians who insist that Imperialism was not a purely late-Victorian phenomenon have been quick to point out that it was a fixed policy of all governments to prevent British North America from falling into the hands of the United States. There was no agreed frontier between the two until as late as 1871, despite various partial agreements in 1817, 1818, 1827 and 1846. Friction both within, and between, the French-speaking provinces and Lower Canada and the increasingly populous English-speaking Upper Canada – the two had been separated by Pitt's Canada Act of 1791 – led to rebellions in 1837 in both provinces which, though easily suppressed, alarmed Melbourne sufficiently to send Lord Durham out to report on the situation. Durham was chosen by Melbourne chiefly to get him out of England because his personal behaviour was tiresome and because he was too popular with the Radicals. The Durham Report that resulted recommended that the two provinces be reunited and this was effected in 1840. The purpose was to ensure that, in this one large province, the French Canadians should in future be outnumbered. The less illiberal suggestion in Durham's report, that internal affairs in Canada should be the sole responsibility of the Canadian legislature, with only matters of imperial concern being reserved to the imperial government, was not acted upon. This has not prevented the report from being hailed as the foundation stone upon which responsible colonial self-government, and finally dominion status, were eventually erected.

But perhaps the real turning point was in 1847, when Canada, as a result of the repeal of the Corn Laws, lost the advantage of the low duties on Canadian wheat. It was to cope with the discontent this caused that the third Earl Grey, in effect, granted the Canadian administration self-government solely on condition that nothing should be done to imperil the political link with Westminster. It was, in fact, in Durham's phrase, 'municipal self-government'. But in 1859, the Canadian legislature went further than that by insisting on the right to depart from the principle of free trade and to impose tariffs on British imports. This claim that Canadians should decide for themselves how they should manage their system of taxation echoed the similar claim made by the Thirteen Colonies in 1765; but this time, the British government contented itself with mere verbal protests. Significantly, Grey, who had granted the Canadians self-government in internal affairs in 1847, strongly opposed the Tory surrender of 1859 on the issue of taxation, which suggests that neither Durham nor Grey envisaged themselves as founding fathers of full colonial self-government.

All these developments were designed to keep British North

America British. There was always a body of opinion both in the United States and in Canada in favour of annexation by the United States. The British lacked the forces either to suppress a Canadian rebellion or to resist a United States invasion; and there were frequent complaints about the cost of such defence forces as were maintained in Canada; but, though the British could not keep Canada British by force, they hoped to do so by their policy. It was the fear that this delicate situation would be jeopardized, if the North won the American Civil War, and rendered much less hazardous, if the war were won by the South, that explains the generally anti-Yankee attitude pursued by Palmerston right up to the point when it was clear that the North would win. Once it had won, Palmerston reverted to reliance on discretion and politeness.[1] Indeed, the British North America Act of 1867 was as much a Canadian as a British answer to the victory of the North. It created a federal 'Dominion of Canada' out of Ontario, Quebec, New Brunswick and Nova Scotia; to it were added Rupert's Land, the North Western Territory and British Columbia between 1869 and 1873, with only Newfoundland remaining outside. The word 'dominion' was used in preference to the word 'kingdom', which some Canadians wanted, because the democratic people of the United States might have been gravely affronted by the reimportation of a monarchical title into 'their' continent.

As a corollary of responsible self-government and the stability which it was presumed would follow Federation, British governments at once began to implement an economy which had always been dear to them. Under the governments of Derby in 1866 and Gladstone, 1868-74, there was a steady withdrawal of the greater part of the British forces which had garrisoned Canada, Parliament having accepted, in Palmerston's last ministry, the view that self-governing colonies should undertake 'the main responsibility' for internal order and 'assist in their own external defence'. It was this bipartisan policy which Disraeli impudently attacked as a wholly Liberal dereliction of duty in his Crystal Palace speech of 1872.[2]

[1] See p. 150.
[2] See p. 209.

The other main colonies of settlement were Australia and New Zealand. Towards both, British governments long adopted a more grudging and cautious policy even than that adopted towards Canada. New Zealand's history as a British colony had beginnings haphazard enough to make Seeley's reference to a 'fit of absence of mind' not inappropriate. Adventurers, missionaries, escaped convicts and land speculators provided the advance guard and, out of their oppressive treatment of the Maoris, there had gradually developed a missionary protest and then a movement for systematic colonization which only really got under way at the start of Victoria's reign as a reluctant response to a threat that France might attempt to acquire part of New Zealand. The government's reluctance was due to its express unwillingness to envisage the cost, the difficulty, and indeed the impropriety, of a course of action which would do damage to the Maoris, who were described as 'a numerous and inoffensive people whose title to the soil and to the sovereignty of New Zealand is indisputable'.

Accordingly, in 1840 New Zealand was formally annexed as a crown colony and the New Zealand Company, founded in 1836 to organize British settlement in the country, had its powers limited by the treaty of Waitangi with the Maoris, British sovereignty having been proclaimed before the signature was completed, in order to check the activities of the settlers themselves. The Maoris gave up their sovereignty, kept their lands and gave the British government the first claim to buy any land they sold. Disputes over land agreements between settlers and Maoris led to an uprising by the Maoris which the Westminster government refused to punish, greatly to the disgust of the New Zealand Company, which insisted in effect that Waitangi should be treated merely as a device for tricking 'savages' and not as a binding legal document. In the company's view, also, uncultivated land could not be regarded as within the sovereignty of 'uncivilized inhabitants'. In 1850, the company was bought out by the British government and by 1856 New Zealand had responsible government. But the land problem produced a Maori war, and although the main fighting was over by 1864, it was not wholly concluded till 1869. Having borne the greater part of the cost of the war, the British government insisted on a less vindictive policy of expropriation by the New Zealanders thereafter.

At the beginning of Victoria's reign, the two Australian colonies already in existence were New South Wales and Tasmania, known as Van Dieman's Land until 1853, both used as settlements to which convicts were transported.[1] Queensland and Victoria had just begun their existence as separate offshoots of New South Wales; and in 1837 a slow start was made on the establishment of a South Australian colony, with Adelaide as its capital. Three things contributed to Australia's development: its growing wool exports, the discovery of gold in Victoria and New South Wales in 1851, and the progressive abolition of transportation which was completed by 1855, save in Western Australia, which was still used for this purpose until 1868. The effect of all three processes is illustrated by the trebling of Australia's population in the years between 1850 and 1860.

Sir George Grey, who contributed so much to constitutional growth in New Zealand as governor from 1845 to 1853, and again from 1861, and as its prime minister from 1877 to 1879, was also governor of South Australia from 1841 to 1845, and performed valuable service of a similar nature at the Cape. It was largely on the basis of proposals put forward by him in the late 1840s that the Australian colonies were given responsible government between 1850 and 1855.

Over the cost of the defence of Australia and New Zealand there was a good deal of grumbling by devoted adherents of free trade ideals and low taxation. These included Cobden and Gladstone and even Sir William Molesworth, who was one of those in public life who was labelled 'Colonial Reformer', whereas Cobden and Gladstone are labelled 'Little Englanders'. But in fact none of them wanted to abandon the colonies, though all three made public utterances that could be so interpreted and Cobden privately thought it absurd that the British should be expected to defend a place as remote as Australia,

[1] See p. 179.

calling it 'as quixotic a specimen of folly as was ever exhibited'. Basically the so-called 'Little Englanders' were opposed less to Empire as such than to the expense that paternalistic attitudes involved; and it was a strong point in the arguments of those who came to be regarded as anti-Imperialists that it was morally wrong for freeborn Britons to be either subject to, or dependent for protection on, a government which was not their own and in which they were not represented. This is fully consistent with Gladstonian theories in general. A point made by Cobden and others, on purely economic grounds, was that the home country derived little or no economic advantages from its colonies of settlement. The volume of British imports from, and exports to, the United States in the 1860s was greater than that with any part of the British Empire, and greater even than British trade with India. The basic thesis of those to whom free trade was a first principle was that political control, with its consequent administrative and defence expenditure, was less profitable to the home country than a complete absence of such control. Direct control, and particularly responsibility for defence, also increased the liability of becoming involved in expansionist wars or wars of doubtful justification against other states or indigenous peoples. India provided the outstanding example of both, but, on a lesser scale, so also did the development of British responsibility in both New Zealand and Cape Colony.

Yet virtually no so-called free trade Little Englander ever seriously contemplated abandoning any part of the Empire. Self-government, and self-reliance in matters of defence, were considered, indeed, the only means of binding the Empire together. This was a point of view appropriate to men who recalled how the eighteenth-century mercantilist trade policy, combined with a denial of responsible self-government, had led to the loss of the American colonies. It was not, certainly, very consistent of them to believe that the colonies should remain within the Empire, given their awareness that trade with the colonies we had lost was greater than that with the colonies they thought we should try to keep; and those who still incline to regard the Victorian years before 1871 as a time when the best that could be hoped for was that the colonies of settlement would one day part company with the home country but, it was hoped, amicably, are perhaps the more reliable interpreters of the pacifically-minded free traders of the time.[1]

The problem facing the British in South Africa was always more complex than in the American and Australasian colonies, though Britain's initial presence there was a positive tactic within an overall imperial strategy. Cape Colony had not been returned to the kingdom of the Netherlands in 1815 because the British wanted it as a strategic port of call on the long sea route to India; but they had no desire to make more of it than that.

Unfortunately, to keep within the simple objective proved impossible, because the Dutch Boer farmers resented the eventually successful British campaign against slavery and because the black Africans on the ill-defined borders of the colony existed in a state of constant warfare among themselves. Caught between the pressure of invading Zulus, and the presence of Europeans to the south of them, the Kaffirs and the European settlers inevitably clashed frequently in the 1830s. The governor of Cape Colony from 1831 to 1837 (Sir Benjamin d'Urban) proposed annexation of the border area in order to keep the peace; Melbourne's colonial secretary, Lord Glenelg, vetoed the proposal, and clashes between settlers and Kaffirs continued. The consequence was the Great Trek, when, between 1835 and 1837, some 5,000 Boer men, women and children crossed the Orange River to found a state of their own, announcing that they expected the British government not to interfere with them. The outcome of the Great Trek was the creation, first, of the Orange Free State and then also the Transvaal. The British objected to these migrations, and when trekking Boers proceeded to settle themselves in Natal, the home government, reversing a previous decision not to do so, proclaimed it a British colony in 1843. The Natal Boers thereupon migrated to the Orange Free State and the Transvaal.

---

[1] It is well known in this connection that Disraeli referred to the colonies of settlement in the 1850s as 'millstones'; what is ignored, however, is that he showed no particular interest in them in the 1870s either.

Renewed conflict between settlers and Kaffirs wrecked British plans for the orderly control of the smallest possible area of southern Africa. British control over Kaffirs as far as the River Kei territory on the eastern frontier of Cape Colony had to be reasserted in 1848 and the Orange River territory was annexed. But, when war with the Kaffirs was renewed in 1850, the cost was so resented at home that the government yet again decided to draw back. The outcome was the Sand River Convention of 1850 with the Transvaal Boers, and the Bloemfontein Convention of 1854 with the Orange Free State Boers, by which both communities should govern themselves. In a further attempt to disengage, the British granted responsible government to Cape Colony in 1853 and set up a separate assembly for Natal in 1856.

It remained the fixed aim of British policy that territorial acquisition should be avoided in Africa. Nevertheless, the security of Cape Colony itself was never allowed to be jeopardized by either Boers or black Africans. Griqualand East and the Transkei were annexed in 1865; Basutoland was annexed in 1868 and absorbed into Cape Colony in 1871, because of continuous conflicts between immigrants and the Basutos; and to control the quarrels caused by the discovery of diamonds in the lands of the Griquas, the British assumed control of Griqualand West in 1871, though it was not formally incorporated into Cape Colony until 1880. A look at the map of southern Africa indicates that, apart from purely local factors, the British annexations were also very obviously designed to keep the Boer territories well away from the whole length of coast between the original eastern frontiers of Cape Colony and Portuguese East Africa.

The fact that it was the security of the long and short sea routes to India that lay behind, respectively, Britain's limited but vacillating South African policy and her more celebrated policy of maintaining her strategic interests in the Straits and the eastern Mediterranean, is a reminder that British control of India was by far the most important element in British imperial policy throughout the nineteenth century.[1] British power was

[1] And usually the most important element in British foreign policy too.

throughout Victoria's reign held to be based primarily on the British Isles and on India, and it is generally overlooked that the greatest extension of British power in India itself after 1815 had taken place by 1858, well before the so-called Age of Imperialism had begun, and indeed mostly before the accession of Queen Victoria. After 1870 the only major additions were on the North West Frontier and the defensive absorption of the Burmese hinterland; the coastal areas of Burma were all in British hands by 1852. Thus, the Age of Imperialism produced nothing more important in the most vital area of British Imperialism than Disraeli's Royal Titles Act.[1] Governments in the Age of Imperialism were more anxious about the defence of India than ever before, and the public was perhaps more conscious of its Indian empire, if only because Kipling would not let them forget it. But by the 1880s, the age of British expansionism in India was already virtually at an end.

As was only to be expected of a people whose prime interest was profit, the British for long ruled India indirectly, in the hope of cutting down costs to the British exchequer. After the India Act of 1784, British control in India was vested officially in the East India Company, subject to a board of control in England whose president, from 1813 onwards, was a member of the Cabinet. In India itself, the affairs of the company were controlled by a governor-general and a council of three. By the India Act of 1833, the company was to cease all its commercial business, the proprietors receiving, in exchange, an annuity paid for out of the Indian revenues. The original monopoly held by the company in trade both in, and with, India and China, had already largely disappeared by that date; it had always been a source of friction and as England moved towards a free trade policy it was inevitably seen as a restriction upon freedom of commercial enterprise. Its profits had in fact been declining for some years before 1833; but from then until the end of the Crimean War, India's exports nearly trebled in value and its imports more than trebled.

When the Victorian reign began, the sense both of mission and of conquest was strong in the governors-general and their

[1] But see p. 412, *infra*.

advisory councils. The company's renewed charter after 1833 (which in effect left it simply as the administrative agent through whom power was exercised in British India) laid down that employment should be denied to no one on the grounds of religion, colour or race. The last pre-Victorian governor-general of India, Lord William Bentinck (1828–35), considered it his duty to stamp out the practice of suttee by which, as part of a married man's funeral rites, his widow's live body should be burned simultaneously with her husband's dead one. Thomas Babington Macaulay was a member of Bentinck's council and it was largely due to him that the decision was taken to teach the English language and use it as the medium of instruction in all state-aided schools in India. Thus, Victoria's reign began with the British committed to acting as guardians, charged with the duty of imposing an Anglo-Saxon culture upon an Oriental one for its own good. From the operations of this white English guardianship there would eventually emerge a brown Indian élite, distinguishable from the English élite solely by the unimportant circumstance of its different skin pigmentation. That a wholly westernized education (as then understood) was not even necessarily appropriate to Englishmen let alone Indians was not of course suspected; still less was it realized at the time that, since words like 'freedom', 'liberty' and 'independence' occur with ringing frequency in most writings in English, the result would be that educated Indians would assume that the ideals, like the language they were expressed in, were also for export. As for the absolute equality of opportunity promised in 1834 (and again in 1858), this was ultimately incompatible with British rule and therefore very little came of it, at any rate in the nineteenth century.

The problem of frontiers was always even more urgent in India than at the Cape and attempts to solve it were clearer because of the abiding Russophobia of the English governments of the time and by the absence of any rival European community like the Dutch Boers in South Africa with their own ideas on how 'the natives' should be treated. As related elsewhere,[1] the reign began with the first of various attempts to

[1] See Chapter 6.

control Afghanistan for fear of Russia. In the years 1843–56
British power advanced dramatically. The whole Indus valley
was conquered: Surat in 1843 and the Punjab in 1849. This
extended British India to the borders of Afghanistan and thereby almost guaranteed there would be even more sensitivity
about Russia's relations with that country. In addition to
completing the subjugation of the Sikhs of the Punjab, Lord
Dalhousie, governor-general from 1849 to 1856, making the
cause of British merchants in Burma his own much as Palmerston had made those of British traders in China, made war on
the Burmese and annexed the province of Pegu, of which
Rangoon was the principal city. Dalhousie then turned his
attention to what he considered the misgovernment of the
various Indian princes (they were numbered in hundreds)
whose states were not part of, but were 'protected' by, British
India. He made extended use of the so-called 'doctrine of lapse',
by which, whenever an Indian prince died without natural
heirs, his state 'lapsed' to the British. He extended it to forbid
the common practice among childless Hindu rulers of bequeathing their states to adopted sons, save with the governor-
general's consent. Alarm at the implications of Dalhousie's
policy was all the greater by reason of the exceptional number
of princes who died without heirs while he was governor-
general. The largest of the several states annexed in Central
India in accordance with the doctrine of lapse was Nagpur, with
a population of four million. His largest annexation, of the
even larger state of Oudh, of which Lucknow was the principal
city, was not an application of the doctrine of lapse. It was
undertaken in 1856 solely on the grounds that the kingdom was
hopelessly misgoverned despite earlier promises of reform. In
addition to all this, Dalhousie was an energetic projector of
railways, roads and canals and a telegraph system, put through
various administrative reforms and concerned himself with
prison reform, forests and the training of engineers. He also
warned the British government that there were too few British
troops in India. Many had been withdrawn for service in the
Crimea, others were in Burma, and others were fighting the
Persians or garrisoning Aden. Within a year of Dalhousie's

return to England, the Indian Mutiny took place and gave the British in India a fright from which it may be said they were never to recover.

Mutinies by small bodies of Indian troops had occurred in the past, and since, when the Mutiny began in January 1857, combatant Indian troops outnumbered the British by over five to one, the most remarkable feature was that it was confined to a small area and was completely suppressed within less than two years. Basically, it was a protest by both soldiers and aggrieved civilians against the rapid and aggressive imposition of an alien culture and an alien government, so that the rising involved privileged Brahmins, dispossessed princes and sepoys all fearful, for a variety of reasons, of being compelled to violate their religious customs and taboos. Indians had seen their social customs and beliefs (or superstitions) vigorously attacked ever since the 1830s, and, given the weakness of the British power at the time, it is not surprising that a miscellaneous group of discontents should have found violent expression.

The suppression of the Mutiny was followed by the Government of India Act of 1858. All the lands and other properties of the East India Company were transferred to the Crown. The governor-general became a viceroy, and the president of the board of control in London now became secretary of state for India. The proportion of British troops was increased and the artillery kept in British hands. Once again, the Indians were promised equality of opportunity, and non-interference with Indian religious beliefs was promised also.

Despite these renewed promises, and despite also the opening of the Indian Civil Service to competitive examination well in advance of the opening of the Civil Service at home,[1] the Mutiny ended the vision of an India becoming Anglicized through the benevolent operation of western education. For one thing, the chance of Indians even sitting for I.C.S. examinations in any number was minimized by the fact that the examination papers had to be taken in London and that the more orthodox forms of Hinduism forbade the undertaking of journeys by sea. Only one Indian candidate entered the I.C.S.

[1] See p. 202.

M

before 1871. The education provided in India was little related to I.C.S. entrance requirements; and Indians were employed only in minor positions and despised for their possession of a mere veneer of education in English. They were 'babus', or 'wogs'. Accordingly, British India was ruled henceforth by efficient and, in its own limited way, enlightened despotism, whose power rested ultimately on an army of about 250,000 men which could easily be expanded at need owing to India's vast reserves of manpower. Not only did the Indian army sustain British rule in India; it was a huge garrison from which men were regularly drawn for the defence of British interests everywhere from the Sudan to Hong Kong (and in 1877 in the Mediterranean).[1] The Indian army was almost wholly outside the control of the Imperial Parliament; and it was paid for by the Indian taxpayer, who thus subsidized not only the occupation of his own country but the defence of British influence throughout the Eastern hemisphere.

The viceroy combined the office his name implied, that of a personal representative in India of the Queen (from 1876 the Queen-Empress) with that of an executive ruler whose powers were more like those of a British prime minister, though one independent of a House of Commons or the whim of a democratic electorate. Indeed he was said officially to 'reign' during his five-year-term of office and in practice he was the most powerful ruler in Asia, exercising more effective control over his empire than either the Czar of Russia or the Emperor of China. His council was a Cabinet composed of senior civil servants; and though he could summon extra members, rendering it in appearance something of a legislative assembly, he could ignore it if he chose. The central government over which the viceroy presided was responsible for India's own system of tariffs and all other fiscal matters, for defence, foreign relations, and posts and telegraphs, all operated by the bureaucracy. The seven great provinces that made up British India had complete control of all other matters, through the I.C.S., and often acted independently of the viceroy, each having a governor, a lieutenant-governor or chief commis-

1 See p. 214.

sioner and a proliferation of bureaucratic departments, all headed by Englishmen. In the detailed paternalism of its activity, India was more like a socialist or at least a collectivist state than anything to be found elsewhere in the area of British control. Within the seven provinces were about 250 districts. These constituted the basic administrative unit in British India, and over each there presided a district officer who was responsible for pretty well everything that went on despite the fact that the post of district officer was a junior one in the I.C.S. His main task was to assess and collect the taxable revenue of his district; but he combined also the function of police chief and chief magistrate. When Kipling wrote of the White Man's Burden he probably had in mind the typical young district officer in the I.C.S., dispensing justice and upholding the majesty of his Queen, perhaps sitting on a camp chair in the open air in front of a collapsible desk.

One other manifestation of the turning away from a westernizing policy after the Mutiny was the abandonment of the doctrine of lapse by 1860. This meant that in the last part of the nineteenth century there were, apart from British India, over 600 princely states, within which lived about one-quarter of the entire population of India. They ranged from such large states as Kashmir, Hyderabad and Mysore to small villages. Each prince was in treaty relationship with the government of India, and was required to act in accordance with the advice of a British resident; the precise degree of supervision to which the princes were subjected varied from state to state. Although in none of these states was there lacking visible evidence of the paramountcy of the government of India, their continuing nominal independence conformed more closely to the more typical 'indirect method' by which the British usually preferred to minimize the financial burdens of administering their imperial power. The survival of the princely states was an Indian parallel to the policy of granting responsible government to the colonies of settlement.[1]

[1] Not that the British ceased altogether to absorb princely states into British India; the process slackened in the 1870s but was renewed quite vigorously in the 1880s and 1890s; see p. 412.

It is always put on the credit side of the balance in assessing the value of Britain's contribution to Indian history that it gave India peace, order and justice where there had hitherto been anarchy. But this was in its own way, in spite of the changed attitude to Anglicization after 1858, a perpetuation of an essentially alien and westernizing policy. When in the 1920s Gandhi was to campaign so melodramatically for a revival of village crafts and culture in India he was asserting an historical fact about British rule, namely that its imposition of a centrally-controlled bureaucracy answerable only to the princely occupants of the Viceregal Lodge had all but destroyed the fabric of Indian village society. Peace and order, and relief operations in times of famine, increased the population without adequately improving the fertility of the soil; Lancashire cotton ruined the Indian village cotton industry; the unfailing tax-collecting activities of district officers increased the peasants' indebtedness, and was accompanied by the certainty of eviction (by due process of law) for non-payment of taxes. There was commercial development to the extent that by 1870 British investment in India amounted to £160 million, by 1895 to £270 million and by 1900 about £305 million. But British investment in India was always less than British investment in the United States; and there was a reluctance to industrialize India for fear of its effects on British exports – a reminder that nineteenth-century advocacy of buying cheap and selling dear could produce an imitation, in a free trade context, of eighteenth-century mercantilism. Moreover, even railway construction, considerable though it was, and valuable in the long term in facilitating some degree of unity in India, was conceived less for industrial than for commercial and strategic purposes. Yet railway construction and a westernized form of education were probably the principal contributions made by the Victorians in the long run to the people of their Indian empire, and also the major contributions to the movement for Indian independence. The direct influence of British power on the mass of the Indian people in the nineteenth century was perhaps less than is sometimes imagined and less beneficial than it became fashionable after 1945 to pretend. And throughout the Victorian era it was the Indians who bore the cost of the British occupation and the British, militarily and financially, who benefited most from it.

The Age of Imperialism therefore had no new impact upon India itself and those who seek to minimize the novelty of late-Victorian Imperialism may perhaps be said to have the best of the argument when they rightly point out that the greatest period of expansion in British India took place not only before 1875 but even before 1857. If there is a turning point in the history of British India it is the Mutiny; this halted the most aggressive phase of British activity in the sub-continent. Late-Victorian Indian history was chiefly a time for the consolidation of what had been secured before 1856; and it was Imperialist (as the word is most commonly used) only in the strengthening of its belief that the British would have to stay in India because the Indians, it was now felt, could not really be trusted. The horrors of the Mutiny were to resound through the recesses of the late-Victorian mind, helping to confirm official (or rather unofficial) Imperialist notions of the inherent superiority of the Anglo-Saxon race and the treacherous unreliability of lesser breeds without the law, particularly if Oriental.

No consideration of the extent of British power overseas is realistic that is confined to an examination of what is formally described as the British Empire. Perhaps the difference between the period before 1880 and the period after it is precisely in the greater attention paid to the 'formal empire' after 1880. Yet from the point of view of trade, investment, and indeed emigration, neither before nor after 1880 was 'the empire' the only, or even the principal, sphere of British influence. Nor is it realistic to attempt any clear distinction at any time in the Victorian period between foreign, colonial and imperial policy. The mere necessity to defend the trade routes to India lay behind the whole foreign policy of the Palmerstonian era in so far as it was anti-Russian in the eastern Mediterranean. The nub of the Eastern Question was, for Britain, that Turkish control of the Near East provided the only sure guarantee for the short route to India. The insistence that independent Greece should in effect be a British satellite and that Egypt should not become a French one, and that Russia should not have the Straits or

Constantinople, were manifestations of a foreign policy that was essentially imperial in purpose. The indifference to Singapore in the twenty years after 1815 was because it was on the farther side of India. The China Wars were acts of imperial policy, arising out of the extension of Indian traders into the China Sea; forcing the Chinese to cede ports, to open others to trade and to agree to normal diplomatic intercourse were acts of power indistinguishable from those which in earlier centuries had initiated the process which led to Britain's empire in India.[1]

True, the size of territory actually annexed was small, but this was in keeping with nineteenth-century commercial theories about trade and empire; a flag that had 'free trade' and 'the open door' inscribed on it was an imperial, not an anti-imperial device. Wherever the British wished for legitimate trade and were denied it, they used force to get their way; just as, wherever after 1815 the British wished to end 'illegitimate' (i.e. slave) trading they also used force to get their way – as in West Africa. But wherever they could have free trade and the open door, i.e. unrestricted access to markets and raw materials, they sensibly refrained from force. Yet even where this seems most obvious, in South America,[2] the precondition of British commercial domination was the exercise of military, diplomatic and naval power during the Napoleonic Wars, and during the colonial revolt against Spanish and Portuguese control in the decade after 1815. Canning's celebrated insistence in 1823 that Britain would not allow the Holy Alliance powers to suppress the Spanish American rebellions was as manifest an act of power as any in the century. It was undertaken because, with South America liberated, the British would achieve those opportunities for unlimited trade in that area which had been one of their principal imperial aims since the times of Drake and Hawkins, and Marlborough and Chatham. Britain's actual recognition of the South American republics in 1824 was also a

[1] The Japanese, too, were punished at Kagoshima in 1863 for their reluctance to allow peaceful trade.
[2] Though the British did use both naval and military forces on occasion in South America in the mid-Victorian period.

counter-measure to the celebrated Monroe Doctrine of December 1823 which had asserted that there should be no European interference in the American hemisphere. Not only did Canning decline to accept this as a principle of general application throughout the Americas; the effectiveness both of Britain's recognition of the republics and of the Monroe Doctrine in the succeeding century depended upon British naval supremacy; and, for all practical purposes, the South American republics became commercial satellites of England. By the end of the century there was more British investment in South America even than in India.

The richest area of British commercial activity throughout the Victorian period, however, was the United States. To the end of Victoria's reign and beyond, the British exported more to, imported more from, and invested more capital in, the United States, than in any part of the Empire; and, by 1880, half England's trade and investments were with the United States, which had long ceased to be a colony, South America which had never been British, and with Canada which by that time was more loosely connected to Westminster politically than any other part of the formal Empire. If the formal Empire itself be considered, it accounted, in the nineteenth century, for less than half of British overseas investment and only one-third of British imports and exports. There were thus strong arguments for the Manchester economist-pacifist and pseudo-anti-imperialist view that annexation and territorial expansion were not greatly to Britain's advantage. Equally valid, however, is that the worldwide extent of British domination depended upon the exercise of power: an unchallenged naval supremacy, supporting, and supported by, the effective garrisoning of strategic points, including above all the army of occupation in India which the British were administratively powerful enough to compel the Indians themselves to pay for.

One of the major British exports of the Victorian period was the vast number of emigrants. The population of the British Isles increased at a greater rate than that of any other European state, and between 1814 and 1840 a million emigrants left the British Isles. By 1840, half these emigrants were going to

British North America and a somewhat smaller proportion to the United States. The troubled 'forties led to a great increase in emigration, particularly from Ireland, and in the second half of the century the total number of emigrants was estimated at ten million, of whom by far the largest proportion went to the United States, with Canada and Australia as the next most popular choices. It was not until after Victoria's reign that emigration to Canada exceeded that to the United States; and not until after the end of the Boer War that there was any sizeable emigration to South Africa. Only 10,000 had gone to Cape Colony by 1840. By the end of the Victorian period the total number of persons of British stock in the world as a whole was estimated at about 140 million, of whom as few as one-third were in the British Isles and as many as one-half were in the United States.

It is possible to argue that a growing awareness of how widely the British had spread themselves across the world was a contributory factor to the spread of imperial consciousness at home. The fact that so many British families had relatives who had settled in the United States must be set against the fact that, after 1880, the proportion of emigrants going to Canada, Australia, New Zealand and South Africa was tending to increase, and that the number of British soldiers serving overseas also tended to go up in this period. The vast majority of emigrants and of the military personnel serving abroad were not members of the upper classes; even the Indian Civil Service (and the Indian army) ranked lower in the social pecking order than the Home Civil Service and the British army. The settlers in the colonies were, by definition almost, people for whom the British Isles, for whatever reason, appeared to offer inadequate scope for adventure and advancement. The colonial societies they set up were looked down on by the upper classes in England, as were, for at least the first three-quarters of the century, those ex-colonials, the Americans. But these colonials appear to have been in fairly constant communication with the Home country and their affection for it (and their home-bound relatives' affection for them) tended in the first generation at least to be deepened by distance. The bonds of sentiment between the Old Country and the emerging dominions must have grown stronger as the Victorian age drew to its close, and the fact would not be recorded in the documents or reflected in the feelings of the still mainly aristocratic chiefs, permanent or political, in the highest circles of government at home. Nevertheless, the growth of imperial sentiment, particularly among sections of the community at home who might be expected to be radical as well, may be regarded as a not unexpected consequence of the growing popular awareness of how many families in the British Isles had real blood ties with the colonies. If Imperialism was 'vulgar' it was perhaps because the Empire itself was populated by 'vulgar' people. The patriotism of the Palmerstonian period perhaps became the Imperialism of Chamberlain's day for the simple reason that so many more patriotic Britons were living in the dominions than in Palmerston's time. Perhaps his awareness of this helped to make Seeley's *Expansion of England* so enduring a work; for in it he exhorted his hearers and readers to think specifically of the empire of settlement as the real Empire of 'Greater Britain', summoning them, as it were, to a greater realization of their opportunity and their duty to fill with men of British stock all that were left of the empty spaces of the earth.

17 · African Scramble
1881–97

> I would annex the planets if I could.
>
> CECIL RHODES

The present population of the British Empire is now said to exceed three hundred and nine millions. And what a golden round of sovereignty shines in those figures. There are the dusky myriads of British India and Ceylon; the peoples of British North America, of Australasia, and South Africa, our dark fellow subjects of the Gold Coast, the West Indies, Honduras, the Straits, Guiana, Fiji and Borneo; there are tattooed Maoris and British blended in New Zealand, pig-tailed Chinese and British at Hong Kong, yellow-robed Buddhists and British in Burmah. Those figures carry the mind from the white rocks of Malta to the black crags of Perim and Aden; over vast seas dotted with the stations of the Queen's flag; from coast to coast, from island to island round the great globe; over expanses so studded with colonies and the appanages of Her Majesty that probably no Englishman lives who could suddenly and precisely enumerate all these jewels of the Imperial crown.

Daily Telegraph, 1887

In any period, what professors, publicists and journalists write can rarely be accepted as descriptions, and even less as explanations, of what governments do. What politicians say, when they are out of office, does not describe or explain what they do when they are in office; and what they actually say when they become members of a government usually describes hardly at all what that government is doing in fact. It is easy to forget that academics, intellectuals, journalists and political speakers are all concerned with the presentation of what they hope are persuasive ideas; governments and their attendant bureaucrats, on the other hand, are concerned with the different task of dealing with situations as they are. In the field of politics, whether domestic or international, there are few situations that are not highly complex; and, in general, few which can be handled by simple reference to a basic principle. In politics, all situations are exceptional situations; those who write about them at the time rarely understand their complexity; those who handle them are, because human, fallible and, because political animals, neither free nor unfettered in their choice of action. Even if they get as far as understanding the causes of the situation that confronts them there is usually little to guide them towards an understanding of what will be the consequences of their actions. Rarely, too, is any act of government, even in the most authoritarian of states, the sole decision of one man; and, in England, every political act in the nineteenth century was the outcome of a conflict of views among cabinet ministers and among their official advisers at home and overseas.

Among the Queen's prime ministers, only Peel and Palmerston ever came near to imposing his own views upon his Cabinet for any length of time, and in both cases because, in particular spheres and for a limited period, each was a master of detail. But Peel drove his team too hard so that it fell apart, while Palmerston triumphed only because he was the greatest of all the persuaders in Victorian history; and even he was outfaced in the end by Bismarck, the greatest of all the masters of detail. Disraeli's principal ministry was in perpetual confusion, and Gladstone was, outside the narrow field of fiscal doctrine and detail, tossed hither and thither by his own unpredictable, messianic temperament. Salisbury survived as long as he did by doing as little as possible on the home front and by saying as little as possible about foreign policy, choosing deliberately to conduct it mainly in the privacy of his own home at Hatfield House. The volume of propaganda and theorizing about Imperialism in the last two decades of the Queen's reign was perhaps as great as it was because nobody could make sense of Gladstone, and because hardly anybody ever knew the mind of Salisbury either. Men could understand Livingstone, Gordon, Wolseley, Kitchener and Roberts; and they knew that, whereas Joseph Chamberlain and Cecil Rhodes believed passionately in Empire, Mr Gladstone had given in to the Boers after Majuba and had let Gordon die. All else was wrapped in mystery; and, in default of genuine information, they waved their Union Jacks, and wove their theories, their fancies and their national self-esteem into the dream-fabric of an Empire on which the sun would never set.

The result has been to obscure for almost a century the reality: that the period regarded as representing the grand climax of Britain's Imperial Grandeur was precisely the period when, for the first time, the currents of world history gradually began to turn against the undisturbed pre-eminence that Britain had enjoyed in almost all parts of the globe since 1815. The Imperialism of the late-Victorian period was a set of haphazard, uncoordinated responses to a whole new series of complications which appeared to threaten the security and survival of British power in almost every part of the world. The very magnitude of the Imperialist propaganda of the time indicates that here was a hitherto triumphantly pre-eminent nation, protesting that everything was getting bigger and more glorious, in a successful attempt to disguise from itself that its preponderance, for a variety of reasons, suddenly seemed to be vulnerable.

Already, by the 1880s, certain of the principal bases of British pre-eminence, outside India and the colonies of settlement, had begun to give way. The events of the mid-seventies had disastrous effects on the Turkish Empire, on whose maintenance as a bulwark against Russia the security of the short sea route to India had been firmly based since before 1815. The impact of westernization had resulted in the Turkish government going bankrupt in 1876; and the upsurge of Balkan nationalism, itself a reflection of western ideas, had confirmed the impression that it could no longer be regarded as a permanent guarantee of British (and French) interests and security against Russia: hence Disraeli's occupation of Cyprus and his guarantee of Asiatic Turkey against Russia. It was because both represented a departure from a long-standing tradition that Gladstone had attacked them so vehemently and refused to maintain the Asian guarantee on his return to office in 1860.

More alarming still, as it turned out, was the collapse of the Egyptian finances under the strain of the Khedive Ismail's ambitious westernizing plans in the 1860s and 1870s, which had produced a twenty-fold increase in Egypt's indebtedness. Disraeli's purchase of Suez Canal shares in 1875 was the first consequence of this breakdown and the first act in the involvement of the British in the direct management of Egyptian affairs. English and French controllers were established to supervise the Khedive's finances in 1876. In 1878 they forced him to accept British and French ministers, to cease to be an autocrat, and to rule with a responsible ministry. This upset Ismail himself, the notables who had to give up their immunity from taxation, the army officers whose jobs were put at risk by westernized notions of economy in public spending, and the peasants who now had the dubious benefits of westernized efficiency in tax gathering. The unrest was so widespread that Ismail repudiated his agreement with the French and the British; he was then, at their behest, deposed by his Turkish overlord in 1879, in favour of his son Tewfik. An international commission was set up to sort out Egyptian finances, the detailed work being carried out by a system of dual control operated by the French and the British. Austria–Hungary, Italy and Germany were all represented on the commission. It was in protest against this European domination, and the humiliating deference to it shown by Tewfik, that, as related earlier,[1] the nationalist movement of Colonel Arabi came into being, with, as its

[1] See p. 226.

outcome, the British bombardment of Alexandria and the battle of Tel-el-Kebir.

Much of the vacillation and apparent humbug which accompanied the British intervention and occupation of Egypt derived from Gladstone's natural revulsion at finding himself compelled to pursue a policy which resembled all that he had found most detestable in the work of Palmerston and Disraeli. Similar considerations apply to his even more disastrous policy towards the Sudan.[1] But the Egyptian occupation was contrary to both the theory and the experience of British policy towards 'backward' people outside India ever since 1815. Naval demonstrations had worked in the past; but in 1881, the Egyptians needed actual armed invasion to bring them to heel; and thereafter, such was the chaos into which their finances and administration had fallen that they required the kind of military activity and subsequent alien administration which had been applied in India. After the experience of the Mutiny in India, it had become almost axiomatic (not merely among Liberals) that the British should never again assume direct rule of a non-European people.

The British action in Egypt was an almost perfect demonstration of all that the free trade Liberals had said was bad about a forward policy of Empire: it led to the inevitable further involvement in the Sudan; it distorted Anglo-French and Anglo-German relations for over twenty years; and it proved to be one of the starting points of the so-called 'scramble for Africa'. On the other hand, there seemed no other way at the time to prevent Egypt either from falling into collapse or coming under the influence of the French. For while occupying Egypt could not keep the Russians out of Turkey, a French occupation of Egypt could endanger the whole British control of the short sea route to India. The record shows that Gladstone's Cabinet, of whom it must be recalled many were Whigs who, along with Chamberlain himself, later became Liberal Unionists, went to extreme lengths in their efforts to avoid doing anything at all. The record also shows that there was no attempt by succeeding

[1] See p. 228.

Conservative governments to regain the Sudan which Gladstone abandoned, until over a decade later.

The occupation of Egypt encouraged the French to compete
with the British in West Africa where the latter had repeatedly
endeavoured to avoid more than the minimum amount of
official responsibility. By 1880, the extent of Britain's formal
control in West Africa was limited to Lagos, which had been
annexed in 1865, partly to stop the slave trade and partly
because of the number of merchants who, as the slave trade had
declined, had begun trafficking in the Niger Delta region for
palm oil. It was for this reason that the area was referred to as
the Oil Rivers. The British had been present in Sierra Leone
since 1788 and had made it a British possession in 1807; but it
was so unprofitable, and so widely referred to as 'the white
man's grave', that complete withdrawal from Lagos, from
Sierra Leone and its dependent colony on the Gold Coast, had
been seriously contemplated in 1865. Since trading interests
tended to increase, however, this recommendation had not been
acted on. In 1874, the Gold Coast was separated from Sierra
Leone and adjoined to Lagos until 1886. The territories to the
north of the Gold Coast were not organized as a dependency of
the Gold Coast until 1897.

The presence of French traders on the Niger had already
provoked a demand in 1881 by the energetic west coast trader,
George Goldie-Taubman, for a charter to enable his National
African Company (founded in 1879) to administer the territories on both sides of the Niger north of the Oil Rivers. This was
turned down. Similar problems existed in the Congo, whose
trade had hitherto been dominated by the British. Under the
aegis of King Leopold II of the Belgians, there was founded an
International Association to exploit central Africa, in which
both French- and Belgian-subsidized explorers (Brazza acting
for the French and Livingstone's discoverer, Stanley, acting for
the Belgians) competed with each other for the trading concessions in the Congo Basin. The English hit on the unheroic
device of a treaty with Portugal, in 1883, by which that country
was to be regarded as sovereign over the Congo and would
allow the British to control its trade. The treaty provoked well-

organized opposition from all the powers with trading interests in the Congo, the French taking the lead. Most decisive was Bismarck's decision to support the whole movement against British influence, not only in the Congo but also in the Niger region. Suddenly, as Gladstone and Granville debated nervelessly about what to do next, Bismarck, in 1884, declared a protectorate over Angra Pequena, Togoland and the Kameruns. Angra Pequena was on the coast immediately to the north of the Orange River boundary of Cape Colony, and was the original point of departure of the development of German South-West Africa. The Togo protectorate brought the Germans immediately within the vicinity of the British on the Gold Coast. That in the Kameruns placed them in a position to move north into the Niger basin and south towards the Congo. However great the diffidence of the British about the African hinterland, domination of its coast was a traditional policy; so was freedom of trade. Both seemed at risk, not only because of what amounted to German annexations capable of indefinite extension, but also because of the probability of exclusion from whatever African trade there was by German protective tariffs. To turn the screw a little more, the Germans and French demanded an international conference about West Africa and the Germans suddenly became extremely obstructive on the matter of an international settlement of the still unsolved problem of the Egyptian debt.

It was fortunate for the British that by the time the Berlin Conference on West Africa was in session in 1884 Goldie[1] had bought out his French competitors on the Niger and secured a number of treaties between his National African Company and the Nigerian chiefs on the Lower Niger. Thus, the Treaty of Berlin of 1885, which emerged from the Berlin Conference of 1884–5, ensured a division of the Congo between France, Portugal and Leopold of the Belgians' International Association; but, though it put the Upper Niger under French control, it left the Lower Niger under the British. Both the Congo and

[1] George Goldie-Taubman assumed the name of Sir George Goldie after being knighted in 1887.

the Niger were to be open to the commerce of all nations; and, more important, any power could lay claim to African territory by 'effectively' occupying it and notifying the other powers.

The Berlin Treaty of 1885 not only shouldered the British out of the Congo; it compelled them to make their occupation of the Oil Rivers and the Lower Niger 'effective'. Despite the energetic pleas of Goldie, the governments of Gladstone and Salisbury from 1885 to 1892 refused to undertake direct annexation. Goldie did get a charter for his Royal Niger Company in 1886; but it failed to make much money and was opposed by British traders in the Oil Rivers, and by the Germans, as a monopoly (and therefore in breach of the 1885 treaty) so that it was never able to do what the Foreign Office really wanted, namely to administer the Oil Rivers and the Lower Niger without cost to the taxpayer. In 1893 the whole region had to be declared a British Niger Coast Protectorate; but it had been laid down in advance by Salisbury that the administrative costs of the protectorate would have to be provided for out of customs duties. In 1897, during the worst period of Anglo-French hostility in international affairs,[1] Chamberlain, as colonial secretary, formed the West African Frontier Force and in 1900 all the Niger Company's political rights were transferred to the crown. Part of the area previously under its control was joined with the Niger Coast to form the Protectorate of Southern Nigeria; the rest formed the Protectorate of Northern Nigeria.

The turn of events in East Africa from the 1860s onwards imposed a similar strain on the capacity of British governments to exercise a sufficiency of imperial security with the traditional minimum of trouble and cost. British hegemony in East Africa operated principally through its influence over the Sultan of Zanzibar, who had suzerainty over a large area of the neighbouring mainland. By treating the Sultan as an ally, the British hoped to keep the French away from the east coast, to further the anti-slave trade cause, and to sustain their strategic command of the long sea route to India that depended also on their

[1] See p. 389.

hold on Cape Colony, Aden (acquired in 1839) and Muscat on the Persian Gulf. This last was also a possession of the Sultan of Zanzibar, who was its imam. British paramountcy in this area had already begun to prove difficult to maintain, after the death in 1856 of the long-reigning sultan-imam, Seyyid Said. Britain was forced to intervene over a disputed succession and in 1861 Zanzibar and Muscat were forcibly separated; but it was still hoped that Zanzibar would become the nucleus of a British-influenced African east coast. The strength of Seyyid Said's successors was, however, weakened by British efforts to stop the slave trade, which was an integral part of Zanzibar's trade and its Muslim culture. More and more, in the 1860s and 1870s, were the British compelled to prop up the Zanzibar sultans against mainland rebellions provoked by their attempts, at the behest of their British protectors, to suppress the slave trade. By 1881 the Sultan did indeed ask for a formal protectorate; but the British government refused. Such penetration of the mainland as there was was due to missionaries and private traders.

By the time of the Berlin Conference of 1884–5 the Germans had become embarrassingly active in the Kilimanjaro region on the mainland, which was, theoretically at least, within Zanzibar's territory; but, once again, Gladstone's government refused to embroil itself on the East African mainland, and in 1885 Bismarck announced Germany's acquisition of the territories which were in a short time to become German East Africa. These German acquisitions of 1885 effectively deprived the Sultan of Zanzibar of most of his possessions in the East African mainland; but when he objected, the British, both Gladstone's government in 1885 and Salisbury's in 1886, gave support neither to him nor to the British traders and businessmen of the British East Africa Association, founded by Sir William Mackinnon, which was bent upon opening up the interior by railway construction. Thus, the Germans were even allowed, with Salisbury's approval, to acquire the port of Dar-es-Salaam by an agreement of 1886 which also formally delimited the British and German spheres of interest in the hinterland of the East Coast hitherto subject to Zanzibar (which still, however, remained formally in control of most of the coast itself). By this agreement the British preserved their control of Mombasa.

After much persuasion, Salisbury agreed in 1888 to give a charter to the East African Association, but only on the understanding that it should receive no financial aid from the government. Salisbury's aim was to preserve what was left of British influence on the coast from extinction by either the Germans or the Italians, who were also seeking to undermine the authority of Zanzibar's sultan. The British East Africa Company had the larger ambition of extending its influence to Lake Victoria and Uganda, but its resources were a good deal less than those of the rival German East Africa Company, controlled by the able and ruthless Karl Peters.

By 1889–90, however, Salisbury was more ready to take positive action in East Africa, chiefly for the sake of protecting the south-eastern flank of the Sudan and the headwaters of the Nile;[1] this meant a determination to acquire Uganda. He was helped in his sudden effort to try for a settlement with Germany by the declining influence of Bismarck in 1889 and his fall in 1890, which brought William II to the direction of German affairs with a policy of friendship with England and Austria–Hungary rather than the previous (and only intermittently successful) Bismarckian insistence on alliance with Russia and Austria–Hungary. Even before he fell, Bismarck had shown more willingness to restrain his colonial adventures than he had in 1884–5. Throughout the Bulgarian imbroglio of 1885–7[2] he had needed British diplomatic support for his policy of restraining Russia and bolstering up Austria–Hungary, and Salisbury had felt the need for Bismarck's support against Russia over the same issue. It was Salisbury's concern, not only with Bulgaria but with Afghanistan and Egypt after 1885, which had prevented an earlier agreement about East Africa. By 1889, also, he was becoming conscious that Imperialism was blowing strong winds across English public opinion, not least because of the widespread publicity

[1] See p. 365.
[2] See p. 217.

given to Rhodes' dream of an 'all-red' route from the Cape to Cairo.

By the agreement of 1890, the British were able to establish a protectorate over Zanzibar, and the western frontiers of German East Africa were recognized as extending as far as the Congo to the north of Lake Tanganyika. The whole area from Egypt to the borders of Lake Victoria[1] was recognized as a British sphere of interest (and for Salisbury this mattered even more than the ending of squabbles about Zanzibar); and the British also acquired the protectorate of the territory immediately west of Lake Nyasa (the Nyasaland Protectorate), which effectively confined German East Africa to the north and east of the lake. The frontier of German East Africa was also drawn in such a way as to preserve British communications between the north of Lake Nyasa and the southern end of Lake Tanganyika.[2] Salisbury did not, however, insist on securing the strip of territory to the east of Lake Tanganyika which would have guaranteed (on the map at any rate) the possibility of the 'all-red' route from South Africa to the North. It was to assure himself of German friendship that he not only dropped this demand, but also ceded Heligoland to the Germans, a bait they found irresistible, especially as their new Kaiser was already beginning to dream dreams about a great German navy. A further concession to Germany was a recognition that the northern frontier of South-west Africa should extend in effect to the borders of Portuguese Angola; but even here Salisbury safeguarded the coast by keeping hold of Walvis Bay, which had been part of Cape Colony since 1878.

Salisbury's other success in assuring British interests in the Nile basin was an agreement with the Italians in 1891. The Italians were establishing themselves in Eritrea and endeavouring to assert themselves against the redoubtable Emperor Menelik in Abyssinia. On balance, Salisbury approved of Italy's attempt to create an East African empire since this was less dangerous than a French empire there. What did disturb him was an apparent Italian threat in the direction of the Eastern

[1] i.e. in present-day terms, the Sudan and Uganda.
[2] This reserved the so-called Stevenson Road to the British.

Sudan;[1] and although at this stage it was not yet possible for the British to reconquer the Sudan after the catastrophe of 1885, Salisbury was determined to keep other European powers out of it. Fortunately, the Italians, like the French and German governments, were never consistently 'imperialist'; they were much more consistently concerned with their status in Europe. The Anglo-Italian agreement defined the respective areas of influence of the two powers, setting respective limits to Eritrea, British Somaliland (declared a protectorate in 1884 at the time of the Berlin Conference) and Italian Somaliland, where the Italians had established themselves in 1889. The Italians were also to keep out of the Eastern Sudan.

Meanwhile, Salisbury had also made a rather less pleasing agreement with the French in July and August 1890. He accepted an extension of French influence in Algeria to as far south as Sokoto, which limited the ambition of the Royal Niger Company by giving France control of the whole of the Upper Niger (the area approximating to twentieth-century Mali and Niger). In return for French acceptance of the British protectorate of Zanzibar, he gave France a free hand in Madagascar and the whole of the area which, on the modern map of Africa, is represented by Chad and Central Africa, and which Salisbury shrugged off in the House of Lords as amounting to 'what agriculturists would call "very light land"; that is to say, it is the desert of Sahara'.[2]

The German acquisition of Angra Pequena in 1884 appeared an even more serious complication for the British than their designs on East Africa. At least, in the latter area, the Germans had no potential allies among the local population; but once in South-west Africa they would soon be encouraged to join the virulently anti-British Boers in the Transvaal, now presided over by Paul Kruger and describing itself as the South African Republic. It was for this reason alone that, at last, the British

[1] That is, what is now commonly called Sudan. Before the 'scramble for Africa' the entire area of the continent between roughly the Upper Niger and Abyssinia was known as 'the Sudan'.

[2] A. L. Kennedy, *Salisbury, 1830–1903* (London, Murray, 1953), p. 225.

gave way to the pressures already being exerted on them from Cape Town to declare a protectorate over the intervening area of Bechuanaland in 1885. They also made haste to absorb the unoccupied territory on the east coast separating Cape Colony from Natal. The dislike of new commitments had been overborne, less by any home-grown desire for imperial glory, than by the long-standing convention that the coasts of South Africa must remain safe from foreign domination. The fact of a German South-west Africa could not be resisted, but it was at once countered by swift action to ensure there would not be a German-Boer South Africa. The fact that the Germans had no naval power in 1885 was a comfort; but it was a comfort that would not last indefinitely.

Matters became worse with the discovery of gold in the Transvaal in 1886. This led to its producing a fifth of the world's gold supply by the end of the century; and made the South African colonies, for the first time, a powerful economic region in their own right, almost doubling their exports to and imports from Britain and multiplying by eight the amount of British capital invested in southern Africa as a whole between 1881 and 1901. But it was Kruger's South African Republic that benefited most, becoming the most prosperous part of South Africa, and there seemed a serious danger that Kruger might create a large federation of anti-British republics from the Vaal to the Zambezi. Kruger was thus seen as a threat to the economic preponderance of the British as well as to the security of their communications with India via the Cape. A fierce competition for expansion developed; from Natal there was a movement to Zululand and Pongola to stop the Transvaalers who were moving to the coast in the same direction, and who might make common cause in that area with the Portuguese. Cape Colonists hastened to expand via Bechuanaland and northwards towards the Zambezi. Anxious to avoid alienating the Transvaal too much (for there were the normally less fractious Boers of the Orange Free State and in Cape Colony itself to consider), the British assigned only the eastern coastal area of Zululand to Natal, the South African Republic being allowed to acquire the rest of it and thus cut Natal off from expansion towards Swaziland. It was deemed sufficient in London to do no more than make sure the Boer republic had no outlet to the sea.

In the outcome, it was Cecil Rhodes who came to the government's rescue. The situation in southern Africa seemed to him to require, if British interests were to survive at all, that men of British stock should strike north from Bechuanaland to the lands of the Matabele and the Mashona (reputedly rich in gold) and even beyond them into Nyasaland, where British missionaries, treading where Livingstone had led the way, were fighting a losing battle for control against both Arab slaves and Portuguese explorers. Only by this means, was it argued, could South Africa become British rather than Boer, and the South African Republic be prevented from becoming, in alliance with the Germans and Portuguese, economically and politically predominant. Further, it was argued, if the British did not advance into these regions[1] the Transvaal Boers inevitably would. All these points of view were pressed forward earnestly by Cecil Rhodes, already a millionaire several times over as a result of his diamond and gold intercsts, a member of the Cape Colony assembly and, in 1884, resident deputy-commissioner in Bechuanaland.

In Rhodes, with his great wealth, and his political influence both in South Africa and with the government at Westminster one is at last confronted by an unequivocal Imperialist, not only in deed but in thought. As fervently as Livingstone had devoted in his life to spreading Christianity in Africa, Rhodes devoted his to spreading the 'Anglo-Saxon' race in Africa. In 1889, he claimed to have the solution to all the problems that beset the South African British, and to all the doubts, fears and financial worries of Salisbury and his nervous colonial secretary, Knutsford. Let there be, he said, a chartered British South Africa Company. It would pay all the cost of annexation and administration out of its profits. Once again, the British would get an enormous accretion of territory to their empire and at abso-

[1] They correspond to the Rhodesia, Zambia and Malawi of the second half of the twentieth century.

lutely no cost to themselves, and the British government could keep South Africa 'Anglo-Saxon' by letting the B.S.A. do all the work – obtain concessions, sign treaties and administer territories. Indeed, it may be said that the Salisbury government, to all intents and purposes, deliberately abdicated its responsibilities in the matter and insisted that there should be no Colonial Office interference in, or supervision of, the company's activities. When to this is added the fact that Rhodes was by 1890 prime minister of Cape Colony, and that within six years of the granting of the charter, the entire area assigned to it, north to Lake Tanganyika and north-east to the Nyasaland protectorate, was the already settled British province of Rhodesia, it can be realized how high Rhodes stood in public esteem both in Britain and in South Africa. In the course of his advance north he had fought and defeated the Matabele and opened their lands to British settlement. Only one setback irked him: that part of the Anglo-German agreement of 1890 which brought German East Africa to the eastern shores of Lake Tanganyika and thus blocked his dream of an all-red route from the Cape to Cairo.[1]

But if the B.S.A. Company prospered, the Imperial British East Africa Association did not. It had been expecting (and was expected) to run Uganda successfully after the Anglo-German agreement of 1890 had put it within the British sphere of influence. Instead, by the end of 1891, despite the expenditure of nearly half a million pounds, it was doing very little trade; and nothing but financial aid and an administrative take-over from Westminster seemed likely to save it. Salisbury let the matter drag on; doubtless, if the I.B.E.A. Company had been led by somebody with the will-power and the millions that Rhodes had, it would have been dealt with in the way that Rhodesia was. Instead, the problem was bequeathed to the Liberal administration of 1892–5, for Rosebery to deal with as Gladstone's bright new foreign secretary.

Rosebery was a Gladstonian Liberal only in respect of Home Rule; though never to become a Liberal Unionist he was always

[1] See p. 364.

a Liberal Imperialist, if not the principal founding-father of that group.[1] For this reason, therefore, he had even more trouble with his colleagues over the Uganda problem than the secretive Salisbury, since all the Gladstonians still hankered after abandoning Egypt and were positively enraged by the suggestion that Uganda ought to be preserved for the sake of British interests in Egypt, and the still not reconquered Sudan. In consequence, all the government would agree to was that the company should stay in Uganda long enough to extricate the missionaries from the bloodthirsty squabbles which had broken out there, involving Muslims, Catholics and Protestants in continuous fighting and revolutions. Only after Rosebery had threatened to resign was a commissioner sent by the government to Uganda in 1893 to report on the situation. Rosebery privately instructed the commissioner, however, that he was not to consider a policy of withdrawal. It was not until Rosebery had replaced Gladstone as prime minister in 1894 that he at last got the protectorate he had all along wanted. In the following year, 1895, two years of protracted negotiations following the death of Mackinnon ended with the territory, hitherto assigned to the I.B.E.A. (and till that time simply referred to as 'Ibea'), becoming the East African Protectorate. The association was wound up £193,000 in debt; but, by 1895, Salisbury was no longer prepared to hesitate. The railway from Mombasa to Lake Victoria Nyanza was begun in 1896, and completed within the next seven years at the cost to the British taxpayer of over £5 million. With the final conquest of Madagascar by the French in 1896 and the defeat of the Italians at Adowa in the same year, which preserved Abyssinia's independence until 1935, only two real issues were still in doubt in Africa: in the north, the future of the Sudan and in the south, the future of the two Boer republics, the Orange Free State and the Republic of South Africa. Both problems, however, were part of a sudden world-wide convulsion of imperialist rivalries affecting all the continents and all the oceans, but whose origins

---

[1] Although Sir Charles Dilke could also claim paternity. His patriotic travel book, *Greater Britain*, published as early as 1868, ran into eight editions by 1885.

have to be looked for in the transformation of the European diplomatic scene after the fall of Bismarck.

It is clear, nevertheless, that the remarkable increase in the amount of African territory between 1880 and 1895 over which the British government assumed control was an increase that the government usually tried hard to avoid. The only prime minister, indeed, in the whole of the last quarter of the century to whom the label 'Imperialist' can be applied with any approximation to the truth was Rosebery; and although there were special reasons why he was determined to avoid a withdrawal from Uganda, he had to fight his Liberal colleagues all the time and eventually behind their backs. The most spectacular and most important acquisition in the period was Egypt, and that had been obtained in spite of himself by that most violent anti-Imperialist, Gladstone. What was acquired under Salisbury's rule was obtained without undue trouble from his Cabinet, but as the result of much delay and distaste on his own part and chiefly as the result of elaborately precautionary negotiations not only with Bismarck but with the French, the Italians, the Belgians and the Portuguese.

Nevertheless, history is not a sum whose total is discovered by striking a balance between the pros and cons, ifs and buts and hems and haws of cabinet papers. The Age of Imperialism cannot be written out of history books because it is not to be found spelled out in the official documents.[1] Nor can it even be written out of them for the rather better reason that large tracts of the territories coloured red on the African map in 1901 were not yet pacified, let alone settled. Those at the receiving end of late-Victorian Imperialism – the Matabele, the Ashanti, the Zulus, the Dervishes, the Bunyoros or even the Boers, to name but a few – can have had no doubt at all that they had been caught up in an Age of Imperialism which was for them an entirely new experience.

By the very nature of English society in the nineteenth

---

[1] The superstition that 'real' history is only what can be proved by reference to Lord So-and-so's papers and Sir Somebody's office minutes and memoranda is, alas, widespread.

century, the Imperialist initiative was bound to be unofficial and entrepreneurial, because Victorian England was always an expanding society, and because in late-Victorian England the divorce between politics and society as a whole was widening. Government remained in the hands of an aristocratic class whose social influence was being whittled away, and whose responses to changes in that society were bound to be defensive and disapproving. As late as 1877 it was still considered rather degrading that a Mr W. H. Smith, who founded the railway station bookstall business, should become a member of a Conservative Cabinet; Chamberlain was never quite able to live down the reputation of being a screw manufacturer. No solicitor and no Methodist was given cabinet rank until as late as 1892, when H. H. Fowler, who was both, became president of the Local Government Board.[1]

The real founders of British Imperialism, all of them nearly always at odds with officialdom, were the missionaries, the explorers, the merchants and traders and, of course, those who, whether consciously or not, had voted against the condition of England by booking their passages in the emigrant ships. With the notable exception of Livingstone (who was, however, dead by 1873), missionaries were almost universally regarded by Cabinet and Foreign Office as tiresome troublemakers always demanding that the home government extricate them from the perils they provoked by their attempts at conversion and their struggles against slavery. Except among the most serious-minded at home they were often unpopular. Dickens poked fun at them and a piece of obscure Victorian doggerel directed against them ran,

> I wish I were a cassowary
> Upon the plains of Timbuktu
> I'd catch and eat a missionary
> Legs and arms and hymn book too.[2]

[1] Lady Bracknell in *The Importance of Being Earnest* is again a useful witness to contemporary attitudes. She expresses her approval of Miss Cardew's family solicitors, Markby, Markby and Markby, by saying 'I am told that one of the Mr Markby's is occasionally to be seen at dinner parties'.
[2] From *Notes and Queries*, 5 September 1863.

Missionaries were also resented on the spot and at home because they were liable to agitate for annexation in order to protect the indigenous population from exploitation by traders. The explorers tended to be dark inscrutable characters like Speke, who discovered the source of the Nile, or showy men like H. M. Stanley who, after his celebrated meeting with Livingstone at Ujiji in 1871, devoted himself to the dubious cause of Congolese exploitation by Leopold II's International Association. The traders and merchants of Africa were disliked by government because they too wanted government defence and administration to make life easier for themselves, because as traders and merchants they were assumed not to be gentlemen, and because their grandiloquent assurances that their undertakings would produce great financial reward were almost always belied by events.

Mackinnon and Goldie and Rhodes were the principal agents of British expansion in late-Victorian times; all three were disliked in varying degrees by government; all three ended up in one way or another as embarrassing liabilities for that government. The companies founded by the first two produced little or no financial return to investors, and Rhodes' British South Africa Company would never have got going without his previously acquired millions, and in strictly financial terms was not the success it was expected to be. From the point of view of England's political rulers, these were vulgar men employing men even more vulgar than themselves for the purpose of making money, and were supported by the more vulgar of the vulgar newspapers. It was as a counter to this governmental dislike and indifference that the association of annexationist imperialism with ideals of service and duty came to be developed. The old Christian missionary spirit was replaced by the secular missionary zeal of those who proclaimed the supreme duty which had been imposed upon 'the Anglo-Saxon' to shoulder the greatest possible part of the white man's burden of civilizing the coloured races for their own good.

The point has been made, and there is substance in it in relation to India in the nineteenth and twentieth centuries, and to Africa from the late 1890s, that for certain sections of the middle classes the spheres of imperial administration provided opportunities for meaningful patriotic service to their country that were closed to them at home. The Indian Civil Service and the Colonial Civil Service always ranked socially below the Home Civil Service as commissions in the Indian army ranked socially lower than those in the army at home; but the sense of service and the opportunity for the exercise of it could be far more greatly nourished in India and Africa than in any but the very highest positions in the public service at home. So could a sense of social solidarity with one's own race be more fully developed through membership of a ruling race abroad. This is the feeling hinted at, naïvely and almost unconsciously, in the words of John Buchan:

> I knew ... the meaning of the white man's duty. He has to take all risks, recking nothing of his life or his fortunes and well content to find his reward in the fulfilment of his task. That is the difference between white and black, the gift of responsibility, the power of being in a little way a king; and so long as we know this and practise it, we will rule not in Africa alone but wherever there are dark men who live only for the day and their own bellies. Moreover, the work made me pitiful and kindly. I learned much of the untold grievances of the natives and saw something of their strange twisted reasoning.[1]

It is easy, in the last decades of the twentieth century, to mock such pretensions and to assert, of even the best of the Imperialist generations, that even when they were doing good they were doing harm. This must inevitably happen when one civilization confronts another in an attitude of armed superiority, however benevolently the superiority may be exercised. What is hard, is to visualize the supreme confidence with which young men went out to administer their imperial heritage at the end of the Victorian age; and it is almost as hard to realize the reluctant unwillingness of their rulers to administer any part of Africa at all as it is to realize how late was the beginning and how short the duration of the British hold on their lion's share

[1] John Buchan, *Prester John*; quoted G. Himmelfarb, *Victorian Minds* (London, Weidenfeld, 1968), p. 259.

of Africa. Hardly less remarkable, and a good deal less admirable, perhaps, is the little that they did with, and for, the huge areas of empire they acquired in the Old World outside India. What Joseph Chamberlain already recognized at the end of the 1890s as 'an undeveloped estate', Lloyd George later not unjustly called 'a slum'. Perhaps when it becomes possible to evaluate that Empire realistically, it may turn out that the wisest heads of all were those in London (and one particular one in Hatfield) who had not wanted the process to start.

18 · A Clash of Empires
1895–98

> Nations may roughly be divided between the
> living and the dying. . . . For one reason or
> another – from the necessities of politics or
> under the pretence of philanthropy – the living
> nations will gradually entrench on the territory
> of the dying, and the seeds and causes of conflict
> among civilized nations will speedily appear.
> These things may introduce causes of fatal
> difference between the great nations whose
> mighty armies stand opposite, threatening each
> other. These are the dangers, I think, which
> threaten us in the period which is coming on.
> It is a period which will tax our resolution, our
> tenacity and imperial instincts to the utmost.
>
> LORD SALISBURY,
> Speech at the Albert Hall, 4 May 1898

From shortly after the signature of the Anglo-German agreements about Africa in 1890 until the end of the Queen's reign,
the international and world scene seemed to turn to Britain's
disadvantage. The twin bases of British world pre-eminence
had been the combination of naval predominance with diplomatic, and in time of war, military alliances in Europe. The
former had never sufficed in wartime without the other. But
by the end of the century it was being challenged, and throughout virtually the whole decade after 1892 England was, for
the first time since the last coalition against Napoleon,
unable to rely on the permanent friendship of any continental
power.

To begin with, Salisbury had been able to maintain fairly close links with the Triple Alliance of Germany, Austria-Hungary and Italy. For all Bismarck's flirtations with colonial affairs in the early 1880s and his tendency to support France against England about Egypt, he had no fundamental desire to quarrel with England from 1885 onwards, since both countries needed each other in order to hold Russia in check during the Bulgarian imbroglio of 1885–7. In the latter year Salisbury signed two Mediterranean agreements with Italy and Austria-Hungary for the defence of the *status quo* in the Mediterranean, chiefly against Russia, but also against France; and both agreements had Bismarck's background connivance. The agreements were not alliances in the sense that the participants promised to go to war; they merely provided for joint consultation. Nevertheless, they were as close as Salisbury could get to an association with the three members of the Triple Alliance and were indeed more specific in their terms than the agreements signed with France in 1904 and Russia in 1907. It was as a result of this close association that Salisbury was able to make the Zanzibar–Heligoland agreement in 1890. Basically, relations between England and the Triple Alliance remained as satisfactory until 1895 as relations with France and Russia were unsatisfactory.

With France, the issue was still Egypt. The French had been extending their hold over Algeria since 1830 and had, with Bismarck's connivance, anticipated Italy's intention to declare a protectorate over Tunis by making it a French protectorate in 1881. The great issue, however, from 1882 to 1898, was the determination of the French, if they could, to outflank the British in Egypt by securing the whole of the Sudan by expansion southwards from Algeria and eastward across Central Africa from Senegal to the Red Sea, where they had already taken care to acquire Djibuti (French Somaliland) on the opposite shore to the British protectorate of Aden. It was for this reason that Salisbury had got the Eastern Sudan recognized by Bismarck as a British sphere, and had sought to buy off the French with 'the Sahara Desert' in 1891; that Rosebery had been at such pains to acquire Uganda in 1895, and that Salisbury was so mortified by the collapse of the Italians at Adowa in the following year. French hostility towards the British in Egypt, with its concomitant requirement that England acquire a firmer hold on both East and West Africa, was, however, only part of the problem.

It was becoming increasingly clear after 1878 that the Turks could not be relied on to keep the Russians out of Constantinople. Accordingly it became impossible for the British to get out of Egypt. The Khedives, as experience in the 1870s showed, could not keep Egypt stable by themselves any more than they could retain the Sudan. So, even though Egyptians in general had no love at all for British manipulation of puppet Khedives, the British found that Egypt had become the strategic centre of their maritime and imperial strategy, but at the cost of the permanent alienation of France, which, ever since 1830 and despite intermittent disagreement, had been England's traditional continental friend. This situation was held to be fraught with danger; for while a traditional friend had become a persistent foe, the traditional enemy, Russia, still remained a traditional enemy. Hence the Mediterranean agreements of 1887. But in that same year, when Salisbury tried to get an agreement with the Sultan of Turkey for a British withdrawal from Egypt within three years, subject to a right to reoccupy it if conditions in the country deteriorated, the combined pressure of both France and Russia induced the Sultan to reject the proposal.[1] Worse followed: a noisy Franco-Italian quarrel in 1888 led to a sudden concentration of the bulk of the French fleet at Toulon and to a demand, by both Italy and Germany, for British naval support for Italy in the Mediterranean. This led to the alarming fear that the British navy would be unable to cope simultaneously with the French navy in the western Mediterranean and a Russian attempt to force the Straits. The result was the Naval Defence Act of 1889 and the adoption of the so-called Two-Power Standard, by which it

[1] This was the second of the so-called Drummond:Wolff negotiations. An earlier attempt at agreement with Turkey about Egypt had failed in 1885.

N

was laid down that the British navy should always exceed in strength the combined strength of the next two largest naval powers.

This was indeed prudent, but it gives rise to two considerations. One is that the passage of such legislation indicates how early and how dramatically British Imperialism was already ceasing to think of itself as invulnerable. The other is that the dangers that provoked the act of 1889 were illusory. The Franco-Italian war was all talk; the notion, much mooted at the time, that the French could invade England at any time was deliberately fostered in Germany to frighten the British into support of Italy; and the absolute failure of the Russians to achieve any gains whatever at the expense of Bulgaria after 1880 hardly suggested they were really about to force the Straits. Although it had a duty to be reasonably far-sighted, the British government may perhaps be open to the accusation of over-reacting to what was essentially a non-crisis. It is a surprising criticism to make of any government headed by Salisbury; but the celerity of his reaction to the possibility of future danger in the Mediterranean is a striking contrast to the snail's pace at which he proceeded in matters African that did not immediately affect Egypt and the Sudan. The explanation may perhaps best be looked for in the two overriding factors in his policy: relations with France and the security of the short sea route to India. It is always a speculative undertaking to try to read Salisbury's withdrawn and exceptionally complicated mind with any exactitude; but it is permissible in this context to recall that it had been as secretary of state for India that he had first made his mark in Cabinet, in 1866, and it had been while still holding that office that he had attended the Constantinople Conference at the end of 1877.[1]

Moreover, the Naval Defence Act had immediate repercussions. France, Russia and, worse still from the British point of view, Germany, all increased their naval expenditure considerably in 1890; and plans for great naval programmes were put in motion by both the United States and the Japanese. It is thus arguable that the naval expansion which Salisbury began in

[1] See p. 211.

1889 created as much danger to British naval supremacy as it prevented; and it marks the end of the days when the British could rule the waves on the cheap. But, punctually, the justificatory theory for naval expenditure by all and sundry was provided by the publication, in 1890, by Captain Alfred Mahan in the United States, of a classic volume entitled *The Influence of Sea Power Upon History*. Avidly read in England and in all European countries, particularly in Germany, it asserted as a fundamental principle that no power could be imperially and commercially great that did not possess a great battle fleet. The widespread acceptance of this theory by every great power (except the Italians who were too poor, and Austria–Hungary which was too landlocked, to act upon it) is a truer indication of the nature and the reality of the Imperialism of the late-Victorian period than any evidence based on the reluctance of British governments to annex territory in Africa.

It was an example of that grandiose thinking of men made slightly megalomaniac by their technology, which lay behind the Imperialist obsession with railway construction that equally characterized this period. The railway had made Canada and united the United States. A railway from the Cape to Cairo would therefore guarantee Britain's mastery of Africa; the Trans-Siberian would (in due course) make the Russians the masters first of Manchuria and then of the government at Peking; a Berlin–Baghdad railway would make the Germans masters of the Near East, threaten the British in the Persian Gulf and the Indian Ocean, and simultaneously keep the Russians away from both. Even the Austrians had their railway plan: a railway from Vienna to Salonika would make them, and not the Serbs, masters of the western Balkans. The imperialism of the last years of the nineteenth century was without question a new imperialism because it was based on the developed technology of the railroad and the great, steam-powered iron battleship, and because it was a race which every great power was everywhere determined to win. It was an imperialism supported by a new corpus of academic theory and a vast amount of popular fiction and journalism and, from the British point of view, expressed in the music halls in the defiant, all-together-now roar of,

> Sons of the sea,
> True British born,
> Fighting every ocean,
> Laughing foes to scorn.
> They may build their ships, my lads
> And think they know the game,
> But they can't build the boys
> Of the bulldog breed,
> Who made Old England's name.

All the same, Salisbury would not add diplomatic commitment to increased naval preparations. The latter would take several years to come into effect, and formal alliances would add to responsibilities at a time when his policy was concerned to reduce them. He showed no interest in an Anglo-German alliance, much in the 1890 agreement to eliminate tensions in Africa, and none at all in a German hope that this would be followed by greater British support for Italy against France in the Mediterranean. Afraid of France, he had no wish to provoke that country; the British presence in Egypt was provocation enough in itself.

From 1892 onwards, Britain's European position took a turn for the worse diplomatically, since, between that year and 1894, there was slowly created a Dual Alliance of France and Russia. Although this looked, from a continental standpoint, like a defensive alliance against Germany, brought about by the refusal of Bismarck's successors to continue in treaty-relationship with Russia, it was, by its mere existence, a potential offensive alliance against England. Given the situation in the Mediterranean, in Egypt and the Sudan and in Central Asia and the Far East it was an alliance of the two great opponents of British Imperialism, a threat made all the more menacing by the virtual collapse of the traditional British influence over the Sultan of Turkey. The Admiralty was pessimistic to a degree; it was impossible, they said, to defend the Straits against Russia owing to the strength of the French fleet at Toulon.

This was the situation which confronted Rosebery as foreign secretary and as prime minister from August 1892 to June 1895. As has already been shown over the issue of guarding the southern borders of the Sudan, Rosebery, for all his neurotic sensitivity, was able to pursue an Imperialist and not a Gladstonian Liberal policy. He was at pains to assert that the Mediterranean agreements, which associated the British with the Triple Alliance, would not be abrogated. He refused to pursue what Gladstone wanted: an understanding with France leading to a withdrawal from Egypt. He supported Admiralty plans for further naval increases as soon as, in 1893, elements of the Russian fleet were dispatched to Toulon as part of the burgeoning alliance between France and Russia; and it was on this issue that Gladstone at last gave up his premiership.[1] Gladstonian Liberalism could not survive in this world that he found so 'mad': a world in which Uganda must be annexed, Egypt must be held in perpetuity and battleships must be multiplied, all regardless of cost and of the higher moral values of liberty and international goodwill. But Gladstonian Liberalism could only co-exist with Empire for so long as the Empire could be defended on the cheap because there was nobody to defend it against. Now that it appeared vulnerable everywhere, time had made Gladstone's 'ancient good uncouth'. Gladstonian Liberalism had dug a grave for itself in Egypt in 1882; had indulged in fatal acts of self-mutilation over Ireland; had been killed off by the Naval Two-Power Standard; and was buried in Uganda, never to rise again.

That Rosebery did not react to the Franco-Russian alliance by closer association with the Triple Alliance was due to a number of causes. Among them was that both Austria–Hungary and Italy were usually too eager to persuade the British to undertake greater responsibilities for the defence of the Straits against Russia, and of the Italians against the French, than the British felt capable of, given their views on their own naval weakness and the much greater naval weakness of Italy. Another reason was that, by and large, the Germans were coolly offhand towards Rosebery, on the grounds that the

[1] See p. 258.

Liberal administration was a merely temporary and exceptionally unstable interlude. They reckoned on the speedy return of
a stable government under Salisbury, who would see clearly
enough the need for association with the Triple Alliance and be
politically strong enough to bring it about. In so far as Bismarck's successors had a policy at all it was that time was on
their side. They had welcomed the Franco-Russian Dual
Alliance because it must, in the German view, have the logical
consequence of making England dependent on the Triple
Alliance. If the Germans waited long enough, England would
be faced with an imperial struggle with France and Russia;
and when that happened the English would be bound to turn
to Germany – and on Germany's terms.

The last months of Rosebery's ministry certainly suggested
that the German forecast was not far wrong. It was becoming
clear that the French were planning an expedition to go from
Central Africa towards the Sudan and the Upper Nile; and
Rosebery was forced to rely on getting the foreign under-secre-
tary, Sir Edward Grey, to announce in the Commons in March
1895 that any French advances into the southern part of the
(modern) Sudan would be regarded as 'an unfriendly act'. This
was to say publicly what the French knew already; but it was a
somewhat meaningless if not desperate gesture when set against
Rosebery's inability to counter either the French campaign in
Madagascar or their encroachments on the Niger at this time.
And although he had got his protectorate over Uganda by now,
it was quite useless for the defence of the Sudan at least until
it had a railway.

At the far end of the earth, British policy seemed to suffer
another setback in May 1895. In 1894, Japan violently detached
Korea from Chinese sovereignty and immediately proceeded
to use it as a base for starting a war against China in August of
the same year. Within a few months, the Chinese armies had
been defeated in Korea and driven across the Yalu river into
Manchuria; the Chinese fleet had been defeated; and both Port
Arthur and Weihaiwei captured. By the treaty which the
Japanese compelled the Chinese to sign at Shimonoseki in
April 1895, Korea, Formosa and the Liaotung peninsula, includ-

ing Port Arthur, were all to be ceded to Japan. In addition, China was to give Japan 'most favoured nation' status in matters of trade.

The Japanese victory and the treaty of Shimonoseki were both a great shock to the European powers, and to Russia in particular, which, with the Trans-Siberian railway under construction, saw Japan's gains as imperilling Russia's own plans to dominate Manchuria and the Liaotung peninsula and Port Arthur. Manchuria was needed by Russia in order to secure the short route for the Trans-Siberian Railway to the Russian port of Vladivostock in the Maritime Province, taken from China in 1860; and Port Arthur would, if acquired, provide Russia with the only port under her control which was ice-free throughout the year; and, owing to its proximity to Peking, it could be a useful base from which to exert pressure on China itself, now the Sick Man of Asia as Turkey was (still) the Sick Man of Europe.[1]

Russia therefore demanded joint European intervention to compel the unmaking of Shimonoseki, and the French at once agreed. The French, who had acquired control of Indo-China, wanted China broken up rather than preserved; but to go along with Russia on the Manchurian issue seemed a useful way of showing that they took the Dual Alliance of 1894 seriously. They assumed there were no risks involved, since England was expected to join in also. Seventy per cent of China's foreign trade was in England's hands and thus England might be expected to have as great a commercial interest in maintaining Chinese integrity as

---

[1] It was all through the Victorian period a great trial to the British that Russian power was physically within striking distance of places important strategically to British imperial influence but not always accessible to British sea power. Russia began by merely being near to Constantinople; by the end of the century Russian territory was physically within striking distance of Teheran, the capital of Persia, Kabul, the capital of Afghanistan, and Peking, the capital of China. The only antidote to the alarm this caused was a greater realization of Russia's weakness than most people possessed, or an acceptance of Salisbury's advice to study the situation only by reference to large-scale maps. But even large-scale maps could not put all that much distance or physical obstacle between Port Arthur and Peking.

she had once had in maintaining the integrity of the Turkish Empire. But Rosebery's divided Cabinet did nothing. Later on, when the Anglo-Japanese alliance was created in 1902, this seemed a brilliant stroke of policy. In fact it was due to Rosebery's inability to persuade his colleagues that any vital issue was at stake. Those Britons with commercial interests in China thought that the opening of more Chinese ports to trade which Shimonoseki provided would be beneficial to them; and public opinion was on the whole favourable to the Japanese, since it made a pleasant change to see somebody other than England's European rivals winning a dramatic victory. In the popular mind, whereas the Chinese were fiendish Orientals, the Japanese were 'an island people like ourselves'.

The Germans, however, rushed in where Rosebery's Liberal colleagues feared to tread; together with Russia and France, they compelled the Japanese to return both Port Arthur and the Liaotung peninsula to the Chinese – for the Russians to seize whenever the moment seemed right. Thus, as things stood when Salisbury returned to power in June 1895, Russia had the cooperation of both France and Germany in the Far East, and England was quite isolated. Much as he would have liked to preserve the Mediterranean agreement, he now felt that Germany could not be trusted, that Italy was a liability and Austria–Hungary hardly less of one; and more important, he was at last coming to the conclusion that if, as the Admiralty said, it was beyond the capacity of the navy to stop the Russians at the Straits, then it might be as well to accept the fact and to abandon for good the traditional policy of supporting Turkey. Chronic misgovernment in Macedonia and the massacre of Armenians by the Turks in 1894, added to the macabre character of the Sultan Abdul Hamid ('Abdul the Damned') merely reinforced Salisbury's twenty years' doubt about such a policy with the further consideration that it was morally impossible to support a régime so brutal and disreputable. Henceforward, the keystone of British imperial policy would be, not Turkey, but Egypt; not Constantinople, but Cairo.

Such a policy tended to make Salisbury move away from the

Triple Alliance, since the purpose of the Mediterranean agreements had been primarily anti-Russian. Relations with Germany
were, however, dramatically worsened in the long term, though
not greatly in the short term, by Germany's fruitless effort to
interfere with British policy towards the Transvaal in January
1896. The Germans had, during the two previous years, begun
to pose as protectors of Kruger's South African Republic.
They had warned the British not to try to seize Delagoa Bay in
Portuguese East Africa for the purpose of preventing Kruger
using it as a railhead connecting his territory to the sea. They
had also announced their opposition to the vigorous campaign,
supported at Cape Town by Rhodes, and in London by the new
colonial secretary, Chamberlain, to force Kruger to grant adult
male suffrage in the Transvaal. This could have swamped the
Boer electorate with the votes of the immigrants, mostly
British, who had been attracted into the Transvaal by the gold
and diamond mines. There appears to have been no doubt,
either in London or in Cape Town, that the Transvaal must be
kept free from German influence. The strategic importance of
Cape Town and the naval base at Simonstown seemed now of
greater importance than ever; now that both the French and
Japanese had fleets in the Far East and the Russians were poised
to pounce on Manchuria and Port Arthur, the British navy had
not only the route to India to defend, but Britain's threatened
predominance in the China Seas. The Germans may be presumed to have been aware of this; and their sudden interest in
the Transvaal was prompted either by a desire to extort com-
pensations from the British as the price of German cooperation
or by a desire to frighten England back into association with
the Triple Alliance.

The British therefore made plans to force the issue. Rather
in the manner of Napoleon III and Cavour at Plombières in
1858 when planning war against Austria, Chamberlain and
Rhodes would incite a rebellion against the Transvaal government by the immigrant 'Uitlanders' (one of whose leaders,
conveniently enough, was Cecil Rhodes's brother, Frank) and
then move in with troops to support the cause of their oppressed
kith and kin whom Kruger was taxing while denying them

the vote. There was force available with which to do this: the armed 'police' of the British South Africa Company and of the Bechuanaland Protectorate.

Suddenly, an international dispute with the United States, already brewing for some months, was inflated to crisis proportions by President Cleveland, who announced, in December 1895, that he would himself arrange the settlement of a long-standing claim by Venezuela to a large part of the neighbouring British colony in Guiana and would impose that settlement on Britain, if necessary, by war. The affair had all blown over by 1897 and a settlement wholly in England's favour was eventually reached in 1899. But it needed all Salisbury's gifts of planned lethargy and phlegmatic calm to achieve this result; and when the storm broke at the end of 1895, England's world position seemed exceptionally isolated. The United States was openly hostile; a renewed quarrel with France over the Sudan had been in the offing ever since Grey's reference to it in the Commons early in the year; the English had been left out of the Far Eastern settlement after Shimonoseki; and now, as well as the unbridled language of the United States, there was Germany's persistent support of a recalcitrant Kruger. As for Russia, reasonable relations with that country depended wholly on the hope that Russia would move neither towards Constantinople nor the Liaotung peninsula; and as one further naval result of the Dual Alliance there was now a Russian squadron in the western Mediterranean at Villefranche.

No moment could have therefore been more ill-chosen from the international point of view than 29 December 1895, the date on which, solely on his own responsibility, the administrator of the B.S.A. Company, Dr Jameson, and his force of 470 mounted men, a handful of maxim guns and even fewer pieces of artillery, launched the Jameson Raid on its 180-mile trip to Johannesburg. Some of the Uitlanders were Americans; others were Germans. They were not sure whether to rebel against Kruger waving the flag of Britain or the flag of the Transvaal. Indeed, there was a strong desire among many Uitlanders to work for a Uitlander-dominated and completely independent Transvaal, not for one that would be limited by membership of a federated South Africa dominated by Cape Colony. They decided not to rise at all. By 2 January 1896 Jameson and his men were rounded up and had surrendered to the Boers.

There is ample evidence that neither Rhodes nor Chamberlain approved or ordered Jameson's Raid on 29 December 1895. There was some evidence that Rhodes had vetoed the raid in advance, owing to the collapse of the Uitlanders' morale; but there was much more evidence that he had planned that some such expedition under Jameson's leadership should take place at an appropriate time. He therefore resigned the Cape premiership. Jameson and his officers were convicted and sentenced to terms of imprisonment by the High Court in London. Jameson got fifteen months. In Johannesburg, the Uitlanders' leaders were put on trial; four were sentenced to death (though the sentences were commuted) and nearly sixty others imprisoned and fined. Although he at once condemned the raid, and communicated his repudiation of it to Kruger, Chamberlain knew something of the sort was being planned even though the report of a select committee of the Commons, issued in 1897, absolved him from all blame. Few were satisfied, either then or subsequently, that the select committee saw, or even insisted on seeing, all the relevant documents. Salisbury himself was aware that Chamberlain and Rhodes were up to something; and no doubt he, like the majority of the British public, thought that Jameson's only real error was not his attempt but his failure.

British opinion was the more inclined to whitewash Jameson, and applaud both Chamberlain and Rhodes, because of the instant reaction from Berlin. The day after Jameson's surrender came the century's most celebrated telegram apart from that from Ems in 1870: the German Emperor, William II, cabled his sincere congratulations to Kruger on having, 'without appealing for the help of friendly powers', maintained the 'independence' of his country against 'the armed hordes' which had invaded it. Not only did this reckless message create an anti-German feeling in the British public that had barely existed before; it called in question a fundamental principle of British policy, namely that the Transvaal was not, despite the Pretoria Convention of 1881, an 'independent' state at all. Control of its foreign relations were, in the minds of Westminster, still reserved to the Imperial government. The British sent a 'flying squadron' of the fleet to Delagoa Bay to overawe the small German force there and the Germans immediately softened their tone, if only because, for all England's isolation, Germany could not get support for a joint protest from either the Russians or the French. The Russians had no desire to add to their quarrels with the British, and the French were interested not in the Transvaal, but in Egypt.

Thus, the Germans made a discovery of fundamental long-term importance out of the manifest failure of the Kruger Telegram to achieve anything better for Kruger than to intensify the British government's belief that there was no way to contain the growing dominance of the Transvaal except by outright war. Germany could not help Kruger in 1896 for the simple reason that telegrams were no substitute for battleships; and it was the British who had the battleships. The Kruger Telegram was a landmark in the history of the German High Seas Fleet. Naval expansion had already begun in Germany, and in 1895 the Kiel Canal had been opened. By 1897 a powerful propagandist organization, the *Flottenverein,* had been set up by Germany's new minister of marine, Admiral Alfred von Tirpitz, a devoted admirer of Mahan.[1] The Kruger Telegram's failure to cause any kind of climb-down in England gave tremendous impetus to the German *Flottenpolitik,* because it was proved in 1896 that Germany could not exercise her 'proper' influence in the world without a battle fleet to back up telegrams with guns.

Hard on the heels of the Venezuelan border dispute and the Jameson raid came two further developments. On 1 March 1896 the Italians were defeated by the forces of the Emperor Menelik of Abyssinia at Adowa. This disaster was so humiliat-

[1] See p. 379.

ing to the Italians that the Germans at once turned to the British for assistance. If the Italians suffered any further losses of the Sudanese outposts of their fragile possession of Eritrea, it would collapse, and with it, perhaps, the Italian monarchy itself, to be succeeded, so it was believed in Berlin (where they were as easily frightened as they were quick to give offence), by a republican régime which would denounce the Triple Alliance and form an alliance with France instead.[1] Almost simultaneously, it became clearer than ever that the French were going to push ahead with their long-awaited plan to send an expedition to the Sudan. What dictated the timing of Salisbury's decision, in that same month of March 1896, to approve a southward advance from Egypt by a nominally Egyptian force led by its British commander-in-chief,[2] Sir Herbert Kitchener, remains in dispute. Salisbury did not want to help the Italians; but Menelik's victory did involve the possibility of a Dervish–Abyssinian combination which would be difficult to dislodge; and it had been British policy for years to regain Sudan, or at the very least to keep everybody else out of it. Furthermore it was becoming apparent by 1896 that although the railway into Uganda from Mombasa would indeed be built, it would take too long to be finished for it to be prudent to await its completion and approach the Sudan from the south. Neither the theory that Salisbury sent Kitchener forward in order to get back into favour with the Triple Alliance or as a response to Captain Marchand's expedition from the west seems wholly convincing. The Italians got very little benefit from the expedition and Marchand did not leave Paris until three months after Kitchener began moving. That Salisbury acted when he did in order to forestall the French rather than to help the Italians or please the Germans is probably the best

[1] It needs to be emphasized that apart from Switzerland, France was at this date the only republic in Europe, a fact which in itself lowered the standing of France with all the other monarchical states of the Continent and explains the always shaky character of its alliance with imperialist autocratic Russia.

[2] Since the British were in Egypt nominally as civil or military servants of the Khedive, who was himself a vassal of the Sultan of Turkey, Kitchener used the appropriate oriental title of 'sirdar'.

explanation of a fairly abrupt decision. But the reoccupation of the Sudan was something that lay in the logic of the decision to centre British strategy upon Egypt rather than on Turkey; and the precise occasion which set the operation in motion is of less significance than the total context of European diplomacy, Imperial strategy and African partition from each of which the decision might be expected to arise and upon each of which it exercised a decisive influence. The general impression Salisbury has left behind him is that the two focal points of his policy were relations with France and the defence of the short and long sea routes to India. With Africa itself, outside the Nile Basin and the security of Cape Town he was, like Rosebery, little concerned; he thought that the problem of China could wait, and that alliance with Germany was out of the question. As it is, he had waited long enough even over the Sudan; and it can be guessed that what happened in 1896 was that that slow brooding mind derived its decision to act when it did out of its own undocumented (and undocumentable) recesses.

In any event the order was to proceed with caution. The declared intention in 1896 was to go no farther south than Dongola in order to prevent, so the Germans were told, an invasion of Egypt. The onward march of civilization had been gravely endangered by the Abyssinian victory at Adowa and by the encouragement this had given to the wild and anarchic Dervishes immediately to the south of Wadi Halfa, which marked the limit of Egyptian control. Characteristically, the Egyptian and not the British ratepayer was to foot the bill; and when the financing of Kitchener's advance out of Egyptian funds was put to the International Commission, Germany, Austria and Italy voted for, but the French and Russians voted against. Salisbury was sufficiently alarmed by Russia's support of France to persuade the Cabinet at last officially to accept the view of the director of naval intelligence that the idea of 'guarding the inviolability of the Dardanelles' was no longer worth 'any important sacrifice'; the only way to maintain British power in the Mediterranean and to continue to hold India was 'by holding Egypt against all comers and making

Alexandria a naval base'.[1] Naval estimates were immediately increased accordingly.

Salisbury chose to follow his decision to go forward with a display of Byzantine caution. Cromer, who was the real ruler of Egypt, had been alarmed by the financial burden the expedition would impose, and Kitchener was annoyed, first, by the suddenness with which he was sent forward, and then by the strict orders that he should go no more than a hundred miles into the Sudan without further instructions; and he was to ensure that, as he went, the engineers built a railway along which he could, if things went wrong, retreat with due celerity. Everybody in government – and in Cairo – remembered the fate of Hicks and Gordon; and though the army (and Kitchener in particular) was grimly resolved to revenge Gordon's death the mere possibility of a third *débâcle* in the Sudan was, given the vulnerability of Britain's diplomatic and naval situation, the recent disaster to the Italians, and the truculent mood of a triumphant Kruger, alarming in the extreme. Marchand's expedition was by now on the move, too; but the Cabinet was still against taking steps to ensure that Kitchener got to beyond Khartoum before Marchand by asking Parliament to approve the expense of sending additional British troops. In fact, when the chancellor of the exchequer steeled himself to ask for the money to pay for Kitchener's railway and his gunboats, the Commons voted overwhelmingly in favour; despite the fact that the total voting strength of the Liberal and Irish opposition was around 200, only 57 of them voted against the proposal.

But once Kitchener had reached Dongola in 1897 the plan got itself bogged down in more diplomacy. To take Khartoum itself would require British troops, and another appeal to the Commons. Salisbury tried to enlist the support of Menelik and to hurry up the Uganda railway so as to send an expedition into the Sudan from the south. By the end of 1897, all these devices had yielded no result; and Marchand was already, though with

---

[1] Ronald Robinson and J. Gallagher, *Africa and the Victorians* (London, Macmillan, 1961), pp. 355–6, and A. J. P. Taylor, *Struggle for Mastery in Europe* (London, O.U.P., 1954), pp. 367–8.

extreme difficulty, moving towards Fashoda, south of Khartoum. Finally, therefore, Salisbury agreed to send British troops to Kitchener in January 1898; and for the first time the British government and the British taxpayer were committed fully to the reconquest of the Sudan.

Believing as he had, all along, that the fate of the Sudan would not be decided by the appearance there of a small French expedition quite incapable of the 'effective occupation' that would establish a title to the area under the terms of the Treaty of Berlin of 1885, Salisbury now made a diplomatic move to accompany Kitchener's ponderous southward advance. This resulted in an immediate failure but a long-term success, at least as far as the Sudan was concerned. In November 1897, the Germans abruptly seized the Chinese port of Kiao Chow,[1] and almost simultaneously announced plans for a vast naval building programme. In the light of these German actions, unpleasant both to Russia and to England, Salisbury approached the Russians in January 1898 with a view to an overall agreement about both the Straits and China. What Salisbury hoped for by this display of amiability was to divert Russia from diplomatic support of France in the Sudan.[2] In the short run he failed; Russia was, in particular, unwilling to agree to a delimitation of her sphere of influence in China as Salisbury asked. Instead, in March 1898, the Russians compelled the Chinese to grant them the lease of Port Arthur, snatched back from its Japanese conquerors in 1895.[3] Their reasons were ambitious. The Trans-Siberian had reached Vladivostock; now they were bent on constructing a branch line from Harben in Manchuria down to Port Arthur through the Liaotung peninsula. In effect, therefore, the Russians proved so determined to concentrate their attention in Manchuria and China that their intervention in the Sudan crisis was now most unlikely. But British opinion bristled; and Chamberlain, having all along pressed for speedier action in the Sudan, was now all for action against Russia. But

[1] Technically, they forced the Chinese to 'lease' it to them.
[2] In 1897 an abortive attempt was in fact made by a handful of French and Russians to reach Fashoda from Abyssinia.
[3] See p. 384.

with a French expedition in the Sudan and a French fleet based on Indo-China, Salisbury would do no more than secure from China the lease of the port of Weihaiwei, also in March 1898. In August 1898, the Germans were sweetened for the moment by an agreement about their future share of Portuguese Africa, then thought to be on the verge of collapse.

In April 1898, Kitchener defeated the Dervishes on the Atbara River within sight of Khartoum. The government had no difficulty in securing the Commons' approval for further large expenditure in June and, in August, Kitchener was instructed that on arriving at Khartoum he should raise the British and Egyptian flags side by side and thereafter send forces up the White Nile to Fashoda, which Marchand had already reached in July. On 2 September 1898, the Dervishes came out of Khartoum, to be mown down in their thousands by Kitchener's maxim guns at the battle of Omdurman. Having then taken Khartoum, Kitchener ritualistically ordered the destruction of the tomb of the Mahdi whose forces had killed Gordon, and suggested that the Mahdi's skull be sent to London to be examined and displayed as a supreme example of a criminal cranium. The Queen vetoed the suggestion.

On 19 September 1898, Kitchener reached Fashoda to find Marchand there with the French flag already hoisted. Kitchener registered a formal protest against Marchand's presence and left a detachment of troops to keep watch on him in view of Marchand's insistence that he could not withdraw without orders from the French government.

It was not until 3 November 1898 that the French finally gave in and instructed Marchand to withdraw from Fashoda. They struggled long to avoid so public a humiliation but the British were in Egypt and the Sudan in force and Marchand had only seven men. Rent by the searing effects of the worst moments of the Dreyfus affair, the French government was desperate to avoid inflaming the army or the Right by a total climb-down. Any inclination Salisbury had to let the French off the hook was prevented by the belligerency of Chamberlain, and others in the Cabinet, who were prepared for war on the issue. Finally, lest the Republican government, like the

Imperial government of Napoleon III, be tempted to seek in war an escape from its weakness at home, the British Mediterranean fleet was given orders to be ready for action if necessary; and within the week Marchand had his instructions to withdraw. The Sudan became an Anglo-Egyptian condominium and there was nothing anybody could do about it.

In the history of public opinion, at any rate, the battle of Omdurman and the enforced retreat of the French at Fashoda represented the high water mark of British Imperialism. Most of the press, most of the politicians and most sections of public opinion, the learned and the unlearned alike, reacted with an enthusiasm so jubilant and widespread that it is impossible to deny that this was indeed a new Imperialism if only because, unlike the old, it provoked so little dissent. Indeed, the lack of contemporary criticism is in ironic contrast with the diffidence with which Salisbury had approached the Sudan question. It was not that, at the age of only sixty-seven, he had begun to lose his grip. It was rather that most of his political life had been spent in the years when at the slightest suggestion of Palmerstonian bullying or Disraelian theatricality towards foreigners there had been a Gladstone or a Cobden or a Bright to thunder in denunciation; hence, to find the leader of the Opposition, Rosebery, emphatic in his support and hardly anybody of importance except for John Morley, or any newspaper except the *Manchester Guardian*, expressing disapproval was a phenomenon for which he was unprepared. Nor, indeed, was it a state of affairs he greatly approved of. The intemperate hullabaloo that caused foreign and home opinion to regard the Russian seizure of Port Arthur as a resounding defeat for England and for himself was personally distasteful to him.

Even more irritating had been the invention at this time of the slogan 'Splendid Isolation' which, starting out in life as a piece of political rhetoric in the Canadian parliament on 16 January 1896, was referred to by Joseph Chamberlain in a speech in London on 21 January, turned into a cross-heading in *The Times* on 22 January, used again in the Canadian parliament on 5 February 1896, reiterated by Joseph Chamberlain six years later, and thereafter elevated to the status of an historic definition of Salisbury's foreign policy. The phrase was first used in Canada in the midst of the twin crises of the Venezuelan border dispute and the Kruger Telegram, and at a moment when Britain was indeed diplomatically isolated; but it was the Cleveland message,[1] with its implication that no European power ought to have any links with any territory anywhere in the Americas, that was obviously uppermost in Canadian minds. The assertion (made by leaders of both Canadian parties) was that though 'isolated' England was still 'splendid'; indeed what was originally described as 'isolated' was not England as such but 'the great mother Empire'. It was important at that precise moment for Canadians to let it be known in Washington that they had a great and splendid (even if 'isolated') Mother and had closer ties with her than any that rich Uncle Sam might claim upon them. From its very birth, therefore, the phrase 'splendid isolation' belonged to the oratory of imperialist propaganda; and Salisbury dismissed it, correctly, as 'jargon'.

From time to time in the 1890s England was isolated as a matter of fact; but as a definition of Salisbury's policy it is wholly without meaning. In that it may be used to indicate that England had no alliance committing her in advance to go to war in association with another European power, in the sense that members of the Triple Alliance and the Dual Alliance were so committed, this is merely to say of Salisbury's policy what could be said of every other peacetime foreign secretary or prime minister from 1815 until Neville Chamberlain's sudden guarantee to Poland in the spring of 1939. Hence arises the chronic difficulty historians have had in deciding what was the terminal point of a 'policy' that had no existence. The Anglo-Japanese Alliance of 1902 cannot have ended England's isolation if it was an isolation from Europe; nor can either the Anglo-French entente of 1904 or even the Anglo-Russian entente of 1907 have done so, since neither of them committed any of the parties to war against anybody. The whole labyrinthine conduct of foreign policy under Salisbury was based on continuous, not to say tortuous, diplomatic involvement with

[1] See p. 386.

the European powers precisely because he believed that the fate of Africa, Egypt, India and China would be decided in Europe. In thinking this, he was vindicated by almost everything that happened in the history of these vast regions during the two succeeding generations.

19 · Recessional

1898–1902

I 'listed at home for a lancer,
Oh who would not sleep with the brave?
I 'listed at home for a lancer
To ride on a horse to my grave.

A. E. HOUSMAN

God of our fathers, known of old,
Lord of our far-flung battle-line,
Beneath whose awful Hand we hold
Dominion over palm and pine –
Lord God of Hosts, be with us yet,
Lest we forget – lest we forget!

RUDYARD KIPLING

The fate of South Africa is a clear exception to the general proposition that the major changes that took place in continents outside Europe in the sixty years after Fashoda were determined by events inside Europe. The struggle in South Africa that developed after the Jameson Raid and culminated in the Boer War arose almost exclusively out of the deepening quarrel between British South Africans and Afrikaner South Africans. It remained a conflict domestic to the British Empire, however, because whereas the government at Westminster was able, though at tremendous cost, to support British South Africans, no other state in the world had the power to support the Afrikaners.

The economic domination of South Africa by Kruger's Republic had become a fact before the Jameson Raid; but the raid, and the whitewashing of the British Colonial Office, and the hero-worship extended to Chamberlain, Rhodes and Jameson, all of them guilty men in the eyes of Afrikanerdom, alienated the Cape Dutch and the burgher Boers of the Orange Free State on whose support Rhodes and the British South Africa Company had previously relied. The struggle to contain the Republic had been hard enough before this. There had been (and still was) a danger that Republican Boers might trek north across the Limpopo into the future Rhodesian territories (then known as Southern Zambesia) and into Swaziland on the west coast. To prevent the former, the British would have to be ready to protect the B.S.A. Company by force; and to prevent the latter it had to partition Swaziland with the Republic so that, although most of it went to the Republic, the coastal area between Zululand and Portuguese East Africa went to Natal.

What the British dearly wanted was to acquire Delagoa Bay from the Portuguese, since it was the terminus of the railway from Pretoria. The Republic's only access to the outside world, vital for its rapidly expanding commerce, would then have to be via the railway to the Cape and thus firmly under British control. By 1895, Rhodes had spent nearly five years trying to buy Lourenço Marques and the Delagoa Bay coast from the Portuguese. But German opposition was so strong that Salisbury and Rosebery, each with his mind on the Sudan, would give him no support. Economically, therefore, Cape Colony's commerce declined, while that of the Republic increased. A further economic factor was that the large hopes the B.S.A. Company had entertained of finding gold in southern Zambesia (i.e. Matabeleland and Mashonoland) had proved baseless.[1] The fortune-hunters were going to the Rand and not to the territories of the B.S.A. Company, and it was for this reason that Chamberlain and Rhodes had begun to pin their hopes on those 'Uitlanders' within the Republic. But these hopes were already fading even before Jameson's disastrous raid. The Uitlanders of the Republic certainly wanted the

---

[1] One of the great myths that history would seem to destroy is the myth about 'hard-headed businessmen'. Rhodes is only one of innumerable examples of a ruthless moneymaker who was as visionary as the most rhapsodic of poets.

franchise; but this did not at all mean that they wanted to be controlled from Cape Colony and, through Cape Colony, by London. The British, therefore, faced a double problem in the Republic; to stop the Boers from controlling it, and to prevent the Uitlanders from controlling it. The former was their public aim, and became even more so once the Jameson Raid had inflamed Afrikaner opinion against the British, both in the Free State and the Cape, as well as in the Republic. But, primarily, the object of policy after the Jameson Raid was to destroy the Republic's political independence in order to restore the political and economic predominance of Cape Colony. The alternative was held to be the domination of all southern Africa, not only its economy but the strategic base at Simonstown, by the Afrikaners in alliance with the Germans.

Fortified by the knowledge that the All-Highest in Berlin was his friend, Kruger's attitude to the British further hardened after the scandal of the raid. He rejected all British claims to interfere between him and the Uitlanders in the Republic; demanded full recognition of his right to an independent foreign policy; began rapidly to increase the Republic's armed strength; and, in 1897, signed an offensive and defensive alliance with the Orange Free State. The Cape Dutch threw Rhodes out of office in Cape Colony. A united states of South Africa led from the Transvaal was held by Chamberlain, and Alfred Milner, the Cape's high commissioner, as inevitable. The only hope left was for the British in the Republic to get the vote. Out of the Republic's estimated total population of 75,000, there were some 50,000 Uitlanders of whom about 37,000 were British. If they got the vote they could sway the balance back towards Anglo-Saxon predominance. Little though Chamberlain liked the Uitlanders, their cause and that of Rhodes in Southern Zambesia, were seen to be the only media through which imperial paramountcy could be reasserted and that, almost certainly, would involve war against Kruger. One last effort to secure Delagoa Bay was made in 1898; but all the Anglo-German agreement of that year provided for was recognition by Germany that the Bay was an Anglo-Portuguese, and would, if the Portuguese collapsed, become a

British, sphere of influence. But the Portuguese declined to collapse in East Africa; they declined yet again to sell Delagoa Bay. Given this agreement, no German aid could reach the Transvaal in the event of war; but this still did not solve the problem of how to re-establish British paramountcy without a war with Kruger.

Salisbury was for extreme caution and Chamberlain, though anxious for action, was alarmed, as were many others in the Cabinet, at the certain cost and probable unpopularity of a war against Kruger for the sake of Johannesburg mine-owners. Given that the Fashoda affair and the Far East dominated the public and the official mind at home, there was little relish for rushing headlong into conflict in South Africa. Milner, as the man on the spot, was all for action. When Kruger did offer concessions to the Uitlanders they remained unsatisfied and petitioned London to come to their aid in 1899. But the Cabinet still demurred. In international law, the Republic appeared to have the complete right to manage its internal affairs as it wished. Chamberlain's proposal, at Milner's insistence, that an ultimatum be sent to Kruger, was also turned down by the Cabinet, in favour of a conference at Bloemfontein in the O.F.S. between Kruger and Milner. By August, Kruger had agreed to enfranchise all Uitlanders with five years' residence and to guarantee them a quarter of the seats in the Republic's parliament; but, in return, he required the British to abandon their claims to suzerainty and all further right to interfere in the Republic's domestic affairs. Chamberlain's reply was to threaten Kruger with an ultimatum if he did not abandon these requirements. Kruger refused to budge. The British response was to send troops to the frontier between Natal and the Republic, and to work out the terms of their ultimatum. As drafted, it demanded the abolition of laws passed since 1881 that discriminated against the Uitlanders; municipal self-government for the mining towns; and a limitation of the Republic's armaments. In return, the British would guarantee to protect the Republic's integrity against any external attack. Kruger's reply was formally to renounce British suzerainty. The British then reinforced the troops in

Cape Colony and Natal; and Kruger sent his own ultimatum on 9 October 1899 requiring the withdrawal of all British troops from the borders of the Republic and the removal from South Africa of all reinforcements sent out since the beginning of June. On the rejection of this ultimatum by the British, Kruger, on 11 October 1899, invaded the territory of Natal, and called on the Cape Dutch to rise in rebellion. At the same time, troops from the Orange Free State invaded Cape Colony.

Any assessment of responsibility for the outbreak of the war must take account of the long-standing hostility of the Boers towards the British in South Africa and the extreme difficulty of eradicating it either before (or after) the war of 1899–1902. The decisive element was that to Boer dislike of the British intruder was added British envy and fear of the Transvaal Boers, once its gold and diamonds made the Republic of South Africa the most powerful state in the whole of Africa. But these general causes would not have produced war had they not been aggravated in the second half of the 1890s by the visionary Imperialism of Rhodes, the impatience of Chamberlain to make the Empire a tighter political and economic force in the world, and the extremist attitude of Milner, the man on the spot.

None of these provocations was sufficiently resisted by London. In a real sense, the war was the consequence of a continuous evasion of responsibility by British governments. There was, first, the evasion of political responsibility in an area known to be highly sensitive politically, which took place when Salisbury gave Rhodes the charter for the B.S.A. Company in 1890. The failure of the B.S.A. Company to find gold, or attract settlers in the number hoped for, intensified the hatred of British South Africans for the more fortunate Boers of the Transvaal; and, without the B.S.A. Company, the Jameson Raid could never have happened, creating, as it did, a situation which made it difficult for either British or Boers to accept the possibility of a peaceful solution. The last evasion of responsibility was Salisbury's failure to insist that the Republic of South Africa be treated with the patient caution with which he and his government had treated almost all its other major problems, both in Africa and elsewhere. It is true that, by 1899, Salisbury's sight was failing and his wife was dying, and that, without him, matters might well have been worse and the war started sooner. The fact remains that, little though Chamberlain wanted the Boer War, it would probably not have occurred without him. He commanded votes in the country, and ever since becoming colonial secretary in 1895 his colleagues, particularly Hicks Beach at the Exchequer, had time and again denied him the resources he had sought for the development and welfare of the African colonies. By 1899 they could hardly go on frustrating much longer a man with so great a reputation and following in the country, unless the prime minister himself assumed full responsibility for the handling of the South African crisis. But Salisbury failed to assert himself; out of fatigue, ill-health, personal misfortune and perhaps, too, out of an unwillingness to interfere in an area of conflict in which he had little personal interest beyond the basic necessity of preserving a secure British presence at the Cape. But, to allow things to drift to a point where Britons believed that the British route to India could be safeguarded only by making war on the Boers, at the behest of gold and diamond mine owners and overblown, over-optimistic land-grabbers with their so-called 'vision of Empire', was a blunder hardly less than that which produced the War of American Independence.

It was not that Chamberlain wanted war. He tried to avoid it. But he was, to a great extent, the prisoner of Milner, the self-appointed champion of the Cape British, and of Rhodes, because he, like both men, was impatient to assert 'Anglo-Saxon' supremacy throughout Southern Africa. No other British minister seems to have been positively Imperialist in the way Chamberlain was. It was his attitude of mind, rather than his particular actions, that brought the war on; whereas, for his colleagues, Empire was a responsibility to be minimized, for him it was a responsibility to be accepted. And so he became an Imperialist dog wagged by a British South African tail.

All the same, the ultimatum which Kruger finally sent to the British was an act of singular recklessness and of an unreasonableness that caused much British opinion to support a war which, but for Kruger's truculence, they might have opposed.

Kruger made a crass mistake in virtually giving the British government no alternative but to fight. It was also fortunate for the British that, though heavily outnumbered by their opponents, and less well-equipped, the Boers, as well as the British, made strategic errors when war began. They concentrated their endeavours on besieging Mafeking in Bechuanaland, Kimberley in Griqualand and Ladysmith in Natal, instead of concentrating on an immediate drive towards Cape Town. This dispersal of Boer forces was matched by a similar dispersal of forces by Sir Redvers Buller, who sent one force to relieve Kimberley, one to the north of Cape Colony, and the other to relieve Ladysmith. In the Black Week beginning on 10 December 1899, all three British forces were signally defeated; and Buller, after advising the defenders of Ladysmith to surrender (advice that was ignored) was replaced by Lord Roberts (of Kandahar), with Lord Kitchener (of Khartoum) as his chief of staff, in February 1900.

By the summer of that year, Kimberley, Ladysmith and Mafeking[1] had been relieved; the three chief Boer towns of Bloemfontein, Johannesburg and Pretoria captured; and both Boer states annexed to the Empire. But the Boers at once turned to guerrilla warfare and, by the end of 1900, British forces had to be reinforced to cope with them. When the Queen died on 22 January 1901, the war was still far from won. Kitchener sought to defend his railway communications by a chain of blockhouses and by destroying the Boer farms and stock while rounding up non-combatants in concentration camps. Even this did not prevent Boer offensives against both Natal and Cape Colony in February 1901, though both failed. Thereafter, more blockhouses, built across the country and connected by barbed wire, eventually wore down Boer resistance; in March 1902, the negotiations began which culminated in the peace of Vereeniging on 31 May of that year. The most notorious aspect of the last year of the war was the neglect and mismanagement of the concentration camps in which the Boer

---

[1] It was always asserted that the jubilation this caused in London added the word 'mafficking' to the language. It would be more accurate to say that it was added to the dictionaries.

women and children were placed, which led to over 20,000 deaths. Hardly less deplorable was the prolongation of the war by the intransigence of Milner as a peace negotiator.

The Boer War proved that the Empire was based in one sense on bluff and in another on sentiment. It had required the expenditure of £220 million,[1] the deaths of 5,774 soldiers in action, and another 16,000, from sickness, merely to add to the Empire two small Boer Republics. Yet the fact that Canada sent 8,400 troops, Australia over 16,000 and New Zealand 6,000, to help the 'Mother Country', showed a degree of attachment to the idea of Empire that perhaps surprised only those who failed to realize how isolated in the world all three colonies would have felt without their Imperial connections.

The most important political consequence of the war was its reawakening of the old dampened fires of mid-Victorian Radicalism. Rosebery had resigned the Liberal leadership in a huff in 1895, and this led in 1898 to the leadership in the Commons passing to Sir Henry Campbell-Bannerman, though Rosebery continued actively to support Salisbury's foreign policy. When the Boer War began, Asquith, like Rosebery, gave it his support, while Campbell-Bannerman was lukewarm about it, and the energetic Welsh Radical M.P., Lloyd George, hotly opposed it in speeches all over the country. With Lloyd George endeavouring to raise feeling against the war and other Liberals not knowing just how far their support of the war went, Chamberlain used the announcement of the annexation of the Boer Republics in 1900 as an excuse to take the internal political war into the enemy's camp by advising Salisbury to hold a general election. In the course of the campaign leading up to this so-called Khaki Election, Chamberlain publicly expressed the opinion that every seat lost by the government would be 'a seat gained by the Boers'. When all the results were in, the Unionist majority rose by four to 134, compared with its position at the dissolution. (In 1895 its majority had been 152.) This hardly argued a nation deep in the throes of Imperialist

[1] This figure has to be set against annual defence estimates of just over £23 million in 1870, just over £25 million in 1880 and just over £34 million in 1890.

frenzy, particularly as, in terms of votes cast, the Unionists, with 2,400,000 votes, obtained only 300,000 more than the Liberals, despite the attempt to smear the latter as 'pro-Boer'. Even those leading Liberals who tended to accept the war's inevitability were inclined to dislike Chamberlain rather more than they disliked Kruger. And as the war dragged on, despite the government's claim that it had been won, Campbell-Bannerman referred to Kitchener's concentration camp techniques in a phrase that resounded even more loudly than the sensational riots created by Lloyd George's 'pro-Boer' speech in Chamberlain's own city of Birmingham during the election campaign. 'We are often told,' Campbell-Bannerman declared in June 1901, that 'war is war.' 'But,' he went on, 'when one came to ask about it, one was told that no war was going on, that it was not war. When was a war not a war? When it was carried on by methods of barbarism in South Africa.'[1] The words sharpened the divisions within the Liberal party and its general dissatisfaction with Campbell-Bannerman's leadership; but it was significant for the future that it was not left merely to John Morley and certain prominent figures in the Labour Representation Committee to make a stand against the war. Hyndman, John Burns, Ramsay MacDonald and Keir Hardie were all strongly pro-Boer.

Of even more long-term importance, perhaps, was the publication in 1902, the year of Vereeniging, of the book *Imperialism, A Study* by the *Manchester Guardian* correspondent, J. A. Hobson, who had been in South Africa just before the Boer War began. It proved impossible, thereafter, to attempt a critique of late-Victorian Imperialism without reference to Hobson's devastatingly hostile analysis of most of its aspects; and few of the later attempts to discredit his work are overwhelmingly convincing since he did not crudely assert that Imperialism was due solely to 'economic' causes and neither did he fail to do justice to the innumerable psychological factors involved. In asserting that there were strong economic factors at work in the 1880s and 1890s, such as a search for new fields of investment and, because of the falling prices of those years, a

[1] Roy Jenkins, *Asquith* (London, Collins, 1964), p. 123.

search also for new markets, he did not assert that these motives were the only ones, or that governments as such were consciously or consistently in pursuit of such motives. He was aware of the very small part played in the country's external trade by the territories, particularly the tropical ones, which had come under British control after 1870. He was aware (and in the hoity-toity manner so characteristic of the newspaper whose correspondent he had been) of the appeal that Imperialism had for the masses (but it was never only 'the masses') as a 'spectator-sport', and the adventurous openings it offered to those who wanted to do more than look on; but, in pointing out the obvious benefits of an expansionist policy for shipbuilding and armament firms and allied manufacturing concerns in heavy industry, as well as financiers who floated loans or played the stock markets as crisis followed crisis, he was looking in the right direction in the search for the most likely pressures which were at work upon the minds both of governments and the public at large.[1] Like all subsequent attacks on Imperialism as the 'culminating stage of capitalism', Hobson's creates something of the impression of his being an intellectual witch-hunter with a tendency towards a conspiratorial theory about 'Big Business' (or at any rule some sections of 'Big Business'). Yet his main thesis, that it was neither a deliberately-planned governmental policy nor a spontaneous outbreak of popular nationalism, can hardly be disputed.

Historically, the most important feature of Hobson's work was that it at last provided what had been lacking for over thirty years – the intellectual basis of an anti-Imperialist attitude. Since it was provoked by the South African War, that war may be regarded as bringing to a close the period when Imperialism was the prevailing creed among Englishmen. For the first time, they had discovered the bloodstained cost of Imperial expansionism; for the first time, Imperialism had ceased to be a mere spectator sport; for the first time it was revealed as having its

---

[1] The argument that there was relatively little profitability in investment in the colonial field at this time seems no argument at all against Hobson. It was the hope of profitable investment, not the fact of it, that counted at the time.

seamy side. The sense that Imperialists thenceforth had that their finest days were over, and that they were now on the defensive, helps to explain the splenetic bitterness and near-treason with which they reacted to the problem of Ulster some ten years later.

While British soldiers were succumbing to the bullets of Boer snipers, or to enteric fever, in South Africa, the British government continued its endeavours to adjust itself to, and protect itself against, the still unfamiliar phenomenon of world-wide competition for Imperial predominance.

In this matter, too, Chamberlain took a hand, as Salisbury's health declined. From 1898 to 1901 Chamberlain angled for a German alliance. Convinced that there could, at any rate as things stood with the Fashoda affair still unresolved, be nothing to expect from France but hostility, and convinced, too, that Russia must be checked in the Far East, he saw (as did the Germans) that association with Germany was the logical response. After the agreement with the Germans about Delagoa Bay in 1898, he tried for an agreement with them to contain Russian ambitions in China, particularly after the annexation of Port Arthur. But Germany had no interest in resisting Russia in the Far East. It was in Germany's interest, indeed, to encourage the growing determination of the Russians to involve themselves in Manchuria; it would prevent their reopening the question of the Balkans, an area in which Germany was pledged, as an ally of Austria–Hungary, to oppose Russia. Chamberlain next, in 1899, decided that an alliance with Germany was desirable on general grounds. Shortly after the outbreak of the Boer War, the Kaiser visited Windsor; in the afterglow of this demonstration of Anglo-German kinship (which was highly unpopular in Germany, where opinion was, as it was everywhere else in Europe, except perhaps Italy, violently pro-Boer) Chamberlain announced in a public speech on 30 November 1899 that the British and Germans were 'natural allies' and referred to the further possibility of a new Triple Alliance – one between 'the two great branches of the Anglo-Saxon race' and the Germans. This idea of Britain, the United States and the Germans (the 'Anglo-Saxons' and the 'Teutons') getting together to resist the wicked Russian 'Slavs' and the presumptuous French 'Latins' well indicates how the Imperialist mind was at once complacently racialistic and grandiose. The idea that the United States was 'a branch of the "Anglo-Saxon" race' and not already a repository for discontented peoples from most of the nationalities of central and eastern Europe was matched in absurdity only by the pretence that, whether Anglo-Saxon or not, the United States had hardly ever been on anything but bad terms with the United Kingdom. (It was also to imply that the thousands of Irish Americans were 'Anglo-Saxons'.) And only because the Black Week of December 1899 in South Africa was still a fortnight away can Chamberlain be partially forgiven the folly of expecting even Germany, let alone the United States, to want an alliance with a state whose army was so vulnerable to the farmers of the veldt. But the idea was a grand one. It looked like a grand solution to the grand problem of ensuring the permanent grandeur of an Empire that, in Chamberlain's view, might stop being grand unless somebody produced a Grand Design for its future. There was no response whatever to Chamberlain's suggestion.

Events in China produced yet another Anglo-German misunderstanding. In June 1900, China was the scene of the chaotic anti-western Boxer rising: European missionaries, merchants and diplomats were attacked and the German minister at Peking was killed. At once the Russians invaded Manchuria to 'restore order'; and to counter this, and avenge the murder of his representative, the Kaiser got general agreement to the dispatch of an international force, under a German commander, to punish the Chinese. When the besieged European diplomats in Peking were released, the Russians demanded the instant withdrawal of all European forces. England and Germany therefore signed an agreement to uphold the principle of the open door in China. The aftermath was yet more frustration: when the Russians then, in effect, demanded political control of all Manchuria, the Germans made no move whatever to implement their agreement with the British. By 1901, the Germans had announced that the agreement of 1900 did not include Manchuria. Hence, by 1902, the British gave up hopes of Germany and signed an alliance with Japan instead. The

Germans lacked the means or the will to do what the British wanted, namely to oppose Russia in Manchuria; the British lacked the means and the will to undertake what Germany demanded, namely full membership of the Triple Alliance and, thereby, a commitment to support Austria–Hungary against Russia. Nor was Germany willing to limit her suddenly increased naval programme, which seemed to the British unnecessary, since Germany's overseas possessions did not need defending; and provocative, since its only field of operations would be the North Sea and the Channel where it must be a danger against which Britain would have to guard by herself expanding her own navy. It was much simpler for the British to turn their backs on the other European powers and to seek to isolate Russia in the Far East by an alliance with Japan that would effectively prevent France from coming to Russia's aid. By this time, Salisbury had given up the foreign secretaryship to Lansdowne (in 1900) and the premiership (in 1902) to Balfour. With the Queen dead, Salisbury in retirement, and Chamberlain about to split the Unionists with his last Imperial dream, that of tariff reform, politically the Victorian years were over.

The flurry of diplomatic activity and the jittery prognostications of doom among both admirals and politicians that characterized the years from 1892 to 1902 seem, on close examination, to have been much in excess of any real need for them. In a much-quoted memorandum, written on 29 May 1901, Salisbury, then almost at the end of his political tether, wrote a comment upon Germany's proposal that England needed to join the Triple Alliance for her own safety that was a comment on all the anxieties of the previous decade, including even his own. He wrote of the German assertion that England's isolation constituted 'a serious danger',

> Have we ever felt that danger practically? If we had succumbed in the revolutionary war, our fall would not have been due to our isolation. We had many allies but they would not have saved us if the French Emperor had been able to command the channel. Except during his reign we have never even been in danger; and therefore it is impossible for us to judge whether the 'isolation'

o

under which we are supposed to suffer, does or does not contain in it any element of peril. It would hardly be wise to incur novel and most onerous obligations, in order to guard against a danger in whose existence we have no historical reason for believing.[1]

But this, which has been described as the final summing-up by Salisbury on his views about 'isolation', is a criticism not only of what Salisbury opposed (i.e. British membership of the Triple Alliance) but also of much that he had supported or proposed since 1890. What historical reason was there for believing that France could, after 1882, somehow dislodge the British from Egypt? There is so little evidence for the view that the French could effectively occupy the Sudan that historians find it increasingly difficult to believe that the decision to fight the Dervishes was related to French ambitions in the Sudan at all.[2] The operation mounted by Kitchener to cope with what, by 1898, was menaced only by Marchand's tiny expedition could well fall under the criticism contained in the last sentence of the Salisbury memorandum of 1901. The same criticism could be applied to the zeal to acquire Uganda, to the chartering of the B.S.A. Company, and to the belief that only by war and the annexation of the two Boer Republics could South Africa and the Cape be saved from foreign domination. The reign ended with the British able to control both Egypt and the Sudan and to fight a long and inglorious war in South Africa without any European power, or powers in combination, being able to interfere in the least. Substantial reasons for being afraid that Russia could mobilize her power effectively anywhere in the world are singularly hard to find in the nineteenth century; the Dual Alliance in the Salisbury era was an alliance between two

[2] See C. J. Lowe, *The Reluctant Imperialists* (London, Routledge, 1967), Vol. 2, p. 126, and A. L. Kennedy, *Salisbury, 1830–1903* (London, Murray, 1953), pp. 331–2.

[1] Ronald Robinson and J. Gallagher, *Africa and the Victorians* (London, Macmillan, 1961), Ch. 12, and Kenneth Bourne, *The Foreign Policy of Victorian England* (London, O.U.P., 1970), pp. 160–1, relate it to the fear of Russia and the chaos produced by Italy's defeat at Adowa. As is indicated on p. 390, the decision to proceed in the Sudan seems, in the present state of knowledge, inevitable or unnecessary according to taste. Hard evidence is lacking.

incompatibles, both of whom were politically unstable and afraid of the Germans.

Even the Admiralty's panic from 1888 onwards was excessive. Joint Franco-Russian activity in the Mediterranean was always unlikely; and even the frenetic German naval programme proposed in 1898 made relatively little difference. In that year, England had 29 battleships against a Franco-Russian total of 28. By 1905, the British had 44, the Germans 16 and the French 12, and the Russian fleets had been destroyed by the Japanese in the Russo-Japanese war with nothing to assist them but a diplomatic holding of the ring by the British.[1] The French, so far from helping their Russian ally had signed an entente with England in 1904 with the express purpose of evading any commitment to Russia in the Far East. All the evidence seems to suggest a government that over-reacted to the novelty of a world in which, for the first time, other powers had not only sizeable armed forces, but new navies and new railways and a desire for overseas territories on a large scale. Britain responded to this new situation, outpacing all the other powers at the cost of assuming vast new defence commitments and vast new territories, none of them ruled other than autocratically, few of them as yet settled or even fit to be settled by the end of the Queen's reign, and few of them a source of anything but danger and expense. It is clear that the principal motive of government was neurotically strategic, and that of unofficial Imperialists over-optimistically economic. The search for a coherent, rational explanation of late nineteenth-century Imperialism is a search for what is probably not there; basically it was never coherent and rarely rational.

This survey of British Imperialism, even in Africa, can make no claim to be comprehensive, since its activities were so ubiquitous. The acquisition of Southern Rhodesia involved bitter and unequal fighting in 1893 with the Matabele, under their chief, Lobengula, and the suppression of a revolt by the Matabele and Mashona in 1896. The expansion of the Gold Coast colony into the hinterland required two campaigns

[1] See A. J. P. Taylor, *Struggle for Mastery in Europe* (London, O.U.P., 1954), p. 426.

against the Ashanti in 1896 and 1900 before they would finally cease their opposition to British authority, and it was not until after the extension of British control to the Ashanti capital, Kumasi, in 1903, that the colony's resources in cocoa, gold and timber were fully exploited, assisted by the railway from Sekondi, completed in 1901. In Northern Nigeria, development through the system of indirect rule used by Lugard had scarcely begun to overcome the chronic problems of administration in 1900; it was not until 1914 that the two Nigerias were united as one colony.

In India, the lull in the acquisition of princely territories that followed the Mutiny was ended after the mid-eighties, and an additional area of over 200,000 square miles was placed under direct British rule by 1901. Not only was Burma annexed in 1886, but half the area of the mountainous Pamir country was acquired to offset Russian advances in that area in 1895. With difficulty, only Siam was preserved as a buffer between the British Indian-Burmese empire and the French south-east Asian possessions of Indo-China. Already by 1867, Singapore, originally an unpopular acquisition first established as a British trading post by Sir Stamford Raffles in 1819, had become a flourishing entrepôt. Ruled from India until 1867, it then became a crown colony. Already possessing footholds on the mainland of Malaya in Penang since 1786 and Malacca since 1824, the British turned Perak into a crown colony, and protectorates were proclaimed over the other Malay states of Selangor, Negri Sembilan and Pahang, all in 1874. Sarawak, Labuan and North Borneo, acquired in 1841, 1846 and 1877 respectively, became a British protectorate in 1888. A constellation of Pacific islands came under British control: notably Fiji, in 1874, and the Solomon Islands, in 1893, in the course of a continuous competition with the French and the Germans.

An extraordinary consequence of these farflung activities was not merely a steady migration of persons of British stock throughout the world but a like migration of non-Anglo-Saxon peoples within the Empire. Indians had been moved in quantity to the Caribbean after the emancipated negroes had shown so little disposition to work for their former owners after 1833; they moved also to Nyasaland, Hong Kong and southern Africa as well as to Aden and to Fiji. Chinese were indentured temporarily and unsuccessfully in the West Indies, but contributed permanently to the population-mix of the Malay Archipelago, and, like Indians, found themselves also in Australia and in South Africa, as well as in London's East End. Singhalese, when Ceylon's coffee crop failed at the end of the 1860s, migrated to various parts of the empire in south-east Asia and Australasia.

The British transported flora and fauna as well as migrants and indentured labourers throughout their Empire: most notably they took rubber for the first time to Ceylon and Malaya, introduced the tea plant to places where it had never grown before, rice to British Guiana, coconuts to the Bahamas and quinine to India; and almost the entire domestic livestock of New Zealand, Fiji and the Falkland Islands as well as Australian sheep came originally from England itself. Less usefully, the onward march of Empire plagued Australia with the over-fecund rabbit, and spread sleeping sickness from the Congo to Uganda, cancer, tuberculosis and syphilis into the South Seas and measles to the Eskimos of Northern Canada.

One successful development at the end of the century was the federation of the six Australian colonies by the Commonwealth of Australia Act of 1900. A unitary system was impracticable owing to the large distances and poor communications of Australia; but some degree of political cooperation was felt essential in view of the need for concerted action to cope with the many problems of the northern territories which might, if left without ordered government, become wholly colonized by non-whites. Australians, with the Chinese and the Japanese, and French and German colonists as relatively near neighbours, needed to assert their nationhood without doing violence either to the long-standing separatism of the colonies themselves or to the Imperial connection. The latter was preserved only in the most tenuous possible form: a strictly limited right of appeal to the judicial committee of the privy council at Westminster.

In the negotiations leading to the establishment of the

Australian Commonwealth, Chamberlain, as colonial secretary, played a useful and tactful part. A first informal conference had taken place between all the prime ministers of the self-governing colonies whom Salisbury had invited to London for the celebration of the Queen's Golden Jubilee in 1887. The initiating factor was an unofficial one, from a short-lived body known as the Imperial Federation League, founded in 1884 and numbering among its supporters W. E. Forster, Lord Rosebery, and Seeley; the deliberations of the conference were barely publicized and it met in the Foreign Office because it could not be accommodated elsewhere. Salisbury told them they needed 'a combination for purposes of self-defence' but the only immediate outcome had been the suggestion that the Queen should be described as Queen not only of the United Kingdom but also 'of the Colonies and Dependencies thereof'. This bore fruit when in 1901 Edward VII's title had inserted into it the words 'and of the British Dominions beyond the Seas'. This, while asserting that the self-governing 'dominions' were no longer 'colonies' in the former sense of the word, failed in fact to differentiate, for example, virtually independent Canada and Australia from 'crown colonies' such as St Helena and Tristan da Cunha.

The decision to celebrate the Queen's Diamond Jubilee in 1897 involved the holding of another colonial conference, presided over this time by Chamberlain, who also arranged for all eleven colonial prime ministers present to become privy councillors. The conference discussed political relations, commercial relations and defence. Chamberlain made proposals with a view to the eventual establishment of a Federal Council for the whole Empire. The colonial prime ministers were unimpressed; a federation might lessen their political independence. They preferred instead to declare that their relations with the United Kingdom were 'satisfactory'; and even to that modest assertion New Zealand and Tasmania declined to adhere. On defence, the Admiralty thought there should be a single Imperial navy, and the army talked on similar lines. The prime minister of Cape Colony impulsively offered to pay the cost of a battleship and had to withdraw the offer as soon as he got home. The Australians contented themselves with offering to continue their small annual contribution to the defence of the Pacific. In commercial matters, the colonies flatly rejected Chamberlain's proposal for an Imperial customs union because it would have ended the protective tariffs the colonies had against one another. Instead, they asked for Imperial Preference, in order to increase their capacity to export to the United Kingdom. But, among other factors, Britain's free trade policy ruled this out too. Thus, although the conferences of 1887 and 1897 set the fashion for periodic conferences of a similar nature for the next century, they established at once their almost unvarying inability to agree on anything more specific than the fact that the countries represented were all virtually, or *de facto*, independent states, whose only common bond was that at some time or other in the past they had all been ruled from Westminster. The only basis on which the self-governing colonies, or as they came increasingly to be called 'dominions', would regard themselves as members of either the Empire, or the later Commonwealth, was the golden rule that they should be treated, regardless of any legal niceties to the contrary, as independent sovereign states.

20 · *New Ways for Old*

1880–1900

> When the righteous man turneth away from his righteousness that he hath committed and doeth that which is a little naughty and wrong, he will generally be found to have gained in amiability what he has lost in righteousness.
>
> SAMUEL BUTLER

> The golden rule is that there are no golden rules.
>
> BERNARD SHAW

Innumerable changes in the 1880s, and above all in the 1890s, indicated that there was developing a more highly urbanized mass society than had existed even as late as the 1870s. With this increased urbanization, the establishment of a more complex system of communications and the great growth of banking and commerce, London regained its pre-eminence as the capital, not only of a kingdom and empire, but of the whole of the world's financial system. Never the centre of a particular branch of commerce and industry to the extent that Manchester and Birmingham were, and never an industrial city in the modern sense, it tended to assume a more dominating position as the City's financial activities assumed more and more importance in the national economy, providing the sole means by which the gap between the country's imports and exports could be made good. The annual adverse balance of trade in commodities was at an annual average of £62·2 million in the first half of the 1870s; but this figure, itself a record, had risen to £160·6 million in the late 1890s; even though the rate at which the gap had widened had slowed somewhat in the 1880s, it was even then over fifty per cent greater than it had been in the 1860s. The income from insurance, banking, and foreign investments continued to increase in the late-Victorian era, and more and more was society becoming aware of the power of finance. The 'bloated capitalist' of the socialist cartoonist was not attired like a manufacturer, but like a City financier. There began to develop the folk-myth of the American share-pusher and the German or German-Jewish millionaire as hidden powers behind the London financial world. It was pointed out in 1890 that the names of Rothschild, Speyer, Stern, Seligman and Frühling were among the weightiest in the City and that other names of importance were S. P. Morgan (American) and Hambro (Danish).

The growing importance and cosmopolitanism of London began, perhaps for the first time in Victoria's reign, to make the great provincial cities appear 'provincial' in the pejorative sense that had prevailed in the eighteenth century, before industrialization had made the new towns of the North and Midlands the most progressive and dynamic centres of the expanding economy. The establishment of a competent system of local government in London, and the long-term consequences of the concentration of the railway system on the capital, also helped to make London not just an 'infernal wen' but something of a true metropolis once more. London became something of an intellectual and artistic cult, the breeding ground for the first time in the Victorian period of a host of new and challenging ideas about social criticism and more adventurous ways of living. At the same time, chophouses gave way to the café and the restaurant; dining out began to be fashionable. For the lower classes, the music hall had now become more respectable, or at least less disreputable. 'Let's all go down the Strand!' was a phrase that began with a music hall song; and, by the time when, a little over a decade after the Queen's death, they went off so cheerfully to be slaughtered in Flanders, singing

> Goodbye Piccadilly, Farewell Leicester Square,
> It's a long, long way to Tipperary,
> But my heart's right there!

it was Piccadilly Circus and Leicester Square where they mostly thought their hearts were, since it was indeed such a long way to Tipperary that most of them had no idea where it was. For the more sophisticated, the Empire Theatre, Leicester Square, where entertainment was for long combined with the parma-violet-scented professional ladies of its promenade, was the most cherished legend of the 1890s; and, for the most sophisti-cated of all, there was the Café Royal in Regent Street where all the best people would claim to have heard Oscar Wilde dispense epigrams and Frank Harris tell lies about his love-life.

The so-called aesthetic and 'hedonistic' movement of the 1890s was almost exclusively a phenomenon of the metropolis. It was almost as an act of open defiance against this new cult of the metropolis that the Fabians went for long, health-giving walks on the Surrey hills, and certain other types with a social conscience built themselves fairly large houses amid Surrey pines and large gardens and rather laughingly called them country cottages. It was much smarter to resume the attitude that the Rev. Sidney Smith had taken in the pre-Victorian age that the country was 'a kind of healthy grave'. The warm cheerful streets that had once consoled Charles Lamb now gave rise to the more lurid myth, in the words of Wilde's Dorian Gray: 'London, with its splendid sins and sordid sinners.' The provinces became, by definition, places where one could not enjoy oneself, where the old early-Victorian concentration on money-making, respectability and artistic philistinism still survived to be condemned as 'behind the times'. A common feature of such typical writers of the 1890s as Shaw, Wells, Wilde and Maugham is their almost complete indifference to the countryside and their wholly metropolitan outlook. Not until twenty years later did Shaw try to depict a country girl, in *Saint Joan*; and Joan's plea at her trial to be allowed the free-dom of the fields and to hear the wind in the trees, the larks in the sunshine and the young lambs crying in the healthy frost is exactly the kind of vacuous bathos that his plays of the 1890s had set out to debunk. Though a countryman by birth, Wells was a Cockney by adoption (and voice) all his life; though Irish in origin, Wilde was wholly metropolitan, and Maugham's earliest work was *Liza of Lambeth* (1897).

More important for more people, because it was not confined to London alone, was the suburbanism made possible, first, by the railway and then by the middle-class omnibus and the working-class tram. Although the suburban way of life embraced most of the classes except the very rich and the very poor, and could include any type of dwelling from poky little terraced houses via every variety of 'villa' from the only-just-detached to the almost-mansion, all its inhabitants were at once condemned, and have been condemned ever since, by the militantly working-class, the scornfully patrician, the angrily progressive and the priggishly intellectual. Even the normally placid pages of Flora Thompson's *Lark Rise to Candleford* become uncharacteristically acid as she writes of her first encounter, as a country girl, with one of the humblest of the new suburban married couples in a 'villa' on the edge of a town as remote from the centres of English life in the 1890s as Buckingham. Little Mrs Green thought some of her neighbours 'common'; she thought (and it was indeed an advanced thought for the 1890s since it had not commanded universal acceptance thirty years later) that aspidistras were 'common'; and that toasting herrings and bloaters was 'common' because of the smell. Even in isolated Buckingham, it was, according to the writer's observation, already 'the thing' to have in one's home 'the latest' in furniture, in preference to things which had 'been in our family for years'; and most bewildering of all to a country girl's ears was to hear her villa-dwelling friend say that she and her husband did not 'intend' to have any more children. This piece of evidence that birth control was already being practised so far down the social scale and so remote from the major urban centres by the 1890s is all the more remarkable in that thirty years later the topic was still shrouded in mystery.

Although the decline of religious observance by the end of the century can too easily be over-emphasized, the general loosening of the old evangelical strait-jacket was evident in most places. The aristocracy had largely ceased the old practice of holding daily family prayers and in young households of all classes it was no longer being continued. Church attendance declined rather more than did attendance at chapel. The character of the established clergy tended to change also. With the decline in land values, on which clergy stipends depended, an incumbency became less financially worthwhile. Graduates were diverted to teaching, the Civil Service and other secular professions. The old Victorian parsonage was ceasing to serve as the village welfare centre, with free, or freely-lent, layettes for labourers' wives, and gifts of food and clothes for the necessitous, now that the parson was no longer *ipso facto* a 'gentleman'. Nonconformity, too, lost to the nascent labour movement or the bureaucracy of the trade unions many who might otherwise have been full-time ministers,.

Even without the (generally overrated) effects of Darwinism and the Higher Criticism, the church-and-chapel-centred social life of the early- and mid-Victorian stereotype gave way before the multiplication of rival attractions. After a long struggle, 1896 saw the victory of efforts to get museums and art galleries opened to the public on Sundays. The growth of free public libraries, stimulated by gifts for the purpose by Andrew Carnegie and James Passmore Edwards, made secular literature more readily accessible. Already, too, long before the so-called 'yellow press' of the 1890s, lurid Sunday newspapers had wide circulations; already, in 1850, Sunday newspapers sold 275,000 copies as against the total circulation of some 60,000 a day for the daily press. By 1896, Sunday newspapers were selling 1,725 million copies, the best-seller being *Lloyd's Weekly News*, which had most of the market. The habit of buying a newspaper only on Sunday survived well after the first world war among the less affluent or less curious. Both *Lloyd's* and the *News of the World* had been founded in the 1840s and their steadily rising circulation before 1896 is enough to dispose of the idea that the Victorian press was 'respectable' and 'solemn' until Harmsworth came on the scene in 1896 with the *Daily Mail*. Not only did the Victorian Sunday press have a large circulation; it mainly concerned itself with crime. The 'respectability' of the Victorian press was, in so far as it existed at all, a temporary manifestation of Victorian middle-class respectability itself. The press had been far from respectable in the loose-mannered eighteenth century and even *The Times* was more ponderous in the Victorian period than it had been earlier; and it always had a small circulation. True, its influence was out of all proportion to that circulation; but it is foolish to suppose that the mid-Victorians read *The Times*, Tennyson and George Eliot whereas their successors read *Tit-Bits* and the *Daily Mail*.

The repeal of the stamp tax on newspapers in 1855 had led at once to the foundation of the *Daily Telegraph*, which sold at one penny and had thereafter bridged the gap between *The Times* and the sensational Sunday press by itself being both cheap and sensational, by its emphasis on the 'human' interest in the news, and by its occasional 'stunts'. By 1890, the *Telegraph* sold about 300,000 copies a day. The 1880s had seen the foundation of two London evening newspapers selling at a halfpenny, the *Evening News* in 1881 (though it was not successful at first) and the *Star* in 1888, both largely catering for the growing interest in sport. Also in the 1880s came Newnes's *Tit-Bits* (1881) and in 1888, Harmsworth's *Answers*. *Answers* soon had a circulation of a quarter of a million, and like *Tit-Bits* was looked down on, both then and afterwards, as ministering to the tendency of the partially educated to be fascinated by purely trivial and snippety bits of information. The real objection to them was that they sought principally to entertain rather than to inform or educate their readers. Anything novel, however, then and since, which aims 'merely to entertain' the under-educated, is condemned first by the well-educated contemporaries and then by those of their well-educated successors who write history books. It was on the basis of his success with *Answers*, then *Comic Cuts* for children and *Home Chat* for their mothers, that Harmsworth was able to buy the *Evening News* in 1894 and found the *Daily Mail* in 1896 with a price of one-halfpenny. Pearson's *Daily Express* came in 1900; its proprietor, too, had started operations with a competitor to *Tit-Bits* and *Answers*, called *Pearson's Weekly*.

By 1900, the *Mail* was already selling 989,000 copies a day, more than twice as many as any other daily paper in the country. For the next thirty years, it was normal for all literate persons to condemn Harmsworth's *Daily Mail* on the grounds that it introduced sensationalism into the daily press and that, by frankly accepting that a mass circulating newspaper could function only by attracting advertising, it also made it its business to espouse whatever was the currently favourite popular cause. It was also said to have exploited war, crime and sport. It was the 'yellow' press; it was the 'gutter' press: in due course it became the 'capitalist' press and the 'press lords'' press. Criticism ranged from Lord Salisbury's observation that it was 'written by office boys for office boys' to the anonymous charge that the *Mail*'s only consistent policy was to advise its readers to sow sweet peas in their gardens every spring; an accusation that was simply not true. The *Mail*'s chief offence was not that it was vulgar and sensational but that it was belligerently imperialist and consistently warned its readers about the threat of the German navy. Its violent anti-French stance during the Fashoda crisis; its strident jingoism during the Boer War; and its strenuous advocacy of naval construction to outdo the Germans thereafter were all part of a quite remarkably consistent policy. The *Mail* was not, in fact, very revolutionary in its lay-out. It was the *Express* and not the *Mail* which first carried banner headlines and put news on its front page. The attraction of the *Mail* was principally that it presented a very wide coverage of news promptly and interestingly to a large audience for the first time. The *Mail* not only helped, in the decade after its foundation, to double the readership of daily newspapers as a whole; as well as attracting some readers from *The Times* and the *Telegraph* it attracted a whole new lower middle-class readership. It was also the start of the age of the newspaper empires, producing or acquiring other daily or Sunday newspapers and periodical publications, and thus still further increasing the hold of a London-based journalism, geared to advertising, upon the country as a whole.

The chief mark of the new press was that it abandoned the language of Victorian self-improvement. While always given to propaganda, it eschewed the impression of wanting to instruct;

though to deny that the new press was in any way informative is wrong. But its existence was said to have helped to widen the gap between the 'educated' and the 'half-educated' and to have accordingly fragmented the common, shared culture of the mid-Victorians (according to Sir George Young)[1] and to have helped make 'cultural class-distinctions more evident' (according to Raymond Williams).[2] These seem dubious propositions. What seems to have happened was that the 'culture' of the 'uncultivated' could be ignored until its expression (or exploitation) by a mass press forced everybody to be aware of it, particularly in London, where it was most in evidence and where it impinged most harshly on sensitive minds who had hitherto supposed that 'culture' was made up of *The Times*, Carlyle and George Eliot, and that nobody read anything else. It has to be remembered, too, that, particularly in industrialized urban societies, all new cultural media begin by being 'vulgar' and are only accepted as worthy of the attention of the cultivated mind when they have ceased to be either novel or popular.[3]

The development of sport into a form of mass entertainment was also well advanced by the end of the century. This resulted from shorter working hours, improvements in transport and communications, and, to a lesser extent, from the missionary activities in the industrial towns of muscular young Christians from the public schools and universities. As early as the 1860s, association football was organized on a national basis. The Football Association had been formed in 1863; the first F.A. cup competition was held in 1871, with fifteen clubs taking part. By 1885, professionalism was officially approved, and many southern clubs withdrew from the association, preferring to preserve the amateur game. League, as distinct from cup,

---

[1] *Victorian England: Portrait of an Age* (London, O.U.P., 1953), p. 159.
[2] *The Long Revolution* (Harmondsworth, Penguin, 1965), p. 225.
[3] Thus, as cinemas emptied and closed down from the 1950s onwards, film societies for 'cultured' people at once multiplied. Jazz was 'negroid' and 'barbarous' until it ceased to be popular; it then became a cultivated cult. The daily press was suddenly found to be greatly worth preserving once it appeared threatened by television; and twenty years after people stopped going to see them, American musicals started to be suitable subjects for historical research.

football began modestly in 1888 with twelve clubs. In 1882, amateur association football endeavoured to stage a come-back with the formation of the Corinthians club, but the great days when it could play professional sides on terms of equality were already passing by the end of the century. Professional football, relying in the first instance on gate-money, was almost as heartily disapproved of as the new 'yellow' press. Not only was its professionalism deplored; so was the fact that the working classes watched it in large numbers. J. A. Hobson contrived to link it with the evils of Imperialism, and other writers were equally hostile to the readiness of working men to take time off to watch weekday soccer matches. The habit began of warning the population, on the totally inadequate evidence of the football terraces, that it was becoming 'a nation of spectators'. The evidence was inadequate even in its application to football in view of the multitude of amateur clubs which did not play before huge crowds. The real basis of the objection to professional football was that it was 'ungentlemanly' and that it brought the working classes together in large crowds, a spectacle which intellectuals and academics have always found distasteful. It was almost a century before cultivated minds could be found to admire, and even philosophize over, the skills of the professional footballer.

Rugby football had first become a serious club game in the 1860s, when the Blackheath, Richmond and Oxford University clubs came into existence; the first Oxford and Cambridge match took place in 1872. A year before that, the Rugby Union had been founded, with a membership of twenty clubs, By 1893, however, there was a breakaway by the Northern Football Union (eventually to be known as the Rugby League) which soon sanctioned full-time professionalism and therefore passed into the limbo of the unforgivable, leaving Rugby Union to preserve, through the social cachet of its amateurism, that freedom from any form of social criticism which was denied to other forms of football.

Cricket had a more ancient organized history than either types of football and although there was always a professional element in the county game, it escaped criticism on that account because management of the game nationally and locally remained firmly in the hands of wealthy amateurs, to whom the professional cricketer stood in much the same relation as the experienced warrant officer did to his commissioned officers. Kipling's scornful conjunction of 'the flannelled fools at the wicket' with 'the muddied oafs in goal' in his poem *The Islanders* indicates the distinction with a probably unconscious nicety: even when rather caddishly criticizing cricketers he calls them 'fools', thus allowing for the possibility of their being wealthy and aristocratic fools; but only common people like footballers could be labelled 'oafs'.

There had been county sides since the early part of the eighteenth century in southern England, and a famous game was played between Kent and All-England in 1744. The Marylebone Cricket Club, with Lord's as its headquarters, had been founded in 1788 and the matches it organized were played for money in an uninhibited eighteenth-century and Regency fashion in great contrast to the aura of sanctity which the game acquired in the late-Victorian period. The county championship, as it was to survive into the twentieth century, was founded by the M.C.C. in 1873 and it was the domination of the game by Dr W. G. Grace of Gloucestershire in the succeeding five years which made first-class cricket into a widely-followed national game. In 1877 came the first test against Australia, played in that country. An English side had first visited Australia in 1861–2, had been composed of professionals and commercially sponsored by the firm of Spiers and Pond. County cricket continued to make generous use of professionals but all counties were captained by amateurs who were also, in the social meaning of the word, gentlemen (or even members of the nobility), and in the 1890s the annual matches between the Gentlemen (amateur cricketers) and the Players (the professional cricketers), which had first been played in 1806, saw the honours evenly divided. The great acclaim which county cricketers enjoyed, whether they were 'gentlemen' or 'players', depended entirely on the transport facilities which enabled both spectators and players to travel to county grounds in large numbers and with considerable frequency. Like professional football, county and test cricket encouraged the proliferation of amateur clubs in both town and village, and schoolboys of all classes played cricket too. Since association football was regarded as socially inferior to rugby by the more famous schools, cricket was, at the end of the century, probably played more widely than soccer or rugby and thus, in a sense, was more genuinely democratic by virtue of its inclusion of all the classes. Cricket was associated with religion: just as freemasons referred to God as the Great Architect of the Universe, young cricketers were taught to think of Him as The One Great Scorer and almost to regard a Straight Bat as second in religious symbolism only to the Cross of Jesus. It was linked, too, with the defence of Empire:

> The sands of the desert are sodden red,
> Red with the wreck of the square that broke;
> The gatling's jammed and the colonel's dead. . . .
> The voice of the schoolboy rallies the ranks;
> Play up! Play up! and play the game![1]

It inspired something rather more like poetry in Francis Thompson, otherwise celebrated for his spiritual poem *The Hound of Heaven*, when at Lord's he remembered the Lancashire professional cricketers of his youth:

> And a ghostly batsman plays to the bowling of a ghost,
> And I look through my tears on a soundless clapping host
> As the run-stealers flicker to and fro,
>   To and fro: –
> O my Hornby and my Barlow long ago![2]

Lawn tennis and cycling were more significant social diversions of the late-Victorian period since, unlike the 'national' team games, they involved women as well as men. Lawn tennis was invented in 1874, and after a period of uncertainty the rules were devised by the M.C.C. and then the All-England Croquet Club at Wimbledon, which added the words 'and Lawn Tennis' to its title in 1877, when the first Wimbledon's men's championship was held. The first women's championship competition followed in 1884. Very soon, a lawn tennis court and lawn

[1] Sir Henry Newbolt, 'Vitai Lampada'.
[2] Francis Thompson, 'At Lord's'.

tennis parties were a normal feature of better-off suburban houses and of the aristocratic country house. A. J. Balfour was a keen player of the game. It helped to enliven the country-house week-end which was such a well-established feature of the lives of the better-off at the end of the century, and quite outfaced the less strenuous game of croquet. It had an influence upon the spread of what was, for the moment at any rate, a mildly graceful athleticism among young women, though there were already some splendidly Amazonian young women among the leisured classes who indulged in archery and the predominantly masculine game of golf, which also allowed female participation after 1885. It made a small beginning to the liberation of women from the excessively trammelling fashions of the Victorian era, which were primarily designed to inhibit movement and which, if they exposed any area of female flesh at all, proclaimed woman's primarily maternal function by revealing white shoulders and a suggestion of heaving bosom. Below the waist they were required to indicate little or no capacity for excessive locomotion, let alone emotion.

More liberating still was cycling, particularly after the adoption of the safety bicycle in 1886 and the pneumatic tyre in 1888. The safety bicycle, wrote Holbrook Jackson retrospectively in *The Eighteen Nineties*,

took its place as an instrument of the 'new freedom' as we glided forth in our thousands into the country, accompanied by our sisters and sweethearts and wives, who sometimes abandoned skirts for neat knickerbocker suits. 'The world is divided into two classes,' wrote a wit of the period, 'those who ride bicycles and those who don't.' But the great novelty was the woman cyclist, the New Woman *rampant*, but she was sometimes very charming also and we immortalized her in our Palaces of Varieties:

> Daisy, Daisy, give me your answer do,
> I'm half crazy, all for the love of you!
> It won't be a stylish marriage,
> I can't afford a carriage,
> But you'll look sweet
> Upon the seat
> Of a bicycle made for two.

The liberating effect of the bicycle, even when (or indeed particularly when) not used *en masse* in cycling club expeditions or by members of the London aristocracy, who descended from their carriages to go for a short spin in Battersea Park, can hardly be exaggerated. It doubled the distance which could normally be covered in a day's outing compared with that possible for a horse and carriage and until the advent of the motor car in the last years of the century the bicycle was the fastest thing on the roads, marking the beginning of the end of a long Victorian quietude.

Besides taking townspeople out into the country and younger village housewives into the nearest town for shopping, the cycling craze brought a new dimension to the problem, alleged to exist already in the 1880s, of 'the New Woman'. It assisted the decline of chaperonage of young women among the upper classes and, more important, it increased the mobility of young women and wives among all but the highest social class. So did the invention of the typewriter and the development of the telegraph and the telephone. By the end of the Queen's reign forty per cent of all employees in the two services were female. The emergence of the lady typist and the lady telephonist, like the increasing employment of women in the state schools, heralded the beginning of the end of domestic service and the tailoring sweatshops as the normal source of employment for poor girls in towns; so did the growing number of the larger retail and departmental stores. These were developments far more pregnant with social change than the middle-class adoption of nursing or the increasing middle-class interest in women's suffrage. It was also the beginning of the end for the normally rather pathetic genteel-poor female occupations of governess[1] or lady's companion; though not, of course, of the 'nannie', who was more in demand than ever as wealthier women felt more and more the need to emancipate themselves

---

[1] Already, by the 1890s, the less well-paid governesses tended to display the incompetence characteristic of an occupation in decline because of better opportunities outside it. But 'staying at home to help mother' was still thought, even down to the level of the better-off artisan class, more 'genteel' than gainful employment outside the home.

from the purely domestic and purely maternal aspects of their lives. High up in the social scale, the New Woman was already being described in society journals in terms like those applied to their daughters and grand-daughters in the 1920s – they were held to be 'sharp, wide-awake, aggressive, self-assertive'; they were said to 'stand no nonsense and need no help' and, if they possessed a sense of shame, to have one 'very different from that recognized by their mothers'. Since these strictures came from *The Queen*,[1] a superior periodical for the greatest of ladies, they are of limited value as evidence of what was happening in general, but they give a hint of what was to come. Not having lived in the 1960s and 1970s, Holbrook Jackson could declare, in 1912,[2] that in the 1890s, 'Never . . . was there a time when the young were so young or the old so old'.

Thus, what marked the last decade of the century was not so much a weary as a cheerful and liberating '*fin de siècle*' spirit. Leisure was more varied and restraints less oppressive. Much of the elaborately-expressed 'decadence' of the aesthetic minority was a pose, but it was none the worse for that, since every artist, like most young men, tends to strike poses of various sorts until he finds one that fits his real self; and the most successful and shameless poseur of the 1890s was neither the exquisite Max Beerbohm nor even Oscar Wilde, but the robustly undecadent and only marginally aesthetic George Bernard Shaw. The 'decadents' rhapsodised about vice because after nearly fifty years of rhapsodies about virtue, there was nothing left to say about it. 'Art for Art's sake' may have begun the process of divorcing art from the mainstream of society; but it had stayed within that stream for so long during the Victorian period that it was all but drowned as a result. Victorian art, with its emphasis on virtue, can only be assessed objectively (if objectively is the proper word to apply to any aesthetic fashion) because those whom it suffocated by its overblown cosiness are now dead. As Samuel Butler had already observed:

[1] They are quoted in Stella Margetson, *Leisure and Pleasure in the Nineteenth Century* (London, Cassell, 1969).
[2] The year when he first wrote *The Eighteen Nineties*.

> If virtue had everything her own way she would be as
> insufferable as dominant factions generally are. It is the function
> of vice to keep virtue within reasonable bounds.[1]

Nor was the dramatically symbolic manifestation of *fin de
siècle* aestheticism, the illustrated quarterly called *The Yellow
Book*, quite the repository of satanic decadence it was held to
be. Renowned for the brilliant and fantastic decorative black-
and-white drawings of the doomed, tubercular Aubrey
Beardsley, who was its art editor in 1894–5 (and who became
instantly famous as a result, but was dead in 1898 at the age of
thirty-six), it numbered among its contributors writers as undecadent as Arnold Bennet, Edmund Gosse and Kenneth
Grahame, author of *The Wind in the Willows*, and such artists
as Wilson Steer and (though he was suspected of being somewhat *outré*) Walter Sickert. Nor do the prose and poetry of
Richard le Gallienne, who also contributed, show many signs of
decadence. In so far as the 'decadence' was 'decadent' at all, it
was a legitimate first step towards extending the range of
human emotions and sensibilities which had been confined for
far too long within the pseudo-morality of respectability and
the complacent philistinism of a society whose principal
philosophy had been the impoverished Christianity of the
advocates of self-help and an emotionally stunting devotion to
hard work and the making of money. Virtually no society,
before or since the Victorian age, worked so hard on the basis,
not of external pressures like those of ancient slavery or of the
totalitarian democracies of the twentieth century, but on the
basis of a grimly cultivated internal compulsion, maintained at
heavy cost to other facets of the human personality. The
aesthetes and the decadents of the 1880s and 1890s went on
strike, not for the individual's right to work, but for the
individual's right to live. Like all strikers, they put slogans on
their banners that were designed to shock, and to decry
established values.

In many was, the 1890s were years of intellectual and artistic

[1] From *Selections from the Notebooks of Samuel Butler* (London, Cape, 1930),
p. 32.

renaissance and years when the arts in England were open to, and more obviously a part of, a European renaissance. It was the decade of the first volumes of Frazer's *Golden Bough*, which was to call in question a whole series of Christian complacencies about the uniqueness of their particular Revelation. Beardsley himself is closely associated with the birth of Art Nouveau, at a time when similar styles to his own were already observable in central Europe. It was the decade that saw the first workings, in poetry and design, of that seminal Scottish mind, Patrick Geddes, the father of twentieth-century ideas on town planning; it produced at its end Mackintosh's School of Art in Glasgow, which was to have important influences on continental, and particularly German, architecture until the time of Hitler. It was the decade of Hardy's *Tess of the d'Urbervilles* and *Jude the Obscure*, the early novels of Wells and the early plays of Shaw. The theatre was also enlivened in the 1890s, not only by Wilde's *The Importance of Being Earnest*, *Lady Windermere's Fan* and *A Woman of No Importance* but also by the less polished but somewhat 'daring' *The Second Mrs Tanqueray* by Arthur Pinero. It saw the first Henry Wood Promenade Concert in 1895; in 1900 came Elgar's 'Enigma Variations'. It was the decade of Kipling's *Barrack Room Ballads* and also of *Stalky & Co*, which spawned all those school stories of the early twentieth century that were so different in style and outlook from the improving ones that sprang from *Tom Brown's Schooldays* and *Eric, or Little by Little* in the mid-Victorian period. In the 1890s also, appeared the first volume of poems by W. B. Yeats, Hardy's *Wessex Poems* and A. E. Housman's *A Shropshire Lad*. The Tate Gallery was opened and the Wallace Collection purchased. The first London tube railway was opened, the Sherlock Holmes stories began to appear in the *Strand Magazine* and in Germany the first Zeppelin flew. In the last year of the Queen's reign came Marconi's first wireless telegraphy message and the first petrol-engined bicycle. There also seeped across from the continent such foreshadowings of the mid-twentieth century as Planck's Quantum Theory and the separation of uranium in 1899. Such developments were paralleled abroad by Freud's *Studies in Hysteria* in 1895 and at home by Havelock Ellis's

Psychology of Sex, which appeared between 1897 and 1900. Perhaps even more indicative of how the future was being prepared for in the 1890s was an invention of 1899: aspirin.

In general it was a buoyant decade. There were bitter strikes from time to time; there was still much poverty and unemployment; but then, as in subsequent periods, these matters did not impinge on the national consciousness as sharply as they might, since nothing is so easy to ignore as the misfortunes of people with whom one need not come into personal contact. And, even if the Boer War did call a temporary halt to the general cheerfulness, there was recovery both in spirits and in prosperity from 1898 until the bad-tempered years from 1911 to 1914. As the Queen grew older, London society more and more took its tone from the restlessly, but always charmingly, self-indulgent Prince of Wales, who consorted cheerfully with German Jews, French actresses and English beauties, exuding portly bonhomie wherever he went as long as he could always have his own way. Earlier, his departures from the narrow path of virtue prescribed by the Queen had caused several public scandals; now, he and the times were better matched. His lady friends were gracious and discreet; and Queen Alexandra was even more gracious and discreet; and also contrived to stay young and charming.

Lower down the social scale, the music halls flourished, signalling their upward ascent from mere rowdy places of drink and entertainment for the shadier sections of society by sometimes calling themselves Palaces of Variety. The lowered cost of food, the shorter hours of work and a communications system advanced enough to enable the stars to do the rounds of the London and provincial halls on the basis of a fairly limited repertoire, but not so advanced that after one brief television series they had given the best of all they had to almost everybody, provided the means by which the cheerful good humour and homely vulgarity of the lower middle class and upper working class could contribute something to society as a whole. The music hall became a part of the national culture; it was no longer a disreputable sub-culture hidden from sight by its lack of respectability. Its leading figures were for the first time national personalities, extending upwards from the lower class something of its broad sense of comedy and its unabashed sentimentality, and something of its disrespect for the old pruderies. For this brief period, too, it was a purely native product. American influence would not be long in coming. The cake walk, foreshadowing ragtime and jazz, was already in existence across the Atlantic by 1900, and the songs of Stephen Collins Foster had long been favourites; but if there was at this time foreign influence it derived mainly from what music hall jargon called 'Gay Paree'. Among the more celebrated of the male stars of the halls was Dan Leno, a comic with oddly wistful spurts of surrealist philosophy ('Ah, what is man? Wherefore does he why? Whence did he whence? Whither is he withering?') and Albert Chevalier, representing the coster-monger as a gentle creature who was kind to the donkey that pulled his barrow and to the 'old Dutch' to whom he had been married for forty years. The leading lady of the halls was Marie Lloyd, attracting such admiration for her cockney vivacity (and 'naughtiness') that Max Beerbohm ranked her as one of the three most memorable of Victorian Englishwomen, the other two being 'the Queen herself and Miss Florence Nightingale'. But the high spirits that characterized the 1890s in particular were most specifically expressed by Lottie Collins who, with a tremendous high kick and a blaze of red petticoat, doubtless as England's answer to the can-can, sang the hit-song, Ta-ra-ra-boom-de-ay:

> Not too forward, not too bold,
> Not too hot and not too cold
> But the very thing I'm told
> That in your arms you'd like to hold –
> Ta-ra-ra-boom-de-ay!

Saucy, silly and vulgar, it ran through the land like an epidemic from 1892 to 1896. But perhaps even more significantly, it did not prove naughty enough. One schoolboy parody ran,

> Lottie Collins lost her drawers,
> Will you kindly lend her yours?

For she's going far away
At the breaking of the day –
Ta-ra-ra-boom-de-ay![1]

But, since the music halls reflected more than one of the characteristic English moods of the time, they produced a song for the Boer War, too. It foreshadowed, in 'Dolly Gray', the way in which they would try to sing their way through the grimmer sacrifices of the years from 1914 to 1918:

Hark, I hear the bugle calling –
Goodbye, Dolly Gray.

[1] There are other versions of this parody, but the first line and the last are constant.

21 · Queen and Mother

May children of our children say,
'She wrought her people lasting good;

Her court was pure; her life serene;
God gave her peace; her land reposed;
A thousand claims to reverence closed
In her as Mother, Wife and Queen.'

TENNYSON, 1851

It is a sufficient measure of the length of Queen Victoria's reign to recall that it began in the year that John Constable died and ended in the year that Walt Disney was born. Nothing but the fact that one reigning sovereign presided over the intervening years could give even the appearance of unity to a period that spanned the gap between two such different lives: one, creative of the still canvases that portrayed the vanishing rural landscape of pre-industrial England, and the other productive of the fast-moving celluloid antics and canned American squawks of Donald Duck. Yet the length of the Queen's reign was not without its consequences. It provided the public mind with a sense of continuity with its past, which was none the less real for being wholly symbolic, and all the more valuable for contrasting so sharply with the dramatic social and economic changes by which that long reign had been marked. Much of the effusive verbiage occasioned by her two Jubilees in 1887 and 1897, and by her death in 1901, was in fact taken up with the astonished recital of all the changes that had occurred since 1837; but, informing most of what was written and said, was a hardly less astonished realization that, all through what had happened, one small, not very clever and certainly not very beautiful, woman had sat securely on the throne, her common sense outweighing her varied absurdities, her lack of brilliance or real power outweighed by the circumstance that her position as Queen and the institution of monarchy became stronger the older she became.

The survival of the the old Queen into the first years of the twentieth century seemed incarnate evidence that human personality, and therefore the English nation itself, was, after all, capable of absorbing changes for whose rapidity and variety history could provide no precedent, and of remaining, so it seemed, basically as sound and as warmhearted as ever. The Queen seemed to disprove what all the best minds had asserted, namely that the change to an industrial society would be destructive of the human personality. True, she had not herself been much inconvenienced by the manifold stresses of the time; but this, in itself, attested not only to her great physical vitality but to the exceptional stability of English society during her long reign. Only the occasional lunatic made an attack on her life, and by 1901, the contrast between her long-lasting reign, at whose end, the Boers notwithstanding, both her crown and her country were still everywhere respected, and the fortunes of other European crowned heads since 1837, was remarkable. The French had overthrown three dynastic sovereigns since her early girlhood and every other European state had been shaken time and again by revolution or assassination or both. The nineteenth century ended with France a distraught republic and Italy a perilously precarious monarchy. Russia remained hardly less autocratic under Nicholas II than under Nicholas I, save that the autocrat himself was now ineffectual and stupid. Austria–Hungary's Emperor presided over an Empire the brilliance of whose scientists, artists and intellectuals failed to disguise its political obsolescence. The convulsions of the 1860s had produced an upstart Empire in Germany which, by 1901, was ruled by an Emperor whose position, as seen from Windsor and from most other places in England, was that of the Queen's most ill-behaved and arrogant grandson. For all its blustering anti-Spanish imperialism at the century's end, the United States was still politically weak in the world, even if powerful economically.

More flattering than these contrasts was the fact that, in the course of her reign, every state in Europe except Russia had acquired representative, parliamentary institutions approximating, in appearance at least, to those in which – though with intermittent outbursts of indignant but unpublicized protest on points of detail – the Queen had for long been the only important European monarch genuinely to believe. Indeed, it was taken for granted that the representative institutions on the English model over which the Queen had presided were the only conceivable form of government to which any state in the world could aspire, the only one in which the processes of political evolution would find their ultimate and inevitable expression.

The length of the Queen's reign, and the juxtaposition in her character of a strong sense of dignity and a lack of pretentiousness, succeeded in strengthening a monarchy and a dynasty which even for some time after her accession had been regarded, ever since its transplantation from Hanover on the death of Queen Anne, as at best a political convenience and at worst a source of public disrepute. The first two Georges had been unloved foreigners. George III, though he began as a more popular sovereign than they, was politically discredited by the loss of the American colonies and, from 1788 onwards, was gradually reduced to a physical condition which, if it was not clinically a state of insanity, looked sufficiently like it for the difference not to be apparent. From 1811 until his death in 1820, at the age of eighty-two, he had lived in pathetic seclusion, blind as well as mad. Even when he was in normal health, his court and his queen were remarkable for the dullness of their Germanic domesticity; though, given the dissolute behaviour of so many of the English nobility and of his own sons, this was the one reason why in the early part of his reign and the sane interludes in the latter part, he inspired some degree of popular, though not political, respect.

Of the dozen of his fifteen children who survived infancy, few of the seven sons seemed capable of producing legitimate heirs and none of his five daughters produced children either. By 1820, the Hanoverians seemed to be in as much danger of extinction through infertile marriages as the descendants of Henry VII or of Louis XIV had been; and, given the public scandals of their private lives, the royal dukes were well on the way to causing the dynasty to be extinguished by its unpopularity if not by its infertility. George III's eldest son, the Prince Regent, and his impossible wife, Caroline of Brunswick had only one child, Princess Charlotte; and she had died, with her child, in childbirth in 1817, so that at that date George III had no legitimate grandchild. Three of the Prince Regent's brothers were persuaded to contract legal marriages with a view to begetting heirs, since the marriage of the Prince Regent's eldest brother, who eventually succeeded as William IV in 1830, was also infertile. Thus George III's third son, Edward, Duke of Kent, reluctantly agreed to part from his mistress at the call of duty and married, in 1818, Princess Victoria of Saxe-Coburg, a sister of Princess Charlotte's widower, Prince Leopold of Saxe-Coburg, for whom Palmerston was to obtain, in 1831, the crown of Belgium. Though he died of exposure to the chill winds of the English seaside in 1820, the Duke of Kent had just had time to become, on 24 May 1819, the father of a daughter who, there being no children to survive either the Prince Regent, who reigned as George IV from 1820 to 1830, or William IV, who succeeded in 1830, duly became Queen regnant in 1837.

The future Queen's childhood was the usual Hanoverian and Germanic chaos of mismanagement, intrigue and inadequate funds, all culminating in strenuous efforts by the Duchess of Kent and the comptroller of her Household, Sir John Conroy, to ensure that the Duchess should become regent, even if William IV did not die until after Victoria reached the age of eighteen, and that Conroy should be the young Queen's private secretary. A grim domestic feud developed, Victoria's only persistent ally being her governess. The Princess was, however, tough enough to hold out against considerable pressure sufficiently long to secure the support of both the Tory, Lord Liverpool, and the Whig prime minister, Melbourne, by the time of the King's death. Both men considered Conroy an adventurer; and Victoria considered he was at least flirting with her mother. Thus, before her accession, Victoria had already revealed her lifelong capacity to combine with her simplicity and her gift on occasion for artless merriment, a remarkable degree of will-power. Her education had been sketchy, her intellectual gifts were few if any; but in her own small way, she had acquired, from the squalid domestic in-fighting of her years as a princess, some of that determination to be mistress of her own affairs which Elizabeth I had acquired so much more dangerously in the lurid years before 1558.

To imply that the Queen always got her own way once she ascended the throne would be far from the truth; but she was sufficiently endowed with Hanoverian hot temper to make it essential for all her prime ministers to handle her with care, treat her with respect, to go to considerable lengths to placate her, and above all to keep her fully informed. The only prime minister with whom she was permanently on bad terms was Gladstone. He alone failed to benefit from her capacity for what, almost to the end of her life, one can only call an immature tendency to develop 'crushes'. She fell instantly for Melbourne; she fell, in the end, for Peel; she fell for Aberdeen, and revered him hardly less than Gladstone did; and, after 1855, she even learned to like Palmerston. After Palmerston, she fell in a big way for Disraeli and, after him, though in a more measured way, for Lord Salisbury. In her widowhood, she came bizarrely under the spell of her favourite Scottish servant, John Brown, so that, just as her fondness for her first prime minister had caused her to be referred to as 'Mrs Melbourne', so her fond-ness for her burly, hard-drinking 'Highland Servant' caused her to be called 'Mrs Brown' in the late 1860s. Within four years of Brown's death in 1883 she had found a replacement. At the time of the Golden Jubilee she acquired an Indian servant, Abdul Karim, who at first merely taught her some Hindustani and cooked curries for her. The favours shown by the Queen to 'the Munshi', as he was officially called, were such as to cause a decade of trouble among her Household staff, her political advisers and her foreign relations, who were shocked by the degree of precedence the Queen demanded they accord to him.

The three principal male influences on her life were, in chronological order, Melbourne, Prince Albert and Disraeli. It was not perhaps wholly to the good that her most impressionable years as a young queen should have been spent under the tutelage of a world-weary Whig like Melbourne; but to the task of giving a little girl of eighteen, who was under five feet tall and looked at times no older than twelve, her first lessons in how to perform the duties of a reigning constitutional monarch, he brought an affectionate patience seasoned not only with an obviously fascinating middle-aged melancholy but also a certain worldy gaiety. She might easily have become shrewish or priggish in less skilful hands. As it was he did her reputation harm over the Bedchamber affair[1] and some personal harm by jealously postponing her marriage.

Unquestionably, Prince Albert, whom she married in 1840, was valuable in sobering her judgment and her manner. Much that was Victorian about Queen Victoria derived from the patient German earnestness of her devoted and intelligent husband. It was his influence that helped to make the Queen less frivolously Hanoverian than she might have been; for despite her well-known childhood promise, 'I will be good', and her highly developed sense of her own dignity as queen, she was always ready for a girlish romp in a way that suggested that she could have been recognizably the niece of her wicked uncles as well as recognizably the mother of her gregariously un-Victorian son, Edward, Prince of Wales.

Albert was a prince who preferred botany to hunting or gambling and who derived evident pleasure from playing, and composing for, the organ. His musical interests did much to improve behaviour and raise standards of musical appreciation among London opera and concert audiences. Operas by Rossini, Donizetti and Bellini were not only attended but listened to seriously by the Queen and the Prince; he did much to encourage Italian opera, which was performed both at Covent Garden, which became known as the Royal Italian Opera House, and at Her Majesty's Theatre, where audiences were enraptured by Jenny Lind. It was further due to the Prince that at concerts

[1] See p. 67.

held by the Philharmonic Society, Mendelssohn, Liszt, Berlioz and Wagner, as well as the very young Joachim all performed, while at Exeter Hall in the Strand sacred choral music was regularly performed to audiences of thousands. Mendelssohn's 'Elijah' had its first performance there and the Queen and Prince were present for the occasion. The royal pair also encouraged Charles Kean who, with his wife Ellen Tree, often performed plays at Windsor, sometimes in a small theatre the Prince himself had constructed. His taste in the visual arts was a somewhat curious mixture. A great admirer of Landseer's 'Monarch of the Glen', he was a collector of the work of the Italian primitives at a time when they were otherwise almost completely neglected. His interests and his influence were well-reflected in Peel's invitation to him to be chairman of the commission for the rebuilding of the Houses of Parliament, by his presidency of the Society of Fine Arts and by the persistence and thoroughness of his work as chairman of the commissioners responsible for the Great Exhibition of 1851. To refine London's musical manners and taste and to encourage the sciences and technical education were not speedy ways of earning popularity, but the Prince's influence in these directions help to explain the Queen's adoration of him and the esteem he won from Peel, Aberdeen and Palmerston.

His love of domestic quiet, which led him to create for himself and the Queen places of retreat at the Renaissance-style Osborne House in the Isle of Wight and a pseudo-Scottish baronial hall at Balmoral, was a reflection of his sensitive awareness that in social intercourse he was awkward in the presence of women or all but the most serious-minded of men. As a result he probably over-developed both the puritanism and the sentimentality in the Queen's nature; and her revulsion from appearing in public after the Prince's death was in one sense a continuation of his own aversion from society.

There is little evidence that the Queen was herself popular until towards the end of her reign. Her youthfulness at her accession made her appear far too visibly under Melbourne's influence; and her obvious devotion to her German husband excited in her subjects a xenophobia that was not placated by his cultural and scientific interests, or his long hours of work as, in effect, the Queen's private secretary. Indeed, in 1854 he was the victim of one of the more lunatic outbursts of English patriotism. He was accused by wilder radicals of being pro-Russian, of being the cause of Palmerston's short-lived resignation from Aberdeen's Cabinet,[1] and was even alleged to have been sent to the Tower as a traitor. There was some fire behind this smoke: the notion that there was a conspiracy among all the courts of Europe, not merely in England and Russia, to get rid of Palmerston, sorted well with his reputation as one who was far too often offensive to foreign sovereigns, and with the fact that Victoria and Albert regarded him as not only internationally dangerous but scandalously immoral in his private life.

After he became prime minister in 1855, however, Palmerston went out of his way to praise in public the assiduousness with which the Prince performed his public duties. Albert was, indeed, a great desk-worker, and this naturally appealed to Palmerston, who liked attention to detail. The Prince's readiness to compose careful memoranda included not only the summarizing of complicated political problems for the Queen but also extended to analyses and recommendations relating to the Queen's sometimes quarrelsome behaviour as a wife. His last act of draftsmanship, performed when he was already a dying man, was to modify the asperity of Russell's bellicose despatch to Washington over the *Trent* affair.[2] It was typical of the Prince to be so conscientiously determined to temper the bombast of a patriotic English Whig with the industrious caution of an unrobust minor German prince, unused to the sweep of seaborne Empire and untouched by the insular pride that went with it. The typhoid germ that killed him some fourteen days later was already at work on him when he dragged himself from his bed at seven in the morning to perform this last of his services behind the scenes. In many ways he had a more consistent sense of duty than the Queen herself. Since she was a queen, she could – and did – have tantrums. He, a

[1] See p. 129.
[2] See p. 149.

sensitive, buttoned-up foreigner, could not afford such regal self-indulgence.

The Prince's death in 1861 plunged the Queen into an orgy of widowhood. Already unnerved by the death of her mother, the Duchess of Kent, earlier in the year, she now allowed herself to sink into a grief and melancholy from which she was careful never completely to free herself for the forty years that were still left of her life and reign. To ensure that nobody else would forget Albert's death, the Albert Memorial and the Albert Hall were in due time constructed in Kensington. Her absorption in private grief fed in her the notion that it was only because Albert had been at her side that she had been able to carry out her queenly duties. Now he was gone, the public could not ask anything from her, for it would be too great a burden for so tragically desolate a widow. At first, she even tried to claim that she could not personally interview her ministers any more. Palmerston overcame this by a display of sympathy that was surprising in a man usually accounted frivolous and offhand; but it was sincere, and the Queen was much touched. Beyond meeting her ministers she would not go; she spent months in seclusion at Osborne and Balmoral. Rumours circulated that the Queen was mad. By 1863, the only public function she could bring herself to attend was the marriage at Windsor of the Prince of Wales to Princess Alexandra of Denmark (or, more precisely, of Schleswig-Holstein-Sonderburg-Glücksburg). Even so, she kept out of the way and in the dark until the ceremony began and withdrew as soon as it was over, lunching alone to avoid the wedding feast. Not until 1866 would she open Parliament in person, and even then she stared stonily ahead of her from her throne while the Queen's Speech was read for her by the lord chancellor. Given that this almost public withdrawal from her public duties coincided with the increasing attention she was paying John Brown it is not surprising that the country grew restive at the little service it appeared to be getting from its monarch. Nobody could deputize for her; she would not allow 'Bertie' (the Prince of Wales) to do so, and her remaining children were almost all married off to foreigners.

With the appointment of a private secretary in 1867 and the impingement on her life of Gladstone and Disraeli, she began to get her second wind and to show a more lively interest in politics. Nevertheless, her obvious preference for Osborne and Balmoral (and in the latter place she was often remarkably energetic) and her insistence on avoiding public appearances because, she declared, her health, and indeed her reason, would break down under the strain, gave some impetus to republicanism in the 1870s. Whether this was in part also stimulated by a desire to emulate the new French Republic or to be derisory at the expense of the King of Prussia's transformation into a German emperor, it would be hard to say. An anonymous pamphleteer demanded to know what the Queen had done with all her money. About fifty republican clubs were established in the provinces; Sir Charles Dilke accused the Queen of failing in her duty, and informed a large audience in Newcastle that the sooner the monarchy was abolished and a republic set up, the better.

Much of this outburst fizzled out when the Prince of Wales suffered a timely attack of typhoid. More robust than his delicate father, he shook it off with some speed, but at Gladstone's insistence a national service of thanksgiving for the Prince's recovery was held at St Paul's. The Queen combined her sensible objection to making a religious show in this way with an insistence on going in an open carriage so that if, as was apparently the idea, the people wanted to see her, see her they should. Great cheers greeted the widowed Queen and once-more healthy heir. Yet as late as 1886, at a Liberal political dinner, many diners ignored the royal toast and others hissed, and there were continuing grumbles in the press that, as ordinarily understood, court life did not exist in London. There were also from 1840 until 1857, when the last of her children was born, and from 1858 until 1884, when the last of them was married, running complaints at the financial cost to the nation of providing for the four princes and five princesses borne by the Queen, and also financial, social or political (not to say family) objections about almost all their marriages.

In their entirely different ways, both Gladstone and Disraeli were responsible for drawing the Queen more closely into political affairs. Both equally wished her to make more appearances in public, but Gladstone so venerated the Crown that he found it impossible to speak intelligibly to the unintellectual little woman who wore it. It was not that he spoke to her as though she were a public meeting or a government department; it was rather that he addressed her as an august and well-nigh sacred institution. To a woman who responded to the rough Scottish manliness of John Brown and had already begun to enjoy the elaborately garlanded compliments of Disraeli, Gladstone was, as he was to other women outside his family circle, frightening in manner and bewilderingly convoluted in utterance. Apart from his manner, his policies also seemed to the Queen hardly less bewildering. This was not because the Queen was a reactionary or a Tory; it was simply that she had by now stored up a fund of political common sense without ever being able to grasp abstract ideas or principles. Thus, it was 'on principle' that Gladstone criticized the cost of erecting the Albert Memorial; but the Queen could hardly be expected to appreciate a 'principle' which flouted her deepest feelings as a widow.

It is not surprising that, when Gladstone proposed that the Queen accept the offer of an Irish residence so that she could spend part of the year there and thus (so Gladstone imagined) endear herself to the Irish people, she insisted that Balmoral alone was suited to her health; equally repugnant to her was Gladstone's proposal that Ireland be rendered more loyal by having the Prince of Wales sent there as a viceroy. That 'Bertie' was too frivolous and unreliable for anything save the frivolous occupations to which he was driven by his mother's refusal to permit him public employment, was one of the Queen's most enduring obsessions. Not surprisingly, therefore, she refused to open Parliament in person in 1869 both on the grounds of her delicate health and her disapproval of the Irish Church Bill.[1] Gladstone besought the Queen to curtail her overlong absences at Balmoral; she in return complained that overwork and worry had killed her husband and that she could

[1] For the Queen's part in enabling the bill to become law see p. 235.

not be expected to be 'driven and abused till her health and nerves gave way'. Long after it became clear that the Queen would agree to none of his plans for her, Gladstone persisted in bombarding her with memoranda, thus producing resentment in the Queen and a melancholy sense of failure in himself. She thought he was trying to be as harsh and dictatorial to her as Bismarck was to the German Emperor; and while he thought he was striving loyally to increase the Queen's standing in the country, she became convinced she could place no confidence in a man of whom she said, shrewdly enough, 'No one can be sure for one moment what he may *persuade himself* to think right.'

By the time he became prime minister for the second time in 1874, Disraeli had already lived down the Queen's disapproval of his opposition to Peel. Disraeli's tributes to the Prince Consort after the latter's death were, like Palmerston's, more sincere than their effusive language suggests. When he had first become prime minister in 1868, the Queen wrote to her daughter in Prussia, how 'proud' a thing it was for a man 'risen from the people' to attain such eminence. It was due, she declared, to his loyalty, his talent, his good temper and his masterly handling of the Second Reform Bill. The Queen was, thus early, as disposed to think kindly of Disraeli as he was to speak romantically to her. The difference between Disraeli, who had 'risen from the people', and Gladstone, who was 'the People's William', was that the former had been so much more 'loyal' – to her widowed feelings. He had also, by 1874, promised a more active foreign policy; and furthermore he had earned additional merit in her eyes because, his wife Mary Anne having died in 1869, he was, like his sovereign, 'Quite Alone'. On his side, whereas her harassed staff referred to her privately as 'Eliza', he spoke of her, much less privately, as 'the Faery'. The two of them were, in their maritally deprived condition, ideally suited. She had always needed a man to lean on; he had always relied greatly on the friendship of elderly women. Best of all, they both knew that each was playing a part. The Queen was warmed by his performances and happily played up to them; and he was as delighted by them as she was. She sent him primroses from Osborne and set in motion a long-lasting legend that they were His Favourite Flower. He, at last, satisfied her wish to be an empress. Hence, whereas Gladstone had failed signally to get the Prince of Wales sent to Ireland, Disraeli succeeded, after a struggle, in getting him sent to India.[1]

A more permanent bond was established between them when Disraeli stood up to the Russians during his second ministry,[2] though he was never as belligerent as the Faery, who was quite beside herself with rage against 'the fiendish Russians' and, indeed, several times in 1877 and 1878 threatened that she would abdicate rather than 'submit' to them. Gladstone's espousal of the cause of the massacred Bulgarians still further strengthened her belief in Disraeli; it made her certain that it was Gladstone who had encouraged the Russians to instigate the Balkan rebellions in the first place. All the same, the Queen's part in the conduct of Disraeli's foreign policy was never more than that of a frenzied supporter sounding off rhetorical advice from the touchline; just as, when Gladstone was in play, her hostile cries were no less unavailingly rhetorical. By the time of his last premiership, Gladstone had got into the habit of starting cabinet meetings by taking a letter of protest from the Queen from his pocket, reading it aloud, returning it to his pocket and then saying, 'And now, gentlemen, to business.'

The experiences of 1874–80 made the Queen a Tory and, to all intents and purposes, an Imperialist; and in this, perhaps, she was at last of one mind with many of her people. This was not merely because of her regard for Disraeli, but also because of her preference for Salisbury when he replaced Derby as foreign secretary.[3] She had found Derby's timidity unendurable. It was characteristic that the last parliamentary session of Disraeli's premiership should have been opened by the Queen in person, and that a resplendent new state coach was used for the occasion. When the Conservatives were defeated in 1880, she renewed her threats to abdicate if she were compelled to

[1] See p. 209.
[2] See p. 210.
[3] See p. 214.

have Gladstone as prime minister. But she did accept Gladstone[1] and she did not abdicate, contenting herself with informing Gladstone that he must not diverge from the previous government's foreign policy. He accepted the instruction meekly and totally ignored it. Soon, she was once more threatening to abdicate. Gladstone became more and more convinced that chief among Disraeli's manifold wickednesses had been that he had poisoned the Queen's mind against him.

In 1881, Disraeli died, allegedly declining a deathbed visit from the Faery with the words, 'It is better not. She'd only ask me to take a message to Albert.' The Queen had a wreath of primroses placed on his grave with the words 'His Favourite Flower' written on a card in the royal hand. She erected a memorial tablet in his church at Hughenden, recording that it had been placed there 'by his grateful Sovereign and Friend, Victoria, R.I.'.[2] This announcement so soon after a general election which had driven the Queen's 'Friend' from office was one further sign to Gladstone of the hold the 'old Jew' had had on the Queen. She had, in fact, continued to correspond with Disraeli after Gladstone had become prime minister just as after 1885 she corresponded with Salisbury on political matters whenever he was out of office. All through Gladstone's second ministry she disapproved violently and helplessly of almost everything he did; but although Disraeli, by his panache, had given the Queen, as he had given the nation itself, a lift of the heart, Gladstone's maniacal condemnation of Disraeli in the 1870s and his messianic muddlings after 1880 were in themselves enough to explain the Queen's dislike of him.

In 1886 came the Colonial and Indian Exhibition, a foretaste of the greater junketings of the following year. As the Queen entered the hall for the official opening ceremony she was greeted by the National Anthem, the first verse being sung in English, the second 'in Sanskrit'. There then followed an ode of little poetic worth by Tennyson, the Poet Laureate, a prayer

---

[1] See p. 224.

[2] After 1876, the Queen delighted to describe herself as Regina et Imperatrix. This was very much a matter of keeping up with the Hohenzollerns, whose head was Rex in Prussia and Imperator in Germany.

from the Archbishop of Canterbury, the singing of the Halle-
lujah Chorus (to which the Victorians were addicted) and as a
fitting close to the ceremony, 'Home, Sweet Home' was sung.[1]
   The Golden Jubilee itself was celebrated in 1887 on a nationwide, indeed Imperial, scale. The women of England contributed a Jubilee Gift of £75,000; the People's Palace was opened
by the Queen in the East End of London (to the accompaniment, alas, of a certain amount of booing); a large assemblage
of European personages was entertained at Windsor. On 21
June 1887 there was a thanksgiving service at Westminster
Abbey, at which the Queen yet again refused to wear anything
more regal than a bonnet, even though it was a bonnet with
diamonds on it. The Crown Prince Frederick of Prussia looked
splendid, but was already speechless with the cancer of the
throat that killed him a year later; the Prince of Wales, to whom
public ceremonial was meat and drink (when he was not eating
and drinking), was a great help to Mama throughout; but the
Prussian Prince William, who would succeed his doomed father
as German Kaiser before 1888 was out, complained that
Uncle Bertie (the Prince of Wales) had taken altogether too
little notice of him. That afternoon there was another state
luncheon at Buckingham Palace; and in the evening there were
fireworks and bonfires all over the land.[2] On 22 June, large
quantities of poor schoolchildren were assembled in Hyde Park
to receive a bun, milk and a Jubilee mug, and to watch balloons
ascending into the sky; and on returning to Windsor, the
Queen was sung to by young gentlemen from Eton College.
There was a Royal Garden Party, at which the Queen was only
just successful in avoiding having to speak to Gladstone; the
Volunteers were reviewed at Buckingham Palace, the army at
Aldershot and the fleet at Spithead. Throughout the kingdom
and empire, there were tea parties; and Jubilee clocks and
drinking fountains and all sorts of other commemorative
edifices were subscribed for.

[1] These details are culled from *The Queen's Resolve: A Jubilee Memorial* by
the Rev. Charles Bullock, B.D., of which it appears at least ninety thousand
copies were sold. The author was editor of *The Fireside* and *Home Words*.
[2] See the first poem, '1887' in A. E. Houseman's *A Shropshire Lad*.

It was hardly possible after this to accuse the Queen of neglecting her royal duties and it is from this time onwards that the role of the monarchy as a purveyor of pageantry began to be established as part of the pattern of London, if not of English, life, and in a way that had no very precise parallel in its early history and none at all in the reign of Queen Victoria. This new, more publicly theatrical, role of the crown coincided with the growth of imperial sentiment and thus made the Queen the symbol of Empire without her ever quite intending to be so in this way. Like many of her subjects and her ministers, she was carried along by a wave of feeling, and willy-nilly, she was perched at the top of it. The statue of Queen Victoria in a public place became the visible sign of British Imperialism wherever, within any part of the Empire, a public place of sufficient dignity could be constructed.

Politically, her last years were disturbed only by the necessity of enduring Gladstone for one last brief period as prime minister. She described him at various times from 1892 to 1894 as 'a dreadful old man', as 'half-crazy', 'half-silly', 'a deluded old fanatic', 'loud', 'unreasoning' and 'wild'. They understood each other so little that they could not even manage a courteous leave-taking when he finally decided to resign. The faults, though, were mainly on Gladstone's side, and he spent the remaining four years of his life brooding in an uncomprehending way on why the Queen had let him go so casually after so many years of what he considered his devoted service to her. Absorbed so utterly in his own sense of righteousness, he failed to see that his whole career since 1868 had been devoted to the political subordination of the Queen to the prime minister. Disraeli had had the tact and feeling to disguise his political independence with the language of love. Disraeli paid the Queen the attentions due to a political mistress; Gladstone treated her like a political wife, whose duty was invariably to acquiesce in her lord and master's plans and to regard, as a sufficient proof of his devotion, the fact that he was prepared to expound those plans to her in language she could not understand. He did not realize that this was how he behaved; but the Queen, who was so much shrewder, did realize it; and resented it. No other prime minister made her so aware of her political impotence.

Once Gladstone had gone, though at first she thought she preferred Rosebery to Salisbury as a man, she felt Salisbury's politics were much sounder. He had, she knew, his 'peculiarities' – as who, indeed, did not know; but he was a trusted and wise statesman and even, indeed, a greater man than Disraeli. Or even, she thought, the best prime minister she had had. Nothing is more bizarre than the circumstance that in the excitable, intellectually and morally experimental last years of her reign, the years of strange ideas and vulgar people, of mass newspapers and far-flung imperial adventures, of Wilde and Ibsen and Shaw, the government of England should have been headed by a couple of ageing recluses: an old queen in her late seventies who could hardly see and hardly walk, and a prematurely aged prime minister in his late sixties who was liable to fall asleep in the middle of framing a dispatch or a memorandum. It says much for the English social and political system that it hardly seemed to matter that, for much of their time, the Queen shut herself away in Osborne and the prime minister shut himself up in Hatfield House.

But, on 20 June 1897, the Queen had broken George III's record by several months and had reigned for sixty years. Her Diamond Jubilee was therefore duly celebrated. On 20 June there was a family thanksgiving in St George's Chapel, Windsor and, since the day was a Sunday, Jubilee services were held in all places of worship throughout the country. On the 22nd she drove from Buckingham Palace to St Paul's for a brief service at the cathedral steps – she was too lame to get up the steps into the cathedral itself. At Chamberlain's suggestion, the procession contained large contingents of troops from all parts of the Empire, thus providing a spectacle which dazzled the London crowds with the glories of their exotic Empire. When, later in the day, the Queen appeared on the balcony of Buckingham Palace in her wheelchair, an anonymous immortality was achieved by that member of the large crowd whose voice was heard to call out, 'Go it, old girl!'

In view of her age (she was seventy-eight in 1897), the

hypochondria of her middle years and the dim vision and arthritis and sciatica from which she now suffered, she remained surprisingly willing to 'go it'. Ellen Terry, Henry Irving, George Grossmith and the D'Oyly Carte Gilbert and Sullivan Opera Company were among those by whom she allowed herself to be entertained in the 1890s. When the Boer War began, she took the average, middle-of-the-road view that Kruger had left the country with no honourable alternative to war; she was stimulated to boldly resolute utterances to her ministers; she reviewed troops and visited hospitals. She drove through London twice in one week to celebrate the relief of Ladysmith, and in April 1900, went on a three-week state visit to Dublin. But, by the end of the year, she began to break up; and on 22 January 1901, she died.

The sense of shock, if not of alarm, as well as loss, which her death occasioned, is understandable. It was no use pretending any longer. Already, well before 1901, the reality of a Victorian age was over; now even its symbol was gone. She had reigned for sixty-four years. By the end of another sixty-four years, even those statues of her that still survived in those distant parts in Asia and Africa where Englishmen had erected them, had most of them become as historically antique as those of the emperors of Rome.

Like most notable Victorians, she was too much an individualist to be easily categorized. Perhaps she was most Victorian (and was seen to be so) in her sentimental absorption in that somewhat suffocating form of family life in which so many Victorians took psychological refuge from (and occasionally revenge against) the changing, demanding world outside. But it was a family life whose major events were all disasters: childbirth, a potential killer in all ranks of society; wedding days, on which, as the Queen wrote of the Princess Royal's wedding, the bride was 'like a lamb led to the slaughter' to have her finer feelings shattered for the sake of male sexual appetite; and death itself – though the Queen did not herself approve of deathbed scenes. For the long, mundane stretches in between these major domestic crises the Queen, again like many of her subjects, was psychologically ill-equipped. She liked babies hardly at all and children not very much. She and her husband needed to be sentimental about their children to compensate for the fact that they often treated them with such misguided harshness, particularly the Prince of Wales, by seeking to impose rigid standards on them at far too early an age. Even in its own right, family sentimentality could easily turn into emotional bullying and the Queen, again like many another Victorian mother, was a practised exponent of this insidious maternal art. The general and necessary Victorian reaction against the careless and neglectful attitude of many wealthy eighteenth-century parents was undoubtedly carried too far both by Victoria and the Victorians.

She was eminently Victorian in the complete divorce that was fixed in her mind between sex and love. That sex should express love was thought rather disgusting; that love could only complete itself by becoming sexual was described as 'giving way to the baser passions'. Sexual desire was an unfortunate and flawing affliction to which even the noblest of men were liable. In her innumerable letters to her eldest daughter after her marriage to the Crown Prince Frederick, the Queen repeatedly expressed this view, lamenting that even Albert the Good was not immune to it. The Queen perhaps exceeded her female subjects in being revolted by the procreative process. It made a woman feel more like a cow or a dog, she said, and it made 'our poor nature . . . so very animal and unecstatic'. It was some time before she could bring herself to share in the common sentimentality about 'bonnie little babies'. To her, they represented too much humiliation and pain; and when the aid of chloroform was made available in childbirth she made no bones about making use of it.

This relegation of sex to the extreme periphery of the personality explains the capacity of the Victorians to express passionate love for one another in circumstances which, if they were to be repeated a century later, would instantly give rise to the most sinister of suspicions. Men effused over their mothers, their fathers, their brothers, their sisters; men effused about other men, women effused about other women, all in a way quite impossible when, in the twentieth century, men and women were expected to place sex at the centre of their personal lives and to see it symbolized in everything. All the sexual abnormalities existed, and in plenty, in Victorian times; but to the pure of that age, far more things were 'purer' than would be possible for their late twentieth-century successors. Thus, the Queen was so pure that she did not even think sisters-in-law would be sexually endangered by the Deceased Wife's Sisters' Bill, which she supported, but which her legislators could not bring themselves to approve until after her death.[1] When, in 1885, all forms of male homosexuality were made illegal, it is said that the exclusion of the female version from the act was due to the belief of ministers that the Queen could not possibly understand that such a phenomenon could exist; and nobody would take on the task of explaining it to her.

In the matter of class and colour, the Queen was again something of an individualist. In her view, there were only two classes: the 'high-born' and 'the people'. Unless the 'high-born' also set a high moral tone, she tended to disapprove of them; though, when Gladstone took exactly the same line, she thought it dangerously radical of him. Outside the aristocracy, she seems to have had no sense of class difference, lumping all the rest of the population together, but showing a particularly sentimental affection for the poor and the simple. This was, of course, a common phenomenon among those sufficiently well-off only to come into close contact with those members of the lower orders who were domestic servants or country people. This found its most notable expression in her two published works, *Leaves from the Journal of our Life in the Highlands* (1868) and *More Leaves* (1884), the latter being dedicated to John Brown. Both are a remarkable exercise in the sphere of sentimental 'human-interest' writing, combining artless anecdotes about the minor happinesses of the domestic life of the Queen and her children on holiday and a few minor mishaps, together with cosy references to the 'simple mountaineers of bonnie Scotland, from whom', she wrote, 'she has learnt many a lesson of resignation and faith, in the pure air and quiet of the beautiful Highlands.' It is typically Victorian that the simple

1 See p. 181.

people in whom she delighted were either country folk or exotics (the Scotch were both). She was much concerned with the welfare of 'our brave soldiers' in the Crimean and Boer Wars; and very much concerned, sentimentally at any rate, about 'the poor natives' of India and Africa. For this reason, she described the Boers as 'a cruel people' and considered that those who objected to the favours she showed the Munshi were prejudiced because of his colour.

What she did best, in the end, was to prove to be her own best public relations officer. Her wearing of a bonnet when she should have worn a crown; her simple chatter about ordinary happenings and ordinary people in her two volumes of *Leaves*, were part of her knack of displaying towards 'the people' an unaffected womanly simplicity which, little though it sorted with the 'Eliza' whose crotchets so disturbed her Household, the 'Faery' whom Disraeli invented, or 'The Queen!' whose sudden appearance in a room could frighten younger members of her huge family clean out of their wits, served finally to reconcile a large part of the population to an institution which, though she left it even more of a political convenience than she found it, they respected in 1901 to an extent that could hardly have been imagined in 1837.

A Number of Books

The list which follows is a modest selection, mainly of works written in the 1960s, from the vast historical output on Victorian England. Some volumes have been mentioned which, according to the most austere standards, are not academic history books at all. Their inclusion, even in so short and partial a list, is deliberate. No serious student of history can afford to limit his reading by having recourse solely to works written by scholarly professionals. To parody a famous phrase, history is too serious a matter to be left solely to historians.

General Works

SIR LLEWELLYN WOODWARD, *The Age of Reform 1815–1870*, 2nd edition (London, O.U.P., 1962) and R. C. K. ENSOR, *England 1870–1914* (London, O.U.P., 1936) have the virtues of comprehensiveness and readability, though Ensor's volume is perhaps a little outdated in parts.

ASA BRIGGS, *The Age of Improvement, 1783–1867* (London, Longmans, 1959), deals with the period solidly, with an adequate balance between political and social history.

Two discursive volumes are G. M. YOUNG, *Victorian England*, 2nd edition (London, Methuen 1953) and G. KITSON CLARK, *The Making of Victorian England* (London, Methuen, 1962). *Victorian England* is felicitous to a degree; *The Making of Victorian England* is a useful guide-book to the difference between old and newer scholarship in the field of early Victorian study.

Religion and Ideas

OWEN CHADWICK, *The Victorian Church*, Vol. 6),1 (196 Vol. 2 (1969), (London, Black). Measured, scholarly, urbane, authoritative and readable.

MURIEL JAEGER, *Before Victoria* (London, Chatto, 1956; Penguin, 1967) lightly sketches the foundations of the 'Victorian' outlook in the half-century before 1837.

BASIL WILLEY, *Nineteenth Century Studies* (London, Chatto, 1949; Penguin, 1964). A fairly stately exploration of early and mid-Victorian intellectual developments.

GERTRUDE HIMMELFARB, *Victorian Minds* (London, Weidenfeld, 1968) ranges from Burke to John Buchan.

RAYMOND WILLIAMS, *Culture and Society 1780–1950* (London, Chatto, 1958; Penguin 1961) attempts an analysis of the connection between culture and society, in studies ranging from Burke to the twentieth century. The same author's *The Long Revolution* (London, Chatto, 1961; Penguin, 1965) also has relevant material on education and the development of the press.

HOLBROOK, JACKSON, *The Eighteen-Nineties* (Pelican, 1913; Pelican, 1939) sympathetically surveys the intellectual and artistic life of the century's last decade.

Economic and Social

PETER MATHIAS, *The First Industrial Nation, 1700–1914* (London, Methuen, 1969) shows a rather better sense of historical perspective than economic historians usually allow themselves. Stimulating even for historians with little knowledge of economics.

S. G. CHECKLAND, *The Rise of Industrial Society in England, 1815–1885* (London, Longmans, 1964). More detail than Mathias, with more social and some intellectual and political history.

HAROLD PERKIN, *The Origins of Modern English Society, 1780–1880* (London, Routledge, 1969) attempts to synthesize economic, social and political history. Needs attentive reading but offers stimulating ideas.

ASA BRIGGS, *Victorian Cities* (London, Odhams, 1964), and *Victorian People* (Harmondsworth, Penguin, 1965). The former is valuable to correct the London-centred character of so many histories; the latter is useful for its concentration on the 1850s and 1860s.

TERRY COLEMAN, *The Railway Navvies* (London, Hutchinson, 1965). A lively 'documentary'.

Q

HENRY PELLING, *A History of British Trade Unionism* (London, Macmillan, 1963).

G. D. H. COLE and RAYMOND POSTGATE, *The Common People, 1746–1946* (London, Methuen, 1946, 4th edn, 1949), being an older book, is often more useful factually about the working class and working-class movements.

J. D. CHAMBERS and G. E. MINGAY, *The Agricultural Revolution, 1750–1880* (London, Batsford, 1966), unfortunately stops too soon, but would seem mandatory reading.

J. F. C. HARRISON, *The Early Victorians 1832–51* (London, Weidenfeld, 1971) and GEOFFREY BEST, *Mid-Victorian Britain, 1851–75* (London, Weidenfeld, 1971) have both been highly praised as social histories. Also, surveying the middle years of the century, is W. L. BURN, *The Age of Equipoise* (London, Allen & Unwin, 1964), which seeks to explain the stability of the time.

Selections from MAYHEW's *London Labour and the London Poor* (London, 1851 and 1861) have been edited by PETER QUENNELL, *Mayhew's London*, from Vols. I–III in 1949 and from Vol. IV in 1950 (London, Spring Books). E. P. THOMPSON and EILEEN YEO, *The Unknown Mayhew* (London, Merlin Press, 1971) includes material by Mayhew not published by him in book form.

A. FRIED and R. ELMAN (eds), *Charles Booth's London* (London, Hutchinson, 1969; Pelican, 1971) contains selections from his *Life and Labour of the People in London*, 1875–1903.

S. E. FINER, *Life and Times of Sir Edwin Chadwick* (London, Methuen, 1952), and ROYSTON LAMBERT, *Sir John Simon and English Social Policy* (London, MacGibbon & Kee, 1963) are both important for the story of public health legislation.

FLORA THOMPSON, *Lark Rise to Candleford* (London, O.U.P., 1954). and GWEN RAVERAT, *Period Piece* (London, Faber, 1952) provide light anecdotal reading; the former deals with growing up in north Oxfordshire in the 1890s, the latter with a Cambridge upbringing in the same period.

Politics and Political Biography

N. GASH, *Politics in the Age of Peel* (London, Longmans, 1952), and *Reaction and Reconstruction in English Politics, 1832–1852* (London, O.U.P., 1965) would appear to be required reading; the latter should perhaps be tackled first. Also essential is DONALD SOUTH-GATE, *The Passing of the Whigs 1832–1886* (London, Macmillan, 1962).

The relevant two-thirds of ROBERT BLAKE's *The Conservative Party from Peel to Churchill* (London, Eyre & Spottiswoode, 1970) should also be consulted. It has a useful bibliography.

DONALD SOUTHGATE, *The Most English Minister: the Policies and Politics of Palmerston* (London, Macmillan, 1966), and JASPER RIDLEY's *Lord Palmerston* (London, Constable, 1970) are both considerable works, the latter being particularly useful on mid-century politics.

ROBERT BLAKE, *Disraeli* (London, Eyre & Spottiswoode, 1966) is a full-scale work; but even more than Palmerston, Disraeli eludes his biographers.

PHILIP MAGNUS, *Gladstone* (London, Murray, 1954; paperback, 1963) seems the most convincing biography of a nineteenth-century prime minister, though the subject's personality tends to overshadow the politics.

For Lord Salisbury, see under Imperialism below.

For the Queen herself, the fullest biography is ELIZABETH LONGFORD, *Victoria R.I.* (London, Weidenfeld, 1964; Pan, 1966). The first fourteen of the twenty-three chapters of PHILIP MAGNUS, *King Edward the Seventh* (London, John Murray, 1964) are also relevant for a study of the Victorian monarchy, since the King did not succeed until he was in his sixtieth year.

Imperialism

Books on the Empire in the nineteenth century are either encyclo-paedically dull or so deeply engaged in interpretational controversy that the student is left with a mind either sated with fact or bemused by argument. The most lucid introduction to late-Victorian Imperialism is in CARLTON HAYES, *A Generation of Materialism 1871–1900* (New York, Harper & Row, 1941; Harper Textbooks, 1963), Ch. VI. This contains an analysis of 'causes' and also a rapid summary of principal facts for both English and Continental Imperialism.

The Historical Association's pamphlet, M. E. CHAMBERLAIN's *The New Imperialism* (London, 1970), gives a quick guide to the main controversies in which historians of Empire have of late been engaged.

A. G. L. SHAW (ed.), *Great Britain and the Colonies 1815–65* (London, Methuen, 1970) is primarily an economic study, and destroys the myth that there was no interest in colonies before 1865 without successfully proving that nothing new happened after 1875, since this is impossible to prove.

RONALD ROBINSON and J. GALLAGHER, *Africa and the Victorians* (London, Macmillan, 1961; Papermacs, 1966) tries to disprove the existence of the 'New Imperialism' by a meticulous examination of the 'Official Mind' designed to show that governments were not 'imperialistic' and that almost everything that happened in the scramble for Africa derived from the British occupation of Egypt.

A broader view, which examines Imperialism within the context of late-Victorian foreign policy as a whole, is in C. J. LOWE, *The Reluctant Imperialists* (London, Routledge, 1967), with a second volume of documents, similarly titled.

Clear and useful is C. HOWARD's *Splendid Isolation* (London, Macmillan, 1967).

The inter-connection of imperial policy, foreign policy and economic policy is examined in C. J. BARTLETT (ed.), *Britain Pre-eminent* (London, Macmillan, 1969).

Useful for its perspectives is G. S. GRAHAM, *The Politics of Naval Supremacy* (Cambridge, C.U.P., 1965).

Reference should also be made to A. J. P. TAYLOR, *Struggle for Mastery in Europe* (London, O.U.P., 1954), which blames the scramble for Africa exclusively on Leopold II of the Belgians but also cuts through a great deal of the nonsense about splendid isolation and its alleged dangers.

For Imperialism, and for foreign policy throughout the reign, reference may be made to KENNETH BOURNE, *The Foreign Policy of Victorian England 1830–1902* (London, O.U.P., 1970). Its 300 pages of documents are valuable; the 195-page summary which precedes them is over-concentrated.

All historians bemoan the absence of an adequate biography of Lord Salisbury. A. L. KENNEDY, *Salisbury, 1830–1903* (London, Murray, 1953), though somewhat devout, is not altogether uncritical, and remains the only convenient one-volume source of information about Salisbury's whole career.

Those whose minds are not insular might well turn to ROLAND OLIVER and A. ATMORE, *Africa since 1800* (Cambridge, C.U.P., 1967), which contains good maps and a detailed bibliography.

A lively recreation of the Empire as it was in 1897 is provided by JAMES MORRIS, *Pax Britannica* (London, Faber, 1968).

Satisfactory and scholarly modern biographies of Cecil Rhodes and Joseph Chamberlain do not appear to exist.

Newer Books

The following could be consulted with advantage:

HAROLD PERKIN, *The Age of the Railway* (Newton Abbot, David & Charles, 1971): JAMES PREST, *Lord John Russell* (London, Macmillan, 1972); NORMAN GASH, *Sir Robert Peel* (London, Longmans, 1972).

Index